TEACHING STRATEGIES
A Guide to Effective Instruction

NINTH EDITION

Donald C. Orlich
Washington State University

Robert J. Harder
Washington State University

Richard C. Callahan
Callahan Associates

Michael S. Trevisan
Washington State University

Abbie H. Brown
East Carolina University

WADSWORTH
CENGAGE Learning™

Australia • Brazil • Japan • Korea • Mexico • Singapore • Spain • United Kingdom • United States

WADSWORTH
CENGAGE Learning

Teaching Strategies: A Guide to Effective Instruction, Ninth Edition
Donald C. Orlich
Robert J. Harder
Richard C. Callahan
Michael S. Trevisan
Abbie H. Brown

Acquisitions Editor: Christopher Shortt

Senior Development Editor: Lisa Mafrici

Assistant Editor: Caitlin Cox

Editorial Assistant: Linda Stewart

Marketing Manager: Kara Parsons

Marketing Coordinator: Andy Yap

Marketing Communications Manager: Martha Pfeiffer

Project Manager, Editorial Production: Susan Miscio

Print Buyer: Arethea Thomas

Permissions Editor: Katie Huha

Production Service: Matrix Productions

Text Designer: Adriane Bosworth

Photo Researcher: Connie Gardner

Cover Image: © Images.com/Corbis

Compositor: PrePress PMG

For product information and technology assistance, contact us at **Cengage Learning Academic Resource Center, 1-800-423-0563**

For permission to use material from this text or product, submit all requests online at **www.cengage.com/permissions**. Further permissions questions can be e-mailed to **permissionrequest@cengage.com**.

Library of Congress Control Number: 2008934718

ISBN-13: 978-0-547-21293-3

ISBN-10: 0-547-21293-3

Wadsworth
25 Thomson Place
Boston, MA 02210-1202
USA

Cengage Learning is a leading provider of customized learning solutions with office locations around the globe, including Singapore, the United Kingdom, Australia, Mexico, Brazil, and Japan. Locate your local office at: **international.cengage.com/region**.

For your course and learning solutions, visit **www.cengage.com**.

Purchase any of our products at your local college store or at our preferred online store **www.ichapters.com**.

Printed in the United States of America
1 2 3 4 5 6 7 13 12 11 10 09

Contents

CHAPTER 5   Sequencing and Organizing Instruction   133

Preface

This revision was guided by the mission of preparing new teachers for the realities of the classroom. We do this by providing an optimal set of classroom-tested models, strategies, techniques and methods to enhance the learning and schooling of all. The institution of education is now being challenged by school and outside sources to provide a higher-quality education. Simultaneously, the field of education is encountering accelerated change and uncertainty, which creates bold challenges for teachers and students. All educators must master the tools of the information age and prepare to teach students who are "digital natives." Teachers must respond to demands for professionalism and reform, and they must help an increasingly diverse mix of students prepare for life in an ever more global and competitive world.

Our ninth edition of *Teaching Strategies: A Guide to Effective Instruction* has been extensively revised to emphasize the classroom teacher's instructional needs and the improvement of the teaching act. Driving the book throughout is the core belief that teachers have the ability to make a profound difference in their students' lives. *Teaching Strategies* helps all prospective teachers to acquire the basics of professional knowledge that are so necessary to facilitate learning for all our nation's children. Using this book, teachers can improve their skills and strategies, learning to blend technical competence with artistic sensitivity as they work to achieve lifelong learning and career success. As you will see, this mission is reflected throughout the text and features in this new edition.

Purpose and Intended Audience

This book has multiple uses. *Teaching Strategies* is designed primarily for use in courses of instruction for those preparing to become elementary, middle, or secondary school teachers. Our hallmark is to treat all topics in depth and provide operational examples, thus preparing preservice or new practicing teachers to master a broad range of competencies required for state and national certification. We strive to contribute to the profession by providing tested and validated theories and methods of classroom instruction, and by showing how best to apply them in the reality of today's classrooms.

The authors illustrate a broad spectrum of instructional models, strategies, methodologies and techniques that work in today's complex classrooms. Novices and experienced teachers alike have found it a valuable source of sound, practical, and humane educational strategies. It is a reliable guide for making logical, effective, systematic instructional choices. In-service teachers have reported that the book is a helpful and easy-to-use resource in areas they previously missed or in which they need some technical brushing up.

New to the Ninth Edition

As a result of feedback we received from our Advisory Board of reviewers, changes in education, and new research, we've made several changes to the ninth edition while adding new features.

Substantial content revisions in Chapters 1, 2, 3, 4, 6, 9 and 10   Reviewers suggested that in this edition we provide only a snapshot about professionalism. Accordingly, we've streamlined Chapter 1, now titled, "Frames of Reference for Teaching," to focus on teaching as a helping profession, systematic instruction, the key contexts of teaching, incentives, diversity in the schools, and the challenge of influences by nonschool groups, reflective teaching, and decision making.

Chapter 2, "The Big Picture in Your Classroom: Focusing the Instruction in a Social Kaleidoscope," provides a holistic view of instruction. Chapter 2 also contains the prototype Epstein/Piaget chart of developmental characteristics and cognitive levels of children from age 5 to adults, as well as the behavioral and cognitive elements of teaching. A section on "Educational Equity as the Big Picture" examines the essential ingredients for providing equity and excellence in every classroom.

Chapter 3, "Objectives, Taxonomies, and Standards for Instruction," is streamlined and contains a section, "Converting Standards to Objectives," which discusses the process of converting state and national standards into concrete learning objectives. We provide a criticism of the current genre of published state standards. This section also introduces a handy tool called "effect size." Effect size is one quantitative gauge by which to determine the extent to which any instructional technique can have a positive impact on student achievement. The importance of understanding the effect size for a given teaching technique is discussed in the text, and effect size data are referenced on our website for virtually all the teaching techniques discussed throughout the text. *Teaching Strategies* is a "research-based" production.

Chapter 4, now titled "Instructional Planning," stresses the critical and key role that proactive teacher planning has on lesson design and implementation.

Chapter 6, now titled "Managing the Classroom" has been completely reorganized and revised in response to reviewers' requests. There is an emphasis on viewing classroom management as a system, not just as an afterthought.

Chapter 9, "Inquiry Teaching and Higher-Level Thinking," has been tightened to focus more closely on the chapter's themes.

Finally, Chapter 10, now called "Classroom Assessment" has been reorganized for ease of use. It focuses on classroom assessments. We also elaborate on student-led conferences, an exciting new development in classroom assessment. An expanded section on formative classroom assessment is also included.

New and expanded pedagogy to prepare for today's classrooms

◆ Our award winning *Video Case* features have been expanded and vividly show students how the material in the text is put into practice in the real world of teaching.

◆ New *Voices from the Classroom* features practicing teachers who share their own real-life experiences related to the chapter's themes.

◆ New and revised *Technology Insight* boxes in each chapter provide insight on technology-based issues and, in some cases, provide links to relevant resources on the World Wide Web. New features on the use of Web 2.0, Wikis, and blogs are included.

◆ New *Building a Career Portfolio* features appear at the end of each chapter to provide preservice teachers with a repertoire of instructionally related ideas that they can use to build a professional portfolio.

New research and data added throughout   The ninth edition has been brought up to date with relevant research, data, and sources. For example, our federal data are from the most recent publications available.

A Walk Through the Coverage in the Ninth Edition

The revised text is organized in three distinct parts. Part 1, titled "Foundations of Instructional Design," examines the culture of the schools and presents the fundamental frameworks within which teachers set goals and make daily instructional decisions. Chapter 1, "Frames of Reference for Teaching," maintains its important role in presenting an overview of the school milieu. In addition, we discuss teaching as a profession in the context of social interaction and then consider the impact of nonschool factors that affect teaching. The all-important concept of teacher as decision maker is highlighted, as is selecting developmentally appropriate content.

Chapter 2, "The Big Picture in Your Classroom: Focusing the Instruction in a Social Kaleidoscope," begins with a discussion and graphic organizer of holistic instruction, a contextualizing section that picks up on the decision-making theme in Chapter 1 and then sets the stage for most of the major topics in the remainder of the book. We present three major perspectives that can guide systematic decision making: developmental, behavioral, and cognitive. Highlighted are two themes: diversity and equity. Each of these sections integrates key material.

In Part 2, "Fundamental Tools for Instructional Planning," we vividly illustrate the basic tools and knowledge base for effective instructional planning. Chapter 3, "Objectives, Taxonomies, and Standards for Instruction," continues to focus on the goals and objectives of instruction. The related discussion of student standards, in response to reviewers' requests, has been shortened and includes samples from various states, looking at how they are converted into daily lesson design. The concept of effect size is introduced as a tool for determining the educational efficacy of any technique. Chapters 4 and 5 continue to define and demonstrate the process of instructional design with a variety of useful planning methods, planning resources, and instructional models. Chapter 4, "Instructional Planning," contains a strong research-based section that illustrates subsequent topics on planning. It also includes a short section on the construction of individual education plans (IEPs). Including this coverage reflects this edition's emphasis on integrating coverage of special-needs educational issues within related text discussions. Chapter 4 concludes with a section on how expert teachers plan, which directly applies the field experiences of award-winning teachers to the knowledge base. The title of Chapter 5, "Sequencing and Organizing Instruction," reflects its emphasis on the two critical planning angles of sequencing and organizing. We show how teachers can adapt their plans using a multi-methodological approach, thus meeting the needs of students with diverse learning styles.

Part 3, "Instruction as a Dynamic Process in Classrooms," presents the dynamic and interactive aspects of teaching and provides the core knowledge base for creating a lively and productive learning environment. Chapter 6, "Managing the Classroom," introduces classroom management as a technique for establishing a positive and supportive environment. Within a more tightly reorganized format, we maintain our presentation of a broad continuum of management systems, illustrated with practical applications. Throughout, we stress the concept of equity and the need to create classroom routines that foster smooth classroom operations—for example, policies for "cell phone" management and cyber-bullying.

Chapter 7, "The Process of Classroom Questioning," continues to provide the most thorough treatment of the questioning process that you will find in any methods textbook. In addition to illustrating the process of classroom questioning, this edition highlights the essential issue of how teachers can better attend to and develop higher-level questioning, as well as reflective questioning.

Chapter 8, "Small-Group Discussions and Cooperative Learning," explores and highlights how to use six basic types of small-group discussion to create exciting lessons and to encourage active student participation. A synthesized section describes in practical terms how to establish and maintain small groups. We also include material on collecting feedback from small groups.

Chapter 9, "Inquiry Teaching and Higher-Level Thinking," opens with a strong, tightly woven discussion of the nature of thinking and how it can be emphasized. We present in practical detail the two primary avenues for teaching thinking: inquiry-based methods and specific techniques that emphasize problem solving and critical thinking skills.

Chapter 10, "Classroom Assessment," focuses on monitoring student progress. This chapter has been revised to provide reflections on the all-important contexts for classroom assessments. We look at purposes for and areas of assessment, simple core definitions, and the relationship of assessment to planning and instruction. A section on "formative classroom assessment" stresses feedback as a critical element that enhances student achievement. The entire chapter emphasizes the classroom teacher's needs. Test item writing and grading, as well as other topics of importance to teachers, receive full treatment.

The entire book has been deliberately reduced in scope to focus more tightly on instructional strategies and teaching techniques. We provide the prerequisite entry technical skills needed to be successful in the classroom.

Overarching themes, such as the use of technology within the classroom and the instructional needs of diverse students, are integrated in discussions throughout the book. You will find a wide array of ideas from which to select the strategies that best meet your instructional goals and the learning goals of your students.

Special Features

We offer several pedagogical features that are designed to organize and illustrate the content and make the text both reality-based and easy to use. This format encourages readers to engage with the information presented, to make it their own, and to expand their professional horizons. These features are described below.

- **Graphic Organizers** serve as concept maps to preview each chapter. The maps identify the key topics in each chapter and serve as handy visual organizational aids.

- **Classroom Snapshot** is a *new* feature that starts off each chapter with a real-life vignette that reflects the topic of the chapter and provides focus questions to guide reading.

- **Instructional Strategies** boxes provide up-to-date strategic ideas and techniques for direct application in the classroom.

- **Video Cases**, expanded and available on the premium website, are presented in the chapters so readers can actually observe a teacher using one of the models or strategies being discussed.

- **Technology Insight** boxes appear in each chapter, introducing relevant technology-related issues and resources.

- **Voices from the Classroom** are stories of practicing and award-winning teachers who validate the instructional techniques that we highlight.

- **Key Ideas** boxes provide periodic breaks in the chapter to summarize key content.

- **Reflect** boxes, which appear at the end of each major section, allow the reader to stop and reflect on the previously learned content and place it in an experiential context, thereby enhancing its personal and professional relevance.

- **Marginal notes** throughout the text highlight key concepts.

- **Key terms** are highlighted in bold print to draw the reader's attention to these important building blocks of a professional vocabulary, and the Glossary at the end of the book contains all the key terms with definitions.

- A **Closing Reflection** concludes each chapter, providing formative questions for thought on the contents of the chapter.

◆ **Building a Career Portfolio** is a *new* feature at the end of every chapter that offers suggestions for items to include in a professional portfolio to help new teachers prepare for job interviews and their first day of teaching.

◆ **Summary Points** at the end of each chapter aid the reader in pinpointing major concepts.

◆ **Print and Internet Resources** at the end of each chapter provide readers with additional resources that can be used for further information on a given topic and to expand their professional competence.

Accompanying Resources for Instructors and Students

We offer a complete package of support material for instructors and students, as described below.

◆ An **Instructor's Resource Manual**. The IRM is offered online to provide the instructor with additional teaching and assessment support materials in an easy-to-use electronic format.

◆ **Expanded companion websites**. Students and instructors can access valuable content any time via the companion website at www.cengage .com/education/orlich. Students can register or purchase access to the Video Cases on the premium website by going to www.cengage.com/ login. At the student website, students will find numerous items of interest—many of which are not found in this book—including additional information on effect size and other key topics such as the legal structure of public schools, school reform agendas, lifelong learning, elements of the school culture, and characteristics of children in the K–12 setting. In addition, we offer other features, such as self-testing questions, reflection questions, and additional Web links, just to name a few. As mentioned, the award-winning *Video Cases* are offered here and are correlated to the text by marginal features. Each Video Case is a 4–6-minute clip that presents actual classroom scenarios depicting the complex problems and opportunities teachers face in the classroom every day. The Video Cases are accompanied by teacher interviews, classroom artifacts, and reflective viewing questions. Instructors will find instructors' resources, such as model syllabi, activities, the Instructor's Resource Manual, PowerPoint slides, discussion starters, and more.

◆ **Course Management Systems**. Support for online courses is available via platform-ready WebCT and Blackboard cartridges through WebTutor. Jumpstart your course with customizable, rich, text-specific content within your Course Management System. WebTutor offers a wide array of resources including access to the Video Cases. Visit webtutor.cengage.com to learn more.

Acknowledgments

The authors express their appreciation to colleagues who contributed to earlier editions of this text. These include Dr. Harry Gibson, Olympia, Washington; Dr. Anne Remaley of Washington State University; Dr. Constance H. Kravas of the University of Washington; Dr. Andrew J. Keough, University of Wisconsin–Marshfield/Wood County; Dr. R. A. Pendergrass, Glenwood, Missouri, public schools; Dr. Donald P. Kauchak of the University of Utah; Dr. Eileen M. Starr of Valley City State University; and Dr. Foster M. Walsh of Gonzaga University. Each helped make the previous editions of the book relevant and useful, and their insights continue to be reflected in the ninth edition.

A number of reviewers on our Advisory Board critiqued this edition. They include:

Lew Allen, University of Georgia
Christine Baron, Salem State College
Joanne C. Burgert, University of Pittsburgh at Bradford
Marilyn Carpenter, University of Arkansas
Alicia Costa, Seton Hill University
Kristen Cuthrell, East Carolina University
Richard A. Giaquinto, St. Francis College
C. Bobbi Hansen, University of San Diego
Cynthia J. Hutchinson, University of Central Florida
Emily Lin, University of Nevada, Las Vegas
Elisa Michals, Sacramento State University
Carolynn L. Reynolds, California State University, Chico
Martin J. Ward, Texas A&M University–Corpus Christi

We would like to thank each member of our Advisory Board, as well as the many students who offered feedback, for their suggestions. The authors wish to thank Sandra Tyacke for her outstanding job of preparing the many manuscripts necessary for this project. The authors express their appreciation to the talented publishing staff, including Lisa Mafrici, Shani Fisher, Janet Tilden, and Amy Whitaker, whose help is more than observable in the final product.

Donald C. Orlich

Foundations of Instructional Design

*P*art 1 is an overview of the foundations of effective instruction, which we systematically expand throughout the remainder of the book. We introduce teaching as a helping profession, discuss the various contexts of the school milieu as a learning community, and explore how social factors affect what is taught and how. We also provide a rationale that illustrates the many interacting components of instruction and their cyclical nature.

In Chapter 1, we discuss various professional, cultural, and outside contexts that will have an impact on the ways that you teach. We make a strong plea for reflective teaching, setting the stage for the key role of teacher as decision maker.

Chapter 2 establishes the big picture of instruction by illustrating how sociopsychological perspectives shape our techniques of presentation. We show how meaningful instruction is cyclical and how all elements of the cycle inform teacher decisions. We stress the need for active learning, instructional equity, awareness of bias, and instructional differentiation.

Frames of Reference for Teaching

Craig Ellis, recently discharged from military service, enrolled in a teacher education program that offered a paid internship when he completed his teaching BA degree. One of the first assignments in his methods of instruction class was to team up with three other class members and prepare a set of discussion questions related to instruction. The focal point of the assignment was "What are some social and professional challenges faced by newly hired teachers?" When Craig and his team met, they came up with the following list of questions:

- What is the current status of public education in the United States?
- How are instructional models and strategies utilized systematically in the classroom?
- What are some outside influences on what a teacher does, and what are other key contexts that affect schooling?
- How are teachers' professional reflections and artistry expressed within the classroom?

Professor Hernandez reviewed the lists from all the teams in the class and assigned Chapter 1 below as background reading for the class prior to their discussions. As you read this chapter, think about how you would respond to each of the above questions.

SECTION 1   A Snapshot of Schooling and the Profession of Teaching

The schools of the United States are its single largest social service institution. Projected 2010 expenditures for all K–12 schools are over $700 billion. Add to that an estimated $300 billion for higher education, and the magnitude of our enterprise accounts for a tidy 7.5 percent of the nation's gross domestic product. Teachers recognize that, as members of a "service industry" that serves almost one out of every four persons, they must have a broad understanding of instruction. Teachers and administrators know they need to analyze how they teach in terms of what they are teaching and to whom they are teaching it. In this chapter, we present a rationale that gives a theoretical and practical structure to guide action in the classroom as it relates to education as a professional endeavor. If all one had to do were stand up front and talk, then teaching would be a snap, but there is far more to effective teaching than this.

Education is the largest social service industry in the United States.

Facilitating the American Dream

By and large, surveys show the American public believes that the nation's schools provide students with the knowledge, skills, and competencies they need to be successful. For millions of individuals, public schools have provided the opportunities that have allowed them to realize their own American dream. Most Americans believe that success comes with education—and from an economic standpoint, there is little doubt that this is often true.

This dream is not uniformly achieved, however. Not all individuals in our society profit equally from public education. The reasons vary, from socioeconomic factors to language diversity. Perhaps the best that we can expect from schools is that they assure every student an equal access to opportunity. The chance to achieve one's dream is a great self-motivator. Thus every educator has an ethical and moral obligation to assist all students to realize their full potential. Embracing those ideals is a professional obligation.

Teachers guide all individuals toward being successful in American society.

Instruction as a Systematic Process

As you just read, teaching is not simply standing in front of a class and talking. The best teachers contemplate the manner in which they will present a topic and have a wide variety of instructional models at their disposal.

Models of Instruction   What is an **instructional model**? Think of it as a broad, overarching descriptor that encompasses several different concepts. For example, when teaching astronomy, the solar system is a model with the sun at the center and all the planets orbiting around it. A few of the concepts associated with the solar model are gravity, orbits, heliocentricity, satellites, and eclipses. You can use this model to picture the solar system in your mind's eye.

What type of instructional models do teachers embrace?

First, there are learning psychology models. Concepts associated with the learning psychology model can be described as behaviorist, cognitive, constructivist, and developmental. We will amplify these models in Chapter 2.

Second, there are organizational models. Concepts included in these models are large groups, small groups, cooperative learning groups, learning communities, and individualized instruction. In Chapters 4 and 8, these models will be amplified and expanded.

The third category consists of classroom management models. There are at least two major ones: self-discipline and imposed discipline. Concepts included within the self-discipline model are Maslow's Hierarchy of Needs, moral reasoning, character development, and reality therapy. The imposed discipline model includes desist strategies, assertive discipline, and behavior modification. All of these concepts are discussed in Chapter 6.

Finally, if one is going to encourage "inquiry" and higher-level thinking, there are several additional models that we will examine in Chapter 9.

As you'll see, we feature a wide spectrum of instructional models that will provide you with a set of instructional skills that are trustworthy, research-based, and designed to help you bridge the gap between your preservice education and your entry into real classroom experience.

Strategies, Methods, and Techniques

Embedded within any model is a set of accompanying procedures—a series of steps to accomplish something—by which a specific aspect of the model is employed. For example, Chapter 7 is devoted entirely to a model for questioning. We could argue that "wait time" is a model with a series of specific procedures or steps used by teachers when conducting recitations. The questioning model is based on a psychological concept that attempts to raise the attention level of all in the class, rather than just one individual, prior to calling on a student. In this text, we use the terms *technique* and *procedure* as synonyms to signify a series of steps that one takes to employ any general model being used in the classroom. When we use the term *method*, it implies some orderly way of doing something. The term *strategy* implies thoughtful planning to do something. Each of these aspects emanate from a broader and more encompassing model.

As you progress through the ten chapters in this text, you will observe a wide variety of strategies being brought into play to embody an overarching model. While each chapter explores a single topic or set of models, together they form a collective whole—a gestalt, as it were—that will become apparent in the final reading. Our intended goal is to illustrate as many workable and trustworthy teaching/instructional methods as is practical so that when you begin to teach you, too, will have an array of models and strategies from which to choose, and of critical importance, you'll know how to employ each and know why you are using that technique at any given moment of the lesson. The lesson is the essence of the act of schooling. Each lesson has a structure, just as a carpenter uses blueprints in building a house. In short, reading this book will give you a holistic view of schooling.

Keep in mind that we are providing a manageable sample of the total instructional spectrum. As you gain classroom experiences, you will learn about other models and strategies. The operational term is **experience**! With experience you can sort out strategies that work well for specific topics and student groups. At this point in your pre-service career, your experiential framework is limited. We understand this, having passed through those same moments. But remember, the best teachers are lifelong learners as well.

Influences on Instruction

As we enter the second decade of the twenty-first century, it is abundantly clear that a wide variety of influences are affecting how, and to some extent what, you will teach. There are books aplenty that examine this issue (see the list on page 7), but we will simply highlight three major influences: (1) politics at the federal level, (2) business groups, and (3) advocacy groups. Collectively these three influences will directly affect many aspects of your classroom.

Federal Politics As pressing national social problems emerge, there is usually a call for the federal government to intervene. Since the nation's founding, a series of acts have been passed to aid the schools. In 1983, The National Commission on Excellence in Education published "A Nation at Risk: The Imperative for Educational Reform." This report ultimately led to the No Child Left Behind Act of 2001, PL107-110. Reauthorization would maintain a large federal footprint in all public school classrooms.

As a result of the No Child Left Behind Act, you will be affected by testing mandates, be required to use a pre-selected national curriculum in reading, and be expected to adhere to specific teaching methods for exceptional children. We will amplify the latter in Chapter 2. Suffice to say, the federal presence as a classroom intruder has never been greater. In the past, projects and programs were federally sponsored, but content and methodologies were not. You will be on stage to observe how this plays out. However, it must be noted that public education is paid for with public funds. These funds are raised and allocated through a political process. In the political forums—local school boards and state legislatures—the citizenry assigns its priorities and establishes rank order. In this respect, David F. Mathews, President of the Kettering Foundation (2003) and former Secretary of the U.S. Department of Health, Education and Welfare, makes a compelling case for understanding the public's role in educational policy making and strongly supports the need for open deliberation in public decision making.

As a teacher, your role is to inform parents, school patrons, and policy-makers of your professional concerns. It is all a part of teaching.

Reflect   With a few peers, discuss the impact of political mandates on public education.

Business Groups   Business groups have long had an influence on the public schools. The most obvious business influence on education has been exerted by publishers of textbooks, materials, supplies, and a wide variety of tests and assessments. The role of business groups has now evolved to exert a stronger influence on policy making. For example, *Achieve, Inc.* (founded in 1996 by state governors and business leaders) stresses higher academic standards and achievement, and endorses most testing and so-called accountability in the public schools. The organization links with governors of all states and has six governors on its board, and it aids statewide business roundtables to carry out its agenda. It strongly supports core business values for the public schools—competition, short-term gains, accountability, and quarterly reports.

In Achieve, Inc., we observe a direct intervention by large business interests into school curriculum content, testing, and standards. Underlying all these efforts is the assumption that employers will have a ready-to-work employee as a high school graduate. Using their financial power, business interests focus on key legislators and elected officials. Keep in mind that if these groups lobbied directly, they would lose their nonprofit IRS status. Despite their indirect influence, they carry strong political "clout."

Among business groups, there is an assumption that technology is the key to school improvement and student achievement. Their stress on accountability models actually implies that the technological successes that business has had will work in school classrooms. Yes, technologies will help students, but real learning involves much more.

As a teacher you will be subtly informed about business values and how these values will help your students. Caveat emptor!

Advocacy Groups   A huge number of different advocacy groups have a direct effect on instruction. First there is a host of professional associations—for example, the National Science Teachers Association is just one of several discipline-related groups. One very powerful group is the Council for Exceptional Children (CEC). The CEC promotes programs for children who have any type of learning disability. In 1975, this group encouraged the U.S. Congress to pass PL94-142, the "Education for All Handicapped Children Act," commonly known as "Individuals with Disabilities Education Act" (IDEA). The IDEA was followed by congressional passage of the "Americans with Disabilities Act of 1990," which took effect July 26, 1992. The ADA defined education of disabled persons as a civil right.

Within all the laws and accompanying regulations are several prescriptions for schools and teachers who have any exceptional or disabled children in their classes. You will be given specific guidelines to follow on your first teaching job, especially with regard to making accommodations for children who have an Individualized Education Plan (IEP). We will discuss all of these topics in later chapters.

In the medical profession, clinical trials are prerequisite to any new treatment or drug being broadly applied, but this is not the case in the education profession. Advocates boldly proclaim their solutions to school problems with little or no substantive or longitudinal research, and both students and teachers then suffer (see Ellis 2005). To summarize, there are many pressure groups that play specific roles in your school and classroom. By being aware of their tactics you and your colleagues can sort out what is good for your students and what is not (see Kozol 2007).

Select Set of Statements About Influences on the Schools

◆ Berliner, D. C., & Biddle, B. J. (1995). *The Manufactured Crisis: Myths, Fraud, and the Attack on America's Public Schools*. Reading, MA: Addison-Wesley.

◆ Bracey, G. W. (2001). *The War Against America's Public Schools: Privatizing Schools, Commercializing Education*. Needham Heights, MA: Allyn and Bacon.

◆ Nichols, S. L., & Berliner, D. C. (2007). *Collateral Damage: How High-Stakes Testing Corrupts America's Schools*. Cambridge, MA: Harvard University Press.

◆ Ohanian, S. (1999). *One Size Fits Few: The Folly of Educational Standards*. Portsmouth, NH: Heinemann.

◆ Orlich, D. C. (2006). *School Reform: The Great American Brain Robbery*. Baltimore: PublishAmerica.

◆ Ravitch, D. (2003). *The Language Police: How Pressure Groups Restrict What Children Learn*. New York: Knopf.

◆ Rothstein, R. (2008). "Leaving 'No Child Left Behind' Behind." *The American Prospect 19*(1): 50–54.

How to Be an Active Educator

◆ Be a systematic teacher

◆ Know and apply models

◆ Become aware of nonschool influences

◆ Inform others

Reflect

◆ Discuss with practicing teachers what instructional models they use and under what circumstances.

◆ Examine a local newspaper to observe outside influences on instruction, especially decisions about what will be taught.

Key Contexts of Teaching

The profession of teaching takes place in a number of contexts that will place demands on your work. Some of these demands reinforce one another, while others are sometimes in conflict.

The Social Context   A sign in the Singapore International Airport reads "Welcome to Singapore: Where Our Only National Resource Is Our People." That sign sums up what our schools should be all about. Institutions are made up of people. Schools consist of systems and subsystems of individuals who collectively conduct the business of schooling. The human interactions among administrators, teachers, parents, and learners forge bonds of trust and mutual support. As teachers, our goal is to enhance human potential for every person associated with the school. The process of education takes place, for the most part, in structured and well-organized schools. This is true even for parents who home-school their children. Schooling, to be effective, has a group orientation about it. The entire process is very social—that is, highly dependent on personal interactions. One of the first things that a child learns in school is that the individual must make accommodations to the group. Within this cultural and social milieu, behaviors are changed, learning takes place, and individuals change. Schools provide a social resource that might be missing for individuals learning on their own.

School as group orientation, complex social network

A celebration of success in schooling.

© Will and Deni McIntyre/Corbis

Embedded within the social context of the school is the concept of *social capital.* **Social capital** is the sum of interpersonal relationships that provide support or encouragement. Sources of social capital include families, communities, public institutions, and ethnic groups. Emanating from these sources come social trust, norms, communication, and collaborative networks, to list only a few outcomes. (See Carnevale 2001; Israel, Beaulieu, & Hartless 2001; Putnam 2000.)

The school is an especially critical source of social capital for its clientele. It provides the physical and social framework for teachers, students, and parents/caregivers to work toward a common good, or to extend the **acculturation** process of children or adolescents. **Norms** (unwritten rules of behavior for specific groups) and normative pressures are part of the school's culture and its vast resource of social capital.

As a teacher, you help to create social capital for all students, especially those whose social capital, for whatever reason, has a near-zero balance. These students may include children growing up in poverty and new arrivals to the United States. You provide information that helps students become a part of social networks. By knowing your students personally, you help them gain experiences with things they don't know. You show the students how to employ all the school's resources—counselors, coaches, sponsors of extracurricular or club activities, the music director, or the school newspaper advisor. By your own actions, you demonstrate that you are in your students' corner. These methods of supporting students socially are all aspects of meeting our professional obligation. Collectively, these social elements of schooling aid in the acculturation processes that prepare students to be successful in our society.

Teachers create social capital.

> **Key Ideas** ➤ **Elements of Social Capital**
> - Families
> - Personal relationships
> - Public institutions
> - Churches
> - Communities
> - Clubs
> - Ethnic groups

Now add to these interactions the phenomenon we call *pluralism,* and you can appreciate the social interactions and conflicts that can be predicted to take place in the schools. The term **pluralism** refers to the fact that our society and our schools are composed of many different types of people, creating a mixture of nationalities, races, classes, religions, occupational groupings, philosophies, value systems, and economic beliefs. Given this broad social spectrum, it is inevitable that you will observe contradictory points of view as a teacher (see Livingston & Wirt 2004). You will observe **intrapersonal** conflicts, in which an individual tries to reconcile conflicts within his or her own value structure. You will also observe **interpersonal** conflicts, in which the values of different individuals or groups openly clash. These kinds of conflicts generate considerable energy. Sometimes the energy is positive and leads to common problem solving and beneficial activities. In other cases, the energy leads to disharmony. As a teacher, one of your major roles will be to foster positive social interactions and relationships.

The Emotional Context   As we said before, the educational enterprise is a helping profession. People who enter teaching tend to do so for altruistic, moral, or ethical reasons. If education is to help all persons achieve their maximum potential, then its practitioners must develop an organization that cares about all individuals in it. That quality of *caringness* adds the human element to impersonal buildings and institutionalized delivery systems. The close interactions among teachers and students forge bonds of trust and mutual support, especially for children who have trouble meeting expectations for achievement (see Noddings 2002).

Emphasize caring and values.

Additionally, caringness is part of the social capital of the school organization. This trait makes it a bit easier to help students of all ages to develop moral and ethical values. Do not be alarmed about the last sentence. Yes, the schools have an obligation to teach those values, and virtually all parents or

Voices from the Classroom

Erin Jones

John R. Rogers
High School

Spokane, Washington

Helping to Create Social Capital

The John R. Rogers High School is located in the Hillyard community of Spokane, which is located in the poorest zip code of Washington State. Many of the students who attend this school come from single-parent homes, are not guaranteed three meals a day, have their electricity or water turned off on occasion, and often do not have access to newspapers or travel outside of the neighborhood. This once-vital community has lost its industry and economic power and remains impoverished because the current members of the community do not have a voice. For the most part, the parents of our students do not have professional jobs, do not belong to social organizations and do not have connections to those in places of power.

Teaching in such a school is perceived by many educators and community members alike as a hazard. How could a teacher make any impact on the poverty and lack of hope that abounds in the lives of the 1700 or so students who walk through the doors every day?

The reality for those of us who teach at Rogers High School is that each one of these students is truly a diamond in the rough. As a teacher at Rogers, I have the opportunity to shave away the rough edges and expose my students to the brilliance that exists within them and within their community, to open doors to the wealth of opportunities that exist right in the city of Spokane, a city boasting two nationally recognized private institutions and several successful community colleges.

Students in my AVID (Advancement Via Individual Determination) class have met the current and past mayors of Spokane. They have met the presidents of three corporations, every member of the school board and the most important district administrators, as well as the state superintendent. They have met college students and other special guests who call Spokane home. By allowing my students to hear the stories of those who struggled for their dreams, my students have learned that their poverty is no excuse for failure and, more importantly, no excuse for hopelessness. They have begun to realize that they have a voice that is just as important, just as valuable as that of a business owner or a politician.

One thing I have successfully taught my students is that our future does not need to be determined by circumstances or upbringing. Excellence and success do not happen by accident but are a result of millions of choices, decisions, and actions. With my help and the help of my classroom guests, the students are beginning to develop their own tool kits to allow them to maneuver between a variety of social and professional settings with confidence.

My greatest hope is that success will breed success, and these students who have never seen themselves as "academic" before will now begin to see themselves as future college students and business owners and politicians and doctors and lawyers.

guardians will strongly endorse them because they fall under the umbrella of becoming a good or virtuous citizen (see Comte-Sponville 2001).

Closely related to these values is a concept called *emotional intelligence*. The term may show up in the literature of teaching. In brief, it means being aware of how you as a teacher feel as you scan a class of students with whom you are engaged. How do you react (feel) toward a specific student? Do you show any biases in your verbal or nonverbal cues? How does a student or group of students react (feel) to some situation? These are aspects of the term. (See J. Clarrochi & J. D. Mayer, *Applying Emotional Intelligence: A Practitioner's Guide,* 2007, for a detailed treatment of this topic.)

The Curricular Context   Just what composes the overall curricular context of our schools? This is a tough question to answer, for it depends on your own educational philosophy. Over the years, the schools have either inherited or subtly adopted a social philosophy aimed at accommodating many social, emotional, and familial needs in addition to educational ones. Yes, the schools still teach the basics. But "the basics" now extend to many topics that were once considered extras. To be sure, reading and writing, communicating, mathematics, science, history, and geography still form the core academic disciplines, but the schools now also teach health and life skills, HIV/AIDS prevention, driving, and a host of other skills, both social and behavioral. This is the complicated montage we call the curriculum today. We will return to the topic of curriculum in Chapters 3, 4, and 5 when we discuss lesson designs.

Redefining the basics

The Collegial Context   Over the academic year, principals or supervisors might spend a total of one or two hours observing and evaluating a teacher, with greater time for a novice and less for a veteran; but the vast amount of service that any teacher performs goes uncritiqued or unnoticed by fellow professionals. When teachers develop personal teaching styles that are not especially beneficial to student learning, it often results from working in seclusion.

▶ VIDEO CASE

View the Video Case "Teaching as a Profession: Collaboration with Colleagues" on the student website to listen in as a group of teachers develop recommendations for their math reporting system and present their ideas at a faculty meeting. After you watch the clips and study the artifacts in the case, answer these questions: (1) How do these teachers define collaboration? (2) What are the benefits of finding and meeting with a "collaboration partner" when you begin your teaching career?

Working in isolation is one aspect of many school cultures that tends to perpetuate the "batch processing" of students—that is, using large classes and large-class techniques. This is especially noticeable in self-contained elementary school classrooms and subject-centered high schools. The physical isolation keeps new ideas from spreading. If you do not have opportunities to observe your colleagues, you may miss out on some great ideas (see Woolfolk-Hoy & Hoy 2003).

Even though you may often work in seclusion, you can use the Internet to facilitate participation in the professional community by linking with professional associations' websites. All state departments of education also have extensive websites. We highlight some useful tips to expand your learning in the Technology Insight boxes found throughout the book, and conclude each chapter with a few select sites for your consideration.

Importance of finding a teacher learning community

You may be fortunate enough to be working in a school where the culture maintains a **learning community**. In these instances, you will seldom be alone, as there is a greater emphasis on teacher-student-administrator collaboration and planning. You will also find teachers conducting research and self-reflecting on their practices. The learning community culture encourages continued studies or professional staff development, and even encourages teaching professionals to seek a National Board Certification. (For details, see the website at http://www.nbpts.org.) Further, there appears to be an attempt afoot to reconfigure schools into smaller, cohesive units through the creation of "schools within a school," "core groupings," and even discrete learning groups. The goal of these techniques is to improve professional interactions and provide an environment conducive to student achievement. Schools tend to develop their own independent **school culture** apart from those of other schools in the same district. Their norms and values may be generated from the inside. As a result, subtle or even intentional pressures may be placed on teachers to conform. The outcome can be positive if the school culture includes healthy values, innovative teaching styles, and respectful communication patterns. If, however, the school culture includes less desirable qualities, this unfortunate tendency to encourage teachers to conform may undermine the profession. Education, like all professions, is rooted in the development of its practitioners' individual expertise. And, indeed, novice teachers have at their disposal a broad range of teaching strategies. This book is designed to help develop the best teachers possible. As you study, keep thinking of ways to influence your environment in a positive way instead of becoming a victim to its negative characteristics. If you take this approach, your school ethos can evolve, encompassing new norms that stress problem solving, active teaching, and positive student expectations. We advocate entering into professional discussions and collaborating with other teachers in your school. Share books and journals with one another. This is one way to shape the intellectual and instructional dimensions of your school's culture.

Each school has its own culture.

Contexts of Schooling

◆ Social

◆ Emotional

◆ Curricular

◆ Collegial (professional)

Incentives of the Teaching Culture

Why do teachers continue to do what they do? Teachers bask in the success of their students, and students' success reflects on their teachers' effectiveness. It is great to be with winners. That statement is true whether you are a second-grade teacher whose pupils have mastered addition or a high school French teacher whose students have grasped the concept of the subjunctive. A teacher's level of functioning is largely determined by the attitude displayed toward the students—whether inviting or disinviting interaction. (See the box on page 13; Purkey & Novak 2009). The highest-level teacher, the one who is intentionally inviting, places a high priority on student success. These teachers reinforce their own most powerful incentive. (See Stanley & Purkey 2001 for a series of studies on invitational learning.)

We introduced the concept of teacher expectations only briefly, but we encourage you to reflect on your own experiences as a student. Which teachers expected you to perform to your highest capacity? Did you have any teachers who were almost insulting to the students who did not perform as expected? These attitudes from teachers carry over in the conduct of the lesson.

In addition to student success, another job incentive is recognition as an excellent teacher (Williams 2003). This recognition is reflected in your students' warmth, enthusiasm, and appreciation. These positive responses provide a strong internal motivation for teachers. Remember how you felt when your teacher helped you complete a tough assignment, or when you accomplished something and shared that feat with the responsible teacher? Yes, that creates a real glow in a teacher's eyes!

Earning the respect of colleagues is another incentive. Phi Delta Kappa, the educational honor society, once had the motto "The esteem of our colleagues is the foundation of power." Such esteem helps make teachers develop a sense of **efficacy**, a feeling that they can get the job done. Effective teachers believe that they control their own classroom destinies, and they show behaviors related to self-actualization and transcendence, which are the very highest of human needs (Maslow, 1970; see Margolis & McCabe 2003 for an excellent discussion of self-efficacy).

You gain respect from your colleagues when your students achieve more than expected, when they are successful in your classes, and when the tough cases are not too tough for you. These accomplishments will result if you use the broad spectrum of teaching strategies we illustrate in the ensuing chapters. Efficacy, in the last analysis, is being able to see yourself doing the job, no matter how difficult or demanding it might be. (See Brouwers & Tomie 2000.)

Another incentive is working with other professionals. As we pointed out earlier, most teachers are isolated from other professionals for most of a typical working day. Part of being a teaching professional is working on school problems, curriculum projects, or instructional designs with your colleagues. These activities allow you to participate in the decision-making processes of the school. Working in a collegial manner with your fellow professionals to improve the environment for learning is one aspect of teacher empowerment, in which the concept of efficacy is moved up one level to collective action rather than referring only to individual excellence.

The school is a complex institution, and the school culture has a profound impact on your teaching. We know of a high school where a large sign in the teachers' lounge proclaims, "School Business Is Not Discussed Here." Do you want to guess what kind of teaching culture has evolved there? (Maybe you'd rather not.) But you immediately become a part of any school's culture, and you can have a positive impact on it. Being efficacious is the quickest way to influence that culture. Use this book to develop a variety of instructional skills that make you the best teacher that you can be, inspiring others to do their best.

Don't be afraid to improve your school's teaching culture.

Teachers' Levels of Functioning

◆ Intentionally disinviting

◆ Unintentionally disinviting

◆ Unintentionally inviting

◆ Intentionally inviting

Reflect

◆ How did your schooling enhance your social capital?

◆ What evidence would you seek to determine the level of caringness in a school?

◆ Choose two of the four contexts of schooling discussed here—social, emotional, educational, and collegial. Compare the two. How might the forces and influences of these two contexts create conflict in your teaching environment? How might they reinforce each other?

Professionalism and Diversity

As educators, we realize that the United States is an amalgam of a broad spectrum of individuals. Schools reflect a diverse range of ethnic, language, racial, and religious groups. Further diversity results from regional influences and physical characteristics in the school-age population: gender, disabilities, physical dimensions such as height and weight, and other observable personal traits. Our national diversity makes it difficult to define a single U.S. culture. While the people of the United States have a common root language and many shared values, we are a culturally plural society.

As teachers, we have a professional obligation to be aware of commonalities and differences in the many cultures represented in our schools. Students and their teachers are similar in many ways and yet different in others. A major question you will face as a teacher is this: Should the selection of instructional objectives and teaching strategies promote unity or celebrate differences? Or should it do both? What resources does your school provide to make necessary accommodations to instruct all students at an optimal level?

For teachers, diversity also means providing a wide range of instructional options. There are age-related considerations regarding the instructional options that you offer to your elementary school students, but middle school classes can be equally diverse, as can an Advanced Placement high school course. We hope you will give your students the broadest possible view of the subjects or areas that you teach. In so doing, you can provide a global view of history, art, or science rather than a narrow, parochial perspective. The transmission of our culture is a key element of teaching. Thinking about diversity in all dimensions makes for a richer educational environment. This topic will be expanded and amplified in Chapter 2, where we will look at the "Big Picture" of the impact of diversity on our nation's schools.

Key Ideas   **Professionalism and Diversity**

◆ Recognize different cultures in your classroom.

◆ Respect all who show up in your classes.

◆ Be cognizant of similarities and differences in groups.

◆ Offer an enriched curriculum.

SECTION 2 The Challenge of Reflective Teaching and Decision Making

As you begin your journey in teaching you will be exposed to many different ideas, values, and theoretical models. In this section, we want to provide you with a series of perspectives so that you may be fully informed when you make instructional decisions.

Teaching as Art and Science

Professional-level teaching is both an art and a science (see Eisner 2003). Like an artist, a good teacher makes decisions from both a technical and a creative perspective. Great artists display a mastery of technical skills—painting, glass blowing, sculpting—that includes a grasp of the science behind how these techniques work. They also know when and in what way to apply their technical skills. They make decisions. That part is the art. Similarly, teachers develop their science by using carefully planned, fine-tuned lessons that reflect an understanding of many different teaching techniques. They apply each technique skillfully to gain the desired intellectual, social, affective, or kinesthetic result. They develop artistry by being aware of what they are doing and how their actions affect their learners. They are constantly aware that the choices they make affect the intellectual, attitudinal, and psychomotor skills of their students. Above all, they make decisions.

Importance of Research-Based Teaching Methods   Nearly all of the instructional techniques presented in this book have an extensive body of research supporting them. You will be a consumer of research and may even contribute to that literature; as you progress through your teacher education program, you may encounter advocates of some golden technique. Ask for empirically derived data—that is, longitudinal experimental and control group results that have been replicated. The educational fads that abound usually have no such data to back them up. Understanding and interpreting research is part of the science of teaching. Using that knowledge appropriately, making the right decisions, is the artistry.

The most effective teaching methods are empirically verified.

One last point on this topic: Robert Marzano (2007) provides research-based evidence that teachers who have a strong professional pedagogical competence also have students who show greater academic achievement. Yes, there is a very powerful link between your instructional knowledge and how well your students will do in the school setting. Having a diverse set of teaching methods gives you an opportunity to blend the art and science of teaching.

National Board for Professional Teaching Standards (NBPTS)   There is yet one more hurdle to surmount on your path to top-level professional recognition. The NBPTS came into being as a consequence of the Carnegie Task Force on Teaching as a Profession in 1989. The NBPTS has established both content and instructional standards for the profession, which are based on the following five "core propositions":

1. Teachers are committed to students and their learning.
2. Teachers know the subjects they teach and how to teach those subjects to students.

3. Teachers are responsible for managing and monitoring student learning.
4. Teachers think systematically about their practice and learn from experience.
5. Teachers are members of learning communities.

Obtaining NBPTS certification is a rigorous endeavor, and most states add a handsome yearly stipend to teachers' salaries for those who pass muster. At least one research study shows that teachers in grades 3 through 6 in Arizona who were NBPTS certified tended to be more effective in terms of student achievement (Vandevoort, Amrein-Beardsley, & Berliner 2004).

As you can see, much is expected of professional teachers, both within the occupation and outside it.

In keeping with our goal of providing you with a basic core of technical aspects of teaching to make your entry into the classroom an informed one, the back inside cover of this textbook provides the Interstate New Teacher Assessment and Support Consortium (INTASC) Standards and shows where in this textbook you will gain the entry-level knowledge to meet this organization's standards for all beginning teachers.

Decision Making and Responsibility

Decisions and judgment put the art in teaching.

Implicit within the concept of decision making is the notion of *responsibility*. Teachers cannot pass the buck. If you make a decision, you must be willing to take responsibility for both the implementation and the outcome. As we mentioned previously, some decisions are made for you—class sizes, time schedules, curriculum guides, lunch schedules. But you make the instructional decisions (see Lashway 2002 for an interesting statement on this topic).

In our opinion, many teachers do not recognize their responsibility for making decisions. They tend to blame the administration or the school board. To be sure, administrative regulations and school board policies do govern some instructional procedures and content. But most classroom instructional decisions are, in fact, the teacher's. It is you who will answer such questions as "Should I spend one period on the map-making activity, or two?" "Shall I have the students prepare poster sessions for small-group presentations?" "How many periods can I allot for a class activity?" On the surface, these are not monumental decisions, but they all have an impact on your students. Take responsibility for making such decisions, and make them logically and deliberately rather than according to impulse.

The buck stops with you.

Teachers who take responsibility for decision making obtain as much information as possible about both students and subject matter and then develop an instructional plan geared for success. This plan is based on their conclusions about the interaction between the subject matter, the students, and the teacher. One way to begin acting more deliberately is to use "if-then" logic in your thinking. Think about causes and effects. For example, *if you*

Act deliberately, thinking cause + effect.

VIDEO CASE

The Video Case "Teacher Accountability: A Student Teacher's Perspective" on the student website explains a national movement that holds teachers responsible for student performance. After you watch the video clips and study the artifacts in the case, reflect on these questions: (1) To what extent do you agree that student performance is your responsibility? (2) How much responsibility rests with administrators, school boards, or the students themselves?

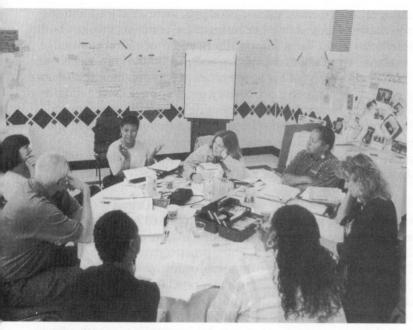

Teachers choosing materials.
© Michael Zide

desire to encourage students to learn through inquiry techniques, *then* you must provide them with the initial learning skills they need to make inquiries. This technique helps raise your level of cognitive awareness; it provides a cognitive map for you to use in generating rules and principles and in thinking about relationships between classroom activities and students.

If there is one indisputable statement about teaching, it is that there is no one "right" way to teach anything or anyone. With alarming frequency, educational authorities and critics announce that they have discovered the answer to the nation's teaching problems. In this book, we will never say that we have discovered *the* teaching method to use in a given situation. Instead, we will present a series of options, all of them practical and able to provide results. This is our way of showing diversity. If teaching is a decision-making activity based on individual teachers' skills, knowledge, and artistry, then there ought to be a variety of means for accomplishing any instructional objective.

Reflect

◆ What topics in your teaching specialty can be used to illustrate teaching as artistry?

◆ How can you determine how well a teaching episode has integrated the technical skills into the art of teaching?

Selecting Developmentally Appropriate Content and Processes

As you plan to teach a subject, you must remember that the processes that students use to master the content of a lesson are just as important as the content itself. Cunard Steamship Lines once advertised that "Getting there is half the fun!" The same idea applies to teaching. Students must know how to accomplish what you want them to learn. And, once they know how to get there, they'll enjoy the journey.

For example, a middle school math teacher wants to teach students how to use ratios. Before they can use ratios, however, the students must be able to understand the meaning of division, to comprehend the concept of whole numbers, to conceptualize the notion of proportions, and to perform basic arithmetic operations. These different kinds of knowledge are typically divided into two categories: **declarative** or **content knowledge** (knowing *what*) and **procedural** or **process knowledge** (knowing *how*).

Content = declarative knowledge
Process = procedural knowledge

In the teaching of ratios to middle school students, there are at least four specific concepts to master, listed above. Mastering these concepts involves both declarative knowledge (rules, facts, information), and procedural knowledge. (Division, for example, entails both declarative and procedural knowledge.) We use this example because many of the academic concepts taught in school are a mix of some content base (poetry, art, history, geography, science) and processes (writing, drawing, analyzing, experimenting). Learning one concept—ratios—calls for a carefully integrated approach that requires students to know and understand both content and processes, when applicable.

You can make your instructional decision-making process more deliberate by being aware of content and process implications.

Grade-Level Considerations: Subject Orientation vs. Child Orientation   When prospective teachers are asked what concerns them most as they anticipate beginning their career, many secondary education majors identify knowledge of subject matter as their chief concern. Thus, prospective secondary school teachers tend to be *subject oriented*. In contrast, prospective elementary school teachers tend to be *child oriented*. Their primary objective is to help children grow and mature mentally and physically, not just to teach mathematics, science, or writing. Accordingly, the activities of elementary school teachers will be oriented toward processes, such as helping children make a smooth adjustment from their home environment to the institutional dimensions of school, rather than content.

Middle school provides the transition from a human-growth orientation to a content orientation. It is critically important for middle school educators to understand that young adolescents are just beginning to emerge cognitively from Jean Piaget's concrete operational stage and are entering the initial formal stage (refer to Orlich 2000). To teach this group effectively, teachers must combine hands-on activities with thinking activities for all major concepts. Techniques such as preparing time lines, conducting experiments, designing charts and graphs, classifying, and sequencing are useful to learners at this age. High school teachers tend to focus on content, a focus endorsed by our society at large.

More than half a century ago, anthropologist Clyde Kluckhohn (1949) concluded that the schools of any society mirror that society. The wishes and beliefs of a society are subtly translated into the values, curricula, and instructions of its schools. In the late 1960s and early 1970s, many secondary school educators wanted to "humanize" secondary schools by making them more process oriented (see Read and Simon 1975). But when journalists, school board members, legislators, and parents began to pressure high school teachers to improve test scores and raise academic standards, those same teachers refocused their efforts on content.

To some extent, processes must be taught along with content, with an eye toward the needs of each student. Occasionally a teacher will say, "Well, if they didn't have the knowledge or techniques before they got into my class, that's too bad!" (This is an example of being intentionally disinviting.) But if students do not have the **prerequisite skills**, then you as a teacher must provide them. If you provide the basics, then your students will be successful. If you do not, then your students will fail. This important decision is yours, and it reflects being intentionally inviting.

Transition from child to subject orientation

Equity Considerations   So far our discussion has focused on decision making based on students' cognitive levels, but your decisions should also be affected by equity considerations. What do we mean by *equity*? In our view, the term means that *every* student in your class has an equal opportunity to learn. It means that you consciously decide to include all members of the class in all activities. This means fairness in asking questions, in delegating student work assignments, and in providing access to resources, such as computer time. In short, it means that you give every student the same opportunity to excel.

Give each child a chance to excel.

We are bothered, quite frankly, by curriculum frameworks designed around a single standard that every child must attain regardless of aptitude. Instead, curriculum frameworks should stress individual excellence. And this is where you come into the process: If you decide to hold every student responsible for doing his or her very best, your students will rise to the occasion.

Reflect

◆ Think about your elementary, middle school, and secondary education. What are some of the processes you learned at each stage of your education? What were some of the content areas?

◆ Were there points at which one aspect—process or content—was clearly emphasized over the other?

◆ Were there points at which process and content were inseparable?

Motivation and Learning

The vast majority of school-age children can master most topics, assuming the content is appropriate and learning is paced appropriately (see Bloom 1984). You, as the teacher, will be responsible for making decisions that will help every student in your class. A particularly important one is to encourage each child to take responsibility for learning. Teachers can teach only if the learner has some desire to learn. We call that desire **motivation**.

Motivation is the inner drive to do something—to finish a book, complete a tough assignment, make the cross-country track team. Motivation is an abstract concept, but it will become very much a part of your vocabulary. Winning coaches have more going for them than good players—they are also great motivators. They can get their players to perform better than the players think they are capable of performing. The same principle applies to great teachers. In the classroom, you try to motivate students to do their best work. You may appeal to their inner selves, hoping that they will do an assignment to please themselves, because they enjoy it, or to meet a challenge. In other words, you appeal to students' **intrinsic motivations**. However, not all students are intrinsically motivated, so we also use a range of **extrinsic motivations**. These include stars on a paper, letter grades, special treatment (a party or time off to do something a student wants to do on his or her own), and even prizes. Part of the

◀◀ ▶ ▶▶ **VIDEO CASE**

Discover the benefits of a student-run school store in the Video Case "Motivating Adolescent Learners: Curriculum Based on Real Life" on the student website. After you watch the video clips and study the artifacts in the case, reflect on the following questions: (1) What are the intrinsic motivations of working in the store? (2) What are the extrinsic ones?

artistry of teaching is in knowing when to use intrinsic motivation and when to use extrinsic motivation. Part of the science of teaching involves determining which ones to use on specific students. (See Cretu 2003 for an interesting treatment of this topic.)

Intrinsic vs. extrinsic motivation

Choosing Technology Wisely

It may surprise you, but we consider the use of high-tech equipment in the classroom an extrinsic motivator. Why? Children and adolescents view the use of personal computers and other peripheral equipment as a game or challenge. That qualifies technology as an extrinsic motivator. Because students enjoy computer use so much, it's important to make sure the time spent on computers is truly worthwhile. Analyze each technology for its usefulness in helping your students achieve their maximum potential. You will make decisions for your students and perhaps others as you plan for the appropriate integration of any technology as an *instructional tool*. All of the modern and not-so-modern technologies are simply tools that make the process of

---

TECHNOLOGY
Insight

Communication with Professional Educators: Listservs, the Web, Blogs, Wikis, and Online Virtual Reality

The Web has made communication among like-minded individuals very easy. A person who wants to become part of the community of teachers has many opportunities to hear from and interact with experienced, professional educators from all over the world. You can use a computer with Internet access to increase your connection to the world of teaching by making use of listservs, the Web, blogs, Wikis, and online virtual reality.

A **listserv** is a special type of e-mail program that allows people who sign up (or "subscribe") to the listserv to send and receive messages. When you send a message to the listserv address, your message is relayed to all subscribers of the listserv. You can find an extensive directory of teaching-oriented listservs at theteachersguide.com (http://www.theteachersguide.com/listservs.html).

Web-based education resources abound. Some of the better ones encourage visitors to post messages on various topics, encouraging lively discussion of topics of interest to teachers. Try visiting eduwonk.com (http://www.eduwonk .com/index.html), Edutopia's Spiral Notebook (http://www.edutopia.org/ spiralnotebook/), or Teachers.net (http://www.teachers.net/) for opportunities to read about and discuss professional issues facing teachers today.

Blogs (short for "Web logs") and **Wikis** (*wiki* is the Hawaiian word for "fast") are methods of Web-based communication that allow users to share ideas in large or small groups without having to learn Web page formatting code (HTML). Blogs facilitate creation of a personal or public journal. Wikis facilitate the process of creating, sharing, and updating Web pages.

Online virtual reality (VR) environments allow individuals to communicate synchronously (in "real time") with other users in a virtual three-dimensional space. If you are interested in meeting and interacting with teachers from around the world, you may want to visit the Teacher Networking Center in Second Life (www.secondlife.com).

learning a bit more efficient. This book offers references available on the Internet and suggests Web-based reflective activities. To learn more about using technology in your classes, consult resources such as Mark and Cindy Grabe's *Integrating Technology for Meaningful Learning* (2007) and Art Recesso and Chandra Orrill's *Integrating Technology into Teaching* (2008).

Obviously, the full potential of the available technological resources has yet to be reached in the schools. We predict that school reform will focus on expanding learning opportunities through electronic media. And you are on stage as the excitement commences.

Teaching as Reflection and Problem Solving

Reflective teaching stems from John Dewey's concept of "reflective inquiry" (Dewey 1998). Dewey viewed the student as an inquirer and an active participant in learning. He assumed that the interaction of subject matter and method of inquiry could not be ignored in schooling. Following this line of thinking, the reflective teacher makes decisions based on a problem-solving paradigm. Problems are not viewed as obstacles to overcome but as opportunities to be met. Teachers reflect on problems, and as part of a learning community, they call on others to reflect on identified problems. In such cases, the staff collectively lists a series of alternatives that they can take. Ultimately, they narrow such lists to sets of actions that are ethical, just, and educationally sound.

Now you might be thinking, "Isn't a lot of problem solving a matter of using intuition?" Actually, it is not. Intuition is subjective and spontaneous. Although reflective teachers may rely on past experiences to solve problems, they tend to make decisions based on what they know about the learner and the content to be mastered. The reflective teacher is deliberate, rational, and organized (see Distad & Brownstein 2004).

Reflective teachers incorporate social aspects in their instructional planning. They cognitively make the necessary adjustments in their instruction so that all students have an opportunity to succeed. The reflective teacher also questions others' decisions that may have negative social impact. For example, in 2001 the parents of students attending a middle school in Palo Alto, California, were asked to purchase for their sixth-graders $2,000 laptop computers ("Calif. School" 2001). Such a policy would not have been implemented if the teachers and administrators of that school had been the least reflective on the negative economic impact it would have on family budgets. Even Palo Alto, a generally prosperous community, has a significant number of families living at the poverty line. (See Ancess 2000 for an interesting case study on this topic.)

The box on page 22 sums up the major characteristics of reflective teachers.

Do you think an air traffic controller has a challenging, fast-paced job? As a classroom teacher, you'll be exceeding air traffic controllers in the number of decisions made per day. As we stress in Chapter 6, a large number of decisions will be made as a consequence of your personal observations of the class—who is doing what, what is being done, what you can anticipate. You are the primary decision maker on how your classroom is organized and managed for instruction.

As you develop the artistry and science of teaching, you will become more aware of how your decisions affect the intellectual and attitudinal development of your students. You alone make the decision to plan, to be organized, and to be well prepared. As national and state standards become more broadly incorporated into curriculum designs, you will find that some of your control over content will be modified. But effective teaching will always involve dynamic interactions between and among teachers and administrators, teachers and teachers, teachers and parents, teachers and learners, and learners and learners, in which all participants are continuously making decisions—including the all-important decision, made by your student, to embrace learning.

Key Ideas

Characteristics of Reflective Teachers

- ◆ Care about students.
- ◆ Understand the social context of schooling.
- ◆ Question assumptions.
- ◆ Know content.
- ◆ Identify problems or issues.
- ◆ Collect relevant data.
- ◆ Construct a plan of operation.
- ◆ Use many instructional strategies.
- ◆ Practice problem-solving strategies.
- ◆ Think prospectively and retrospectively.
- ◆ Realize that reflection is cyclical.
- ◆ Evaluate the results and processes used.

Reflect

A Closing Reflection

- ◆ "Harm no one." How does this motto apply to teacher decision making?
- ◆ Plan a short study to determine how many decisions a teacher makes in a day.
- ◆ What motivational techniques are espoused in your teacher education program?
- ◆ How would being a reflective teacher affect your plans to teach?
- ◆ How does your teacher education program address instruction?

Summary Points

1. Teaching is a profession with its own body of knowledge, models, and techniques.
2. Schooling takes place within many contexts, including social, emotional, educational, and collegial or professional.

3. Public schools are subject to outside influences, such as political, business, and advocacy groups.
4. Teaching is a science because it requires knowledge of technique. It is also an art because it requires decision making.
5. Effective teachers take responsibility for their decisions.
6. Teachers should select content and processes on the basis of developmental appropriateness and educational equity.
7. For both teachers and students, intrinsic motivation comes from within, and extrinsic motivation comes from outside sources.
8. Teachers should employ careful decision making in evaluating and using technology.

Building a Career Portfolio

As you begin your journey toward excellence in teaching, consider developing a file or portfolio of items that will have some immediate use when you walk into your first class. To help get you started, at the end of each chapter we will make a few suggestions for your career portfolio.

- Compile a list or search the Internet for a listing of instructional questions that you consider "Big Questions": questions that you want to answer prior to having your own classroom.

- What kinds of social and educational information about your school district and students will you need to know before you begin your first teaching job?

- List some classroom practices that will encourage "reflective thinking" by all students, and explain why you chose them.

Resources

PRINT

Danielson, C. *Enhancing Professional Practice: A Framework for Teaching* (2nd ed.). Alexandria, VA: Association for Supervision and Curriculum Development, 2007, 208 pp.
Charlotte Danielson describes 22 broad components of successful teaching. In one sense, this book summarizes the spectrum of teacher education standards.

Distad, L. S., & J. C. Brownstein. *Talking Teaching: Implementing Reflective Practice in Groups.* Lanham, MD: Scarecrow Education, 2004, 88 pp.
In a very few pages the authors present the concept of reflective teaching, with practices and case studies.

Green, T., A. Brown, & L. Robinson. *Making the Most of the Web in Your Classroom: A Teacher's Guide to Blogs, Podcasts, Wikis, Pages, and Sites.* Thousand Oaks, CA: Corwin Press, 2007.
This book is designed to familiarize teachers with the Web and provides tools for incorporating the Web into classroom instruction to support

learning. It shows teachers how to meet International Society for Technology in Education (ISTE) technology and other content standards, and includes "need to know" aspects of using the Web with students, including a brief history of the Web, the language of the Web, Web tools to enhance learning, Web-editing software, student safety, and "netiquette."

Kozol, J. *Letters to a Young Teacher.* New York: Crown Publishing Group, 2007, 304 pp.
Jonathan Kozol provides a social commentary covering a range of topics, including segregation, high-stakes testing, predatory business and political interventions. The storyline is developed through the eyes of a first-year urban teacher. Kozol encourages teachers to be advocates for children and challenges all comers who are not.

Michie, G. *See You When We Get There: Teaching for Change in Urban Schools.* New York: Teachers College Press, 2005, 224 pp.
An essential book for those who will teach in inner-city schools. The author weaves personal experience with relevant vignettes.

Purkey, W. W., & J. M. Novak. *Inviting School Success: A Self-Concept Approach to Teaching, Learning, and Democratic Practice* (4th ed.). Belmont, CA: Wadsworth, 2009, 222 pp.
This little book may be the most important statement about positive school interactions that you will ever read. We invite every middle school and high school teacher to read it.

Thomas, D. B., Editor. *Reflective Teaching: A Bridge to Learning.* Ann Arbor, MI: Pierian, 2004, 176 pp.
This book features a collection of papers expanding on the concept of reflective teaching.

INTERNET

Go to the website for this book at www.cengage.com/education/orlich to find live links to resources related to this chapter.

◆ The U.S. Department of Education provides an extensive listing of education-related Internet resources.
   http://www.ed.gov/

◆ The two major teachers' organizations in the United States, the American Federation of Teachers and the National Education Association, maintain websites devoted to a variety of issues of interest to K–12 teachers.
   http://www.aft.org
   http://www.nea.org

◆ Teachers.net is a commercial resource for teachers. The site includes a wide variety of professional development opportunities and resources from preschool to adult education.
   http://www.teachers.net/

◆ The **International Society for Technology in Education (ISTE)** is a source for advancing the effective use of technology in PK–12 and teacher education. It is also the sponsor of the National Educational

Technology Standards (NETS) and the Center for Applied Research in Educational Technology (CARET).
http://www.iste.org

◆ For an expanded treatment of instructional design models, go to Martin Ryder's site. Ryder is a professor at the University of Colorado in Denver. His presentations of instructional design models are must reading.
http://carbon.cudenver.edu/~mryder/itc_data/idmodels.html.

References

Ancess, A. (2000). "The Reciprocal Influence of Teacher Learning, Teaching Practice, School Restructuring, and Student Learning." *Teachers College Record* 102(3): 590–619.

Bloom, B. S. (1984). "The 2 Sigma Problem: The Search for Methods of Group Instruction as Effective as One-to-One Tutoring." *Educational Researcher* 13(6): 4–16.

Brouwers, A., & W. Tomie. (2000). "A Longitudinal Study of Teacher Burnout and Perceived Self-Efficacy in Classroom Management." *Teaching and Teacher Education* 16(2): 239–253

"Calif. School Rethinks Mandatory Laptops." (2001, Nov. 5). *USA Today*, p. 11A.

Carnevale, A. P. (2001). "Investing in Human Capital." *School Administrator* 58(3): 32–35.

Comte-Sponville, A. (2001). *A Small Treatise on the Great Virtues* (translated by Catherine Temerson). New York: Metropolitan.

Cretu, D. (2003, April). "Students' Motivation in Class." *Thinking Classroom* 4(2): 21–28.

Dewey, J. (1998). *How We Think* (revised and expanded edition). Boston: Houghton Mifflin. (Originally published in 1910 and republished in 1933 as *How We Think, A Restatement of the Relation of Reflective Thinking to the Educative Process*, by D. C. Heath, Boston.)

Distad, L. S., & J. C. Brownstein. (2004). *Talking Teaching: Implementing Reflective Practice in Groups.* Lanham, MD: Scarecrow Education.

Eisner, E. W. (2003, July). "Artistry in Education." *Scandinavian Journal of Educational Research 47*(3): 373–384.

Ellis, A. K. (2005). *Research on Educational Innovations* (4th ed.). Larchmont, NY: Eye on Education.

Grabe, M., & C. Grabe. (2007). *Integrating Technology for Meaningful Learning* (5th ed.). Boston: Houghton Mifflin.

Israel, G. D., L. J. Beaulieu, & G. Hartless. (2001). "The Influence of Family and Community Social Capital on Educational Achievement." *Rural Sociology 66*(1): 43–68.

Kluckhohn, C. (1949). *Mirror for Man: The Relation of Anthropology to Modern Life.* New York: Whittlesey House.

Kozol, J. (2007). *Letters to a Young Teacher.* New York: Crown Publishing Group.

Lashway, L. (2002). *Trends in School Leadership. ERIC Digest.* ERIC Clearinghouse on Educational Management, Eugene, OR: EDO-EA-02-09.

Livingston, A., & J. Wirt. (2004). *The Condition of Education 2004 in Brief* (NCES 2004–076). U.S. Department of Education, National Center for Education Statistics. Washington, DC: U.S. Government Printing Office.

Margolis, H., & P. P. McCabe. (2003, Summer). "Self-Efficacy: A Key to Improving the Motivation of Struggling Learners." *Preventing School Failure 47*(4): 162–169.

Marzano, R. J. (2007). *The Art and Science of Teaching: A Comprehensive Framework for Effective Instruction.* Alexandria, VA: ASCD.

Maslow, A. (1970). *Motivation and Personality* (2nd ed.). New York: Harper and Row.

National Commission on Excellence in Education. (1983). *A Nation at Risk: The Imperative for Educational Reform.* Washington, DC: Author.

Noddings, N. (2002). *Educating Moral People: A Caring Alternative to Character Education.* New York: Teachers College Press.

Orlich, D. C. (2000). "Education Reform and Limits to Student Achievement." *Phi Delta Kappan 81*(6): 468–472.

P.L. 107-110, "No Child Left Behind Act of 2001." Washington, DC: 107th Congress, 1st Session, January 8, 2002.

Purkey, W. W., & J. M. Novak. (2009). *Inviting School Success: A Self-Concept Approach to Teaching, Learning, and Democratic Practice* (4th ed.). Belmont, CA: Wadsworth.

Putnam, R. D. (2000). *Bowling Alone: The Collapse and Revival of American Community*. New York: Simon and Schuster.

Read, D. A., & S. B. Simon, Eds. (1975). *Humanistic Education Sourcebook*. Englewood Cliffs, NJ: Prentice Hall.

Recesso, A., & C. Orrill. (2008). *Integrating Technology into Teaching: The Technology and Learning Continuum*. Boston: Houghton Mifflin.

Stanley, P. H., & W. W. Purkey. (2001). *Abstracts of Published Research Articles, Dissertations, and Master Theses Concerning Invitational Theory and Practice*, 2001. ED 450 329

U.S. Department of Education. (1997). *Mini Digest of Education Statistics 1997*. http://nces.gov. See Table 6.

U.S. Department of Education. (1999). *Mini Digest of Education Statistics 1999*. http://nces.gov. See Figure 3.

U.S. Department of Education. (2008). *Projections of Education Statistics to 2008*. http://nces.ed.gov/pubs98/. See Tables 1, B8, 34, 37, and chap. 6.

U.S. Department of Education. National Center for Education Statistics. (1997). *The Condition of Education 1997*. NCES 97–388. Washington, DC: U.S. Government Printing Office, 1997.

Vandevoort, L. G., A. Amrein-Beardsley, & D. C. Berliner. (2004, Sept. 8). "National Board Certified Teachers and Their Students' Achievement." *Education Policy Analysis Archives* 12(46). Retrieved July 13, 2005, from http://epaa.asu.edu/epaa/v12n46/.

Williams, J. S. (2003, May). "Why Great Teachers Stay." *Educational Leadership* 60(8): 71–74.

Woolfolk-Hoy, A., & W. K. Hoy. (2003). *Instructional Leadership: A Learning-Centered Guide*. Needham Heights, MA: Allyn and Bacon/Longman.

The Big Picture in Your Classroom: Focusing the Instruction in a Social Kaleidoscope

1   A Holistic View of Instruction
The Holistic Instructional Cycle
Bases for Instructional Decision Making

2   Three Perspectives on Instructional Decision Making
Developmental Perspective
Behavioral Perspective
Cognitive Perspective
Active Learning

3   Educational Equity as the Big Picture
Ethnic Diversity
Racial and Socioeconomic Diversity
Physical Diversity
Multicultural Perspectives
Language Diversity
Ability Diversity: Who Is Exceptional?
Encouraging Equity in the Classroom Environment
Gender Equity: Awareness of Bias
Differentiating Instruction or Multi-Methodology

Janis Green considered a degree in the health professions, but sitting in on an Introduction to Education course convinced her to become a teacher. In her pre-student teaching class, she wondered why she was being exposed to so many different instructional and learning perspectives. Then, while observing her student teaching mentor, she understood why teachers needed to know several different learning models. The master teacher was applying multiple instructional models and making use of a variety of psychological theories as the lessons were taught.

When Janis began teaching her own middle school class, she had some experience, professional knowledge, and educational theory on which to base instructional decisions. More important, during her lesson planning Janis was able to consider the "big picture" as the details fell into place. As she gained more professional skills and confidence, her teaching subtly changed to incorporate newly learned ideas and research-based practices.

In Chapter 1, you got a glimpse of systematic instruction and some of the external forces at work on the classroom. Now let's go inside the classroom and explore the learning frameworks and other considerations that directly influence your instructional decision making. As you read, think about how you would respond to the following questions.

◆ How do I envision a dynamic instructional cycle?

◆ How might I apply different learning perspectives in my instructional decisions?

◆ What elements are needed to ensure instructional equity for every student?

SECTION 1 A Holistic View of Instruction

Instruction is the key ingredient of schooling, but it is one of many components of providing quality education to all. Below is a vision of how systematic instruction takes place to provide that "best of educations."

The Holistic Instructional Cycle

As Janis realized, dynamic instruction must be viewed as a *big picture* as well as a collection of details. This is the notion of a **holistic instructional view**. As a teacher, you simultaneously shift back and forth from the big picture that you have for your students to the specific parts that you want mastered. This thinking begins on the first day of school.

By thinking about several instructional aspects at once, you are considering variables that can affect both your teaching and the students' learning. Your vision helps you to be organized and systematic. As this chapter unfolds, you'll realize how theory and practice interact in teaching. For example, this textbook emphasizes the procedural, or technical, aspects of instruction. Taken collectively, all ten chapters interact with the attitudinal and psychological components of teaching plus that all-important learner. Figure 2.1 illustrates this phenomenon, as does the Key Ideas box on page 30.

Holistic teaching: big picture + detailed implementation

Bases for Instructional Decision Making

Observe the dynamic interaction that takes place between the four elements in Figure 2.1. Each element informs the others.

The main point is that you try to envision the entire teaching scenario before you ever begin teaching it. For example, when you begin a new unit of instruction, you want to establish some common experience for the entire

FIGURE 2.1

A Holistic Model of Instruction

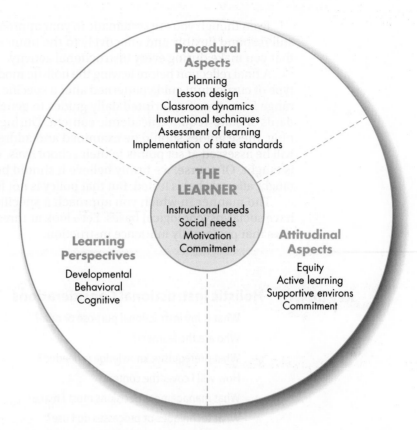

THE LEARNER

Instructional needs
Social needs
Motivation
Commitment

Procedural Aspects

Planning
Lesson design
Classroom dynamics
Instructional techniques
Assessment of learning
Implementation of state standards

Attitudinal Aspects

Equity
Active learning
Supportive environs
Commitment

Learning Perspectives

Developmental
Behavioral
Cognitive

class. Establishing common experiences is going to be a very important part of your instructional planning as uniform and mandatory educational standards are fully implemented. Often the term "set" is used for this common experience, meaning that you set the students' expectations for what is to be learned. We will revisit this topic in Chapter 3.

You might decide to show a video or take the class to the computer center to "surf the Web." Then, after making this decision, you ask yourself, "What purpose does this introductory activity serve for the lesson as a whole?" You also ask yourself what big ideas you are trying to stress in this unit. Or you might be working with a team of teachers, and as a group you'll brainstorm ideas. In addition, you need to consider the learning perspective from which you might approach either the entire class or subgroups within the class. You also need to consider the content to be learned. The easy part of teaching is to cover content. The hard part is deciding what is to be covered (or deleted), how fast, by whom, and in what degree of depth. In the Key Ideas box on page 30, we list some of the big-picture considerations that you must make to be an effective instructor.

Obviously, the learner and the learner's needs are always at the center of this model. It is for the learner that you use different instructional techniques. The learner's successes help to create the conditions by which all the elements coalesce. As you progress through this textbook, you will be provided with in-depth coverage on the principal procedural components of Figure 2.1.

Even though you are systematic in your approach to instruction, you must still respond flexibly and effectively to the numerous on-the-spot decisions that you make during every instructional activity.

A final reflection before leaving the holistic model: Most schools have some type of curriculum guide patterned after a specific set of state standards. They range from specific, scripted daily guides to general statements about standards or state-required academic content. During the holistic phase of planning, these guides should be examined and addressed because the students will be assessed at set points in their school lives. Yes, the tests do affect what is taught. Of course, we firmly believe it should be the reverse—that what is taught affects what is tested. But that policy is not for us to decide just yet.

The manner in which you approach a specific concept or standard will have social-psychological bases. Let's look at three such theoretical perspectives that profoundly influence instruction.

Key Ideas   Holistic Instructional Considerations

- ◆ What is my instructional purpose or goal?
- ◆ Who are the learners?
- ◆ What prerequisite knowledge is needed?
- ◆ How will I cover the content?
- ◆ What management decisions must I make?
- ◆ What techniques or processes do I use?
- ◆ How will I share responsibilities with others?
- ◆ What instructional resources do we have?
- ◆ What special student considerations must I take into account?
- ◆ How can I ensure instructional equity?
- ◆ What state standards must be addressed?
- ◆ How will I assess learning?

Reflect

- ◆ Recall a time in your teacher education when you suddenly saw the big picture of what you were learning. How did the big picture and the smaller elements fit together?
- ◆ Think about an area in which you anticipate teaching. What would be the big picture for one unit? What are some smaller ways to achieve the holistic goal?

SECTION 2

Three Perspectives on Instructional Decision Making

From your study of educational psychology, you know that several learning theories or perspectives can guide teaching and learning. Three perspectives in particular tend to have a great impact on what is taught and how it is presented: the *developmental, behavioral,* and *cognitive* perspectives. The specific teaching model, or set of instructional procedures, that you use probably will be based on one of these three or on an **eclectic** model—one that borrows from or mixes several approaches. Let's briefly explore how learning theories apply to instructional strategies. You can refer to a standard educational psychology text for more detailed information about each theory.

Developmental Perspective

Piaget's Developmental Stages   A very popular teaching and learning model is the *developmental* approach, most often associated with Jean Piaget (1896–1980). This model assumes that humans develop intellectually in various overlapping stages. In Piaget's model (1969), there are four stages or periods of development—the **sensorimotor stage** from birth to 2 years; the **preoperational stage** from 2 to 8 years; the **concrete operational stage** from 8 to 11 years; and the **formal operations stage** from 11 to 15 years and up. The last stage is what schools attempt to reach, what we loosely call the "thinking and analyzing stage." However, the bulk of students in middle and high school are still at the concrete operational stage, and thus they require many illustrations, models, pictures, and activities. The developmental stages in Piaget's model are not fixed for any one individual or group; instead, they tend to overlap. In the middle school grades, for example, you will find a wide range of developmental levels, from students who are not yet in the early concrete operational stage to students who have already reached the formal stage. High school students also show a range of intellectual development. Additionally, the developmental stages are not uniformly attained by the same individual within different academic disciplines: A student might be at the formal stage in the social sciences but only at the concrete stage in mathematics.

For intellectual growth to occur, teachers must provide students with key experiences or activities.

Vygotsky's Socially Mediated Learning   Another well-respected learning theory was proposed by Lev Vygotsky (1896–1934). His **schema**, or model, of intellectual growth centers not on developmental stages but on what he terms the zone of proximal development and on patterns of social interaction (Vygotsky 1962).

The **zone of proximal development (ZPD)** is the difference between the intellectual level a child can reach on his or her own and the level he or she can potentially reach if aided by an expert peer or adult. How do you know where a given child's zone falls? You find out somewhat by trial and error. When your instruction is appropriate for the child's zone, learning occurs rather rapidly. Instruction outside the zone is not effective. Learners in their ZPD move easily from what they now know to what they can do next. You also might determine

Piaget: Age-based, but possibly overlapping, thinking stages whether some concept or knowledge is lacking by giving a short pretest on the prerequisite knowledge. The results of the pretest will show whether you need to provide more introductory material. Having prerequisite knowledge is a condition for the ZPD.

In Vygotsky's theory, there are no maturation levels such as those implied by Piaget's stages of growth. If a child does not learn some concept, according to Piaget's theory, the child was not developmentally ready. For a Vygotskian, the instruction was outside the child's zone of proximal development. (See Shayer & Adey 2002 for an excellent discussion.)

The second aspect of Vygotsky's theory is that learning has a social quality. As a child listens to a discussion, the child can think along. Eventually, the child will **internalize** the ideas and can then work individually. Social interaction is a key to learning. Piaget and Albert Bandura (1977, 1997) also observed this quality (see Becker & Varelas 2001; Kozulin 2003).

Vygotsky: what the child can learn with adult's help

Social interaction is key

Implications for Instructional Decision Making

In Piaget's theory, two concepts for instructional effectiveness are critical: age and individual appropriateness (see Adey & Shayer 1994; Bredekamp 1997; Shayer & Adey 2002). If you subscribe to Piaget's stages of growth, then you will attempt to find age-appropriate materials. That means for grade 4 you need materials that can be mastered by 9- or 10-year-olds. The same idea would apply to instructing 15-year-old high school sophomores.

As a Piagetian, you would first introduce some activity that has learning value. After the children experience the activity, you would label the concept being taught so that your students could understand the experience and the formal term together. For example, if you were teaching the concept of time zones, you might show students a map of the United States and tell them what time it is in various cities. Then you would have the children come to some conclusion about what happens to times as you move from east to west or vice versa. Once students had gained experience with this exercise, you would label the zones Eastern, Central, Rocky Mountain, and Pacific.

How would you approach the time zone lesson using Vygotsky's model? First, you would assess your students' zone of proximal development to determine whether introducing the concept would be worthwhile or futile. In the early primary grades, for example, you can teach children how to tell time, but the concept of time zones is simply beyond their zone of proximal development. No matter how hard you might try to teach the concept, the children would not understand it.

But if the children were ready, say by the sixth or seventh grade, you probably would divide the class into small discussion groups and provide each team with maps, markers, and time information for various cities. The groups would be actively and socially involved in trying to visualize some pattern related to times. Finally, with your help, one group would come to the conclusion that there are four distinct time zones in the continental United States. Each group would share this finding. Finally, each learner would understand the concept on an individual basis.

But suppose two students still could not solve time zone problems alone. What would you do then? You would continue the social interaction aspect by assigning peer tutors to the students who had not mastered the time zone concept and hope that further social interaction would complete the learning cycle. We will expand this treatment of constructivism in Chapter 9, where inquiry and higher-order thinking strategies are presented.

Table 2.1 shows an array of ages, grades, and developmental levels. Let us assume that you want to introduce a concept that is clearly at a formal level of thinking. The data in Table 2.1 (synthesized by Herman Epstein, noted Piagetian scholar) show that, even in the junior and senior years of high school, a large percentage of the students are not yet at that cognitive level. In Chapter 5, we illustrate some techniques that will help you teach difficult concepts.

As you examine Table 2.1 it becomes obvious that not all high-school-aged students are thinking at a formal cognitive level. The National Assessment for Educational Progress (NAEP) tests validate the data in Table 2.1 by showing wide discrepancies in various levels of learning in math, science, reading, and writing. The NAEP test questions are designed to reflect five levels of thinking. However, the percentages of students meeting those levels at grades 4, 8 and 11 all decline. These declines would appear to be predicted from the data in Table 2.1. (See NCES 98-530, Tables 1–4; these are the latest data published.)

TABLE 2.1		Percentage of Students at Piaget's Cognitive Levels				
Age	Grade	Intuition (a)	Entry Concrete (b)	Advanced Concrete (a)	Entry Formal (b)	Middle Formal (b)
5.5	P	78	22			
6	K	68	27	5		
7	1	35	55	10		
8	2	25	55	20		
9	3	15	55	30		
10	4	12	52	35	1	
11	5	6	49	40	5	
12	6–7	5	32	51	12	
13	7–8	2	34	44	14	6
14	8–9	1	32	43	15	9
15	9–10	1	15	53	18	13
16	10–11	1	13	50	17	19
16–17	11–12	3		47	19	12
17–18	12	1	15	50	15	19
Adult	—	20	22	26	17	15

1. Level a in each category is composed of children who have just begun to manifest one or two of that level's reasoning schemes, whereas level b refers to children manifesting half a dozen or more reasoning schemes.

Source: Table derived by Herman T. Epstein, personal communication, June 8, 1999. Sources used are J. Smedslund, *Concrete Reasoning: A Study of Intellectual Development* (Lafayette, IN: Child Development Publications of the Society for Research in Child Development, 1964); P. Arlin, personal communication with H. T. Epstein; T. D. Wei, et al., "Piaget's Concept of Classification: A Comparative Study of Socially Disadvantaged and Middle-Class Young Children," *Child Development* 42 (1971): 919–924; J. W. Renner, D. G. Stafford, A. E. Lawson, J. W. McKinnon, F. E. Friot, and D. H. Kellogg, *Research, Teaching and Learning with the Piaget Model* (Norman: University of Oklahoma Press, 1976); M. Shayer and P. Adey, *Towards a Science of Science Teaching* (London: Heinemann, 1981). Reprinted with permission of Dr. Herman T. Epstein. (For a detailed discussion, see Herman T. Epstein, "Biopsychological Aspects of Memory and Education," in *Advances in Psychology Research*, Volume 11, S. P. Shohov, editor, New York: Nova, pp. 181–186.)

But at this point we simply want you to be aware of planning for instruction. We also encourage you to use reflective thought about providing instruction and experiences at the cognitive levels where the bulk of your students reside. (See also Shayer & Adey 1981.)

Providing experiences essential in both theories

Reflect

◆ Prepare a chart that illustrates the key elements of Piaget's and Vygotsky's theories. Where are they different? Where are they similar?

◆ Examine a school district curriculum guide for a selected grade level. Do you find terms such as *developmental* or *age appropriate* in the guide? If so, how are they used?

◆ State standards assume that every child, at any grade level, will master every topic. Discuss this assumption with your classmates and your education professors in light of the NAEP data.

Behavioral Perspective

Overview   According to the **behavioral perspective**, learning can be defined as an observable change in behavior. The modern behavioral movement was initiated by B. F. Skinner (1938). However, Ralph W. Tyler (1949), with his use of behavioral objectives to guide lesson design, instituted a major educational application of behaviorism. One might even be so bold as to suggest that the twenty-first century's enthusiasm for standards and accountability is simply an extension of Tyler's behavioral objectives. Behaviorism is usually aimed at students who display some inappropriate behavior or who have emotional disorders. Behaviorism is a very complex model, with many ramifications and applications to life outside education. One element of the theory is **transfer of learning**. This term refers to the **application** of something learned in some specific situation to a novel or new setting. For example, you have just completed instruction on ratios. One of your students comes up to you and says, "Do you realize it is cheaper per ounce to buy a twenty-ounce bottle of soda pop than a ten-ounce bottle?" You ask the student to tell you more. The student then shows how, by setting up ratios to determine per-ounce costs, the relative unit values can be computed. You smile! (We will discuss this technique in relation to behavioral management in Chapter 6.)

The behavioral perspective provides a theoretical foundation for many approaches to teaching and curriculum construction. It is not simply a behavior management model. For example, a very popular elementary science program, *Science: A Process Approach* (SAPA), is structured entirely on behavioral principles. *Instructional Theory Into Practice* (ITIP), popularized by Madeline C. Hunter (1982), was designed from this perspective.

Direct Instruction   When you apply behavioral theory to instruction, you will find yourself establishing specific learning objectives and building a sequence of learning activities that proceed from simple to more complex. More than likely, you will adopt a teaching model called **direct instruction** (see Carnine 2000). This model is based on behavioral principles. It is a popular technique, and we illustrate it here as an application of the behavioral perspective. (Keep in mind that many "constructivist" strategies, such as cooperative learning groups, are based on behavioral assumptions and implications.)

Direct instruction is often called "whole-group" or "teacher-led" instruction. Basically, the technique involves academic focus, provides few optional choices for student-initiated activities, tends to be large-group oriented, and emphasizes factual knowledge. In response to those who have criticized direct instruction as being oriented toward rote learning, one study showed that elementary school pupils taught via direct instruction showed progress in the higher-order intellectual areas associated with problem solving (Elliott, Busse, & Shapiro 1999). A review of the research indicates that direct instruction does transfer skills across a broad range of learners and subject areas (Adams & Engelmann 1996). The technique is used to increase on-task learning time, thinking skills, problem solving, computer literacy, writing skills, and science learning. Sara G. Tarver (2003) and others provide a comprehensive review of issues related to direct instruction. Arthur K. Ellis (2005) provides a detailed analysis of the research basis for direct instruction. He concludes that the evidence ranges from simple advocacy to data-driven empirical evidence.

Martin A. Kozloff et al. (2001) summarize steps for using the technique effectively. These steps and the strengths of the system are listed in the boxes below. Direct instruction is often used when teachers are required to use "scripted lessons." These lessons prescribe every detail for a teacher to follow, and they tend to be found in special education classes in some schools.

Direct instruction relies on the application of behavioral principles

Not a rigid, low-level instructional model

Key Ideas **Strengths of Direct Instruction**

- Content is delivered to entire class.
- Teacher controls focus of attention.
- Process maximizes use of available time.
- Feedback assesses class understanding of learning.
- Teacher focuses on class objectives.
- Teacher provides clarity through explanations.
- Less teacher preparation is required.
- All students work on same task.

Steps for Direct Instruction

1. Review and check previous work.
2. Present new material in small units.
3. Provide for guided practice.
4. Provide feedback and correctives.
5. Supervise independent seat-work.
6. Review concepts every week and every month.

Programmed Instruction When you use computer-assisted instruction, the basic learning theory supporting the technique is grounded in the behavioral concept of **programmed instruction**. That technique provides for small, discrete increments of instruction plus immediate reinforcement for correct responses. When you use lessons that are subdivided into achievable components or modules, you use behavioral principles. We will expand on these topics in Chapters 3 and 4.

Cognitive Perspective

Cognitive Psychology   We want to provide you with a framework for analyzing any instructional model or curriculum to discover its theoretical basis. You can then align your teaching methods with the content, thereby helping your students be more successful learners. So far we have briefly explored selected aspects of the developmental and behavioral theoretical perspectives that will affect your instructional decision making.

Over the past several years, a school of thought known as **cognitive psychology** has emerged. The goal of this model is to develop student academic and thinking skills from a novice level to a more expert level. Obviously, it takes maturity and time for this transition to occur. One way to help it along is to teach students how to think about thinking and how to make plans to learn new information more efficiently.

A second major goal of the cognitive model is to provide adequate experiences in which students structure the learning and teaching themselves. Obviously, students will need to have access to knowledge, know how to organize it, and be self-motivated to learn. The box below gives a quick overview of the cognitive model (from Ashman & Conway 1993).

Move students to expert level; teach students about thinking

Some Principles of the Cognitive Model of Instruction

- ◆ Students engage in active learning and problem solving.
- ◆ Students use a wide range of learning strategies.
- ◆ Time is allocated for students to apply new skills.
- ◆ Responsibility for learning and problem solving is transferred from teacher to student.
- ◆ Strategies to be learned by students are clearly specified.
- ◆ Rate of student learning is determined by the teacher.
- ◆ Teacher is responsible for instructional decisions.

Tips for Cognitive Instruction   As you examine the list in the box above, you will undoubtedly note that some of these principles overlap with those of other learning theories. Further, you might even infer that school environments play a major role in motivating students to become active learners. Yes, they do, and there are some interactive elements in all learning theories. But what strategies should you use to incorporate cognitive ideas into your teaching? Let's just list a few that are used in **information processing**.

The first process is one called **mnemonics**—the use of some memory-aiding device. A mnemonic device commonly used in science is "Roy G. Biv." This reminds students of the order of colors in the spectrum and in the rainbow—red, orange, yellow, green, blue, indigo, and violet. This mnemonic also arranges the colors from the longest wavelengths to the shortest. Surely you have used mnemonic devices to remember a series or chain of events.

A second strategy is to create visual or graphic organizers such as charts or time lines. Enter a middle school history class, and you will probably see a time line skirting the entire perimeter of the classroom. This helps students visually place historical events in order. Similarly, at the beginning of each chapter in this book we provide a concept map. This tool is an information-processing device to help you learn and remember what each chapter covers.

Visualizing is often used in physical education as well. Participants try to understand just how they will dance, run a course, take a turn on a ski hill, or complete some game strategy. Visualization techniques are also helpful when a student is setting up laboratory equipment or solving a multistep problem. Remember, it is your responsibility to teach your students how to use these cognitive devices. Linda Campbell (2003) provides over 100 instructional tips for teaching science with cognitive strategies.

Learner-Activated Instruction One of the more difficult tasks you will face as a teacher is how to structure your classroom in a way that will let your students initiate learning. Throughout your teaching career you will need to make decisions about how much instructional control to maintain. At one end of the instructional spectrum (see the diagram below) is **student-initiated learning** (or self-directed learning), where students determine how to reach the desired learning outcomes. A classroom that uses student-initiated learning will be a maze of activity: small groups, working groups, and individuals working on projects or activities simultaneously. There is little sequencing of instruction, and the teacher can be observed moving about the room acting as a prompter, question asker, clarifier—in short, a facilitator of learning. (See Agran et al. 2003 for details.)

How much control?

The Spectrum of Instructional Control

Student-Initiated Learning ◄----------► Direct Instruction (Teacher Initiated)

At the other end is teacher-initiated instruction, or direct instruction, which we have already introduced. In this mode you will find an academic focus, little choice of activity for individual students, large-group instruction, and teacher domination over most curricular and instructional decisions. Table 2.2 contrasts these two approaches. The table is included for comparison purposes only; actual practice may be quite different.

In addition to student-initiated learning, there is also the practice of **independent study**. Independent study, as described by John Marlowe (2000), is neither home-schooling nor in-class work. A successful independent study program allows students to work alone on a project or problem. The teacher helps the student plan, but the student has multiple options by which to accomplish the purposes prescribed. (See Alvarado & Herr [2003]; Tate [2003] for strategies associated with student-based learning.) According to the North American Council for Online Learning (2008), more than a million students—including those in private schools and home-schooled students—are enrolled at "virtual schools" across the country. (All of these students would be classified as using independent study. With virtually all public schools now online, this number can be expected to increase.

However, we must add a word of caution. With the advent of state and national standards prescribing curriculum, the perspective of student-initiated

TABLE 2.2	Student-Initiated Instruction Versus Direct Instruction
Student-Initiated Instruction	**Direct Instruction**
Flexibly arranged furniture	Somewhat fixed arrangements
Emphasis on individual or small-group work	Delivery to entire class
Teacher as facilitator	Teacher as controller
Little concern about time	Time used efficiently
Varied assessments	Prompt delivery of feedback
Emphasis on exploration	Emphasis on fundamentals
Flexible classroom structure	Tight classroom structure
Simultaneous activities	All students on same task
Time-consuming preparation	Minimal preparation time

Source: Adapted from Kohn 1996.

learning can be expected to decline precipitously. The extremely prescriptive nature of state and national standards and high-stakes tests means that teachers will have little time to allow students to pursue their own interests. (See Amrein & Berliner 2002 for compelling evidence.) The use of independent learning outside the classroom may be a possible solution to this dilemma.

Obviously, there are many more facets to these two models of instructional control. That is where you come in. You make the decisions, for the most part, concerning how to structure the content and the processes by which it is delivered. Clearly, you need to examine several models of instruction. You need to identify the key features and relative strength of each model. We strongly support using as many different instructional techniques or methods as possible. Why? Because it helps you make decisions deliberately about the best instructional practice for any given content or student need, it helps you involve students actively, and it helps you choose the best level of instructional control for the situation at hand (see Cunningham et al. 2000; Wells 2001).

Constructivist Theory and Practice

Constructivist philosophy, which has evolved over the last half of the twentieth century, is a subset of the cognitive perspective. As educators and others begin to seek a more student-centered instructional model, they tend to be drawn toward the *social-constructivist* camp summarized in the box on page 40. Views of that camp are summarized in the box on the same page (Anderson et al. 1994).

Constructivism is not a monolithic philosophy or methodology—it encompasses a range of beliefs and pedagogical approaches (see Bandura 1977, 1997; Gagnon & Collay 2001; Phillips 2000; Richardson 2003; Shapiro 2000). Our discussion here is of pure or theoretical constructivism; what you find in actual practice will cover an entire spectrum, including limited use, selected use, mixed use, and even inappropriate use of the concept. Here are some of its hallmarks.

VIDEO CASE

◀◀ ▶ ▶▶

In the video "Constructivist Teaching in Action" on the student website, you will see high school teacher Sarabinh Levy-Brightman prepare her students for a debate on Jeffersonian democracy. After you watch the clips and study the artifacts in the case, discuss the following questions: (1) How would you describe Sarabinh's role in this process and the way she structures the learning experience? (2) In what ways is Sarabinh applying constructivist learning theory?

1. Emphasis on Prior Experience   The foundation of the constructivist model is the idea that learners bring with them prior knowledge and beliefs. Learning builds on what learners have already constructed in other contexts.

2. Personal Construction of Meaning   Another hallmark of the model is that learners must construct what they learn. For example, just giving students vocabulary exercises in science and social studies may not result in their assimilating those concepts. The model calls for learners to be active. Rote memorization is antagonistic to the constructivist. However, learners can construct and use memorization strategies on their own. For example, constructivists hold that children can understand multiplication tables at once if they see them as arrays.

3. Contextual and Shared Learning   The constructivist model requires concrete experiences rather than abstract presentations. In addition, learners deepen their knowledge by shared experiences. Cooperative learning and discussions are key strategies (see Chapter 8).

4. Changing Roles for Teachers and Learners   In the constructivist model, learners and teachers learn from one another. Teachers look for signals from learners so that they may facilitate understanding. The teacher is not perceived as the sole authority; rather, the teacher facilitates learning, guiding and supporting learners' own construction of knowledge.

The hallmark of the constructivist philosophy is student-to-student interaction with minimal supervision by teachers. Critics view this practice as *laissez-faire* non-teaching (Richardson 2003).

In our search for longitudinal, quantitative, experimental-control group research studies on constructivist teaching methods, we drew a blank. Nevertheless, constructivism techniques do ensure student involvement and participation in learning, which is supported by educators and qualitative studies.

Voices from the Classroom

Véronique Paquette,
Kenroy Elementary School,
East Wenatchee,
Washington

Integrating Curriculum/Active Teaching

When I began teaching, I would plan my curriculum on a daily basis. However, it became apparent that if I used a theme as a planning guide, my second-grade students would be immersed in not only reading and writing, but in observing how different topics are interrelated. This type of integration is not unusual; what makes my curriculum stand out is the choice of themes. All the themes studied during the school year are science based. Each unit builds upon the first unit, developing prior knowledge that encapsulates the entire year. The units focus on the various habitats and environments of the earth. We begin with the smallest environment, using insects and their life cycles as the basic theme. As the year progresses, we expand to the vastness of space.

Each unit is closely related and connects to the unit that follows. All of my students use reading, writing, mathematics, art, social studies, and computer technology to help reach an inquiry level of learning. Students' project-based units incorporate the critical areas of learning into their knowledge base, and we use graphic organizers aplenty. As the last months wane, we all discuss the connections that have occurred during the school year. My students do the summarizing, and they realize how important each piece of learning is to every life cycle.

Key Ideas

Tenets of Modern Social Constructivism

◆ Learning depends on the prior conceptions the learner brings to the experience.

◆ The learner must construct his or her own meaning.

◆ Learning is contextual.

◆ Learning depends on the shared understandings learners negotiate with others.

◆ Effective teaching involves understanding students' existing cognitive structures and providing appropriate learning activities to assist them.

◆ Teachers can use one or more key strategies to facilitate conceptual change, depending on the congruence of the concepts with student understanding and conceptualization.

◆ The key elements of conceptual change can be addressed by specific teaching methods.

◆ Greater emphasis is placed on "learning how to learn" than on accumulating facts. In terms of content, less is more.

◆ Students are motivated through modeling.

Reflect

Are you leaning toward a particular perspective (developmental, behavioral, or cognitive) in your own teaching philosophy? If so, why? How will this inform your teaching?

Active Learning

Active learning encompasses a wide range of teaching strategies, all of which engage the learner in the actual instruction that takes place. Seat-work is passive. Students working on problems in small groups is active.

Regardless of your theoretical orientation, you probably will structure your classroom to enhance interaction between you and your students. You likely will set up a cheerful, inviting classroom, covering the walls with student work and posters appropriate for your class. Think of your classroom as a pleasant environment for work. School is the work of youth. And if you stress that students take pride in their work, you will get it. An active learning classroom is a learning community where all participate, including the teacher.

Active learning engages the learner and increases participation

A Baker's Dozen Activities for the Active Learning Classroom

◆ Cooperative learning groups

◆ Inquiry-oriented activities

◆ Teacher demonstrations

◆ Teacher–student joint planning

(continued)

- ◆ Use of hands-on, minds-on activities
- ◆ Use of Internet resources
- ◆ Use of instructional manipulatives
- ◆ Small-group discussions
- ◆ Student-conducted demonstrations
- ◆ Student-initiated projects
- ◆ Student portfolios
- ◆ Student presentations of work
- ◆ Student self-evaluations

Reflect   ◆ Compare direct instruction and active learning. How might you use them? How and when can each be effective?

SECTION 3   Educational Equity as the Big Picture

The past two decades have seen a rise in the volume and rhetoric of arguments, pro and con, concerning diversity, multiculturalism, and other emerging social issues. No one is arguing that the racial and ethnic makeup of the United States and its schools is not diverse. However, the proper educational approach to take in light of this diversity is subject to debate. As a future teacher, you will need to consider various viewpoints before you weigh in on this debate. Awareness of student diversity is an important element of responsive instructional decision making. In this section, we spotlight some aspects of diversity and equity that will affect your instructional planning. In subsequent courses, your teacher education program will cover these topics in great detail.

As noted author Arthur M. Schlesinger, Jr., so ably stated, "Our public schools in particular have been the great instruments of assimilation and the great means of forming an American identity. What students are taught in schools affects the way they will thereafter see and treat other Americans, the way they will thereafter conceive the purposes of the republic. The debate about the curriculum is a debate about what it means to be an American" (Schlesinger 1993, p. 17).

The diversity of our students is our most compelling strength and also our greatest challenge. Until our educational institutions evolve a strategy for maximizing the potential of all our youth, regardless of gender, race, ethnicity, or disabilities, we will have a country of haves and have-nots. This is an institutional challenge; in the meantime, teachers can make a difference on a personal level.

First you must understand clearly the many factors that will contribute to diversity in your classroom. During 2003 for example, 28 percent of the students in U.S. central-city schools (grades K–12) were African American and

30 percent were Hispanic (Kewal-Ramani et al. 2007). Of all children aged 5 to 17 in U.S. schools, 20 percent speak a language other than English at home (NCES 2007-039). Moreover, the children who speak a language other than English at home score below their classmates on standardized tests (NCES 97-472, p. 1). The United States is an amalgam of diverse ethnic, language, racial, and religious groups. Further diversity results from the broad spectrum of physical characteristics in the population (physical characteristics include gender, disabilities, physical dimensions, and traits). This diversity makes it difficult to define a single U.S. culture. Although the people of the United States may have a common root language and many shared values, we are truly a culturally plural society. We are similar in some ways and different in many others. The question you will face as a teacher is this: Should the selection of instructional objectives and teaching strategies promote unity or exalt differences? Or should it do both?

Emphasize commonalities or differences?

Lest you conclude that diversity is a concern only for central-city schools, let's examine a bit of data from a small rural community in Washington State with a K–12 student enrollment of under 500. There are Russian-Ukrainian students, Hispanic students, Native American students, and Asian students, accounting for almost one-half of the district's students. With the exception of the Native American students, English is not the language spoken at home by any of these students.

One of our goals in this section is to broaden the scope of discussion on diversity. Accordingly, we address not just ethnicity and race, but also language diversity and physical diversity. Although we address these different facets of diversity as distinct topics, it is important to recognize their overlapping nature. Note that we focus on the concept of *equity* as being all encompassing. **Equity** means that all students are treated equally well and that school resources are shared equally. We realize that each topic in Section 3 has several books devoted to it, full courses taught in schools of education, and even areas of graduate specialization. We present these topics only to establish an overview. (See Mandara 2006 for an interesting treatment of the topic.)

Equity: all students treated equally

Ethnic Diversity

Challenge—to balance diversity with achievement, norms

An ethnic population is a group of people classed according to common traits, customs, or social views (Cashmore 2004). Common ethnic traits include heritage, values, and rituals. *Heritage* refers to inherited cultural models for housing, foods, clothing, music, family structure, and education. Values include group behavioral norms, ethics, religious beliefs, and commonly held attitudes. An ethnic group's rituals frequently include aspects of festivals, dance, sports, medicine, and religion.

The challenge you face is to balance a concern for ethnic diversity with an equal concern for academic and social norms. The educator's task is to provide a developmentally appropriate instructional program that values diversity while fostering achievement. The box on page 43 provides a few ideas for incorporating students' ethnic heritage into your instructional plans.

◄◄ ► ►► VIDEO CASE

Watch second-grade students from diverse ethnic backgrounds collaborate on Japanese Kamishibai books in the Video Case "Diversity: Teaching in a Multiethnic Classroom" on the student website. As you watch the clips and study the artifacts in the case, reflect on the following questions: (1) What impact do you think the activity has on the Japanese students in the class? (2) What impact does it have on the non-Japanese students?

The essence of ethnic inclusion is to stress that the United States is built on a foundation of diverse participation and contributions. Examination of the roles of diverse ethnic groups in U.S. history and culture should encompass both positive and negative impacts (Banks 2002).

INSTRUCTIONAL *Strategies*

Incorporating Students' Ethnic Heritage into Instruction

◆ Discuss diverse ethnic groups' heritages, values, and rituals.

◆ Use local representatives of ethnic groups as resources and role models for achievement, demonstration, and explanation.

◆ Incorporate activities and materials that reflect local traditions and appropriately augment the more traditional curriculum.

◆ Acknowledge and affirm each student's unique ethnic background and show how it adds to our national character and unity.

◆ Discuss different ethnic groups' participation in historic events and provide literature that illustrates different ethnic groups' heritages, values, and rituals.

Racial and Socioeconomic Diversity

Although race is the most recognizable element of diversity, it is frequently the most misunderstood. Members of specific racial groups have distinct experiences in society and common perceptions of it, and this is where racial difference has an impact on the schools. Much of this difference can be accounted for by history, economics, and environment. John U. Ogbu (2003) also shows how the role models that students emulate can have both positive and negative consequences on school behaviors. Research has demonstrated that educational achievement is influenced by economic and social factors: A stable family, educated parents, and a higher household income are clear predictors of educational success (see Knapp & Woolverton 2004; Orlich & Gifford 2005). In the United States, racial minorities have often been denied these advantages. In 2007, a total of 15.7 percent of all families with children under 18 had incomes below the federal poverty level. The percentage will vary depending on the specific school locale, but you will have at least one of six students whose families are poor. In grade 4 alone, 41 percent of all students are eligible for free and/or reduced lunch, which is the proxy for familial poverty (NAEP 2550, Data Explorer).

Minorities sometimes affected by socioeconomic disparity

As indicated by the evolving categories of race used by the U.S. Census Bureau, the exact definition of race may face continued debate. But the implication of race for our classrooms is clear: Educators have an obligation to find the best methods and materials to achieve the best result for *all* students. You can suggest adaptations to the school curriculum that reflect the racial identity of all your students and the historical and literary contributions that have been made by members of all races. To create a positive educational environment that promotes racial unity, consider the points in the Instructional Strategies box titled "Working Toward Racial Unity in the Schools." (For detailed discussions of this topic, see Banks 2004; Greene & Abt-Perkins 2003.)

INSTRUCTIONAL
Strategies

Working Toward Racial Unity in the Schools

◆ Encourage parental participation and responsibility within the institutional framework of the schools.

◆ Open channels of communication among schools, communities, and parents that encourage the use of programs aimed at improving family stability and achievement for all racial groups.

◆ Help all students to participate in class activities.

◆ Discuss with students the economic risks of dropping out of school.

◆ Provide short- and long-term instructional plans that stress expectations of academic success for all students.

Physical Diversity

Diversity includes age, sex, appearance, ability

Inclusive classrooms welcome all learners.

© Ian Shaw/Getty Images

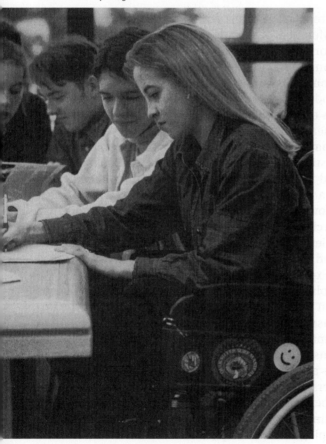

Whereas great attention has been paid to gender and racial discrimination in recent years, relatively little attention has been given to the **physical diversity** of the population and to discrimination based on physical characteristics. People do lose jobs, find career and social opportunities limited, and feel a general lack of societal acceptance due to various physical attributes. The elements of physical diversity include age, sex, physical condition, physical attributes such as height and weight, and physical impairments and disabilities.

Your job is to ensure that all students have equal access to instruction and essential services, and that discrimination based on physical attributes and other characteristics is not tolerated. Raymond Orkwis (2003) shows how using "universal design" for instruction can allow you to accommodate all types of differences in abilities. Being organized and flexible are but two concepts that he develops. (See the box on page 45.)

Multicultural Perspectives

A quote from James A. Banks is a good starting point for our discussion of multiculturalism. Banks asserts that multiculturalism will promote the sharing of power by encouraging students to "participate in social change so that the marginalized and excluded racial, ethnic and cultural groups can become full participants in U.S. society and the nation will move closer to attaining its democratic ideals" (2005, p. 253).

It is within this context of prior exclusion and future participation that educators like you must seek to balance multiculturalism with academic goals and norms. William Sierichs, Jr., underscores the balance educators must achieve when he states: "There is much the world

Aspects of Universal Design

◆ All students have equal access to resources, especially those with diverse abilities.

◆ A wide range of individual preferences and abilities are accommodated.

◆ Instructional strategies are uncomplicated and simple to understand.

◆ Instruction must be perceptible to all learners.

◆ There is a high tolerance for error or unintended actions.

◆ Assessment is flexible.

can learn from the West. Rejecting Western culture is a form of intellectual self-mutilation as severe as rejecting multiculturalism" (Sierichs 1994, p. 114). In other words, it is self-defeating to exclude Western culture and literature in favor of another brand of ethnocentrism. Our educational policy should encourage inclusion, not exclusion. Clearly, we can all agree that minority groups have contributed mightily to the country we have become, and thus schools at all levels can and should be doing more about teaching minority group history and culture. Most educators will grant that having pride in one's people plays a vital role in building self-respect, and this can translate into academic achievement. *Include all, exclude none!*

It is not difficult to include multicultural education in your classroom. It takes nothing away from Shakespeare or Emily Dickinson to include the dramas of August Wilson and the poetry of Langston Hughes in the school curriculum. (For details refer to Banks 2005.)

Draw from European, North and South American, and other cultures in your teaching.

Language Diversity

Language is the vehicle for most learning and communication in a classroom. Therefore, if the educator fails to understand and respond appropriately to the language of the student (and vice versa), academic achievement will suffer. Language barriers are the greatest impediment to social and economic advancement in our country. If obtaining an advanced education in the United States depends on the individual's success with standard English, then failure to master standard English dooms the individual to the economic underclass (Ogbu 1990) because personal income tends to rise with education (see Table 2.3). Mastery of this country's common or standard language is thus essential for its inhabitants' economic and social progress. Over 3 million children in our schools are classified as having limited English proficiency (National Center for Education Statistics, August 2004, NCES 2004-035).

Learning English is key to social and economic advancement in the United States.

However, as the twenty-first century progresses, a critical set of decisions is being made, primarily at the state level, to shift from a **bilingual education** model, in which students are taught their first and second languages simultaneously, to immersion. The immersion approach is to enroll non–English-speaking students in a "crash course" of English and then integrate the students into the English-speaking classrooms as quickly as possible. Decisions about which model to follow are being made state by state (Rossell 2003).

Learning in two languages at once

As a new teacher, you may not be familiar with the first languages or cultures of many of your students. We suggest that you consult with your principal and district English-language learner (ELL) specialist for helpful learning techniques for your charges. The Instructional Strategies box below provides several suggestions.

TABLE 2.3	Actual 2006 Median Earnings of Year-Round, Full-Time Workers, 25 Years or Older, by Years of School	
	Median Income ($)	
Years of Education	Male	Female
Less than 9th grade	22,708	18,133
9 through 12, with no diploma	27,653	20,130
High school graduate	37,031	26,737
Some college, but no degree	43,834	31,954
Associate degree	47,072	35,159
Bachelor's degree	60,906	45,408
Master's degree	75,432	52,438
Doctoral degree	100,000	76,242
Professional degree	100,000	70,519

Source: U.S. Bureau of the Census, Current Population Survey, 2007, Annual Social and Economic Supplement, 2007, Table PINC-03, Charts 136 and 262.

INSTRUCTIONAL *Strategies*

Integrating ELL Students into Your Classroom

1. Provide a warm, encouraging environment by using techniques such as the buddy system and group work, which allow students to practice language skills and receive assistance from peers.

2. If possible, use satisfactory/unsatisfactory grading until students can successfully complete assignments.

3. Avoid forcing students to speak up immediately. Students may need a long wait time, especially when being introduced to new concepts.

4. Have meaningful, relevant print material available in your classroom. Many ELL students read better than they speak.

5. Record important lessons or lectures on tape for use by students.

6. Start classroom interaction with questions that can be answered with a simple yes or no.

7. Try to talk individually with students.

8. Encourage students to use their bilingual dictionaries.

9. Become informed about students' culture.

10. Incorporate and recognize students' culture whenever appropriate.

Reflect

◆ A culturally pluralistic curriculum is a necessity in an ethnically diverse society. How can you balance the need for incorporating other cultures with the teaching of U.S. and European cultures? How will you as a teacher know if you've gone too far in one direction or the other?

◆ How can various cultures and languages be incorporated specifically into some of your lessons? What specific problems might your students have with the subject matter due to cultural factors? What will you do to help them overcome their difficulties?

Ability Diversity: Who Is Exceptional?

IDEA: free, appropriate learning for students with disabilities

On December 3, 2004, H.R. 1350, the Individuals with Disabilities Education Act of 2004 (IDEA) was signed into law. This law renews a federal act for five years. The essence of the act is that all children with disabilities have available to them a free and appropriate public education. We would like to expand that definition to include gifted students and students with learning disabilities. Our focus is on how to adapt your instruction to meet the learning needs of a diverse school population.

◀◀ ▶ ▶▶ VIDEO CASE

Observe a third-grade inclusion classroom through the Video Case "Inclusion: Classroom Implications for the General and Special Educator" on the student website. As you watch the clips and study the artifacts in the case, reflect on the following questions: (1) What categories of exceptionality exist in this classroom? (2) What adaptive tools and strategies are being used on behalf of these students?

There are many definitions of **exceptionality**—up to 27 different categories of it (Ysseldyke, Algozzine, & Thurlow 2000). In the box that follows, we explain six generally agreed-on categories that can be used to describe the range of students that may be present in your classroom (Kirk, Gallagher, & Coleman, 2008). You can teach to all these groups by adapting your basic instructional strategies.

Categories of Exceptionality

◆ *Intellectual* Includes both students who have superior intelligence and those who are slow to learn

◆ *Communicative* Students with specific learning disabilities or speech or language impairments

◆ *Sensory* Students with auditory or visual disabilities

◆ *Behavioral* Students who are emotionally disturbed or socially maladjusted

◆ *Physical* Students with orthopedic or mobility disabilities

◆ *Multiple* Students with a combination of conditions, such as cerebral palsy and dyslexia

---

You are not alone when helping any child with disabilities or giftedness. The inclusion principle has caused a shift in the deployment of school personnel from individual teachers to collaborative efforts. For help with exceptional children in your classes, turn to specialists such as speech therapists, social workers, school nurses, resource room specialists, and school psychologists. In special cases for hearing-impaired or visually impaired students, you may request a *signer* or a *reader*. Your collaborating team members will help you adapt your curriculum for selected students. A large number of options are available to you for adapting your instruction. Today's teaching professionals recognize the need to build on students' strengths and learning preferences as a way of remedying their weaknesses. Happily, many approaches and curricula are available to support your goals for all learners (see Florian 2007; Hardman, Drew, & Egan 2008). The box below lists a few sample strategies and tools. You will be required to enroll in classes or seminars that cover the IDEA and state regulations in depth.

Strategies and Tools for Adapting Instruction to Meet Special Needs

- Mastery learning
- Study/strategy skills training
- Tutoring
- Cooperative learning
- Computer-assisted programs
- Listening labs
- High-interest books
- Large print or Braille materials
- Task groups
- Buddy systems
- Special teachers

Voices from the Classroom

William J. McMaster

Norwalk-La Mirada Unified School District

La Mirada, California

Teaching in a Non-school Setting

My wife, Sue, and I work in the Health & Welfare & Attendance section for the Norwalk-La Mirada School District, California. We might be assigned students who cannot go to regular schools because of physical, mental, or emotional problems. The students might be cancer patients or have broken limbs. Some are young mothers recovering from childbirth. Others might have been victims of gang violence and waiting to recover from gunshot wounds before being sent to juvenile detention facilities.

Our job is to go to students' homes and help them keep up with their classwork before they return to school. Needless to say, this requires a great deal of coordination with their schools and teachers. We also deliver appropriate books, textbooks, and additional material that may be available in the regular classroom—workbooks, remedial materials, records, tapes, tests.

It is a challenge sometimes just to find the student. And it is a pleasure to work with those who want to achieve and a frustration and sadness with the loss of some who tried their best but did not survive.

(continued)

Voices from the Classroom

William J. McMaster

Norwalk-La Mirada Unified School District

La Mirada, California

Teaching in a Non-school Setting—Cont'd

We have compiled a garage full of courses of study and additional materials that work with some students and not with others. We try new approaches until we find something that does work in our one hour per day spent with each student.

Not all school districts provide this service, so our students are lucky. It can mean that these students do not fall behind. If they are really willing to work, they can actually be ahead of the class.

◀◀ ▶ ▶▶ VIDEO CASE

Join a fourth- and fifth-grade inclusive classroom in studying the maps, food, music, and flags of the Caribbean in the Video Case, "Inclusion: Grouping Strategies for Inclusive Classrooms" on the student website. As you watch the clips and study the artifacts in the case, reflect on the following questions: How does teacher Sheryl Cebula (1) observe her students, (2) set the tone, and (3) involve others to make sure each child succeeds?

Encouraging Equity in the Classroom Environment

To create an **inclusive classroom**, you must strive to create an inclusive, interactive classroom environment (see also Ciaccio 2004; Rex 2003). Three important skills will help you to be successful.

1. Observe Carefully An inclusive classroom is a volatile social milieu. One emotionally disturbed child, in one explosive outburst, might ruin the entire day for you and all the other students. We acknowledge that potential problem. But, by continuously observing students and paying attention to their behavioral clues, you can avoid, perhaps even predict, unwanted interruptions (refer to Chapter 6).

2. Set the Tone You must set the tone for the classroom so that inclusion is not undermined. Under your direction, teamwork, cooperation, independence, autonomy, and competition are all brought into action. You make the decision to adapt instruction to help every child. The Instructional Strategies box on page 50 lists several specific ways you can install and maintain a diverse and inclusive classroom. (We will cover these in more detail in subsequent chapters.) Be prepared to adapt your instruction to meet individual needs every day, all day long.

3. Involve Others Discuss your plans with the principal, the school counselor, the school nurse, the social worker, and other support personnel. You are not alone. A wide range of specialists can provide that extra effort—just when the load seems too heavy to lift. Master teachers develop a collaborative network of assistants who can make the classroom environment positive, caring, productive, and equitable (see Sergiovanni & Starratt 2002).

For successful inclusive classroom: observe, set tone, involve.

Teachers use interactive instructional methods in an inclusionary classroom.
© Jean-Claude Lejeune.

INSTRUCTIONAL *Strategies*

Adapting Instruction to Promote Success for All

- ◆ Promote autonomy.
- ◆ Promote student-initiated learning.
- ◆ Organize support groups.
- ◆ Use multi-methodology.
- ◆ Illustrate a caring attitude.
- ◆ Celebrate learning.
- ◆ Instill pride in workmanship.
- ◆ Rearrange the room for positive interactions.
- ◆ Stress student responsibility.
- ◆ Accommodate students with special needs.
- ◆ Vary the pace of instruction.
- ◆ Collaborate with colleagues.

Gender Equity: Awareness of Bias

Bias against women needs to be openly discussed in a book such as this because such bias affects one-half of the student population. David M. Sadker and Ellen S. Silber (2007) provide studies of subtle and not-so-subtle ways women and girls are shortchanged by educational materials. Back in 1991, Myra Sadker, David Sadker, and Susan Klein described several signs of gender bias that are still present today. We note a few in the following box.

Signs of Gender Bias in Educational Materials

◆ Women and girls tend to be vastly underrepresented in textbooks, and that tendency grows worse at higher grade levels.

◆ Males outnumber females by as much as six to one in stories and folktales commonly used in schools.

◆ In history texts, traditionally male activities (hunting, for example) are discussed in depth, whereas traditional women's activities receive a scant sentence or two.

◆ Newbery and Caldecott medals are awarded far more frequently to boy-oriented books than to girl-oriented books.

◆ Boys or men are usually portrayed as heroes, whereas women or girls are shown as selfish or dependent.

The list of indications of gender bias could be expanded (see *The Jossey-Bass Reader on Gender in Education* 2002), but what are the implications for classroom instruction? The Jossey-Bass authors cite study after study showing that in elementary schools boys receive more praise, criticism, and rewards from teachers than do girls. Young girls tend to receive "neutral" teacher reactions. In general, teachers expect less from girls, and therefore girls develop a **learned helplessness**. That condition is notably described by David Bartz and Gary Mathews (2000–2001).

Girls overlooked in textbooks and by teachers

Gender bias is perhaps most serious in mathematics and the sciences, fields in which women are vastly underrepresented (Linn & Hyde 1989). The National Science Foundation is currently making an all-out effort to recruit women and minorities into math, science, and engineering programs, so perhaps this will change. Girls need to be encouraged to complete science and mathematics courses in high school in order to assume leadership roles in the nation's best jobs. The important question, the one that will affect your teaching career, is how do you ensure that every boy and every girl in your classes receives **instructional equity**? The answer should be familiar by now: You must make your classes intentionally inviting—for everyone.

◀◀ ▶ ▶▶ **VIDEO CASE**

Watch the Video Case "Gender Equity in the Classroom: Girls and Science" on the student website to learn how middle school teacher Robert Cho provides role models and mentors to prevent girls from losing interest in science. As you watch the clips and study the artifacts in the case, reflect on the following questions: (1) What do you think turns girls off science in the middle school years? (2) How does the "Girls and Science" program try to address the problem of gender bias?

TECHNOLOGY *Insight*

Technology and Gender Bias

The effect of gender bias on classroom behavior, learning, and achievement is a cultural construction. In many societies, girls and boys are expected to behave differently. Boys are supposed to be active and curious, and aggressive and competitive behavior from boys is widely tolerated. Girls are expected to be more collaborative and supportive. Boys are encouraged to pursue studies in disciplines like engineering and computer science, while girls are encouraged to study disciplines that focus on personal aesthetics—for example, fashion. In the classroom, boys typically use computing tools more often than girls. Boys often receive encouragement to use computers as toys as well as to accomplish specific tasks, while girls are more often expected to use the computer just to accomplish specific tasks. Regardless of the roles boys and girls are expected to play, research indicates that girls and boys are equally capable of developing computing skills (Bray, Brown, & Green 2004).

INSTRUCTIONAL *Strategies*

Promoting Gender Equity in Your Classroom

- ◆ Call on girls as often as you call on boys.
- ◆ Rotate classroom responsibilities and leadership roles between girls and boys.
- ◆ Use wait time in your questioning (see Chapter 7).
- ◆ Make no distinctions between boys and girls in assigning problems. (Some teachers assign easy problems to girls and difficult ones to boys.)
- ◆ Add to reading lists stories or books about women prominent in the subject area being studied.
- ◆ Assign research reports on women's contributions to the topics being studied.
- ◆ Place equal numbers of girls and boys in small discussion and cooperative learning groups (see Chapter 8).
- ◆ Organize a brainstorming session to answer this question: How are girls treated in our school as compared with boys?

Misinformation and Low Expectations   Socialization and cultural mores have a powerful effect on girls in school, and gender stereotypes and the media tend to perpetuate misinformation regarding girls' abilities (Coley 2001). People assume that girls will suffer from math anxiety, so the girls oblige. Thus it is extremely important for teachers to communicate high expectations to girls and to be intentionally inviting to improve girls' motivation and success in mathematics and science classes (see Fennema 2000).

Classroom social interactions can contribute to the development of dependent behaviors and a lack of confidence in young girls. By grade 6, young girls report less confidence in their mathematical ability than boys, even when the girls achieve at the same level as boys (Fennema 1987). This research should send up a red flag for any teacher who works with girls, minority students, or non–English-speaking children. If you show preferences or lowered expectations for any group or individual, you are reinforcing learned helplessness. **Sex-role stereotyping** can be reduced or eliminated in classrooms by talking about it openly, stressing the value of learning, and communicating high expectations for everyone. All students must be given an equal opportunity to succeed because research has shown that interest in a subject is a by-product of success (Bloom 1968). For too long, educators have operated on the erroneous belief that success is a by-product of interest.

Instructional Implications of Gender Equity As a teacher, you must provide leadership opportunities for both girls and boys. If boys are always asked to lead or to set up apparatus in science classes, then girls will simply assume dependent roles. Obviously, complex social and emotional processes take place in classrooms. The manner in which a teacher engages every student has potential learning overtones. This means that you must be consciously aware of your verbal and nonverbal actions and reactions to every class member, every day! Use the suggestions in the Instructional Strategies box on page 52 to promote gender equity in your classroom.

Reflect

◆ List the elements of instruction that you can control that will ensure instructional equity among the races represented in your classes.

◆ Examine a middle school curriculum guide for American literature. What evidence do you find that an attempt is being made to provide a multicultural perspective?

◆ Do you agree with the research that shows that girls are shortchanged in schools? In your experience in elementary, middle, and high school, were girls shortchanged? Were boys? What steps can you take to avoid subjecting your future students to gender bias?

◆ How can you plan for an inclusive classroom environment that meets the intent of IDEA?

Differentiating Instruction or Multi-Methodology

Throughout this chapter we have implied that you, as a classroom teacher, will be faced with a challenge to meet the instructional needs of all students who enter your class. To be most effective requires a bit of flexibility on your part and thus, you need to consider what you will do to help different learners master the content. At this point, we simply introduce the concept of **differentiated instruction** or as we prefer to call it, **multi-methodology**. (See Tomlinson & Cooper 2006 for details.)

The key word here for a solution is "accommodation." How do you make accommodations to your instructional methods or strategies so that every student in your class can enjoy the thrill of learning? Realize that you will have students with Individual Educational Plans (IEPs) and those plans will specify in very detailed terms the instructional accommodations that must be made—note the stipulation "must be made." Suffice it to say here that you

Differentiate instruction by using multiple methods.

will want to master a host of different ways of reaching all children, and we will develop this theme in subsequent chapters.

A basic assumption of the concept of differentiating instruction (multi-methodology) is that as a teacher you can maximize student achievement (Langa & Yost 2007). As a teacher you can vary the content, the methods of instruction, student activities, and the final outcomes or products expected of the students. This is not an easy task. Your author team was involved in a novel high school project in which three sets of learning objectives were designed for every class. The difficulty levels included basic knowledge, applied knowledge, and complex knowledge. Needless to say, this was a time-consuming adventure. The critical feature of this scheme was providing immediate feedback to the student.

You might differentiate instruction by individuals, small groups, or even the whole class. And as you are probably thinking, this takes careful and systematic planning. We would suggest that you discuss any plans for differentiating instruction with your principal and your colleagues prior to implementation. They can help you avoid pitfalls.

Technology has an impact on the ways we teach. Yet, with the advent of new teaching technologies, we must not forget that teaching and learning are very human dimensions. The human element of schooling is one of the messages we have woven into this chapter. The more humanely we treat those who enter the classroom, the more positive our impact will be on those individuals with whom we come into contact (see Fredua-Kwarteng 2005).

When addressing any diversity issue, values and value systems come into play. The messages in this chapter are all affectively oriented; that is, they challenge our basic value structure and the attitudes we express through our words, actions, and deeds. Our job is to instill a love of learning in every student. If our teaching is biased, we may unintentionally alienate some of our students from the disciplines we teach. This, in turn, may adversely affect their desire to learn. Perhaps the observation made by Robert F. Mager (1968), the person who popularized behavioral objectives, is an appropriate way to end this section. He wrote, "If I do little else, I want to send my students away with at least as much interest in the subjects I teach as they had when they arrived" (p. i).

Don't let your attitudes turn students off learning.

Reflect   A Closing Reflection

◆ How much and what type of background would a teacher need to use holistic planning? Discuss with a group of peers.

◆ Picture an active learning model that reflects in some way all three educational perspectives—developmental, behavioral, and cognitive. What does it consist of?

◆ What types of attitudes would help a teacher and his or her class to embrace the concept of instructional equity and make it work in the classroom?

◆ Think of three films, books, museum exhibits, or other works of art that you've experienced in the past year that express a different culture. Are any of them developmentally appropriate for the grade you expect to teach? How might they be incorporated into a multicultural teaching activity?

Summary Points

1. Instructional decisions have two components: holistic vision and detailed implementation.
2. Instructional decisions are predicated on the learner's needs.
3. Piagetian theory assumes that learners develop in stages and that instruction should be developmentally appropriate.
4. Vygotskian theory asserts that there is a right time to teach any concept and that learning requires social interaction.
5. Behavioral perspectives emphasize that learning causes a change in behavior.
6. The cognitive model of instruction assumes that students can learn how to learn.
7. Social constructivism posits that prior experience and shared learning are part of the instructional context.
8. For a significant number of students, educational success depends on their school's sensitivity to and respect for equity, defined in terms of diversity, ethnicity, race, language, disability, or gender.
9. The skillful and deliberate inclusion of multicultural activities in the classroom promotes appreciation of all cultures, as well as pride, self-respect, and dignity for all students.
10. In the United States, proficiency in English is a prerequisite for success in school and beyond. Therefore, schools have a responsibility to increase students' proficiency in English.
11. Gender biases have been found in textbooks, educational activities, and classroom interactions. Gender equity is an important goal of the inclusive classroom. Teachers must be aware of the danger of placing low expectations on girls.
12. Differentiating instruction is one technique that can help you meet the learning needs of all your students.

Building a Career Portfolio

As we noted in Chapter 1, we want to provide you with a repertoire of instructionally related ideas to add to your career portfolio. Be sure to incorporate your own observations from this chapter, in addition to the following suggestions.

List some ways in which common experiences can be incorporated prior to teaching a new unit of instruction.

Examine the data in Table 2.1 to be used as a metric to assess the potential for student success on selected state standards.

List some handy Web-based resources that illustrate differentiated instruction so that you will have an initial set of techniques or methods to try when you are in your own classroom.

Resources

PRINT

Thousands of papers and books have been written on the topics discussed in this chapter. The following sources are of particular value.

Banks, J. A. *An Introduction to Multicultural Education.* Boston: Pearson/ Allyn and Bacon, 2008.
A long established expert in the field provides a wide range of instructional principles for teaching in a multicultural school.

Glasgow, N. A., & C. D. Hicks. *What Successful Teachers Do: 91 Research-Based Classroom Strategies for New and Veteran Teachers.* Thousand Oaks, CA: Corwin, 2003, 210 pp.
The authors list tricks of the trade for structuring an inclusive classroom environment.

Good, T. L., & J. E. Brophy. *Looking in Classrooms* (10th edition). Boston: Allyn and Bacon, 2007, 523 pp.
Two prominent educational researchers provide firsthand observations of what transpires in classrooms.

Howard, G. R. *We Can't Teach What We Don't Know: White Teachers, Multiracial Schools.* New York: Teachers College Press, 1999, 141 pp.
Howard presents a journal of his several years of teaching in racially diverse schools. His work stresses the need to create caring and humane schools—a major thesis of this book.

Klein, S., B. L. Richardson, D. Grayon, L. H. Fox, C. Kramarae, D. S. Pollard, & C. A. Dwyer, Eds. *Handbook for Achieving Gender Equity Through Education.* New York: Routledge, 2007, 754 pp.
A detailed resource that covers virtually all areas related to gender differences, equity, and strategies for teaching.

Tomlinson, C. A., & J. M. Cooper. *An Educator's Guide to Differentiating Instruction.* Boston: Houghton Mifflin, 2006.
A brief how-to-do-it primer with many practical examples.

INTERNET

Go to the website for this book at www.cengage.com/education/orlich to find live links to resources related to this chapter.

◆ The University of Washington sponsors Project DO-IT (disabilities, opportunities, Internetworking, and technology). The goal is to increase representation of individuals with disabilities in science, mathematics, and technology academic programs and careers. Dr. Sheryl Burgstahler is the project director.
http://www.washington.edu/doit

◆ Columbia University's Institute for Learning Technologies maintains a website that features documents and projects on increasing student motivation.
http://www.ilt.columbia.edu/

◆ The Jean Piaget Society database is an online source of information and publications on Piagetian developmental ideas.
http://www.piaget.org/

◆ The National Clearinghouse for Bilingual Education provides assistance for issues involving linguistically and culturally diverse students.
http://www.ncela.gwu.edu/

◆ Two excellent sources that present a wide variety of graphic organizers are listed below:
http://www.edHelper.com
http://www.eduplace.com/graphicorganizer/

References

Adams, G. L., & S. Engelmann. (1996). *Research on Direct Instruction: 25 Years Beyond DISTAR*. Seattle: Educational Achievement Systems.

Adey, P., & M. Shayer. (1994). *Really Raising Standards: Cognitive Intervention and Academic Achievement*. New York: Routledge.

Agran, M., M. E. King-Sears, M. L. Wehmeyer, & S. R. Copeland. (2003). *Student-Directed Learning. Teachers' Guides to Inclusive Practices*. Baltimore: Brookes.

Alvarado, A. E., & P. R. Herr. (2003). *Inquiry-Based Learning Using Everyday Objects: Hands-On Instructional Strategies That Promote Active Learning in Grades 3–8*. Thousand Oaks, CA: Corwin.

Amrein, A. L., & D. C. Berliner. (2002, March 28). "High-Stakes Testing, Uncertainty, and Student Learning." *Education Policy Analysis Archives 10*(18): 1–52. http://epaa.asu.edu/epaa/v10n18.

Anderson, R. D., et al. (1994). *Issues of Curriculum Reform in Science, Mathematics and Higher Order Thinking Across the Disciplines*, OR 94-3408. Washington, DC: U.S. Department of Education, Office of Research.

Ashman, A. F., & R. M. F. Conway. (1993). *Using Cognitive Methods in the Classroom*. New York: Routledge.

Bandura, A. (1977). *Social Learning Theory*. New York: General Learning.

Bandura, A. (1997). *Self-Efficacy: The Exercise of Control*. New York: Freeman.

Banks, J. A. (2002). "Race, Knowledge Construction, and Education in the U.S.A.: Lessons from History." *Race Ethnicity and Education 5*(1): 7–27.

Banks, J. A. (2004). "Multicultural Education: Historical Development, Dimensions, and Practice." In J. A. Banks & C. A. M. Banks, Eds., *Handbook of Research on Multicultural Education* (2nd ed.), pp. 3–29. San Francisco: Jossey-Bass.

Banks, J. A. (2005). "Approaches to Multicultural Curriculum Reform." In J. A. Banks and C. A. M. Banks, Eds., *Multicultural Education: Issues and Perspectives* (5th edition update), pp. 242–264. Hoboken, NJ: Wiley.

Bartz, D., & G. Mathews. (2000–2001). "Enhancing Students' Social and Psychological Development." *Here's How 19*(2): 1–5.

Becker, J., & M. Varelas. (2001, August-September). "Piaget's Early Theory of the Role of Language in Intellectual Development: A Comment on DeVrie's Account of Piaget's Social Theory." *Educational Researcher 30*(6): 22–23.

Bloom, B. S. (1968). "Learning for Mastery." *Evaluation Comment 1*(2): 2.

Bray, M., A. Brown, & T. Green. (2004). *Technology and the Diverse Learner: A Guide to Classroom Practice*. Thousand Oaks, CA: Corwin.

Bredekamp, S., Ed. (1997). *Developmentally Appropriate Practice in Early Childhood Programs Serving Children from Birth Through Age 8* (revised edition). Washington, DC: National Association for the Education of Young Children.

Campbell, L. (2003). *Mindful Learning: 101 Proven Strategies for Student and Teacher Success*. Thousand Oaks, CA: Corwin.

Carnine, D. (2000). *Why Education Exerts Resist-Effective Practices*. Washington, DC: The Thomas B. Fordham Foundation.

Cashmore, E. (2004). *Encyclopedia of Race and Ethnic Studies*. New York: Routledge.

Ciaccio, J. (2004). *Totally Positive Teaching: A Five-Stage Approach to Energizing Students and Teachers*. Alexandria, VA: Association for Supervision and Curriculum Development.

Coley, R. J. (2001). *Differences in the Gender Gap: Comparisons Across Racial/Ethnic Groups in Education and Work*. Princeton, NJ: Educational Testing Service.

Cunningham, J., C. Kroll, N. Land, & S. Russell. (2000). "Motivating Students to Be Self-Reflective Learners Through Goal-Setting and Self-Evaluation."

Chicago: Master of Arts Action Research Project, St. Xavier University, ED 446 872.

Elliott, S. M., R. T. Busse, & E. S. Shapiro. (1999). "Intervention Techniques for Academic Performance Problems." In C. R. Reynolds & T. B. Guthin, Eds., *The Handbook of School Psychology* (3rd ed.), pp. 664–685. New York: Wiley & Sons.

Ellis, A. K. (2005). *Research on Educational Innovations* (4th ed.). Larchmont, NY: Eye on Education.

Fennema, E. (1987). "Sex-Related Differences in Education: Myths, Realities and Interventions." In V. Richardson-Koehler, Ed., *Educator's Handbook*, pp. 329–347. New York: Longman.

Fennema, E. (2000, May 22). "Gender and Mathematics: What Is Known and What Do I Wish Was Known?" Fifth Annual Forum of the National Institute for Science Education, Detroit.

Florian, L., Ed. (2007). *The SAGE Handbook of Special Education.* Thousand Oaks, CA: SAGE.

Fredua-Kwarteng, E. (2005, Nov.). "A Perspective on Gender Disparity in Mathematics Education." ERIC, ED493750.

Gagnon, G. W., Jr., & M. Collay. (2001). *Designing for Learning: Six Elements in Constructivist Classrooms.* Thousand Oaks, CA: Corwin.

Greene, S., & D. Abt-Perkins, Eds. (2003). *Making Race Visible: Literacy Research for Cultural Understanding.* New York: Teachers College Press.

Hardman, M. L., C. J. Drew, & M. W. Egan. (2008). *Human Exceptionality: School, Community, and Family* (9th ed.). Boston: Houghton Mifflin.

H.R. 1350. (2004). The Individuals with Disabilities Education Act (IDEA). Washington, DC: 108th Congress, 2nd Session, December 3, 2004.

Hunter, M. C. (1982). *Mastery Teaching.* El Segundo, CA: TIP Publications.

The Jossey-Bass Reader on Gender in Education. (2002). San Francisco: Jossey-Bass.

Kewal-Ramani, A., L. Gilberton, M. A. Fox, & S. Provasnik. (2007, Sept.). *Status and Trends in Education of Racial and Ethnic Minorities.* NCES 2007-039.

Kirk, S. A., J. J. Gallagher, N. J. & M. R. Coleman. (2008). *Educating Exceptional Children* (12th ed.). Boston: Houghton Mifflin.

Knapp, M. S., & S. Woolverton. (2004). "Social Class and Schooling." In *Handbook of Research on Multicultural Education* (2nd ed.), pp. 656–681. J. B. Banks, editor, and C. A. M. Banks, associate editor. San Francisco: Jossey-Bass.

Kohn, A. (1996). "What to Look for in a Classroom." *Educational Leadership 54*(1): 54–55.

Kozloff, M. A., L. LaNunziata, J. Cowardin, & F. B. Bessellieu. (2001). "Direct Instruction: Its Contributions to High School Achievement." *The High School Journal 84*(2): 36–54.

Kozulin, A., Ed. (2003). *Vygotsky's Educational Theory in a Cultural Context.* New York: Cambridge University Press.

Langa, M. A., & J. L. Yost. (2007). *Curriculum Mapping for Differentiated Instruction, K-8.* Thousand Oaks, CA: Corwin Press.

Linn, M. S., & J. S. Hyde. (1989). "Gender, Mathematics and Science." *Educational Researcher 18*(8): 17–27.

Mager, R. F. (1968). *Developing Attitude Toward Learning.* Palo Alto, CA: Fearon.

Mandara, J. (2006). "The Impact of Family Functioning on African American Males' Academic Achievement: A Review and Clarification of the Empirical Literature." *Teachers College Record 108*(2): 206–223.

Marlowe, J. (2000). "Learning Alone." *American School Board Journal 187*(12): 56–57, 62.

NAEP Data Explorer. Retrieved from http://nces.ed.gov/nationsreportcard/nde/viewreults.asp? Pid.

National Center for Education Statistics, National Assessment of Educational Progress (NAEP). (1998). *Report in Brief, NAEP 1996 Trends in Academic Progress.* Revised 1998, NCES 98–530, Tables 1, 2, 3 & 4, pp. 9–12.

North American Council for Online Learning. (2008). *Fast Facts About Online Learning* (2008). Retrieved June 21, 2008, from www.nacol.org.

Ogbu, J. (1990). "Understanding Diversity: Summary Comments." *Education and Urban Society 22*(4): 425–429.

Ogbu, J. U. (2003). *Black American Students in an Affluent Suburb: A Study of Academic Disengagement.* Mahwah, NJ: Lawrence Erlbaum Associates.

Orkwis, R. (2003). *Universally Designed Instruction. ERIC/OSEP Digest.* ERIC Clearinghouse on Disabilities and Gifted Education. Arlington, VA: ED 475 386.

Orlich, D. C., & G. Gifford. (2005)."The Relationship of Poverty to Test Scores." *Leadership Information 4*(3): 34–38.

Phillips, D. C., Ed. (2000). *Constructivism in Education: Opinions and Second Opinions on Controversial Issues.* National Society for the Study of Education, Part I. Chicago: University of Chicago Press.

Piaget, J. (1969). *Psychologie et Pedagogie.* Paris: Denoel/Garnier.

Rex, L. A. (2003). "Loss of the Creature: The Obscuring of Inclusivity in Classroom Discourse." *Communication Education 52*(1): 30–46.

Richardson, V. (2003). "Constructivist Pedagogy." *Teachers College Record 105*(9): 1623–1640.

2 2

2 2

2 12

12
212

12
2 22

Rossell, C. H. (2003). *Policy Matters in Teaching English Language Learners: New York and California.* ERIC Clearinghouse on Urban Education. New York: ED482 922.

Sadker, M., D. M. Sadker, & S. Klein. (1991). "The Issue of Gender in Elementary and Secondary Education." In C. Grant, Ed., *Review of Research in Education*, Vol. 17, pp. 269–334. Washington, DC: American Educational Research Association.

Sadker, D. M, & E. S. Silber, Eds. (2007). *Gender in the Classroom: Foundations, Skills, Methods, and Strategies Across the Curriculum.* Mahwah, NJ: L. Erlbaum Associates.

Schlesinger, A. M. (1993). *The Disuniting of America: Reflections on a Multicultural Society.* New York: Norton.

Sergiovanni, T. J., & R. J. Starratt. (2002). *Supervision: A Redefinition* (7th ed.). Boston: McGraw-Hill.

Shapiro, A. S. (2000). *Leadership for Constructivist Schools.* Lanham, MD: Scarecrow.

Shayer, M., & P. Adey. (1981). *Towards a Science of Science Teaching: Cognitive Development and Curriculum Demand.* London: Heinemann Educational.

Shayer, M., & P. Adey, Eds. (2002). *Learning Intelligences: Cognitive Acceleration Across the Curriculum from 5 to 15 years.* Buckingham, England: Open University Press.

Sierichs, W., Jr. (1994). "Multicultural Education Is Helpful." In F. Whitehead, Ed., *Culture Wars: Opposing Viewpoints*, pp. 109–115. San Diego: Greenhaven.

Skinner, B. F. (1938). *The Behavior of Organisms.* New York: Appleton-Century-Crofts.

Tarver, S. G., Ed. (2003). "Direct Instruction News: Effective School Practices, 2003." *Direct Instruction News 3*(1–2): 1–78.

Tate, M. L. (2003). *Worksheets Don't Grow Dendrites: 20 Instructional Strategies That Engage the Brain.* Thousand Oaks, CA: Corwin.

Tomlinson, C. A., & J. M. Cooper. (2006). *An Educator's Guide to Differentiating Instruction.* Boston: Houghton Mifflin.

Tyler, R. W. (1949). *Basic Principles of Curriculum and Instruction.* Chicago: University of Chicago Press.

U.S. Bureau of the Census. (2007). Current Population Survey, 2007 Annual Social and Economic Supplement, PINC-03, Washington, DC.

U.S. Department of Education. (2004, Aug.). *Issue Brief: English Language Learner Students in U.S. Public Schools: 1994–2000.* Washington, DC: Institute of Education Sciences (NCES 2004-035).

U.S. Department of Education, National Center for Education Statistics. (2005). *The Condition of Education 2005.* Washington, DC: U.S. G.P.O. (NCES 2005-094).

Vygotsky, L. S. (1962). *Thought and Language.* Cambridge, MA: MIT Press.

Wells, G., Ed. (2001). *Action, Talk, and Text: Learning and Teaching Through Inquiry.* New York: Teachers College Press.

Ysseldyke, J. E., B. Algozzine, & M. L. Thurlow. (2000). *Critical Issues in Special Education* (3rd ed.). Boston: Houghton Mifflin.

Fundamental Tools for Instructional Planning

*P*art 2 presents you with the basic tools for instructional planning. Objectives, taxonomies, lesson and unit planning, and sequencing are the most static elements of teaching. We also illustrate how much teacher planning and work it takes to convert standards to teachable objectives. But as Michelangelo's *David* illustrates as he stands poised to throw a rock at Goliath, thought and contemplation precede action, and they may have a brilliance in their own right. Planning provides the basis for the dynamic, interactive phases of teaching. We also introduce the concept of *effect size* as one gauge by which to measure the worthiness of any instructional strategy in terms of its influence on student achievement.

In Part 2 you will be introduced to instructional planning models, strategies, and techniques oriented toward effective lesson design. Chapters 3 through 5 provide you with the entry-level skills you will need to plan successful lessons and to discuss instructional planning with any experienced teacher or would-be educational reformer.

Objectives, Taxonomies, and Standards for Instruction

As a high school and college student, Carlos often wondered why his teachers did not clearly communicate their instructional goals to their students. He remembers thinking, "Why don't teachers tell us what they really expect from us? Why don't they present material in a more systematic manner?"

After graduating from college, Carlos was hired to teach in an inner-city high school. Being new, he had four different class preparations. Carlos was overwhelmed with the task of organizing the first week's lessons. Here are just a few of the questions buzzing in his head: How much material can I cover in one period? How is the content of my courses related to other courses? How do I use the state standards, curriculum guides, textbooks, and all the information I learned in college? How do I plan for survival? How do I incorporate differentiated instruction with over 120 students?

This chapter, together with Chapter 4, will show you how to solve problems similar to those raised by Carlos. We provide basic information that will help you put instructional planning in perspective. In Chapters 4 and 5, we go into the specifics of instructional design. As you read this chapter, think about how you would address the following questions.

◆ What processes do teachers use to plan successful instruction?

◆ How can I use a cognitive taxonomy of objectives as an instructional guide?

◆ How can I write clear objectives for my learners that will guide them to success?

◆ How can standards be converted into appropriate and learnable objectives?

◆ What are the National Assessment of Educational Progress (NAEP) five achievement levels and how should I use them?

◆ How can I determine whether the teaching strategies I want to use are really effective?

SECTION 1   A Rationale for Planning as a Tool

Planning for Successful Instruction

One hallmark of teaching as an organized activity is the process of planning. If you wish to instruct in a systematic manner, then you will need to devote a substantial proportion of your time and activity to **planning**—deciding what and how you want your students to learn. Master teachers exhibit three common traits: They are well organized in their planning, they communicate their instructional objectives effectively to their students, and they have high expectations for their students.

The more systematic your instructional planning, the greater the probability that you will succeed. Planning instruction or lessons means establishing priorities, goals, and objectives for students. **Goals** are really statements of intent, stated in broad and general terms. For example, one commonly stated goal of education is "to produce a literate citizenry." This is a noble goal, and it shows intent. But to achieve a goal, a series of specific action steps is needed, which we'll call **objectives**. One such objective, to meet the goal of producing a literate citizenry, would be that "formal reading instruction will be delivered in grades 1 through 6." Written **lesson plans** set out in advance illustrate your priorities concerning time, learning materials, objectives, and types of instruction. They are tools for success, both for you and for your students. Let's look more closely at lesson plans.

Goals state intent; objectives lay out the steps.

Time—we have only so much of it. Even master teachers cannot add a single extra second to the day, but master teachers do *control* time by systematically and carefully planning its productive use for instruction. Teachers prepare lesson plans to help them organize and deliver their daily lessons efficiently. Numerous studies have shown that being well organized correlates highly with teachers' effectiveness (see Astleitner 2005; Bost & Riccomini 2006; Stronge 2007; Stronge & Hindman 2003).

The types of lesson plans used by teachers vary widely, reflecting the teacher's experience, the grade level, and the subjects being taught. Writing lesson plans is similar to learning to ride a bicycle. Beginners concentrate on maintaining balance, keeping their feet on the pedals, and holding onto the handlebars. They complete only short trips. With experience, however, pedaling and balance become automatic, and the focus is on safety, comfort, and fun, not to mention on getting somewhere. Similarly, new teachers tend to overplan—that is, to prepare very elaborate lesson plans, being careful not to omit any point they will make in the lesson. To be effective and systematic in your planning, you must become aware of the decision areas and techniques of lesson preparation. The goal of this chapter is to provide the basic information you will need to make instructional plans as well as a rationale for using a wide variety of teaching techniques and models. In Chapter 4, we build on this foundation with more specific information and present an instructional planning model that will help you format actual written lesson plans.

As a new classroom teacher, you probably will begin making detailed plans by imitating a favorite teacher. Later, after further study and experience, you will expand or adapt the basic planning skills you have acquired to reflect your students' specific needs. Classroom innovations will come to you once you are in your own classroom with your own set of learners, have developed your own instructional resources, and have had a chance to experiment with various strategies. Although the fundamental steps in lesson planning remain the same, the basic formula is always modified to suit individual teachers' objectives and style.

Planning is more than thinking about what you want to accomplish. You think about the details, such as who does what, when, for what length of time, and what opportunities will be created for effective student learning. Note that we said *opportunities*. This is a good spot to introduce you to Louis E. Raths's classic dictum (1967, pp. ix–xi). As a teacher, you are responsible for providing opportunities for changing behavior. Students may or may not change. If they don't, that's not the teacher's responsibility. Teachers do not manipulate children to change. Teachers model, demonstrate, and encourage. Any changes are up to the student! The responsibility is a two-way commitment.

The main goal of lesson planning is to ensure that all activities and processes provide a supportive educational environment for the learner. Teachers sometimes forget about the learner and concentrate on the teaching process or on what is being taught. If lesson planning is to be a useful task, it must always focus on the interaction between what is to be learned and the learner.

Like the cyclist who knows where he or she is going, teachers who develop highly structured and detailed plans rarely adhere to them in lock-step fashion. Indeed, such rigidity probably would hinder rather than help the teaching and learning process. For example, you may plan for a 20-minute student activity, only to discover it requires 60 minutes to complete. You would then make the appropriate adjustment in your plan to ensure student success. The planning tools described in this chapter should be thought of as guiding principles and aids rather than as blueprints to systematic instruction. Although you have

- - - - - - - - - - - - - - -
Experienced teachers adjust plans as they go.

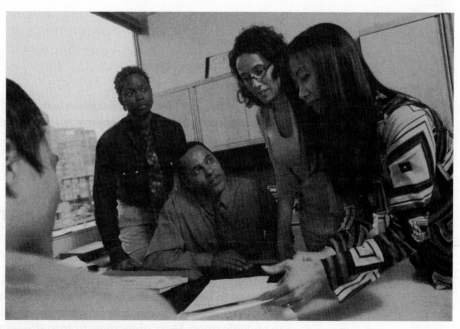

Planning cooperatively for student success.

© ColorBlend Images/Corbis

prepared carefully (perhaps precisely) to teach a lesson effectively, you must allow for flexible delivery. During the actual classroom interaction, you need to make adaptations and add artistry to each day's plan.

Elements of Planning

In Chapter 1, you learned that the process of planning is a reflective experience. As a teacher, you will spend a great deal of time reflecting on what and how you will teach. You will also find yourself planning with your students for various student-led activities. And you will find yourself planning with your colleagues. Look back at the Key Ideas box on page 30 of Chapter 2 that summarizes "Holistic Instructional Considerations." Those 12 items are really the questions that one asks as the planning process is initiated. The list below provides an overview of additional process components.

Planning Process Components

◆ Student characteristics

◆ Standards being met

◆ Goals

◆ Theme or unit

◆ Time allotted

◆ Specific objectives

◆ Cognitive level check

◆ Assignments

◆ Special needs

◆ Assessment

◆ Reteaching as needed

Reflect

◆ Interview a few selected teachers with varying years of experience to learn how they plan. Do you observe any trends or differences?

◆ Interview a school principal to determine what principles or procedures are required for teacher planning in that school.

SECTION 2 Using a Cognitive Taxonomy as an Instructional Guide

Introducing Bloom's Taxonomy

Identifying and developing instructional objectives takes time and planning. One way to begin is to start with broad goals and then work toward specific objectives. This is a deductive process: You proceed from general statements to specific ones. Most objectives fit into three broad instructional areas: the cognitive, affective, and psychomotor domains. Tables 3.1, 3.2, and 3.3 outline the general categories and levels of the three domains.

The **cognitive domain** encompasses objectives that deal with the recall or recognition of knowledge and the development of intellectual abilities and skills. Most curriculum development focuses on the cognitive domain. Objectives within this domain are most clearly defined using descriptions of student behavior (Bloom et al. 1956).

The **affective domain** comprises attitudes, beliefs, and the entire spectrum of values and value systems. For example, committing to follow ethical or moral behavior is an affective value. This is an exciting area that curriculum developers are now reexploring (Krathwohl, Bloom, & Masia 1964).

The **psychomotor domain** involves aspects of physical movement and coordination. It integrates cognitive and affective events with bodily actions

TABLE 3.1	General Categories of the Cognitive Domain
Category	Cognitive Implication
Knowledge	Knows facts, concepts, symbols, principles
Comprehension	Understands meanings
Application	Transfers knowledge to new settings
Analysis	Reduces complex issues to components
Synthesis	Blends older ideas into novel or creative uses
Evaluation	Generates criteria for judging

Source: From Benjamin S. Bloom et al., *Taxonomy of Educational Objectives Book 1: Cognitive Domain,* 1st ed. Published by Allyn and Bacon, Boston, MA. Copyright © 1984 by Pearson Education. Adapted by permission of the publisher.

TABLE 3.2	General Levels of the Affective Domain
Level	**Characteristics**
Receiving (attending)	Willing to listen to some message and point
Responding	Willing to make choices about issues
Valuing	Willing to exhibit a behavior that shows a commitment to a principle
Organization	Willing to defend values
Characterization by a value or value complex	Willing to allow values to drive behavior

Source: From Krathwohl, David R., Benjamin S. Bloom, & Bertram B. Masia, *Taxonomy of Educational Objectives, Book 2: Affective Domain.* Published by Allyn and Bacon, Boston, MA. Copyright © 1964 by Pearson Education. Adapted by permission of the publisher.

TABLE 3.2	Levels of the Psychomotor Domain
Level	**Performance**
Imitation	Models skill development
Manipulation	Performs skill independently
Precision	Exhibits skills effortlessly and automatically

Source: K. D. Moore & C. Quinn, *Classroom Teaching Skills,* McGraw-Hill Companies, © 1998.

(Moore & Quinn 1994). For example, developmental physical education programs have objectives drawn from the psychomotor domain of instruction.

Taken collectively, the three domains are often referred to as "learner outcomes." Labeling the objectives as "outcomes" implies the use of a behavioral psychological perspective. We point this out since the developmental perspective is not embraced in field testing or preparation of the various statements of state standards. You need to be aware of this because many standards are beyond the capacity of the average student.

In this book, we emphasize the cognitive domain because most of what teachers explicitly do fits into this category. State and national standards are also cognitively driven.

Bloom's taxonomy is a system that classifies cognitive behaviors into six categories, ranging from fairly simple to more complex. These categories are briefly described in Table 3.4. Like other taxonomies, Bloom's is hierarchical, with learning at higher levels depending on the prior attainment of prerequisite knowledge and skills at lower levels. We begin our discussion of the taxonomy with a description of the first level, which is knowledge.

Knowledge The **knowledge** category emphasizes remembering—either by recall or by recognition. An example of a recall operation is a fill-in-the-blank exercise; an example of a recognition operation is a multiple-choice exercise requiring the recognition of information previously encountered. Both processes involve the retrieval of information stored in the mind. The

---

Three instructional areas: intellectual, values, physical

Knowledge focuses on memory.

TABLE 3.4	Characteristic Behaviors of the Cognitive Domain
Level	**Characteristic Student Behaviors**
Evaluation	Making value decisions about issues, resolving controversies or differences of opinion
Synthesis	Creating a unique, original product that may be in verbal form or may be a physical object
Analysis	Subdividing something to show how it is put together, finding the underlying structure of a communication, identifying motives
Application	Problem solving, applying information to produce some result
Comprehension	Interpreting, translating from one medium to another, describing in one's own words
Knowledge	Remembering, memorizing, recognizing, recalling

Source: From Benjamin S. Bloom et al., *Taxonomy of Educational Objectives Book 1: Cognitive Domain,* 1st ed. Published by Allyn and Bacon, Boston, MA. Copyright © 1984 by Pearson Education. Adapted by permission of the publisher.

information is retrieved in basically the same form as it was stored. For example, if an elementary school social studies teacher tells his or her students that Washington, DC, is the capital of the United States, then an appropriate knowledge-level question to ask on the next day would be, "Name the capital city of the United States." In answering this question, the student would be retrieving the knowledge in the same form as it was received.

The primary focus of knowledge-level objectives is the storage and retrieval of information. In answering a knowledge-level question, the student must find the appropriate signals in the problem: those that most effectively match the relevant knowledge stores. The student is not expected to transform or manipulate knowledge, but merely to remember it in the same form as it was presented. Knowledge-level activities may consist of

1. Recalling specific *facts* or *bits of information* (for example, "Who was the first president of the United States?")
2. Recalling *terminology* or *definitions* (for example, "What is a noun?")

Although the knowledge level forms the factual foundation for the rest of the categories, its overuse in the classroom causes a number of problems:

1. Simply recalling information does not actively involve the learner. Students are often poorly motivated when much of their work consists of memorizing facts.
2. Because knowledge-level questions usually have only one right answer, they do not lend themselves to classroom sessions in which students work together to discuss and solve a problem. Consequently, students' interpersonal and problem-solving skills are not adequately developed.

Knowledge-level objectives do have their place, since they provide background knowledge. Effective-schooling studies provide evidence that attention to background knowledge skills helps students learn higher-order skills more effectively (see Marzano 2004). A general rule to use in judging which knowledge-level objectives should be included in the curriculum is to ask yourself, "Will this knowledge be useful to the student at a later time in one of the higher categories?" If the answer is no, you should possibly redesign the lesson.

Comprehension   The basic idea behind the comprehension category is for students to understand the material, not just memorize it. For example, memorizing the Pledge of Allegiance falls into the knowledge category, but understanding what the words mean falls under comprehension. However, unlike some of the higher categories, the comprehension level does not ask students to extend information but merely to integrate it into their own frame of reference. In other words, if students rephrase material into their own words, or if they organize it to make sense to themselves personally, they probably will learn the material more quickly and retain it longer (see Fisk & Hurst 2003).

Comprehension: understanding, not memorizing

The comprehension category is an essential gateway to higher levels; if students don't understand something, they can't use it to engage in the higher-level processes of analyzing and solving problems (L. W. Anderson et al. 2001; Wenglinsky 2000). It is worth your time and effort to ensure that all students understand an idea before you ask them to use it in more complex activities (see Wiggins & McTighe 2008).

In Bloom's taxonomy, the comprehension category is divided into four components: interpretation, translation, examples, and definitions. In this section, we describe each component and provide examples of questions for each one.

Interpretation   **Interpretation** involves the student's ability to identify and comprehend the major ideas in a communication and to understand the relationship between them. For example, a student who is asked to relate one idea in an essay to another must go through the process of interpretation: giving meaning to a response by showing its relationship to other facts. This relationship may be shown by comparing and contrasting or by demonstrating similarity. "How" and "why" questions often call for some type of interpretation. In answering these questions, the student relates major points and, in doing so, shows an understanding of them. Following are some examples of **interpretive exercises**. Note that the italicized key words may be used in a variety of disciplines to frame comprehension objectives or questions:

◆   *What are some similarities between* French and German sentence structure?

Interpretation: show meaning, relationships

◆   *What differences exist between* the high school curricula of today and those of the 1980s?

Translation   **Translation** involves changing ideas from one form of communication into a parallel form while retaining their meaning. Reading a graph or describing the main point of a pictorial cartoon are examples of translation. Another example of translation is summarization. In summarization, the student translates a long passage into a shorter, more personal form. Translation questions require the student to construct or change the material into a different form:

◆ Describe in your own words the first paragraph of the Declaration of Independence.

◆ Record the results of your laboratory findings in tabular form and summarize your findings.

Examples   One of the best ways a person can demonstrate comprehension of an idea is to give an **example** of it:

◆ Give an example of a quadratic equation.

◆ Name two countries that are constitutional monarchies.

In asking students to provide examples of an abstraction, the teacher should require that those examples be new or previously undiscussed. Otherwise, the student will be operating only at the knowledge level, remembering examples from previous classes.

Definitions   Providing a **definition** requires students to describe a term or concept in their own words. This involves more than just repeating verbatim a textbook or dictionary definition. The teacher expects students to formulate the definition with words that are familiar and meaningful to them; for example:

◆ Define in your own words the knowledge category.

◆ Explain in your own words the meaning of the term *photosynthesis*.

Note that these examples call on the student to do more than just open the dictionary and copy meaningless words or synonyms.

> ***Reflect***
>
> ◆ When should you use knowledge or comprehension-type questions?
> ◆ How can you determine whether comprehension-type questions are appropriate to your students' grade or developmental level?

Application   The **application** category involves using information to arrive at a solution to a problem or situation. In operating at the application level, the student typically is given an unfamiliar problem and must apply the appropriate principle or method to it without being told to do so. The student must therefore choose the correct method and apply that method correctly. When evaluating an answer to an application problem, you should check both the solution and the process because how a student solves a problem may be more important than the answer he or she obtains. To be sure that a question reaches the application level, you must make the problem unique or novel. If the class went over the same problem the day before, the task for the student would involve mere recall, not application.

The two-step application process can be visualized as shown in Figure 3.1. In the first step of the process, the student encounters a new problem and recognizes it as a type of problem solved before. During the second step of

- - - - - - - - - - - - - - - -

Application: use the information in a situation or process

FIGURE 3.1
Application Problems as a Two-Step Process

solving an application-level problem, the student selects an appropriate solution and applies it to the data at hand. This solution can consist of an algorithm, a formula, an equation, a recipe, or a standardized set of procedures for handling a specific type of problem.

If you view application problems as a two-step process, you can analyze students' responses and diagnose problems on the basis of error patterns (see Dickie 2003; Sprenger 2003). If students are having difficulty recognizing certain equations, then you need to give them a wide variety of these types of problems to recognize and solve. However, if students can recognize equations but cannot plug the values in the problem into the correct formula or equation, give them practice in the computational aspects of the problem. This is another instance of how the taxonomy keeps teachers adapting instruction to meet diverse student needs.

Typically, an application problem has one solution, but there may be alternative ways to solve the problem. These usually involve using formulas or principles that have been learned previously, with the student selecting the appropriate application to solve the problem.

For instance, students may encounter a problem in which the formula $a^2 + b^2 = c^2$ should be used. To evaluate performance at the application level optimally, wait a few weeks after the original presentation of the content and then introduce a new problem dealing with right triangles. This will ensure that students can demonstrate the knowledge in a unique and novel situation. They are doing more than using a formula on a math test because it was the only topic covered for the previous three weeks.

Analysis   Application involves bringing together separate components to arrive at a solution. **Analysis** is the reverse of that process; it involves taking apart complex items—such as speeches, written communications, organizations, or machines—and explaining their underlying organization. The emphasis in analysis-level operations is on explaining how the various parts of a complex process or object are arranged or work together to achieve a certain effect.

Analysis can be differentiated from comprehension by means of the depth of processing involved. Comprehension involves finding similarities and differences in making comparisons. Basically, the task at that level is to show relationships that can be discovered by understanding the communication itself. Analysis, however, involves looking beneath the surface and discovering how different parts interact. In this sense, analysis involves working backward: taking a situation or event and explaining how all the parts fit together to produce a total effect. Comprehension, on the other hand, involves primarily describing what that effect is.

Analysis: explain function of parts

We can divide the analysis category into two subcategories: *identifying issues* and *identifying implications*.

Identifying Issues   In this type of analysis operation, students subdivide a broad communication into its constituent parts. This entails discovering the "skeleton" of a communication because the issues involved are sometimes not explicitly stated in the communication. In this sense, identifying the issues means going beyond the information in the message to show the relationship between assumptions and key points, stated or otherwise.

Following are examples of questions that ask students to identify issues.

◆ Using the six campaign speeches of the presidential candidates, point out the major differences between the candidates, relating the differences to specific sections of the speeches.

◆ Explain the main points of the Bill of Rights in terms of current injustices.

Identifying Implications   Stating implications requires students to identify the relationship between two propositions. The relationship may be expressed in terms of influence, association, or necessary consequences, and it need not be stated directly. It should be noted that inferring an implication does not necessarily mean cause and effect. Following are examples of questions that ask students to state implications.

◆ What were some of the motives behind the NATO interventions in Bosnia?

◆ Why do many organizations keep lobbyists in Washington, DC?

Reflect

◆ Give an example of an application problem from your own field of study.
◆ Under what circumstances would you use analysis questions that ask students to identify examples? To state implications? Give examples of both.

Synthesis   **Synthesis** entails the creative meshing of elements to form a new and unique entity. Because its key is creativity, the synthesis category may be the most distinctive and one of the easiest to recognize—but it may also be the most difficult to teach. Synthesis is the process of combining parts in such a way as to constitute a pattern or structure that did not exist before. A research paper can belong to either the application or the synthesis category, depending on the level of originality it displays. If the paper is comprehensive and thorough but does not add new knowledge to the topic, we would consider the writer to be operating at the application level. If, however, the writer puts ideas together in new or unique patterns or creates new idea configurations, then we would consider the writer to be engaging in a synthesis-level activity.

Synthesis: creating something new from existing elements

Because of the stress on creativity, operations at the synthesis level are usually difficult to grade objectively. You will need to use more subjective judgment in evaluating synthesis operations than in evaluating operations at other levels. However, be sure your judgments are based on appropriate criteria; otherwise, your comments may stifle creativity. To encourage creativity, give your students ample leeway in their creative expression.

Like the other levels, synthesis can be subdivided in terms of the type of processing involved and the products of those operations—*unique or original communication, plans for operations*, and *creating abstractions*.

Unique or Original Communication   In one type of synthesis, the product or performance is a unique type of communication. Examples are an essay, a speech, or an original art form, such as a poem, a painting, or a musical composition. Students' originality and creativeness are among the criteria used in evaluating these products (see also Ennis 1985; McAlpine et al. 1987; Paul 1985).

Plans for Operations   The second subcategory of the synthesis level involves developing a plan or a proposed set of operations to be performed. These operations result in the creation of a tangible product. This tangible product and the creativity displayed in creating it are the two distinguishing characteristics of the synthesis level.

Creating Abstractions   The third type of synthesis involves creating a set of abstract relations. This typically involves working with observed phenomena or data and forming patterns that did not exist before. For example, you might ask students to experiment with liquids of different densities and then formulate hypotheses about what they observed. In social studies, after students have studied the constitutions of a number of different nations, you might ask them to formulate principles for drawing up a workable constitution.

Evaluation   **Evaluation** requires making decisions on controversial topics and substantiating these decisions with sound reasons. Judgment is to evaluation what creativity is to synthesis. Evaluation questions ask students to state their judgments and to give the criteria on which they are based. To function at the evaluation level, the student must (1) set up appropriate standards or values by which to make a judgment and (2) determine how closely the idea or object meets the standards or values.

The evaluation category projects the analysis category into another dimension. An evaluation question requires the student to make a judgment in addition to analyzing. The criteria for judgment must be clearly identified, and the quality of the evaluation response should be graded according to how well the student has met the criteria.

An evaluation response should consist of two parts:

1. The student should establish criteria on which to base his or her judgment.
2. Using the prescribed criteria, the student should state his or her own judgment.

For example, if you ask the question, "To what extent should the federal government regulate health care?" you are asking the student first to decide what regulatory role the federal government should play and then to determine to what extent that role should apply to health care. There will be some difference of opinion about the role of the federal government. This brings out the subjective and creative component of evaluation. The student

Evaluation: making and substantiating decisions

must exercise judgment in matching these criteria with the subject being evaluated.

Evaluation criteria usually originate from one of three sources:

1. Cultural or social values
2. Religious or historical absolutes
3. Individual justifications

Examples of criteria based on each source follow:

1. "The expectations for twenty-first-century public schools are excessive." This statement could be answered in several ways, depending on which social or cultural values the person answering it believes to be important.
2. "Should abortion be legal?" To some people, this is a religious question and is couched in absolute values; to others, it is a decision based on personal morals; and to still others, it is a medical decision.
3. "To what extent are educational standards useful or useless?" Different people probably would arrive at varying answers based on their value systems.

Please note how the evaluation category of the cognitive domain tends to overlap with the lower levels of the affective domain. There is a **correlation** among feelings, attitudes, values, and the way we select criteria by which to judge or evaluate.

Because your students will have different values, you will receive varied responses to the same evaluation question. You can use evaluation questions to help students learn to live with and accept the different views of others, thus preparing them to live in a pluralistic society. You can also prepare students to take a stand on issues by asking evaluation questions such as "What do you think is best/worst or more/most important?" But a word of caution is in order: Always require a *rationale*. Opinions, for the most part, are irrational.

Reflect

◆ The last three items in the cognitive taxonomy—analysis, synthesis, and evaluation—are often called "higher-order skills." What makes them "higher-order"?

◆ How could you encourage your students to use these skills when you teach controversial subjects?

◆ Examine Table 2.1 and categorize the various levels via Bloom's taxonomy.

◆ Of all the skills listed in Bloom's taxonomy, which have you been most successful using in your own schooling? Which have come most naturally to you? Which are more challenging?

Responses to Bloom's Taxonomy

In the 50-plus years that Bloom's taxonomy has existed, it has been widely used and accepted by educators at all levels. Research on the taxonomy, as well as research in cognitive psychology, has generally supported the ideas behind the taxonomy but has also raised some questions about its internal structure. This section focuses on that research.

Questions and Concerns   Despite its widespread acceptance and use, Bloom's taxonomy has raised some persistent questions. One question is about its comprehensiveness. Some critics state that the taxonomy is too narrow and does not include all the important goals taught in our schools (Furst 1994). When you think about the broad range of goals existing in such diverse areas as home economics, art, music, and physical education, you can see that this concern is probably valid. As this chapter points out, teachers in these diverse areas can still use the taxonomy, but they will have to adapt it to their own classroom. In fact, all teachers seem to do this—they customize an educational idea to make it their own (see A. Anderson 2001).

A second concern centers on whether the levels in the hierarchy are discrete or overlapping. You may have encountered this problem yourself as you tried to keep the levels separate. For example, is application of a formula knowledge, comprehension, or application? Though a problem for researchers, this concern is not as great among individual teachers who use the taxonomy to guide their teaching (see L. W. Anderson et al. 2001).

Uses of the Taxonomy   The taxonomy has been widely used in curriculum and test construction, as well as in general curriculum design and alignment (Aviles 2001; McLaughlin & Phillips 1991; Pratt 1994; van der Wal & van der Wal 2003). Applications include providing stimulating experiences for preschoolers through technology (Morgan 1996).

Instructors at all levels have used the taxonomy to determine cognitive levels for classroom activities (McCormick & Whittington 2000), to categorize question-asking (Schurr 2001; Shaunessy 2000), and to assist in differentiating instruction (Distad & Heacox 2000). It has been used to assess the cognitive levels of test bank questions (Masters et al. 2001) as well as the test questions posed in textbooks (Risner, Nicholson, & Webb 2000), and to classify levels of classroom questions (Magner 2000). Another novel use has been to encourage greater cognitive complexity in counselors in training (Granello 2000). Researchers have found Bloom's taxonomy to be a useful analytic tool as well. For example, the six conceptual levels in the taxonomy were used to relate data obtained from a satellite remote sensing exercise. Concepts and principles associated with the satellite images were arranged in hierarchical order in categories ranging from simple data (knowledge) to interpretations and evaluations of data (Marks, Vitek, & Allen 1996). Other researchers have made use of the taxonomy for analyzing verbal interactions in a classroom (Fisher & Hiebert 1990).

Perhaps the taxonomy's greatest contribution has been in the development of a professional language. Teachers and administrators who describe and analyze instruction know that terms such as *knowledge level* and *higher levels of learning* will be understood by educators everywhere. This universal vocabulary, reflecting a specialized body of knowledge, was an essential step in the professionalization of teaching (Danielson 2007).

The importance of the comprehension category as a gateway to the other levels is also becoming clear. In a retrospective review of this area of cognitive psychology, Raymond Nickerson (1985) argued convincingly that

Concerns: not broad enough; levels sometimes overlap

Broad applications within and inside of teaching

comprehending an idea or a concept is an essential prerequisite to applying it, analyzing it, or using it creatively or evaluatively. Thus teachers need to make a special effort to ensure that students understand an idea before asking them to use it. Don Orlich (1991) has raised some questions about the sequence of the levels. Though he supports the general idea of increasing cognitive complexity, he questions whether progress through the taxonomy occurs in six uniform steps. His observations led to the conclusion that comprehension was the key to upper categories. This is a practical problem that you can test by making observations and collecting data in your own classes, a process called "Action Research." (See Mertler 2006 for an extended treatment of the topic.) The overriding message is clear. If your students are to learn effectively, you need to plan and implement strategies that require internal processing of information. Establish goals, lay a knowledge base, and teach actively toward higher cognitive levels.

At this point we will note that an adaptation of Bloom's taxonomy is apparent when you examine the National Assessment of Educational Progress (NAEP) reports. One report is titled "The Nation's Report Card." The NAEP is a congressionally mandated project to provide data on student performance in reading, mathematics, science, history/geography, writing and other areas. These reports intermittently summarize student achievements in five numerical levels, which closely correspond to the six levels of Bloom's taxonomy. Toward the end of this chapter, we will elaborate in detail the five levels, their uses, and how you as a classroom teacher might use them. (The NAEP website can be found at http://nces.ed.gov/naep.)

Using Taxonomies as Planning Tools

Teaching can be envisioned as a triad of strategies, outcomes, and evaluations, as illustrated in Figure 3.2. In this model, the formulated outcomes, or objectives, determine both the teaching strategies and the evaluation procedures—each element affects all the others. A taxonomy can be used in each of these activities: in formulating outcomes or objectives at an appropriate level, in

FIGURE 3.2
A Model of Teaching Alignment

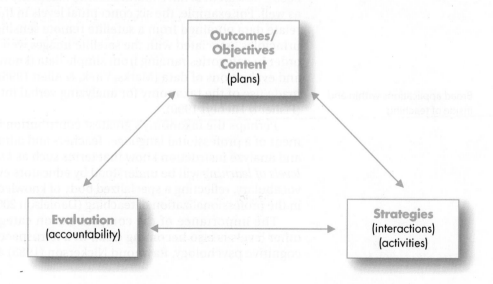

Outcomes/
Objectives
Content
(plans)

Evaluation
(accountability)

Strategies
(interactions)
(activities)

developing classroom questions and learning exercises, and in constructing evaluation instruments congruent with the outcomes and strategies to be employed. In other words, you can use taxonomies to decide what to teach, how to teach, and how to evaluate the effectiveness of your teaching (see Marzano, Pickering, & Pollock 2001).

You can make a broad array of adaptations with the taxonomy. However, for our immediate purpose, we focus only on planning because other topics are amplified in subsequent chapters. Effective teaching requires that teachers think strategically about the taxonomic level of objectives, questions, and test items when they plan. Five different ways that a taxonomy can help in the planning process are listed below. (You may want to add your own items to the list after reading ours.)

1. *Provides a range of objectives.* A taxonomy provides a range of possible outcomes or objectives for any subject. Closely examining the categories may prevent you from overemphasizing one dimension of learning, such as knowledge, in your teaching. In this respect a taxonomy not only adds variety to your repertoire, but also gives greater breadth to your objectives.

2. *Sequences objectives.* An analysis of learning tasks suggests the learning experiences necessary for the student to obtain the intended outcomes. A taxonomy provides one means of sequencing learning from simple to complex outcomes.

3. *Provides a cognitive structure.* Research has shown that students learn and retain information better if it is organized into some type of cognitive structure rather than presented as isolated items (Hohn 1995). Taxonomies can provide cognitive structure to students by showing them how facts can be used in the application, analysis, synthesis, and evaluation of other ideas.

4. *Provides a learning model.* By experiencing a series of learning activities in a sequence based on a taxonomy, students are able to perceive that learning is logical and sequential, thus obtaining a model of learning that they can use even after they leave the classroom (see Dyment & O'Connell 2003).

5. *Reinforces learning.* Because each category of the taxonomy is subsumed by the next-higher category, reinforcement of previous learning occurs if learning experiences are sequenced in terms of a taxonomy. Further, activities can be focused on a specific level.

INSTRUCTIONAL *Strategies*

Using the Taxonomy as a Planning Tool

◆ Provide a range of objectives.

◆ Sequence objectives from simple to complex.

◆ Show the relationship of objectives.

◆ Plan for logical and sequential activities.

◆ Build on previous learnings.

◆ Plan for appropriate levels of instruction and assessment.

SECTION *3*   Using Objectives to Guide Learners

So far we have considered two sources teachers can draw on in writing objectives and planning instruction: (1) goals and standards and (2) cognitive taxonomies. We turn now to a third major resource teachers need in planning: knowledge of how to write appropriate educational objectives. The purpose of creating objectives, both long- and short-term, is to provide intent and direction to your instruction. Students need to know where they are going and why. In this section, we provide guidelines for writing and evaluating objectives.

Objectives tell students where they are going.

You can use several techniques to state objectives. We demonstrate first the most specific formats because they add the greatest clarity and structure. This type of objective, called a *performance objective*, was popularized by Robert F. Mager. Throughout our entire discussion of objectives, keep in mind that there is no right way or wrong way to state outcomes or objectives. The key point is that you must alert the students to what they are to learn. Instructional fairness is the essential prerequisite in specifying learning outcomes, objectives, or anything else.

Writing Performance Objectives

Performance objectives are very precise statements of what you expect the student to do (Mager 1962, 1997). Although performance objectives are written in a wide variety of styles, three elements are generally included (see Figure 3.3):

1. The statement of an observable behavior, or performance, on the part of the learner
2. A description of the conditions under which learner behavior or performance is to occur
3. The prescription of a minimally acceptable level of performance, or criterion, on the part of the learner

Performance Statement   The first element of a performance objective is an **outcome**, generally a verb that indicates what the learner is to perform, do, or produce. Verbs such as *match, name, compute, list, assemble, write, circle*, and

FIGURE 3.3
Three Elements of a Performance Objective

Condition	▶	With the use of a protractor,
Performance	▶	the student will construct a right triangle
Criterion measure	▶	that meets a 3, 4, 5 ratio.

classify describe observable learner behaviors or outcomes, which will help you evaluate student achievement of performance objectives. For example, if you state that the student must name the capital cities of ten states listed, the student's behavior is manifested when this performance takes place; everyone will know that the student has attained the stated objective or outcome.

The specifications of the performance come from the general goals, of course. If you teach social studies in the United States, one goal always will be to provide instruction about the U.S. system of government and the Constitution. An intermediate goal surely will be to study the Bill of Rights. Specific performance objectives may be as follows: The learner will

1. Paraphrase the first ten amendments to the U.S. Constitution
2. Distinguish between statements that are from the Bill of Rights and those that are not
3. Conduct a survey to determine how many students in the high school can identify the Fifth Amendment

Words such as *know, understand, analyze, evaluate, appreciate, comprehend*, and *realize* are not action verbs. Although such terms are important in describing the processes of learning and behaving, they are not observable actions and thus cannot be used when writing performance objectives. However, these terms are used plentifully in state and national standards documents. Such terms may be used when you specify goals, as noted in our discussion of taxonomies. Remember that you make the decisions about the kind of performance you think is most appropriate or relevant. Thus the first and most important element of any performance objective is selecting the action verb and its direct object.

Elaboration of Conditions   The second element in prescribing a performance objective is elaboration, or description, of the conditions under which the learner is to perform the behavior. The **conditions** refer to the circumstances under which the learner must perform. Generally, conditional elements refer to

1. How the performance may be accomplished—for example, using memory, a textbook, a computer program, or calculator
2. Time elements (although time may also be used in evaluation)
3. Location of the performance (for example, in the classroom, in a gymnasium, or in the library)
4. What materials may be used to perform the tasks

For example, in "With the aid of the periodic table, the student will list the atomic weights of the first ten elements," the conditional statement is "with the aid of the periodic table." This tells students that they need not memorize the atomic weights; they should simply identify them from the periodic table. We often refer to the conditional component of a performance objective as a "statement of givens": "given this" or "given that," the learner will accomplish something.

The conditional element of a performance objective is the "fair-play" part of the instruction. As a student, did you ever arrive in class to find that, when the teacher said to "study" a poem, what he or she really intended you to do was to "memorize" the poem? Such imprecision can be confusing, if not

---

Outcome stated with action verb

Conditions: how, when, where, with what

demoralizing. We recommend that you always present this element of instruction to students explicitly, whether you use performance objectives or not.

The list below provides examples of a few conditional statements that could be included in the appropriate performance objectives.

Sample Conditional Statements

◆ "From memory, . . ."

◆ "Using a map, a compass, a ruler, and a protractor, . . ."

◆ "On a computer disk, which describes, . . ."

◆ "Given six different material samples with labels, . . ."

◆ "From the notes taken while viewing, . . ."

◆ "Within a 10-minute time span and from memory, . . ."

◆ "Using IRS Form 1040A, . . ."

These are some examples of the conditions under which a student can achieve a desired performance objective. The teacher sets the conditional statement in advance and gives it to the student. We recommend that the condition be the first component of the performance objective. For instance, if you were to assign a short essay, a reasonable conditional element would be: "With the use of a dictionary, . . ." We believe the conditional element has a significant impact on instructional planning and teacher behavior, so it should never be omitted.

Conditions must be realistic. Even though feasible, "reciting the Declaration of Independence from memory in 5 minutes" would be an inappropriate condition. One must always ask, "What is my main priority for the objective?" If memorizing is the priority, then that condition will define the attainment of the objective. If identifying the key ideas in the Declaration of Independence is the priority, then a condition less rigorous than memorization would be more compatible with the objective.

An integrated social studies and language arts outcome might be written as follows:

> Students will read the two essays [specify essays] found on the Internet. Orally, they will analyze the main points, showing how figures of speech and metaphors enrich the meanings. Each student must prepare a one-page, written summary of the historical and social events that affected each author, using the reference books reserved for this unit. Students will prepare their reports during class time on the computers scheduled exclusively for class use. Before final drafts are prepared, each paper must be critiqued by two members of the working group for grammar, spelling, and punctuation.

Criterion Measure   The third element of a performance objective—the definition of an acceptable standard of performance—is perhaps the most difficult to write. This standard may be referred to as the **criterion measure**, level of performance, minimum criterion, or minimum acceptable performance. Whatever term is used, the designated level is the minimum or lowest level of acceptable performance. When this is specified, students know in advance the standards by which their work will be judged.

Following is a list of clearly written criterion measures (the condition and the performance verb are missing from the statements):

1. "... 70 percent of a given list of problems."
2. "... within 2 mm...."
3. "... nine out of ten of the elements...."
4. "... within 5 minutes, with no more than two errors of any kind."
5. "... the project will be compared to the two models completed by the instructor."
6. "... without any grammatical or spelling errors."
7. "... containing one dependent and one independent clause."

Each of these criterion elements states a well-defined standard for which the student can strive. These standards are always devised so that students have a high probability of achieving them and will thus be encouraged to continue to strive toward meeting the established criterion. A word of caution: Many teachers expect far too much from their students and set standards that are too high or impossible to reach. You must know at what level your students are working so that you can establish reasonable minimum standards—a skill that is part of the artistry of teaching.

Frequently an instructor will require 100 percent of the class to attain 100 percent of the objective—that is, for everyone to demonstrate complete mastery. This is called a *100/100 criterion measure*. There are many areas in which an instructor will require mastery, such as basic reading skills, math facts, using equipment, or learning safety procedures. In these cases, mastery is the minimum acceptable level of performance. The mastery criterion is most appropriate when completing prerequisite or entry-level tasks because later skills are contingent on successfully performing the initial ones.

Although carefully defined standards of student performance are essential to a well-written performance objective, we recognize that much of what is taught in the classroom focuses on activities or experiences. Providing meaningful criterion measures for instruction of this type will be easier if you keep two things in mind. First, remember that activity, experience, or competency learning experiences are made up of previous learning that can be given clear standards of student performance. For example, the activity of playing volleyball is made up of a number of specific behaviors that can be isolated and given clear criterion measures. Competence in building a multimedia presentation is preceded by many skills that more easily provide clear standards of student performance. Performance objectives that focus on activities, experiences, or competencies are often more global in scope, and criterion measures for them can be difficult to write. However, they are always preceded by smaller increments of learning, for which clear standards of performance can be written. In effect, the totality of all the objectives that precede an activity, experience, or competency objective make up the criterion measure for that objective.

Second, to write only narrow, skill-based performance objectives would destroy much of the richness that should be a part of every classroom. Many times, it is the activity—the interdisciplinary or experientially focused instruction—that gives a classroom spice and interest. Do not avoid writing objectives because the criterion measure is not as precise and tight as you might like. Broadly stated objectives in which the criterion measure is less

Criterion measure defines level of acceptable performance.

well defined can be desirable as long as they flow from a sequence of clearly articulated objectives. For example: "Describe at least four conditions of the Great Depression of the 1930s that were missing in the recessions of the 1980s and 1990s." As you will learn, much of the most exciting, high-level learning comes from mastering the lower-level material and the skills that precede it (see Rohwer & Sloane 1994). The box below summarizes the approach to use for complex tasks.

Objectives for Complex Tasks

◆ Focus on prerequisite knowledge and skills.

◆ Use broadly focused objectives for complex tasks.

◆ Proceed from simple to complex.

Criterion Grading   A word of caution about criterion levels: Far too frequently, the teacher prescribes a percentage or a time as the evaluation element of the performance objective. For example, if time is a critical factor in the real world—as in CPR, braking actions (that is, in a car), or manipulating machinery—then a timed criterion is appropriate. But to set a time for student learning experiences that is identical to that of professionals in the field is inappropriate. Skills can be built or improved by using variable criterion measures, just as they can with any systematic method. Thus a criterion measure of 30 seconds for a skill in the first experience may be reduced systematically as learners improve. When providing keyboarding skills, teachers have observed this principle in action many times. As time goes by, students are allowed fewer mistakes per time period. In short, the standards for an A or even a C grade are shifted to higher levels of achievement as the course progresses.

Use increasing criterion measures for skills development.

Some educators have criticized performance objectives for seemingly forcing them into giving "A" grades for minimal student performance. This need not be the case. As a teacher, you may write performance objectives with clear criterion measures and make the meeting of those objectives worth any letter grade you choose. For example, you may state that meeting the criterion measures in your objectives will earn your students a C grade. Not meeting the criterion measures in your objectives will earn students a grade of less than C, and performing beyond your objectives will earn a grade higher than C. We provide a detailed discussion about grading in Chapter 10.

Tying criterion measure to grade

Several alternative methods are available for using performance objectives and grades. You may choose to write several performance objectives for a single sequence of instruction. Each objective can be progressively more difficult, with each worth a higher letter grade. Thus meeting performance objective 1 earns a grade of D, meeting objective 2 earns a grade of C, and so on. Rather than pressuring the teacher into giving a high grade for mediocre performance, carefully phrased performance objectives enable the teacher to prescribe a precise value and meaning to grades in terms of overt learner performance.

Key Ideas

Performance Objectives

◆ Performance statements are precise.

◆ Conditional elements are the givens.

◆ Criterion measures alert students to expectations for success.

◆ Assignment of grades can be based on objective criteria.

Recognizing the Limits of Objectives

Even well-written objectives are not an educational panacea that will re-solve all learning problems. Objectives have limited purposes; they are only a means to an end, not an end per se. The purpose of the objective is to com-municate the exact intent of the lesson. The objective is one component of the lesson plan. The teacher can construct technically correct objectives but can fail completely in the classroom because of a lack of teaching skills and interpersonal competencies or strategies.

When developing lessons that use objectives, the teacher must accept the following four assumptions.

1. Learning is defined as a change in the learner's observable performance.
2. Behavioral changes are observable in some form and may be measured by *appropriate* measuring devices over a specified period of time.
3. Observed learner outcome is directly linked to the teaching strategies, the content, or the media used.
4. The majority of children at all ages can master appropriate subjects at some acceptable developmental level if they are given enough time; adequate, appropriate learning experiences; and necessary materials.

Reflect

◆ As you think about writing objectives for your own lessons, what kinds of objectives do you believe will prove more useful to you as a teacher? Would your response change if you were to focus instead on which objectives would prove more helpful to your students? Why or why not?

Curriculum Alignment

Another rationale for performance objectives centers around the concept of **curriculum alignment** (Cohen 1987, 1995; Steinbrink & Jones 1991). In its simplest form, a curriculum consists of all the subject matter that is taught, together with objectives, instruction, and assessment, as illustrated in Fig-ure 3.2. When all three elements match—that is, when instruction and assess-ment focus on stated objectives—the curriculum is in alignment. Curriculum alignment is much more difficult to attain than it seems. Teachers emphasize different learning experiences based on their skills and interests. Students have varied talents and have mastered different skills at different levels. Teach-ers have a variety of materials to use for instruction. Performance objectives

Objectives, instruction, assessment all in line

do provide a key, however, that teachers can use to align the instruction in their own classrooms. For that matter, performance objectives are essential for alignment at the district and building level, as well as aligning with any set of standards.

The basis for successful curriculum alignment is in the process of carefully analyzing the skills, competencies, and other measures of student learning that you want to result from instruction. You test what you teach, and you teach what is in your objectives—this is an idea that is simple to state but difficult to carry out without carefully planned and written performance objectives. Curriculum can be aligned from either end of the process—the objective end or the assessment end. Too often, what teachers teach is influenced by what they know or anticipate will be on the tests. To make instructional decisions based on what is to be tested is to pervert the process. Done correctly, assessment flows from the decisions you made about what is best for your students to learn. Start from the objectives and make the rest of the process fit. If your objectives are clear and sharp, instruction and assessment will be aligned. The box below summarizes curriculum alignment.

When all parts of the curriculum—performance objectives, activities, instruction, and assessment—are congruent (in alignment), student learning improves dramatically. Curriculum alignment has been identified as a principal sign of effective schools (see Kelly 1991). Curriculum alignment has been shown to be a major tool in changing less successful schools into successful ones (see Martin 2006).

All in all, curriculum alignment is a powerful concept—one that begins with identifying your objectives (English & Steffy 2001).

Curriculum Alignment

◆ Start from your objectives, not from assessment.

◆ If your objectives are clear, instruction and assessment will be aligned.

◆ Curriculum alignment is a recurring cycle.

Reflect   Some authors on curriculum alignment state that you can begin with the assessment and work backwards. Discuss the implications of this position.

Reflecting on Planning

Effective planning has a positive impact on student achievement. Planning is a time-consuming process for the beginning teacher. Although you have spent many hours in the classroom as a student, you probably have never been responsible for student learning. As you gain experience, you will begin to know which activities require detailed planning and which do not.

Knowing when to abandon plans and to take advantage of an unintended learning opportunity is a master teacher's skill. A good plan provides you with the context for this decision. Does this new opportunity (teachable moment) contribute more positively to the objectives of the lesson? Are you meeting a student's important need with a lesson detour? A teacher must exhibit a balance between preparation and flexibility in executing the plan. That, of course, is part of the artistry of teaching.

Addressing individual differences is extremely difficult. Even experienced teachers struggle to meet the learning needs of all their students. Initially, students in your class will need to adapt to your teaching style. As you gain experience and confidence in the teaching and learning processes, you will begin planning for and addressing individual student needs, and eventually accommodate your teaching style to match the students' needs.

Planning is a dynamic process. In fact, it often seems downright chaotic. The United States is unique in that responsibility for planning and teaching at the classroom level rests with you, the teacher. In most countries, teachers are told what to teach and often even how to teach. With this in mind, you should be even more aware that—if state standards shift from general statements to specific learner objectives—you might be responsible only for the "how" part.

In this chapter we have described the basic planning tools of goals, taxonomies, and objectives, and provided examples of how to use these tools to develop instructional plans. Don't be afraid to refine, modify, or experiment with these tools. You are the technician; the tools are there to serve you and those all-important students.

Plans are dynamic, not set in stone.

SECTION 4 — Converting Standards to Objectives

The Significance of Standards

With the advent of federal legislation enacted in 2001/2002, the No Child Left Behind Act (PL 107-110) and its anticipated renewal, all states must establish "challenging academic standards." One component of the standards movement has been the *high-stakes test* phenomenon. Such tests are called "high-stakes" because teachers, students, and schools are rewarded or penalized on the basis of the students' scores. National and state standards have a huge effect on what is being taught in the schools and how it is being taught.

National Education Standards

Momentum for contemporary U.S. school reform and the subsequent academic standards movement can be traced to the 1983 report *A Nation at Risk: The Imperative for Educational Reform*, sponsored by the National Commission on Excellence in Education (1983). One of its most often-quoted lines states, "If an unfriendly foreign power had attempted to impose on America the mediocre instructional performance that exists today, we might well have viewed it as an act of war." By using a war metaphor, the national commission intentionally created a crisis of confidence, which is amply documented by David C. Berliner and Bruce Biddle (1995) in their book, *The Manufactured*

A crisis of confidence?

Crisis: Myths, Fraud, and the Attack on America's Public Schools. Gerald W. Bracey's (2003) *What You Should Know About the War Against America's Public Schools* amplifies the debate.

Background and Perspective   During the 1980s, educational reform had at least eight factors driving it:

◆ Global economic competition

◆ Disparities between socioeconomic groups

◆ Declining wages

◆ Exporting of jobs overseas

◆ New technologies

◆ Renewed business-sector interest in education

◆ Perceived decline in student achievement

◆ Demographic changes in the schools

None of these factors alone could provide impetus for reform, but collectively they caused public education to become a focal point for social and economic changes. As early as 1986, Bill Chance reported that there were more than 275 educational task forces organized in the United States, generating scores of reports to "fix the schools" (1986). The current enthusiasm for educational reform and standards is politically motivated; that is, the drive and energy come from two nonschool sources: (1) policy-makers and (2) professional associations desiring to enhance academic rigor. All states have adopted their own standards. The broad subject areas for which standards have been adopted tend to be in civics, English, fine arts, geography, history, language arts, mathematics, performing arts, science, work skills, and world languages.

Professional groups and associations are involved in establishing educational goals. The National Science Education Standards, by the National Research Council (1996), and *Atlas of Science Literacy*, by the American Association for the Advancement of Science (2007), are two attempts by science education professional groups to provide guidance through educational standards—that is, to provide criteria against which performance may be judged. The goals of these national education standards are to produce students who are able to do the following things:

◆ Use scientific principles and processes appropriately in making personal decisions.

◆ Experience the richness and excitement of knowing about and understanding the natural world.

◆ Increase their economic productivity.

◆ Engage intelligently in public discourse and debate about matters of scientific and technological concern.

The push for standards is inspired by many factors, but most importantly by heightened global competition in an increasingly technological world. (See also Jennings's 1998 discussion about the politics involved and how political and business leaders, not educators, advocated national standards and high-stakes tests.)

What exactly are standards? The term **standards** has multiple meanings and applications. For example, no distinction is made between the standards and educational objectives. Standards can be criteria by which to judge the quality of what students know and are able to do, the quality of programs available to them, the quality of teaching they receive, the quality of the system that supports their teachers and programs, and the quality of their school's assessment practices and policies. Unless carefully designated, these five aspects of schooling are lumped together. In these cases, the same data—usually test scores—are used as the only yardsticks for measuring the success of five distinct and independent activities, at which point we must ask, "How can one measure on a test be valid for evaluating five very disparate phenomena?"

Standards also refer to a vision of learning and, as you saw in Chapter 1, teaching. In both capacities, as performance criteria and as an educational vision, standards tend to provide conflicting expressions. (See Bracey 2004 for a thought-provoking critique.)

A National Adaptation of Bloom's Taxonomy—National Assessment of Educational Progress (NAEP)

As we noted earlier in this chapter, the carefully designed NAEP assessments are systematically conducted using a sampling technique. Approximately 100 public schools per grade and per subject are tested, with approximately 2,500 students in each state.

This sampling technique then provides an accurate "snapshot" of educational trends. Every few years, a long-term trend assessment is conducted on a national sample. Thus, the NAEP tests are designed for a sampling of students and/or not designed to test every student, in every state, every year (White, Smith, & Vanneman 2000).

However, the NAEP uses an adaptation of the six-level Bloom cognitive taxonomy in classifying its assessment questions. The levels are numbered 150, 200, 250, 300, and 350, with the first three corresponding to knowledge, comprehension, and application (150, 200, and 250). The NAEP levels 300 and 350 encompass the "higher cognitive levels" of application, synthesis, and evaluation.

Table 3.5 illustrates in detail the NAEP levels for mathematics with an operational description of what student outcomes are expected (see Campbell, Voelkl, & Donahue 1998; [NCES 98-530] for detailed descriptors in science, reading, and writing).

To provide one example, see Table 3.6, which shows how students perform in mathematics at ages 9, 13, and 17 or in grades 4, 8, and 12. Notice that at levels 150 and 200 virtually all eighth- and twelfth-graders master the content, with students in grade 4 doing very well. At level 250, observe the sharp decline of students' achievements. Examine levels 300 and 350. Virtually no fourth- or eighth-graders can answer those questions correctly. Even among the twelfth-graders, the percentage is very low.

Now return to Table 2.1 in Chapter 2 and review the Epstein-Piaget developmental table. Do you see the close correlation between those data and the percentages shown in Table 3.6?

TABLE 3.5	National Assessment of Educational Progress (NAEP) Mathematics Performance-Level Descriptions

Level 350: Multistep Problem Solving and Algebra

Students at this level can apply a range of reasoning skills to solve multistep problems. They can solve routine problems involving fractions and percents, recognize properties of basic geometric figures, and work with exponents and square roots. They can solve a variety of two-step problems using variables, identify equivalent algebraic expressions, and solve linear equations and inequalities. They are developing an understanding of functions and coordinate systems.

Level 300: Moderately Complex Procedures and Reasoning

Students at this level are developing an understanding of number systems. They can compute with decimals, simple fractions, and commonly encountered percents. They can identify geometric figures, measure lengths and angles, and calculate areas of rectangles. These students are also able to interpret simple inequalities, evaluate formulas, and solve simple linear equations. They can find averages, make decisions based on information drawn from graphs, and use logical reasoning to solve problems. They are developing the skills to operate with signed numbers, exponents, and square roots.

Level 250: Numerical Operations and Beginning Problem Solving

Students at this level have an initial understanding of the four basic operations. They are able to apply whole-number addition and subtraction skills to one-step word problems and money situations. In multiplication, they can find the product of a two-digit and a one-digit number. They can also compare information from graphs and charts, and are developing an ability to analyze simple logical relations.

Level 200: Beginning Skills and Understandings

Students at this level have considerable understanding of two-digit numbers. They can add two-digit numbers but are still developing an ability to regroup in subtraction. They know some basic multiplication and division facts, recognize relations among coins, can read information from charts and graphs, and are able to use simple measurement instruments. They are developing some reasoning skills.

Level 150: Simple Arithmetic Facts

Students at this level know some basic addition and subtraction facts, and most can add two-digit numbers without regrouping. They recognize simple situations in which addition and subtraction apply. They also are developing rudimentary classification skills.

We take great pains to illustrate these data because the plethora of state standards have never been field-tested against the NAEP performance levels. As you view the samples of state standards that follow, you may be shocked to realize for the first time that the standards lack empirical testing and tend to deny the existence of the developmental perspective.

State Standards

A Sampling of State Standards   With all 50 states now having standards for instruction, let us examine just a tiny sample of them—keeping in mind that, in total, thousands of pages are on file.

TABLE 3.6	**Percentages of Students Performing At or Above Mathematics Performance Levels, Ages 9, 13, and 17, in 1978 and 1996**					
		AGE 9		AGE 13		AGE 17	
Level		Percent 1978	Percent 1996	Percent 1978	Percent 1996	Percent 1978	Percent 1996
350	Can solve multistep problems and use beginning algebra.	0	0	1	1	7	7
300	Can compute with decimals, fractions and percents; recognize geometric figures; solve equations; and use moderately complex reasoning.	1	2*	18	21	52	60*
250	Can add, subtract, multiply and divide using whole numbers and solve one-step problems.	20	30*	65	79*	92	97*
200	Can add and subtract two-digit numbers and recognize relationships among coins.	70	82*	95	99*	100	100
150	Knows some addition and subtraction facts.	97	99*	100	100	100	100

* Indicates that the percentage in 1996 is significantly different from that in 1978.

Source: National Center for Education Statistics, National Assessment of Educational Progress (NAEP). *Report in Brief, NAEP 1996 Trends in Academic Progress.* Revised 1998. NCES 98–530, Table 2, p. 10.

Mathematics

Arizona

The Grand Canyon State spells out in detail the mathematics standards by grade level. At the high school level, the "strands" relate to "number sense and operations"; "data analysis, probability and discrete mathematics"; "geometry"; and "logic." Below are two examples:

1. Apply subscripts to represent ordinal positions.
2. Interpret the relationship between data suggested by tables/matrices, equations or graphs.

Ohio

The Buckeye State standards include the following:

Grades 5–7

1. Relate mathematical ideas to one another and to other content areas; e.g., use area models for adding fractions; interpret graphs in reading, science, and social studies.
2. Explain how inverse operations are used to solve linear equations.

Grade 8

Demonstrate an understanding that the probability of either of two disjoint events occurring can be found by adding the probabilities for each and that the probability of one independent event following another can be found by multiplying the probabilities.

Grade 9

1. Define the basic trigonometric ratios in right triangles: sine, cosine and tangent.
2. Use theoretical and experimental probability, including simulations or random numbers, to estimate probabilities and to solve problems dealing with uncertainty; e.g., compound events, independent events and simple dependent events.

Social Science

California

The following are from the Golden State's History-Social Science Content Standards.

Grade 5

1. Describe the competition among the English, French, Spanish, Dutch and Indian nations for control of North America.
2. Identify the significance and leaders of the First Great Awakening, which marked a shift in religious ideas, practices and allegiances in the colonial period, the growth of religious toleration and free exercise of religion.

Colorado

The Centennial State has a Model Content Standards: Economics.

Grades 5–8

Describe how different economic systems affect the allocation of resources (for example, steel production in the former Soviet Union was determined by economic planners. This affected the allocation of many resources: coal, labor, etc. In the United States, all of these resources are allocated by the market).

English/Language Arts   Published standards in this arena are copious. Here's a random sampling.

Florida: Grades 6–8

Determine main concept, supporting details, stereotypes, bias and persuasion techniques in a non-print message.

Massachusetts: Grade 7

1. Students will identify, analyze and apply knowledge of the themes, structure and elements of myths, traditional narratives and classical literature and provide evidence from the text to support their understanding.
2. Identify and analyze similarities and differences in mythologies from different cultures (for example, ideas of the afterlife, roles and characteristics of deities, types and purposes of myths).

North Carolina: Grade 12

1. Recognize common themes that run through works, using evidence from the texts to substantiate ideas.
2. Relate the cultural and historical contexts to the literature, identifying perceived ambiguities, prejudices and complexities.

Texas

In the Lone Star State, the standards are included in the Texas Administrative Code, giving them a legal status. This excerpt is from the Grade 5 English Language Arts and Reading Standards, and provides a good example of specificity:

> (4) Listening/Speaking/Culture. The student listens and speaks to gain and share knowledge of his/her own culture, the culture of others, and the common elements of cultures. The student is expected to:
>
> (A) connect his/her own experiences, information, insights, and ideas with the experiences of others through speaking and listening (4-8);
>
> (B) compare oral traditions across regions and cultures (4-8); and
>
> (C) identify how language use such as labels and sayings reflects regions and cultures (4-8).

Teaching to Standards   Here is a list of steps you can take to convert a standard into teachable lessons. Visit our website at www.cengage.com/education/orlich for a more detailed illustration of this process.

1. Create a series of specific and discrete objectives from the general standards statement.
2. To visualize relationships, sketch flow charts showing connectedness between objectives and standards.
3. Identify appropriate print, nonprint, and Internet-based materials.
4. Plan appropriate lessons, including a variety of teaching strategies and accommodations for special education students or ESL learners.
5. Integrate assessments into the lesson design.
6. Draft a calendar showing time commitments.
7. Evaluate the entire process to optimize student achievement.

This sequence is obviously labor intensive. There will be few shortcuts. And no state has prepared a series of print materials such as textbooks that align with the adopted standards. We encourage you to discuss the implications of state standards for instruction in your education classes.

Looking Critically at State Standards   State standards cover a wide range of topics, concepts, and subjects. Most appear to be randomly generated, even though several states note in their documents that they are modeled after the many nationally published sets. Reading them, one wonders if any of the standards were field-tested to determine developmental appropriateness (refer to Table 2.1). In most cases, the lengthy lists are not arranged in any meaningful sequence or any hierarchical order. The standards collectively do not have flow charts or illustrate how a student or teacher progresses from one standard to another. In numerous instances, the standards do not set a benchmark that teachers would find adequate; rather, they tend to be performance objectives without a statement of the conditions. Most disturbingly, there is often a 100/100 criterion for the standards: Every child in every state must meet every standard. (NCLB dictates that every child must pass a state test by 2013/2014.)

Standards are one of two aspects of educational reform. The second one is **accountability**, which is defined by testing the children at grades 3–12. Arizona has developed an Arizona Instrument to Measure Standards (AIMS) to use in assessing math skills. When first given in late 1999 and early 2000, at grade 10, the AIMS failure rate was extremely high, approaching 90 percent for all test-takers and 97 percent for students of color. As late as 2002, more than 80 percent of the minority students failed and 66 percent of all test-takers failed (see Amrein & Berliner, Note 46, 2002). So Gene V. Glass and Cheryl A. Edholm (2002) conducted a survey to test the validity of the math skills being assessed in the AIMS tests. They wished to determine how relevant the tests and test results were to a student's future success in the workplace.

Glass and Edholm sent questionnaires to 54 managers in 10 different categories of industries in the greater Phoenix area. Forty-three completed their questionnaires (a respectable 80 percent return rate). The results were not encouraging for those who assert that tests and standards lead unequivocally to school improvement. The range of "mathematics used in daily work" ranged from a high of 26 percent to a low of 7 percent. Although politicians support standards as necessary for developing forward-looking job skills, employers in Arizona suggested that the tested skills were irrelevant to their work forces. Concluded Glass and Edholm, "The overall conclusion is undeniably one in which these managers regard the mathematics tested by Grade 10-AIMS mathematics test as irrelevant to the functioning of their employees" (2002, p. 3).

To add one more insight to the position that state standards lack internal scrutiny, let us cite just one more example from Grade 5 science for the state of Washington: "(5) Compare the strength of one force to the strength of another force (e.g., a 5-Newton pull from a spring scale is like the weight of a 1-pound object." (*K-10 Grade Level Expectations: A New Level of Specificity,* p. 30.) One of the co-authors of this book (Orlich) has implemented hands-on, minds on, elementary science programs for 33 years, has had over 20 NSF grants, and cannot answer that question. Can you?

A Final Word About Standards   In January 2005, the very conservative Thomas B. Fordham Foundation issued letter grades for all the published sets of state standards in mathematics and English. The Fordham group established a set of criteria by which they judged the various state standards. They looked at qualities such as clarity, content, reason, teachability, and consistency. "Scathing" would be the best description of this critique (see Finn 2005). The average grade given for math was a D, with a C being the average grade for English standards. We cannot overemphasize that you must critically examine all standards to determine their validity and developmental appropriateness before applying them in your classroom.

You will be faced with hundreds of such standards. We encourage you to take up the challenge from Jonathan Kozol (2007) to be an advocate for your students and fight for fairness. We are in your corner.

Reflect

◆ How do the National Science Education Standards seek to address the increasingly competitive nature of the world economy?

◆ Are there common elements or themes in the collective set of goals that have been recently published?

(continued)

Reflect

◆ What issues do your state's education goals or standards address? How are they related to national standards? Examine your state standards in your area of specialization. How general or specific are they?

◆ To what extent have state standards been fully analyzed for developmental appropriateness in your education classes?

◆ If every child must pass a state test, what are the implications for Individuals with Disabilities Education Act (IDEA) students and English-language learners (ELL)? Discuss with your colleagues and instructors.

◆ In your view, is the purpose of education to train students for future employment? If not, then what is it? What standards might you devise to suit this goal?

TECHNOLOGY
Insight

Using Computers in the Classroom: Good News and Bad News

Planning instructional activities that make use of computers and the Internet can add a great deal to a learning environment. However, these additions present both benefits and challenges.

Using the computer can be highly motivating: Students can produce reports and presentations that look exceptionally good, and the computer allows students to experiment with multimedia production with ease. According to *The Horizon Report* (2008), sponsored by the New Media Consortium, using the computer to collaborate on, present, and distribute classroom projects in a variety of forms and through multiple network venues using "Web 2.0" tools such as blogs, Wikis, and social spaces (e.g., Facebook) is becoming more common and is generally encouraged. However, it may be difficult to evaluate an individual student's contribution to collaborative efforts.

Also, while the computer will help students perform tasks such as formatting text and images, and adding color, movement, and sound, problems may sometimes arise from students' spending too much time on form and too little on content (for example, making the video about triangulation may become much more engrossing than learning the concepts of triangulation). It is important to strike a balance between learning new concepts and formatting the report that indicates learning has occurred.

Using the Internet as a resource has advantages and disadvantages as well. Research indicates that teachers who encourage their students to make use of the Internet develop their own abilities to teach in a constructivist manner. Instructional activities that make use of the Internet often result in students' choosing to perform more research for longer periods of time. The problem with this is that more time is needed to participate in constructivist-oriented learning activities. This includes the extra time it takes to discuss how best to conduct research using the Internet and avoid abuses of Internet privileges. Teachers must find ways to adjust schedules to better fit the activity.

Many teachers feel it is worth the extra time and effort to plan for the use of computers and the Internet in their instruction. However, most teachers also agree that planning for this use requires extra time and effort.

For more information on this topic, see *The Horizon Report* (2008) at http://www.nmc.org/pdf/2008-Horizon-Report.pdf

Effect Size: One Tool for Gauging Instructional Effectiveness

Because you will be learning about several new teaching techniques, you need a quantitative tool by which to judge the relative learning worth of each; that is, what proves that a *specific teaching strategy* has a positive impact on student achievement? One useful gauge is **effect size**. Intuitively, we know that certain instructional treatments have a positive effect on student learning. Effect size (Cohen 1988) tests results by applying a formula to before-and-after test scores once a teaching strategy has been used.

1. To determine effect size, you need a control group (pretest) and an experimental group (posttest), the test scores yield averages (means), and standard deviations. (The formula for computing a standard deviation is located in any statistics book, or search for "standard deviation" on the Internet.)

2. To calculate the effect size, subtract the mean score of the pretest from the mean score of the posttest, and then divide the difference by the standard deviation of the pretest.

    Example:
    90 posttest mean score
    − 80 pretest mean score
    = 10 difference
    ÷ 8.0 standard deviation
    = 1.25 effect size

3. An effect size of 1.0 means a gain of 1 standard deviation based on a normal curve for the treatment group. Effect sizes less than 0.2 are usually not important. An effect size of 0.25 begins to show importance. At 0.3, an effect size becomes useful or important. An effect size of 2.0 would be phenomenal. In the example above, the effect size was 1.25. If you get a result like that from one of your teaching techniques, stick with it—it's a winner!

4. Effect sizes are cumulative but not additive. You can use several teaching strategies and expect a total effect to be greater than any single one. A combination of techniques will seldom go beyond an effect of 2.0. However, that effect size is large enough that a child who is classified as learning disabled would be achieving at an above-average level after being provided with several tested techniques.

For each major technique that we discuss in this book, we provide the published effect size on our website at www.cengage.com/education/orlich. We generally use the effect sizes reported by Benjamin S. Bloom (1984) in his classic paper; those computed by Herbert J. Walberg (1999), for which he and his collaborators reviewed thousands of studies with relevant student data from elementary and secondary schools; and the work of Robert J. Marzano et al. (2001). We encourage you to examine these studies, especially Marzano's. By knowing where to find effect size data, you have access to information far beyond that held by the vast majority of practicing educators.

Further, an effect size is one more professional tool that gives you an estimation of the learning effect you might expect if you use a specific instructional technique as described in the literature. As already noted, effect sizes are not additive; that is, if you use several high-effect-size techniques, you will not be able to add their sizes and expect phenomenal results. But you can predict that, based on previous reports, the technique you use has already demonstrated improved student achievement. Also be advised that effect sizes can be converted to percentiles. For example, an effect size of 0.25 would mean a move of 10 percentiles. An effect size of 0.5 would yield a move of 19 percentiles, while an effect size if 1.0 means a 34-percentile gain. Understanding the effect size and its percentile equivalent provides you with a means to determine instructional efficacy. Conversely, a negative effect size means a learning loss (see Marzano 2007).

Stephen Olejnik and James Algina (2000) point out some precautions on using effect size. With small samples there may be large standard errors. That is, an effect size may be less reliable with smaller numbers—say, under 25. Samples with wide heterogeneity may not give a true measure. For example, comparing one small class to an entire school may not be valid due to the differing sizes of sample populations. However, effect size statistics do provide a useful tool when you cannot meet the assumptions of more complicated statistical measures.

Effect sizes help determine instructional efficacy.

A Closing Reflection

Reflect

◆ Does planning allow you to become more or less spontaneous?

◆ List the pitfalls and advantages of using a planning device such as a cognitive taxonomy.

◆ With all the thinking you've done about standards so far, how will you use them to aid in your planning? What would you do if you found a state standard that was impossible to teach?

◆ How can you be sure that your planning reflects what your students should really learn and are capable of learning?

Summary Points

1. Instructional planning requires a careful consideration of student needs, content goals, and instructional techniques.
2. Goals are broadly stated intentions; objectives or outcomes are specific expectations.
3. Instructional planning follows a cycle ranging from prelesson planning to postlesson reflection.
4. Instruction can be planned around the cognitive, affective, and psychomotor domains.
5. The cognitive domain tends to be the focus of school curricula.
6. Performance objectives show learners what is expected, how the work will be done, and what are the minimum standards.
7. Curriculum or instructional alignment ensures that objectives, content, activities, teaching techniques, and assessment are congruent.

8. National standards are in vogue and guide state and local efforts to plan instruction.
9. Standards must be converted into student objectives.
10. Effect size is a professionally accepted means of gauging effectiveness of a teaching strategy.

Building a Career Portfolio

As we noted in Chapter 1, we want to provide you with a repertoire of instructionally related ideas to add to your career portfolio. Be sure to incorporate your own observations from this chapter, in addition to the following suggestions.

◆ Prepare a checklist of essential planning elements for use in your first teaching experience.

◆ Apply the five performance levels of the NAEP to a set of your own state standards that you may teach, and determine their level of predicted difficulty.

◆ Compile a list of effect sizes for various instructional models and techniques as a gauge to evaluate a current trend in instruction.

Resources

- -

PRINT

Anderson, L. W., & D. R. Krathwohl, Eds. *A Taxonomy for Learning, Teaching, and Assessing: A Revision of Bloom's Taxonomy of Educational Objectives.* New York: Longman, 2001, 352 pp.
This book traces the development of the cognitive taxonomy and illustrates in great depth a new and complete cognitive psychological perspective for classifying school learning.

Brown, J. L. *Making the Most of Understanding by Design.* Alexandria, VA: Association for Supervision and Curriculum Development, 2004, 205 pp.
The author provides a model for applying instructional design principles as a framework to improve student achievement and teacher efficacy. Two chapters address teaching to standards and promoting student understanding.

Carr, J. F., & D. E. Harris. *Succeeding with Standards: Linking Curriculum, Assessment, and Action Planning.* Alexandria, VA: Association for Supervision and Curriculum Development, 2001, 204 pp.
The authors illustrate in great detail techniques by which a classroom teacher can address standards.

Nichols, S. L., & D. C. Berliner. *Collateral Damage: How High-Stakes Testing Corrupts America's Schools.* Cambridge, MA: Harvard Education Publishing Group, 2007, 250 pp.
Two American educational researchers provide compelling documentation that the reform era penchant for high-stakes tests is corrupting the

integrity of our education systems. A must-read book for all teachers, administrators, and policy-makers.

Silver, H. F., R. W. Strong, & M. J. Perini. *The Strategic Teacher. Selecting the Right Research-Based Strategy for Every Lesson.* Alexandria, VA: ASCD, 2007, 300 pp.
This team tackles the Herculean job of attempting to provide the underlying research bases for a wide spectrum of teaching strategies.

INTERNET

Go to the website for this book at www.cengage.com/education/orlich to find live links to resources related to this chapter.

◆ The URL below will provide information and a list of several Internet sites related to Bloom's taxonomy.
http://www.uct.ac.za/projects/cbe/mcqman/mcqappc.html

◆ The current status of Goals 2000 and related educational issues are provided via an online database managed by the U.S. Department of Education.
http://www.ed.gov/pubs/EPTW/eptwgoal.html

◆ A listing of 10 research-based instructional strategies with their effect sizes is provided by Robert Marzano.
http://www.pkmet.com/newmex/pdf/Marzano10Strat.pdf

References

American Association for the Advancement of Science. (2007) *Atlas of Science Literacy: Project 2061.* Washington, DC: AASA and NSTA.

American Association for the Advancement of Science. (1993). *Benchmarks for Science Literacy: Project 2061.* New York: Oxford University Press.

Amrein, A. L., & D. C. Berliner. (2002). "High-Stakes Testing, Uncertainty and Student Learning. *Educational Policy Analysis Archives* 10(18): 1–56.

Anderson, A. (2001). "In the Process." *Clearing House* 74(5): 285–286.

Anderson, L. W., et al. (2001). *A Taxonomy for Learning, Teaching, and Assessing: A Revision of Bloom's Taxonomy of Educational Objectives* (complete edition). New York: Addison Wesley Longman.

Astleitner, H. (2005). "Principles of Effective Instruction: General Standards for Teachers and Instructional Designers." *Journal of Instructional Psychology* 32(2): 3–8.

Aviles, C. B. (2001). *Curriculum Alignment: Matching What We Teach and Test Versus Teaching to the Test.* Buffalo: Buffalo State College. ED 448 402.

Berliner, D. C., & B. J. Biddle. (1995). *The Manufactured Crisis: Myths, Fraud, and the Attack on America's Public Schools.* Reading, MA: Addison-Wesley.

Bloom, B. S. (1984). "The 2 Sigma Problem: The Search for Methods of Group Instruction as Effective as One-to-One Tutoring." *Educational Researcher* 13(6): 4–16.

Bloom, B. S., M. D. Engelhart, E. J. Furst, W. H. Hill, & D. R. Krathwohl. (1956). *Taxonomy of Educational Objectives: The Classification of Educational Goals. Handbook I: Cognitive Domain.* New York: McKay.

Bost, L. W., & P. J. Riccomini. (2006). "Effective Instruction: An Inconspicuous Strategy for Dropout Prevention." *Remedial and Special Education* 27(5): 301–311.

Bracey, G. W. (2003). *What You Should Know About the War Against America's Public Schools.* Boston: Allyn and Bacon.

Bracey, G. W. (2004). *Setting the Record Straight: Responses to Misconceptions About Public Education in the U.S.* (2nd ed.). Portsmouth, NH: Heinemann.

Campbell, J. R., K. E. Voelkl, & P. L. Donahue. (1998). *Report in Brief, NAEP Trends in Academic Progress, Revised Edition.* (NCES 98-530). Washington, DC: National Center for Education Statistics.

Chance, W. *The Best of Educations.* (1986). Chicago: The John D. and Catherine T. MacArthur Foundation. (Released in 1988 by the Education Commission of the States, Denver.)

Cohen, J. (1988). *Statistical Power Analysis for the Behavioral Sciences* (2nd ed.). Hillsdale, NJ: Erlbaum.

Cohen, S. A. (1987). "Instructional Alignment: Searching for a Magic Bullet." *Educational Researcher* 16(8): 16–19.

Cohen, S. A. (1995). "Instructional Alignment." In L. W. Anderson, Ed., *International Encyclopedia of Teaching and Teacher Education* (2nd ed.), pp. 200–204. Tarrytown, NY: Elsevier Science.

Danielson, C. (2007). *Enhancing Professional Practice: A Framework for Teaching* (2nd ed.). Alexandria, VA: Association for Supervision and Curriculum Development.

Dickie, L. O. (2003). "Approach to Learning, the Cognitive Demands of Assessment, and Achievement in Physics." *Canadian Journal of Higher Education* 33(1): 87–111.

Distad, L., & D. Heacox. (2000). "Differentiating Instruction Using a Matrix Plan." *Southern Social Studies Journal* 25(2): 70–76.

Dyment, J. E., & T. S. O'Connell. (2003). "Getting the Most Out of Journaling: Strategies for Outdoor Educators." *Pathways: The Ontario Journal of Outdoor Education* 15(2): 31–34.

English, F. W., & B. E. Steffy. (2001). *Deep Curriculum Alignment: Creating a Level Playing Field for All Children on High-Stakes Tests of Educational Accountability.* Lanham, MD: Scarecrow Education.

Ennis, R. H. (1985). "A Logical Basis for Measuring Critical Thinking Skills." *Educational Leadership* 43(2): 44–48.

Finn, C. E., Jr., et al. (2005). *The State of English Standards 2005. The State of Mathematics Standards 2005.* Washington, DC: Thomas B. Fordham Foundation. Retrieved at http://www.edexcellence.net/foundation.

Fisher, C. W., & E. W. Hiebert. (1990). "Characteristics of Tasks in Two Approaches to Literacy Instruction." *Elementary School Journal* 91(1): 3–18.

Fisk, C., & B. Hurst. (2003). "Paraphrasing for Comprehension." *Reading Teacher* 57(2): 182–185.

Furst, E. J. (1994). "Bloom's Taxonomy: Philosophical and Educational Issues." In L. W. Anderson & L. A. Sosniak, Eds., *Bloom's Taxonomy: A Forty-Year Retrospective,* pp. 28–40. Chicago: University of Chicago Press.

Glass, G. V., & C. A. Edholm. (2002, Oct.). "The AIMS test and the Mathematics Actually Used by Arizona Employers." Education Policy Studies Laboratory, Arizona State University, Tempe, Education Policy unit. EPSL-0209-119 EPRU. Retrieved at http://edpolicylab.org.

Granello, D. H. (2000). "Encouraging the Cognitive Development of Supervisees: Using Bloom's Taxonomy in Supervision." *Counselor Education and Supervision* 40(1): 31–46.

Hohn, R. L. (1995). *Classroom Learning and Teaching.* White Plains, NY: Longman.

Jennings, J. F. (1998). *Why National Standards and Tests? Politics and Quest for Better Schools.* Thousand Oaks, CA: Sage.

K-10 Grade Level Expectations: A New Level of Specificity. (2005). Olympia, WA: Office of Superintendent of Public Instruction.

Kelly, T. F. (1991). *Practical Strategies for School Improvement.* Wheeling, IL: National School Services.

Kozol, J. (2007). *Letters to a Young Teacher.* New York: The Crown Publishing Group.

Krathwohl, D. R., B. S. Bloom, & B. B. Masia. (1964). *Taxonomy of Educational Objectives. The Classification of Educational Goals. Handbook II: Affective Domain.* New York: McKay.

Mager, R. F. (1962). *Preparing Instructional Objectives.* Belmont, CA: Fearon.

Mager, R. F. (1997). *Preparing Instructional Objectives: A Critical Tool in the Development of Effective Instruction* (3rd ed.). Atlanta: Center for Effective Performance.

Magner, L. (2000). "Reaching All Children Through Differentiated Assessment: The 2-5-8 Plan." *Gifted Child Today Magazine* 23(3): 48–50.

Marks, S. K., J. D. Vitek, & K. P. Allen. (1996). "Remote Sensing: Analyzing Satellite Images to Create Higher Order Thinking Skills." *The Science Teacher* 63(3): 28–31.

Martin, R. A. (2006). "Wake-Up Call Brings a Jolt of Alignment to the Curriculum." *Journal of Staff Development* 27(1): 53–55.

Marzano, R. J. (2004). *Building Background Knowledge for Academic Achievement.* Alexandria, VA: Association for Supervision and Curriculum Development.

Marzano, R. J. (2007). *The Art and Science of Teaching: A Comprehensive Framework for Effective Instruction.* Alexandria, VA: ASCD.

Marzano, R. J., D. J. Pickering, & J. E. Pollock. (2001). *Classroom Instruction That Works: Research-Based Strategies for Increasing Student Achievement.* Alexandria, VA: Association for Supervision and Curriculum Development.

Masters, J. C., et al. (2001). "Assessment of Multiple-Choice Questions in Selected Test Banks Accompanying Textbooks Used in Nursing Education." *Journal of Nursing Education* 40(1): 25–31.

McAlpine, J., S. Jeweler, B. Weincek, & M. Findbiner. (1987). "Creative Problem Solving and Bloom: The Thinking Connection." *Gifted Child Today* 10: 11–14.

McCormick, D. F., & S. M. Whittington. (2000). "Assessing Academic Challenges for Their Contribution to Cognitive Development." *Journal of Agricultural Education* 41(3): 114–122.

McLaughlin, M. W., & D. C. Phillips, Eds. (1991). *Evaluation and Education at Quarter Century. Nineteenth Yearbook of the National Society for the Study of Education, Part II.* Chicago: University of Chicago Press.

Mertler, C. A. (2006). *Action Research: Teachers as Researchers in the Classroom.* Thousand Oaks, CA: Sage Publications.

Morgan, T. (1996). "Using Technology to Enhance Learning: Changing the Chunks." *Learning and Leading with Technology 23*(5): 49–51.

Moore, K. D., & C. Quinn. (1994). *Secondary Instructional Methods,* Madison, WI: WCB Brown & Benchmark.

National Commission on Excellence in Education. (1983). *A Nation at Risk: The Imperative for Educational Reform.* Washington, DC: National Commission for Excellence in Education.

National Research Council. (1996). *National Science Education Standards.* Washington, DC: National Academy Press.

Nickerson, R. (1985). "Understanding Understanding." *American Journal of Education 93:* 201–239.

Olejnik, S., & J. Algina. (2000). "Measures of Effect Size for Comparative Studies: Applications, Interpretations, and Limitations." *Contemporary Educational Psychology 25:* 241–286.

Orlich, D. C. (1991). "A New Analogue for the Cognitive Taxonomy." *The Clearing House 64*(3): 159–161.

Paul, R. (1985). "Bloom's Taxonomy and Critical Thinking Instruction." *Educational Leadership 42*(8): 36–39.

P.L. 107-110, "No Child Left Behind Act of 2001." Washington, DC: 107th Congress, 1st Session, January 8, 2002.

Pratt, D. (1994). *Curriculum Planning: A Handbook for Professionals.* New York: Harcourt Brace.

Raths, L. E. (1967). *Teaching for Thinking: Theory and Application.* Columbus, OH: Merrill.

Risner, G. P., J. I. Nicholson, & B. Webb. (2000, Nov. 15–17). "Cognitive Levels of Questioning Demonstrated by New Social Studies Textbooks: What the Future Holds for Elementary Students." Paper presented at the Annual Meeting of the Mid-South Educational Research Association, Bowling Green, KY. ED 448 108.

Rohwer, W. D., Jr., & K. Sloane. (1994). "Psychological Perspectives." In L. W. Anderson & L. A. Sosniak, Eds., *Bloom's Taxonomy: A Forty-Year Perspective.* Ninety-Third Yearbook of the National Society for the Study of Education, Part III, pp. 41–63. Chicago: University of Chicago Press.

Schurr, S. (2001). *How to Improve Discussion and Questioning Practices: Tools and Techniques. Staff Development Kit # 2.* Westerville, OH: National Middle Schools Association. ED 453 196.

Shaunessy, E. (2000). "Questioning Technique in the Gifted Classroom." *Gifted Child Today Magazine 25*(5): 14–21.

Sprenger, M. (2003). *Differentiation Through Learning Styles and Memory.* Thousand Oaks, CA: Corwin.

Steinbrink, J. E., & R. M. Jones. (1991). "Focused Test Review Items: Improving Textbook-Test Alignment in Social Studies." *The Social Studies 82*(2): 72–76.

Stronge, J. H. (2007). *Qualities of Effective Teachers* (2nd ed.). Alexandria, VA: ASCD.

Stronge, J. H., & J. L. Hindman. (2003). "Hiring the Best Teachers." *Educational Leadership 60*(8): 48–52.

van der Wal, R. J., & R. van der Wal. (2003). "Assessing Life Skills in Young Working Adults—Part 1: The Development of an Alternative Instrument." *Education + Training 45*(3): 139–151.

Walberg, H. J. (1999). "Productive Teaching." In H. C. Waxman & H. J. Walberg, Eds., *New Directions for Teaching Practice and Research,* pp. 75–104. Berkeley, CA: McCutchan.

Wenglinsky, H. (2000). *How Teaching Matters: Bringing the Classroom Back into Discussions of Teacher Quality.* Princeton, NJ: The Milken Family Foundation and Educational Testing Service.

White, S., C. Smith, & A. Vanneman. (2000). "How Does NAEP Select Schools and Students?" *Education Statistics Quarterly 2*(3): 1–3.

Wiggins, G., & J. McTighe. (2008). "Put Understanding First." *Educational Leadership 65*(8): 36–41.

Instructional Planning

Roberta had just had her signature notarized on her first teaching contract. It was an exciting moment during her final term before graduation. After taking care of business, she headed back to the Education Library. As she walked, she thought about the first days of school that were approaching in late August. She had demonstrated her knowledge of various standards, performance outcomes, and the domains of learning. But now Roberta began to ponder the importance of preplanning and devising ways to implement those plans with all of her students.

Her coursework and student teaching had already given her a reality check on instructional planning, so she began to list a few major implications of what she had learned. She thought about organizing instructional time to ensure covering at least the cognitive and affective taxonomies, how to make time for relevant activities, and of critical importance, how to apply the concept of "universal design."

Our purpose for this chapter is to provide you with practical guidelines for systematic planning so that you will be able to create effective long-range plans, unit plans, and lesson plans, just as Roberta needs to do. This chapter continues the discussion begun in Chapter 3, covering three main topics: preparation, planning procedures, and the planning practices of expert teachers.

New concepts and techniques introduced in this chapter will help you answer the following questions.

- What factors must I consider for instructional planning?
- What are planning levels, and how do I connect them?
- How can I create an effective unit plan?
- How can I devise a wide range of lesson plans to implement my unit plans, and also use technology effectively?
- What can I learn from the planning techniques of master teachers?

SECTION 1 Overall Considerations for Instructional Planning

As noted in Chapter 3, teachers have a primary responsibility to design and implement instruction. They prepare plans that aid in the organization and delivery of their daily lessons. These plans vary widely in style and degree of specificity. Just as there are many ways to teach and learn, there are many ways to plan—there is no single "best" way. Some instructors prefer to construct elaborately detailed outlines; others rely on brief notes in the weekly lesson plan book. Probably most teachers fall somewhere between these extremes. But regardless of the format they choose, master teachers use planning to select the content and methods that will most help their students achieve predefined learning goals. Without effective planning by their teachers, students are less likely to achieve those goals. As one Washington State high school teacher put it, "Less planning leads to less learning" (Walsh 1992, p. 114). Further, Marlow Ediger (2004) noted that students know if a teacher is well prepared or not, and being unprepared leads to student disinterest.

Planning for a lesson is like planning for an automobile trip. Most drivers, before leaving on a trip to a new area, carefully study a road map and, while driving, continue to check the map. The driver who has taken the same trip many times needs to consult the map less often. Similarly, the first time you teach a lesson, you develop a detailed lesson plan and you continue to

Planning: content + methods to achieve goals

consult the lesson plan while teaching the lesson. After you gain experience, you will depend less on the written plan.

Factors Affecting Planning

As you can well imagine, you have much to consider in planning instruction. Summarized below are some of the initial areas you need to think about. These topics are not listed in any order of importance because each is equally important. You will find it useful, especially at the beginning of your planning, to write down your thoughts about each topic. This will help you focus your thinking and confirm that you are considering your situation thoroughly. An excellent source to help with these steps is an article by Amy Baylor, Anastasia Kitsantas, and Hyunmi Chung (2001) (see the References at the end of this chapter for source information).

Use these questions to begin planning.

◆ *Student considerations.* Students are the reason for and focus of your instruction. What do you know about them, individually and as a group? Are they easy or difficult to motivate? What do they already know about the subject you're planning to teach? How might they best learn? What accommodations will be needed for special students?

◆ *Content and process considerations.* What main ideas and concepts are involved? Will you need to teach skills as well? In what order should the instruction be arranged? Can you devise a variety of learning activities and instructional methods to teach the material?

◆ *Time considerations.* How much time is available for this part of the instruction? Are other school functions—assemblies, plays, extracurricular activities—or holidays and vacations likely to interfere? Do you need more than one day or one period?

◆ *School considerations.* Are there district or state learning outcomes or standards to be considered? Graduation requirements? Legal requirements for special students?

◆ *Resource considerations.* In addition to school textbooks and supplementary materials, are other resources available in the community, such as historical sites, museums, art galleries, or other special places? Are there people within the community who might provide a perspective?

◆ *Teacher considerations.* How knowledgeable are you about the material you're planning to teach? Can you present what you know in terms that students will understand?

◆ *Technical considerations.* Does your school have computer-assisted instructional resources that will aid your students to communicate via technological means? (Many schools require teachers to post course outlines and assignments online and students to submit their work online.)

Reflect

◆ How might you incorporate a district goal such as "reads different materials for a variety of purposes" into your subject?

◆ How do lesson plans vary by area of discipline or grade level?

Planning Resources

Numerous resources are available to help you with instructional planning, and we will discuss several of the major ones later. Keep in mind, however, that effective teachers do not limit themselves to resources specifically designed for planning or for the education professional. They fill file drawers, cabinets, and computer files with materials that they have found useful or that simply look as if they might be useful in planning a lesson or unit. One secondary school history teacher has a large collection of pictures of wooden sailing ships, showing the masts and rigging in detail and describing how the ships were operated. Together with other materials, these pictures help students visualize and understand the reality of Columbus's journey and other "voyages of discovery." A middle school art teacher stores photos of her previous students' artwork on a compact disc. She uses these examples in lesson demonstrations and makes them available for students to view and study on their own.

Effective teachers collect materials over the long term.

Curriculum Guides   Most schools have **curriculum guides**—statements detailing what should be taught in each grade and in each content area. These guides are created by the state and sometimes by the district as standards or "essential student learnings," but they are almost always written by teams of teachers after careful consideration of the aims and goals of local schools. Curriculum guides should be the first place to look when you are considering what to teach and how to plan instruction. They provide a framework—in terms of both time and subject matter—for organizing instruction. Guides spell out, often in great detail, the specific knowledge and skills students are expected to

Technology use is a planned activity.

© LWA/Stone/Getty Images

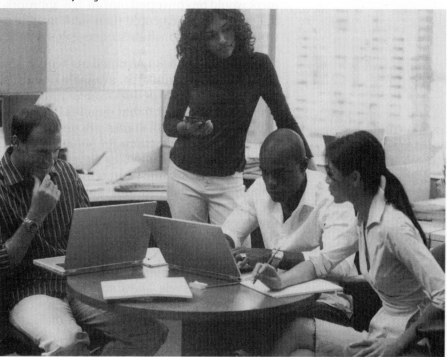

attain and the attitudes they should exhibit. These guides tend to be arranged by grade level for elementary schools and by content area for middle and secondary schools. Of particular benefit to new teachers, they identify what instruction your students have already had as well as what will be expected of them upon completion of your grade or course. (See also Tyler 1949 for a rationale on instructional planning that has stood the test of more than half a century.)

The example goal statements below were written by several groups of teachers in Washington State to meet local needs. Curriculum guides are often phrased in broad terms such as these, thus giving individual teachers freedom to develop appropriate unit and lesson plans. (See criticism of curriculum guides in English 1986/1987.)

Essential Academic Learnings in Reading, #3

The student reads different materials for a variety of purposes. To meet this standard, the student will:

- Read to learn new information.
- Read to perform a task.
- Read for career applications.
- Read for literary/narrative experience in a variety of genres. (Washington State Commission on Student Learning, 2007)

Notice in the above example that "reads different materials for a variety of purposes" is a goal statement, as explained in Chapter 3. Each bulleted statement above shows what students must do to reach the goal. This very desirable goal applies to all levels and subjects in the curriculum. It is as relevant to first-graders as it is to high school physics students, and it can be approached at a variety of levels, from simple to complex, in all grades. Each goal statement would be converted into an age-appropriate instructional objective. The bulleted statements could then state specific performance objectives of how students will demonstrate evidence of mastery, as described in Chapter 3.

Standards and Goals   As noted in Chapter 3, Section 4, you will find that national and state standards, available in most subject areas, are an excellent source of goals to aid or direct you in your planning. The federal "No Child Left Behind Act" legislation that requires benchmark testing in reading and math in third though eighth grades will undoubtedly influence the curriculum because of possible sanctions for poor test scores. This controversial legislation may be expanded through the eleventh grade (Lively & Emerling, 2005).

National academic centers and associations also have developed useful standards and goals for most subject areas. For example, in 1995 the Center for History in the Schools specified this standard: "Students should be able to demonstrate understanding of the Americas by describing the social composition of early settlers and comparing their motives for exploration and colonization."

Every state has standards and goals for most subject areas, with testing at selected grade levels. These standards and goals provide a context for benchmark testing. Many states are also proposing graduation requirement testing.

National and state standard and goal statements can be a significant help in organizing instruction. But even though you find yourself implementing state and national goals and standards, you should feel free to include other

---

Try curriculum guides first.

Sources of useful standards: federal government, states, academic associations goals that are particularly relevant to your students, your district, or your school, reflecting what you believe is important in the subject you teach.

Textbooks   Another source for planning is the text or texts adopted by your school. Especially for elementary teachers, these can offer useful insights into the curriculum and how to plan for and teach it. School districts often buy a series of elementary school texts from a single publisher—a set of materials to teach math, for instance, from kindergarten through grade 6. Teachers often say, "We're using FOSS Science," or "We've had much success with Houghton Mifflin Harcourt's literacy program."

These textbook series generally provide a structured sequence of lessons. They specify instructional objectives, provide a variety of teaching suggestions, offer supplementary readings and practice aids, and include an evaluation program. Many also provide lessons designed specifically to help with cooperative learning, thinking processes, decision-making skills, and a variety of problem-solving techniques. Assuming that the materials meet your objectives, they can be an extremely useful resource, helping you make the best use of your planning time. Publishers' aids deserve much study and consideration.

To illustrate our point, visit http://www.eduplace.com to view a listing of selected resources that come with the adoption of an elementary textbook program from Houghton Mifflin Harcourt Company. The information is arranged by state. Some of the resources are found in the program's components, while others are available on the website.

Much valuable assistance is available from publishers, but be sure that the materials match your objectives, and don't be overwhelmed by the quantity—nobody uses all of the materials for a particular subject. Decide which items are most appropriate for your objectives, your students, and the time available.

Other Resources   Beyond formal school curriculum guides and the supplementary materials associated with textbooks, there are myriad sources of materials that successful teachers use to bring life to their lessons. The following list is suggestive, not comprehensive. Your imagination and the experience of one year of teaching and thoughtful planning should double its length.

- *Colleagues*. Most other teachers will be more than willing to help you find resources and to discuss what works well for them. School librarians can be especially helpful, not only in suggesting resources but also in helping you determine how to include them in your instruction (see especially Wolcott 1994). Along these same lines, Jef Johnston et al. (2007) illustrate how teachers can work as teams to foster academic achievement.

- *The Internet*. A tremendous amount of educational material can be found on the Internet, including unit and lesson ideas for all subjects and grades. If you are selective and can adapt the materials you find to fit your students and objectives, then cyberspace can be a positive force in your planning. We provide suggested sites at the end of each chapter.

- *Local libraries, museums, and historical sites.* Each of these can offer considerable aid in structuring a lesson.

- *Government agencies.* From local police departments to county agencies to the Library of Congress, government agencies can help the thoughtful teacher to make learning a hands-on and stimulating activity.

Publishers' materials can help save time.

SECTION *2*   Instructional Planning Procedures

From a consideration of planning materials, we now turn to a detailed description of useful planning steps. Experienced, successful teachers do not follow a standard planning procedure. All teachers, however, wrestle with common factors that determine the success of their instruction. Refer to Figure 4.1, which illustrates planning steps in the form of a cycle. We discuss these steps in the order they appear on the chart, but remember that teachers do not necessarily consider each factor in the same order. Planning is more a recursive than a linear process: Teachers consider instructional objectives in terms of learning activities and then reconsider each activity in terms of time and student abilities. All parts are interdependent; a change here will likely require a correction there.

> Planning is a recursive process with interdependent parts.

As stated earlier, much instructional planning is done mentally and may never appear on paper. Effective teachers, especially after several years of experience, rehearse much of their instruction in their heads or by talking to themselves. Plans are never far from their minds, and more than one unit or lesson plan has been worked out in the shower or at the shopping mall (Kagan & Tippins 1992; Sardo-Brown 1988). One outstanding high school teacher notes, "Planning is not just when I am sitting at my desk and writing. Planning includes plenty of think time when I am considering possibilities" (Walsh 1992, p. 198). We noted earlier that as a beginning teacher, you are well advised to write out your plans in some detail and store them in your

FIGURE 4.1
The Instructional Planning Cycle

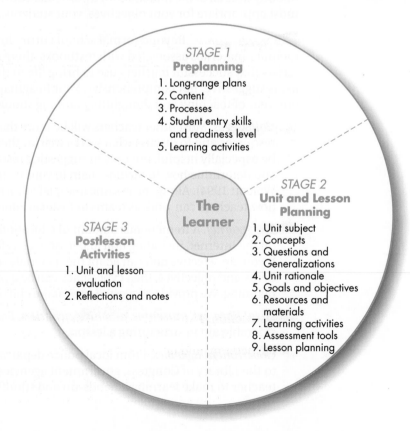

STAGE 1
Preplanning
1. Long-range plans
2. Content
3. Processes
4. Student entry skills and readiness level
5. Learning activities

STAGE 2
Unit and Lesson Planning
1. Unit subject
2. Concepts
3. Questions and Generalizations
4. Unit rationale
5. Goals and objectives
6. Resources and materials
7. Learning activities
8. Assessment tools
9. Lesson planning

STAGE 3
Postlesson Activities
1. Unit and lesson evaluation
2. Reflections and notes

The Learner

personal computer by topic or date. The writing process itself helps you focus your thinking and detect confusion or inconsistency that otherwise inevitably would come out during instruction. A written record of your planning provides a foundation for teaching the lesson. After the lesson is taught, you can note the changes that should be made before you teach the lesson again.

Mental rehearsal augments written planning.

Preplanning

As Figure 4.1 shows, it is useful to consider several general concerns before focusing on unit and lesson planning.

◆ *Long-range plans.* In this grading period, semester, or year, what days are available for instruction, and which are taken for other purposes?

◆ *Content.* What is the content to be taught?

◆ *Processes.* What processes will most effectively reinforce the content?

◆ *Student entry skills and readiness level.* What must your students know to be successful in the planned course of instruction? Do they need prerequisite instruction?

◆ *Learning activities.* What learning activities seem most relevant to the content and your instructional goals?

Developing Long-Range Plans   A useful beginning, before school starts, is to create a long-range planning calendar, using a large sheet of paper for each month. (This is a planning technique borne out by the research of Sardo-Brown 1988, for example.) Mark what you already know on your calendar—holidays, in-service days, dates for each grading period, semester end dates, and any other pertinent data. The remaining days make up the time available for instruction. How can you fit everything you want to teach or must accomplish into those remaining squares? Try to fit all of your instructional major topics into the calendar. Do you have too many? Is there not enough time for all? You have just faced one of teaching's biggest problems—there just isn't time for all we need to do. You now begin assigning priorities, deciding what topics to include, which to deemphasize or combine with others, and which to omit. This is one of your most important responsibilities as a teacher, so consider the choices carefully. We will return to the calendar idea when we consider unit and lesson planning.

Start with a big calendar and then break it down.

The importance of designing long-range plans is underscored by Heidi Hayes Jacobs (2004). She suggests using *big ideas* around which to structure content and *curriculum mapping*, which requires a collaborative effort among teachers to integrate various topics where applicable. We might add that the mapping technique requires a great deal of planning time and effort. The process begins with a system of data collection. Data are collected on your students, their background knowledge and all resources that you have for instruction. The key idea behind mapping is to utilize all the talent in the school and align your instruction with what is known about the students, with the curriculum, and finally with the assessment plan (see Guskey 2005).

Deciding on Content   Providing content is the essence of most lessons. Textbooks are content rich (sometimes too rich), requiring you to be selective about what you will stress. Consider text material carefully. The only content you need is what is relevant to the theme or concept you are developing. You probably have endured classes that were overloaded with content; they had more facts and details than anyone could ever remember. Don't let yours be one of those classes. Delete content that is irrelevant to your major idea. But work hard to find and include activities and examples that make clear to your students the main ideas of your focus topic.

Choose content that focuses the topic.

Deciding on Processes   As we noted in Chapter 1, processes are as important to teach as content. Thinking processes—imagining, problem solving, comparing and contrasting, analyzing, organizing, classifying, and numerous others (can you think of additional thinking processes?)—are critical to almost any subject or topic you are teaching. As you identify content for your units and lessons, note also what thinking processes your students might reasonably need to understand the material. Then make it a point to identify these processes during instruction, helping students to become more aware of deliberate uses of their own thought processes. Consider the following example.

Help students make their thinking explicit.

In planning a social studies unit on the U.S. Civil War, you want to include material on the several causes. One way to approach this material is to ask students to consider this question: "What reasons would *you* need to justify killing an acquaintance, a friend, or even a family member (as happened in the Civil War)?" In discussing the question, students can respond by analyzing reasons, classifying and categorizing ideas and arguments, determining importance, and justifying decisions. By planning ahead for this attention to process, you can be sure to include it.

Identifying Students' Entry Skills and Readiness Levels   Another important task, at the early planning stage as well as at all subsequent ones, is to identify your students' **entry skills** and **readiness** levels. (Refer to Table 2.1 on page 33.) What will students need to know to understand what you will be teaching? Are their basic skills adequate for the planned activities, or must you also teach these? As much as 50 percent of the variability in achievement among students can be attributed to insufficient knowledge or skills (Bloom 1976, p. 167; House, Hurst, & Keely 1996).

Are students ready for your unit or lesson?

The sixth principle of the Coalition of Essential Schools (founded in 1984 by Theodore R. Sizer to create a consortium of collaborating schools that would model effective and humane learning communities) requires all students entering high school to have sufficient skills or to receive remediation to gain the necessary skills to be successful (Sizer 1996, p. 154). It is possible that the widespread adoption of constructivist learning theory, with its emphasis on prior knowledge and teaching for understanding, has the potential to reduce the problems related to insufficient entry skills and knowledge. (See Wiggins & McTighe 2005.)

In general, elementary and middle school teachers and schools accept a student's promotion as confirmation that he or she is ready for the next grade, although emergent literacy is often assessed each year at the primary levels. For high school students, whose instruction is arranged by subjects rather than grade level, placement testing is sometimes done, especially in math and English. In most cases, however, placement within a grade or class is assumed to indicate readiness until evidence to the contrary accumulates.

Classroom technology leads to student–teacher interactions.

© Syracuse Newspapers/Greenlar/The Image Works

An effective way to identify entry levels is to give a pretest. Ask yourself what knowledge and skills a student would need, beyond reading level, to understand the proposed instruction. If you can identify several skills or pieces of information, write a short quiz and administer it to see if most students are ready. Remember, you are determining the skills students need to *begin* the new unit—not the skills they should learn from it!

Experience will soon show you which entry skills should be assessed. In the meantime, you will find that most current standard instructional materials provide a range of grade-appropriate options, although you will need to make some changes for some students.

Gauges of readiness: placement, promotion, pretest

Incorporating Learning Activities   **Learning activities** are hands-on, interactive experiences such as experiments and role playing. These should be considered in your long-term planning, although they will play a larger part in your unit planning. As a beginning teacher, you have to find or create such activities; after a few years' experience, you should have several file drawers full of activities that have worked with past students. As you construct your long-term calendar and consider the goals you need to work toward, try to block out time for those activities that were (or are expected to be) particularly useful in helping students succeed, or note the activities that were not successful and need to be changed (see Brophy & Alleman 1991; Pressman & Dublin 1995; Price & Nelson 2003).

Unit Planning

As teachers, we divide instructional time and topics into pieces to make learning manageable. Because we can't teach everything all at once, we sort content into blocks called **units**, and we arrange these across time using our long-range planning calendar. However, having subdivided our instruction into pieces to make it *manageable*, we must also be careful to allow time to pull the pieces together again to make the content *understandable*. "Unit planning is the most important as well as the most time-consuming level of planning for each teacher" (Walsh 1992, p. 178).

An eighth-grade social studies teacher planning a yearlong course in U.S. history serves as a convenient example. To make learning the subject manageable, the teacher divides it chronologically: the pre-Columbian era, colonial times, the revolutionary period, and the present. (Note that chronology is neither the only nor necessarily the preferred way to organize history classes; it is simply used as a familiar example to illustrate a point about instructional planning.) Teachers of other grades and subjects might use **topics** as an organizer. In science, topics such as matter, sound, electricity, leaves, and waste disposal can all serve as organizers. Language arts teachers might organize their ideas around topics such as love, friendship, or heroes to integrate literature and composition. Primary and lower elementary grades do much the same with seasons, holidays, or special events.

After identifying units, the teacher makes a subjective judgment—on the basis of his or her content knowledge, student readiness levels, and the desired outcomes—about the relative importance of each topic. Those deemed more important will need relatively more class time. Working with the planning calendar and topic list, the teacher then arranges the topics in the desired order (sequences them), leaving time within each unit to analyze the topic and combine it with other material as needed.

This method of planning seems reasonable and logical, yet in practice it can become messy and frustrating. The basic problem, as we noted previously, is that you will inevitably want to cover more material than you can fit into the available time. The big questions, then, become "What must be included?" and "What must I omit to make enough room?" All teachers, at all levels, face this dilemma—and no one answers it easily. The penalty for teachers not answering these questions at the planning stage, though, is that they may inadvertently omit some important material or dwell too long on less important matters.

Having identified major topics and worked them into your planning calendar, you are now in a position to make detailed plans to provide instruction for each topic. Most teachers call these **unit plans**.

Unit planning is the mainstay, the bread and butter, of teachers at all levels—both teachers of self-contained elementary school classes and teachers of content-specific middle and secondary school classes such as science and history. And although teachers plan in a variety of ways, the unit plans they develop contain a number of common elements.

Although we will discuss these elements separately, in practice you are more likely to move back and forth among them recursively than to proceed in a straight line through them.

Defining the Unit Subject   Unit subjects or topics vary across both grade levels and content areas. Often, as in the example of history, the subject seems apparent—the Civil War or the Great Depression. Mathematics also seems self-explanatory—fractions, division, polynomials. These are reasonable topics, and effective units certainly can be built around them. You can create many similar examples within your own subject field.

Organize the year by unit or topic.

Voices from the Classroom

Patricia A. Bailey
Seattle Public Schools
Seattle, Washington

Using Multi-Methodology

It is fashionable for report cards to no longer list "spelling" as a separate category. Spelling is folded into "conventions" and not treated as a discipline needing systematic work. While I wholeheartedly support the practice of students using best-guess-spelling for creating writing sessions, fundamental knowledge in spelling goes a long way to make writing more successful and more enjoyable for students as they advance through the grades. Using spell-check for every other word is a tedious process. Spell-check does not appear to help when students have no ideas how to spell words. Below are some examples of how I use many different methods, i.e., multi-methodology.

I use phonics spelling lessons in class using words that have the same pattern (cake, bake, snake, lake, etc.) and words with the same vowel sounds (ape, tape, ate, late, etc). In this way, children learn to look for words that follow patterns and also receive individual practice applying phonics rules.

For spelling homework, students are given "The Most Used 165 Words in Writing" at the beginning of the school year. The words are divided into groups of five. They only need to learn five new words each week, but the list is cumulative. In addition to the five words assigned in any given week, five past spelling words are chosen at random for a total of 10 words per spelling test. By the end of second grade, students are spelling with amazing accuracy in their writing, because I use several methods to teach this skill.

Possible unit topics: a chronological period, an interdisciplinary concept, a question

Concepts   Teachers at all levels find they can often tie content to student interests by building units around concepts. We explore this idea more deeply in Chapter 5, but for now think of **concepts** as "category" words, enabling us to group many individual objects or ideas under a common label. For example, *desk* is a word (concept) that stands for all the objects we see that have "desky" characteristics. (Can you name some characteristics?) Because a desk is a concrete object, it's easy to get agreement on most of its characteristics. As concepts become more abstract, however (love, democracy, friendship), people often have vague and different ideas about their characteristics. These abstract concepts are ones that students often are confused by or simply find interesting. Thus concepts almost automatically become useful unit topics.

For instance, a language arts teacher might select "friendship" as a unit concept or topic. Students could then read and write short stories, plays, poems, biographies, and other works that would help them better understand the topic, themselves, and others. Alternatively, teachers might have students suggest concepts that interest them, perhaps with different small groups or individuals making explorations and reporting to the class. Notice, by the way, that this approach appeals to students' interests and builds knowledge from their present level—which is one basis of constructivist learning theory (see Hurst 2001). The box on page 112 lists some possible themes or concepts for U.S. history units. Note that the themes focus on people, ideas, and trends rather than chronology.

Examples of Historical Concepts

◆ Elections
◆ Economic depressions
◆ Immigration and emigration
◆ Changing laws for changing times

Elementary school teachers, particularly those in self-contained class-rooms, often include ideas from several content areas in their thematic units, thus developing an **interdisciplinary thematic unit**. For instance, in the "friendship" unit, in addition to the language arts activities, the teacher might include social studies by helping the children develop questionnaires and make a survey of what other students in the school consider to be characteristics of friends. During art time, students might create pictures illustrating types of friendship—people with animals or animals with animals, for instance, as well as the varieties of friendship among people. Math might be included by making charts and graphs of the results from the questionnaires. The concept could even be integrated into lunchtime. Only the teacher's and students' imaginations limit the possibilities (see Castanos 1997; Martin 1995; Martinello & Cook 2000; McDonald & Czerniak 1994). Patricia L. Roberts and Richard D. Kellough (2004) have published a very practical source for developing thematic or inter-disciplinary units. Refer to their work for lesson plans, ideas, and models.

Interdisciplinary teaching involves a conscious effort to apply knowledge, principles, and values to more than one academic discipline simultaneously. The disciplines may be related through a central theme, issue, problem, process, topic, or experience. The framework for such instruction is the creation of themes that specify what students are expected to learn as a result of the experiences and lessons that are a part of the unit (from Houghton Mifflin Harcourt, http://www.eduplace.com, 2005).

Language arts tends to be a major area for interdisciplinary teaching. Integrated through a common theme—for example, television advertisements—are listening, speaking, reading, writing, and critical thinking. A broader kind of integration attempts to encompass several curricular areas.

Interdisciplinary teaching provides one technique in which students can use knowledge learned in one context as a knowledge base in other contexts in and out of school. Student motivation for independent learning is a spin-off from this model.

Students can be involved at all levels—selecting the concept and determining what content areas might be involved, what activities are appropriate, and even what instruction (or instructional methods) might be most useful (see Johns 2003; O'Connor-Petruso 2003). Student participation in preplanning requires teachers to account for these activities in their long-range plans. Having the students help preplan instruction is not a spontaneous act.

VIDEO CASE

Interdisciplinary teaching requires cooperation and a lot of planning from the teachers involved. In the video case "Reading in the Content Areas: An Interdisciplinary Unit on the 1920s" on the student website, you'll see how two teachers join forces to create a History/English unit focused on the Roaring 20s and "The Great Gatsby." After watching the video clips and studying the artifacts in the case, answer the following questions: 1. What strategies did the teachers use to integrate the subject matter? 2. Describe the benefits of interdisciplinary study for the students. How did it increase their learning in both subject areas?

Consider involving students in planning.

Questions and Generalizations   Although concepts make excellent unit organizers and planning tools, they are not your only choices. A well-worded question can also effectively focus your unit (or lesson). Consider the following question: "In what ways was the participation of the United States in the War of 1812 and the Vietnam War similar?" What information would be useful in a response? A detailed description of each war is not necessarily relevant, nor is a lengthy discussion of causes and results—unless such information is relevant to the question. Notice how the focus and content of the unit are almost dictated by the wording of the question.

Here's another example that could organize biology or ecology by examining evolution and extinction: "Who will survive?" Again, notice how usefully the question focuses and organizes content. Such a unit allows plenty of room for investigation of both historical evolution and current threats to species. (See Hanifi, Kelly, & Zeegers 2003 for a model that incorporates student questions.)

In addition to questions, generalizations (a full discussion is presented in Chapter 5) can be useful for organizing unit content. **Generalizations** are inferential statements that express a relationship between two or more concepts, can be verified, and have a predictive value. Here are two examples: "As you shorten or lengthen a vibrating string, the pitch of the sound becomes higher or lower, respectively." "Cold fronts cause a temperature drop in the affected geographic areas." Notice how instruction is almost automatically selected and organized by making clear the concepts involved and exploring the relationships. Notice also that questions and generalizations provide built-in motivation because they present students with a question to be answered or a problem to be solved rather than just a statement of "learn this." Using generalizations often stimulates thinking and problem solving. The Instructional Strategies box below gives two examples of generalizations that could be used as unit topics.

INSTRUCTIONAL
Strategies

Generalizations Used as Unit Topics

◆　The development of the personal automobile revolutionized social and family behavior.

◆　Waterways, as paths of transportation, determined much of the course of colonization.

As you consider organizing units, try to identify what you hope the students will remember long after they leave your class. Certainly, much information will be soon forgotten, but if you have helped them organize knowledge in ways that clarify concepts, answer questions, and explain relationships in terms they understand, they will have truly learned. (See Jacobs 2004 for examples of *big ideas*.)

Reflect　　What are some useful focusing questions or big ideas in your subject area?

Defining the Rationale　An educational **rationale** answers the question "Why is it important to your students to learn this material?" The response should be a reasoned one, not just "It's good for them," "It's required at this grade," or "They have to have it to get into another class." These reasons might be true, but you need to identify a more substantial one, and you need to be intellectually honest with yourself, your students, and your profession. If a parent asks why you are teaching certain material, he or she deserves a thoughtful response based on the importance of the content to the student. So do your students. (And they, at least in high school, are apt to be more blunt in their request: "Hey! How come we gotta learn this stuff?") In the Instructional Strategies box below, we provide two example rationales.

Why learn this?

INSTRUCTIONAL *Strategies*

Example Rationales for Units

Primary Science Unit

Understanding scientific principles and processes is important for every student. Helping students become interested in science at an early age will increase their motivation to want more science as they get older. Additionally, doing science at an early age is an excellent introduction to higher-order thinking processes such as observing, classifying, making inferences, and withholding judgment until sufficient data have been gathered. Thus this unit on water, besides having many informative, interesting activities, will help prepare students mentally for enjoying their observation of the world around them.

Ninth-Grade Literature Unit

Through a study of Greek mythology, this unit helps students build a foundation for understanding imagery and symbolism in literature. Additionally, students should gain appreciation for differing worldviews and human diversity as they examine ancient peoples' perspectives on life and nature. Mythology lies at the source of many themes, images, and symbols in both classical and modern literature. Learning to understand and enjoy these ancient tales will help students understand and interpret all literature.

Defining Goals and Objectives　In planning units and lessons, teachers need to develop learning outcomes in the three areas of *content understanding* (as opposed to simply memorizing facts), *skills/processes*, and *attitudes*. These three areas drive instruction at all levels, although the emphasis among them may shift across the grade levels and for content areas. The focus in elementary school may be on skills/processes with content being stressed more in middle school; by high school, most of the focus is in the content realm. At all levels, however, instruction must integrate skills and processes with content understanding.

Define unit objectives in terms of content, skills/processes, and attitudes.

Attitudes—such as willingness to share or cooperate, to enjoy reading or music or dance, to suspend judgment until sufficient facts are known, and to tolerate ambiguity in decision making—are not specified as objectives as often as content and process. Nonetheless, they are important for students to recognize and deserve more teacher attention than they seem to receive.

At the risk of repetition, we emphasize that these three areas of content understanding, skills/processes (especially thinking processes), and attitudes are interrelated. We probably don't teach or learn purely in any one of them without involving at least one of the others. "Thinking" obviously requires something to think about (content) as well as a willingness to do so (attitude). It is simply convenient for planning and instruction to separate these and emphasize one part or another. Students (and teachers) need to be reminded frequently, however, that learning and understanding are integrated, holistic acts.

What should unit outcomes be? They are best stated as general instructional objectives. (You might want to check back through our full discussion of objectives in Chapter 3.) Try to include objectives from each of the areas: content, skills/processes, and attitudes. These objectives should be attainable (not necessarily mastered) in perhaps as little as a week or as much as three or four weeks. A unit lasting longer than this should have logical dividing points, both for understanding and for manageability. The example outcomes in the box below are typical.

INSTRUCTIONAL *Strategies*

Example Unit Outcomes

Examples of Subject Matter/Content Outcomes

◆ The student understands the relationships among current, resistance, and voltage in a simple series electrical circuit.

◆ The student knows the significance of Presidents Kennedy, Johnson, and Nixon in involving the U.S. people in the war in Vietnam.

◆ Students understand how developments in naval architecture prior to 1500 made possible the "discovery" and colonization of Africa below the Sahara and of both the Americas.

Examples of Skill/Process Outcomes

◆ The student demonstrates satisfactory competence in using the Internet as a research resource.

◆ Each student uses appropriate skill in gathering and classifying data to make inferences for a history project.

◆ The student states an appropriate series of steps in diagnosing and repairing an automobile that won't start.

Examples of Attitude Outcomes

◆ Students show progress (indicated by the teacher's anecdotal records) in delaying a decision until sufficient data have been assembled.

◆ Students achieve a level of personal satisfaction (indicated in self-reports) from completing the history project.

◆ Students apply a "decision tree" (evidenced by student journals and self-reports) in making several personal decisions.

The example outcomes imply that at least several lessons will be required to achieve the level of competence indicated. Notice also that, from the wording, both the necessary instruction and the proper evidence of achievement (for evaluation) are implied. For attitudinal outcomes, evaluation tools are indicated because these outcome goals are less frequently seen in unit plans (and, in some locales, might be subject to citizen criticism for encroaching on personal thoughts or feelings).

In summary, your unit objectives will target specific contents, skills/processes, and attitudes. It is useful to state content objectives as concepts, questions, or generalizations. Skills/processes should include those related to learning, communicating, thinking, decision making, and relationships with other people. Attitudinal objectives, particularly concerning self-esteem and relating oneself to others, need to be deliberately built into unit plans so students can be "set up" for success. Finally, objectives are statements of *student outcomes*, not teacher behaviors. "In this unit I will teach about time zones" is a statement of teacher intent, not a student learning outcome (see Yelon 1996; Zemelman, Daniels, & Hyde 1998).

Selecting Resources and Materials   We have discussed resources in Section 1 of this chapter as part of the preparation stage, but remember their importance. Each unit you create should have as many appropriate resources as you can find to support your instruction and to provide as many ways as possible for students to connect their experiences to the unit. Keep an index of the resources you use; as you gain teaching experience, you can save yourself many hours of searching by having a handy record of sources and items you have used in the past. Resources are entered into the unit plan most conveniently as a list, with perhaps a note about location or intended use.

By the fall of 2003, nearly 100 percent of U.S. public schools had access to the Internet (Parasad & Jones 2005). Teachers are reporting that computers and Internet connectivity are readily available to them in their classrooms, and teachers are generally expected to have at least basic computer literacy to effectively integrate computing tools into their lesson plans. Computers are powerful tools that can be used for communication, creation, and administration (Hansen & Brown 1997). Using the computer as part of an instructional plan is not a spur-of-the-moment decision. You plan for computer use just as you plan the use of textbooks, crayons and paper, or videotaped programs.

As with any instructional tool, some teachers are more likely to incorporate computers into their instructional plans than are others, for a variety of reasons. (See Smerdon et al. 2000 for insight.) Teachers with an active learning orientation are more likely to make use of computers for instruction. Whether hardware and software are readily available in sufficient numbers and whether the teacher feels that he or she is a competent user will also affect how and if computers are included in instructional activities (Becker 2000).

Computer usage should be planned, not impulsive.

TECHNOLOGY
Insight

Finding Lesson Plan Resources on the Internet

A great many Web-based resources exist for teachers. Using a search engine and combinations of Boolean terms such as "lesson plan" and "multiplication + grade 4," it is possible to locate many suggestions for specific instructional activities. A good teaching resource should include some evidence of a positive impact on student achievement. (See the Technology Insight box entitled "Not All Information Is Created Equal: Validity and Reliability of Information," on the student website.)

The best websites for teaching resources tend to be those that are organized and controlled by professional educational organizations or edited by groups of educators. Two of the most respected teaching resources on the Web are the

(continued)

TECHNOLOGY
Insight

Finding Lesson Plan Resources on the Internet—Cont'd

Gateway to Educational Materials (http://www.thegateway.org) and the Apple Learning Interchange (http://edcommunity.apple.com/ali). The Gateway to Educational Materials states that it is dedicated to providing a *comprehensive* collection of resources and is sponsored by the National Education Association. The Apple Learning Interchange describes itself as a social network for educators that provides a wide range of lesson plans and curriculum materials and is sponsored by Apple Computer. Knowing the sponsoring agencies and the organizations' intentions makes it easier to decide how best to make use of these resources.

Creating Your Own Learning Activities   Learning activities were introduced briefly in the discussion on preplanning. Like resources, however, they also play an important part in the unit-planning process. This section will give you some specific aids in creating and finding activities beyond the textbook that will reinforce your instruction.

One of the most useful aids in planning unit and lesson activities is the **Kaplan matrix**, created by Sandra Kaplan (1979). The matrix, illustrated in Table 4.1, is used to plan outcomes and activities at the several levels of Bloom's cognitive taxonomy. Such planning is extremely important if you are to avoid instructing and assessing students primarily at the knowledge level. Use of this matrix forces you at least to consider the other taxonomic levels; if you then choose to remain at the knowledge level, it will be an intentional decision rather than an oversight.

Correlate new activities with Bloom's taxonomy.

The matrix idea can be used in many ways. Table 4.2 shows it in use as a work plan, indicating objective levels, teacher activities, learning experiences,

TABLE 4.1	The Kaplan Matrix for Extending the Curriculum				
Performance Objectives and Related Student Activities					
Content or Concepts	Knowledge	Comprehension	Application	Analysis	Synthesis
Volcanoes	List facts about the Mt. Saint Helens devastation.	Compare Mt. Saint Helens to the volcanoes of Hawaii.	How could we use the piles of volcanic ash?	What do the people near Mt. Saint Helens feel?	Make a volcano model for our class.
Minerals and gems	List the important gems found in the Northeast.	Contrast the hardness of the minerals found in the Northeast.	Field-test the hardness of 10 minerals.	What would happen if the government imposed tougher mining regulations?	Grow crystals of various shapes and colors.
Space travel	Name all the people who have gone to the moon.	Compare the Russian space program to the U.S. space program.	If you were an astronaut, what would you study about space?	What do you think would happen if we found life elsewhere?	Make a rocket and fly it.
Weather and climate	Name the different types of clouds.	Contrast the climates of the Southwest and the Southeast.	Chart the amount of rainfall for the next week.	What effect did El Niño have on the world's weather?	Create a wind generator.

Source: Adapted from Kaplan 1979, with permission of the author.

TABLE 4.2		**Teacher-Student Work Plan**		
Content	Level of Objective	Teaching Activity	Learning Experiences	Student Product
Places of origin	K	Lecture/recitation Reading assignment Worksheet	Note taking Reading	Completed worksheet
Places of origin	C	Demonstration of how to construct graphs	Note taking Constructing a graph	Graph
Places of origin	AP	Small-group presentation	Each group makes a prediction and presents it to the class.	Presentation by small groups to whole class
Places of origin	AN	Presentation of assignment Discussion of resources Description of final product Breaking class into groups	Each group focuses on one immigrant group and is responsible for explaining its motives for coming to the United States, using references, filmstrips, and other resources.	Report to class

Source: Adapted from Kaplan 1979, with permission of the author.

and student products. Again, the act of making such a planning document is itself a positive planning activity—it forces you to think about student outcomes and the types and levels of activities that will most likely help students achieve those outcomes.

Learning activities help you get your students involved in the lesson—in as many ways and through as many senses as possible. Your imagination (right hemisphere) is the key, but a planning matrix (left hemisphere) will help you organize and sequence this important piece of your teaching.

Formulating Assessment Tools   The final portion of your unit plan is assessment of student progress. Because planning is a recursive activity, you need to consider assessment throughout the planning process. Indeed, some teachers find it useful to consider it first—How will I measure what my students can do?—and then create appropriate instruction and activities. In other words, they create a test and teach to it. We urge you to consider assessment throughout your planning. Good instruction entails appropriate assessment.

Key Ideas ➤ **Parts of a Unit Plan**
- ◆ Subject or topic
- ◆ Rationale
- ◆ Instructional objectives
- ◆ Content
- ◆ Processes
- ◆ Resources
- ◆ Learning activities
- ◆ Evaluation

Because Chapter 10 focuses in detail on assessment, we provide only some general guidelines here. First, and perhaps most important, is to remember that the purpose of assessment is to provide evidence of the degree of achievement *each* student has made toward *each* objective. Whatever your system, it must provide that type of individual data. Second, it is important to think of assessment as occurring throughout your units—it is not simply "a big test at the end." If your units include some skills/processes as objectives (and they should), you can assess these as students complete them, using rating scales or checklists. Attitudes can be assessed with your own anecdotal records throughout the unit and periodically by student self-report forms. Particularly for a unit that includes many concepts or much complex information, understanding of content should be assessed with short quizzes at several points during the unit rather than all at once at the end.

Finally, explain your assessment methods to your students—they want and need to know how their performance will be judged. Knowing the ground rules helps them clarify their efforts and probably will result in higher achievement. If your state uses high-stakes assessments, then model some of your test questions after the state required items

VIDEO CASE

In the video case "Assessment in the Elementary Grades: Formal and Informal Literacy Assessment" on the student website, Chris Quinn, a second-grade teacher, uses a variety of assessment tools with her students. After you watch the clips and study the artifacts in the case, answer the following questions: 1. How is assessment used as an instructional strategy? 2. How is assessment used as a planning strategy? 3. How is assessment significant to student learning?

- - - - - - - - - - - - - - - - - - -

Assess frequently, not just at the end.

Reflect

◆ We usually think of assessment as tests of subject matter knowledge. What other areas of student progress are important for you to monitor?

◆ To assess student achievement at the application and analysis level using the Kaplan matrix, what types of assessment tools, other than subject matter tests, would be useful?

INSTRUCTIONAL *Strategies*

A Model Lesson Plan Format

Teacher _____

Course Title _____

1. Unit
2. General Instructional Objectives
3. Specific Learning Outcomes
4. Rationale
5. Content and Skills/Processes
6. Instructional Procedures
   (a) Focusing Event
   (b) Teaching Procedures
   (c) Student Participation and Activities
   (d) Formative Check
   (e) Closure

(continued)

INSTRUCTIONAL *Strategies*

A Model Lesson Plan Format—Cont'd

7. Assessment
8. Materials, Aids, and Computer Needs
9. Notes/File Comments

(The intent of each part is probably clear to you, but some amplification of several parts may help and is provided below.)

1. *Unit:* Record your unit title here.

2. *General Instructional Objectives:* As discussed earlier, these are the unit outcomes that this lesson is meant to reinforce. A general instructional objective might be "Each student will understand the relationships among voltage, resistance, and current in an electrical circuit." A lesson typically will reinforce several objectives. Thus this lesson might focus on content but could also reinforce skills and attitudes.

3. *Specific Learning Outcomes:* These are the specific objectives of this lesson. You might have several in a lesson. An example might be "Using Ohm's Law for calculations, the student will correctly determine the needed values in each of the following circuits: (a) Current is 3.0 amps; resistance is 5,000 ohms. (b) Voltage is 9 volts; current is 0.3 amps. (c) Resistance is 10k ohms; voltage is 6 volts."

4. *Rationale:* This is the same as the rationale for the unit plan but stated in a way that relates this lesson to the unit. In other words, a rationale for a lesson would explain why this particular lesson is important in achieving the unit goals: "To use electricity safely in the home, shop, and business, it is necessary to understand how current, voltage, and resistance are related. The physical relationship can in part be understood mathematically. This lesson will help the student achieve this understanding."

5. *Content and Skills/Processes:* It is important to separate in your mind (and on paper) the content and skills you want students to learn and the procedures or techniques you will use to teach them that content and those skills. This lesson plan format helps you do that. Under "Content" you list the specific concepts or ideas you want students to learn in the lesson. Content for the above lesson in electrical circuits might include working with the following:

Circuits	Ohm's Law	Resistance
EMF	Currents	Amperage
Volts	Inverse ratios	Ohms

6. *Instructional Procedures:* In this section, you list the specific methods you will use to teach each part of the lesson. For our lesson on electrical circuits, for example, some parts might be done by questioning to review an earlier lesson and establish focus on this one. Other parts might have students experiment with a circuit in small groups or view a video and take notes.

7. *Assessment Procedures:* Include a brief explanation of what you will do to determine whether students have reached the objectives. For our sample lesson, students' answers to the computations and explanations of how the problems were solved would be sufficient for assessment.

Lesson Planning

General Plans   Although it is often treated as a separate topic, lesson planning is simply an extension of unit planning. Individual lessons are one way to help students achieve desired unit learning outcomes (objectives). The model lesson plan box on page 119 illustrates the elements a lesson plan should include and some ways to arrange those elements, but you must determine what methods work best for you.

Think of a **lesson** as a piece of a unit, not as a block of time (see Bryant & Bryant 2000). Lesson plans are not the same as activity schedules for the school day. Student teachers are often confused when they see their cooperating teacher's "lesson plan" book and find that it contains mostly notes like the following:

Think of lessons in terms of meaning, not time.

Tuesday, 8th-grade English, 1st period

1. Review spelling words.
2. Dictate test—be sure students make answer sheet first.
3. Introduce Poe's "Tell-Tale Heart." Discuss mental aspects first.
4. Silent reading, Poe.
5. Announce preparations for dismissal at 9:55.

This example is not a lesson plan; it is a schedule of what the teacher intends to do during a class. Lesson plans, like unit plans, are statements of what *students* will do. A good lesson plan contains most of the elements of a unit plan, but on a reduced scale. See the Instructional Strategies box on pages 119 and 120.

Experienced teachers frequently do not write comprehensive lesson plans, although they may expect you, as a student teacher or novice, to do so. An experienced teacher probably spent several years writing similar plans but now has them largely in his or her head, jotted down in margin notes in textbooks, and summarized in brief notes regarding the several activities a lesson might contain. Also, an experienced teacher's unit plan or outline may contain much of what a novice would put into lesson plans. Thus, even if an individual teacher's lesson plan book looks much like the above example, he or she probably did do the planning.

There are many different lesson plan formats from which to choose; the best one to use is determined by your specific instructional goals and teaching strategies. The authors of this text, and many of their students, have found the lesson plan format shown in the box to be useful. The importance of lesson plans and the unit plans they support cannot be overstated. As one high school teacher puts it, "The better the teacher plans, the better the teacher" (Walsh 1992, p. 97). (Excellent examples of lesson plan formats and other considerations are found in Johns 2003; Little 2003; O'Connor-Petruso 2003; Pappas 2003; and Price & Nelson 2003.)

Universal Design and Differentiated Instruction   The schools of today have a more diverse student population than ever. As a teacher, your goal is to reach every student. Accomplishing that Herculean task means applying a concept often called **universal design** or **differentiated instruction**. We simply call it **multi-methodology**. Regardless of the label, this concept means that you plan for multiple means of lesson representations so all learners can acquire the information or knowledge. It also means there are multiple avenues of expressing what students know and engaging them in meaningful activities (Kunkel 2008; Rose & Meyer 2002, 2006; Tomlinson & McTighe 2006).

The San Jose State University Teacher Scholar Project (Hagie et al. 2006) provides a few teacher tips for instituting a universal design by creating a learning community. The team notes that a teacher knows every student by name and develops a trusting relationship. A safe environment with an atmosphere of camaraderie is critical, as is creating a climate of intellectual inquiry. Obviously, these conditions will encourage multiple viewpoints and multiple avenues by which to express them. As we noted, accomplishing all these feats requires the use of a broad spectrum of teaching styles, methods, and models.

Constructing IEPs   All children with disabilities, by federal law, must have **individual education plans** (IEPs) written for them. The IEP is a special and extended adaptation of a lesson plan. We have seen them typed in as few as four pages and as many as 20! Your employing school district will provide the specified format for you to follow. However, just to illustrate their complexity and attention to detail, we present Table 4.3, which simply lists all the key descriptors or key elements mandated by federal law. As you examine the table, keep in mind that, for each item listed, a complete justification or detailed description is required for a total of 39 separate points. Did we mention that IEPs are labor intensive? And, most likely, at least 12 percent of your students will be legally classified as disabled.

But don't give up in despair! You aren't alone. There will be specialists available to help with the planning and delivery of services. (See Bateman & Linden 1998–2000; Hardman, Drew, & Egan 2008; and Ysseldyke, Algozzine, & Thurlow 2000 for detailed models of IEPs.) You *will* be able to prepare IEPs.

The key term in this section is **inclusion**. There is no question that you will have students with special needs and you will be expected to treat them as equals to other students in your classroom. An inclusive classroom requires that you as teacher make accommodations for learning. In the previous section on universal design, we implied accommodations for success. You may have to request assistive technology for some students. Assistive technology can be hearing aids, special computer keyboards, or technologies specifically adapted to a specific handicapping condition.

You will want to incorporate multi-methodologies in your classroom to assist all to become successful in school learning. It will be important for you to also collaborate with the principal and other teachers in the school to bring inclusionary classes to a successful fruition (see McNary, Glasgow, & Hicks 2005).

Response to Intervention Model   Before leaving this topic we will add one more model that you will hear discussed in relation to learning disabilities. With the renewal of the IDEA act in 2004, it was clear that regular classroom teachers could assist in helping children with specific learning disabilities to succeed. The model being espoused is the *Response to Intervention Model* or *RTI* (see Hardman et al. 2008). The RTI model requires all classroom teachers at all levels (K–12) to assess student learning more systematically, as we discuss in Chapter 10. There are three tiers of intervention in the RTI system.

TABLE 4.3	Elements of an Individual Education Plan Required by Federal Law

◆ Student's personal information (age)

◆ Grade level

◆ Statement that parent or surrogate agrees or disagrees with plan

◆ Signatures (parent, student, teacher, district representative)

Services

◆ Special services needed

◆ Frequency—hours or times per week

◆ Expected duration

◆ Responsible persons by position or title

◆ Special media and materials or modifications

◆ Adaptations for physical education

Placement (Least Restrictive Environment)

◆ General education class

◆ General education class with consulting services

◆ General education class with pull-out related services

◆ General education class with pull-out special education services

◆ Special education class with integration into general education class and/or community

◆ Self-contained special education class

◆ Residential school

◆ Home instruction

◆ Hospital instruction

Recommendations and Placement

◆ Neighborhood school or close to student's home

◆ Opportunities for extracurricular or school-sponsored nonacademic activities

◆ Transportation

Levels of Performance

◆ Present levels of performance

◆ Annual goals

◆ Short-term objectives

◆ Objective criteria

◆ Evaluation procedures to be used

◆ Schedule to determine how often objective is achieved

◆ Objectives achieved

FIGURE 4.2
**The Response to
Intervention Model**

From Kirk, *Educating Exceptional
Children*, 11th ed. © 2006 Wadsworth,
a part of Cengage Learning, Inc.
Reproduced by permission.
www.cengage.com/permissions.

Response to Intervention Model
focuses on specific learning
deficits.

Tier I is the regular curriculum where most students make adequate academic progress, i.e., 80 to 85 percent. Tier II interventions require more intensive and supplemental services to enhance student academic progress, i.e., 10 to 15 percent of the typical school. Tier III interventions require intensive and specialized instruction, accounting for about 5 percent of all students.

Obviously, this textbook is written with methods that definitely work with Tier I and II students. Tier III students need very specialized instructional strategies. We close this section with a reminder that you will encounter the RTI model on your first teaching job. The model requires clear planning and observational data, plus formative evaluation. Again, discuss this aspect with your principal or department head before school begins so you can be proactive.

Figure 4.2 illustrates the basic aspects of each tier of the RTI model.

Postlesson Activities

Evaluating Unit and Lesson Plans

What worked and what didn't?

Up to this point in this chapter, we have used the term *assessment* several times to indicate monitoring of student progress. However, we also wish to monitor our own progress as teachers. In this section, we use the term *evaluation* for this process.

At the conclusion of every class session, ask yourself a series of questions about the effectiveness of your lesson and unit plans: Were the objectives realistic and appropriate? Did the instructional methods work? For which learners and to what degree did they work? What components of the lesson succeeded? What aspects could be improved? Write your thoughts regarding your lesson plan in a journal or in your textbook's margins to help you identify difficulties experienced by learners and to relate these problems to specific elements of the lesson and unit.

Keeping Planning Notes and Reflecting on Future Planning Needs

Be sure to jot down any notes or comments about the lesson or unit that will help you the next time you teach it. Master teachers refer to the previous year's notes and resource files as they plan their lessons (Walsh 1992). In fact, one of the greatest distinctions between novice and expert teachers is that the experts have large quantities of previously gathered material to draw on—*and they use it continually.*

Lesson and unit plans should be thought of as *emerging documents;* the first ones you construct will be at only the earliest stage of development. After your initial use of these plans, the actual classroom conditions (learner entry skills, teaching procedures, and learner outcomes) need to be compared to the planned situation. The resulting data will allow for refinement and recycling, making the unit and lesson plans more effective instructional tools. You will continue to evaluate your instructional plans each time you use them, always attempting to improve content, activities, and methods.

An emerging document that you can continually improve

Reflect

Instructional planning can be envisioned as a grid with a series of principles and strategies. This grid includes deciding what to teach, how to teach, and how to communicate realistic expectations as key principles for instructional planning (Ysseldyke & Elliott 1999).

Under the component of managing instruction, the grid highlights instructional preparations, productive use of time, and the establishment of a positive classroom environment. Obviously, we concur. Do you? List several specific classroom management benefits you believe might flow from good instructional planning.

SECTION 3 How Expert Teachers Plan

We close this chapter by describing some planning behaviors that separate expert and novice teachers, then summarizing what the research shows. If you are aware of good planning practices and research when you begin to teach, you will have less to learn through experience to become an efficient and effective classroom planner and teacher.

In general, three areas separate the novice and expert planner: (1) planning routines and interdependent planning levels (McBer 2000; Ornstein & Lasley 2004), (2) reflective practice, and (3) a treasury of teaching materials (Walsh 1992, pp. 12–24). We will consider each of these in some detail.

Differences in planning between novice and expert

Planning Routines

Many repetitive tasks will confront you each day as a teacher. These **routines** include activities such as gathering and dispensing papers, recording tardiness and absences, recording participation in activities, checking assignments, and giving all students an equal chance to respond to questions. Expert teachers devise and revise plans to simplify and systematize the accomplishment of such tasks. For instance, students can be assigned on a rotating schedule to

Use student workers to save
time.

distribute papers and to take roll. A student can be assigned to mark on a class roster which students you call on to help you avoid missing any or calling on some too often (see Clement 2000).

Expert teachers work out many aids like these, frequently involving student help when appropriate, and thus save a few (or perhaps quite a few) minutes of instructional time each day. Consider: Five minutes saved daily is 25 minutes a week, or 900 minutes in a 180-day school year. Your students deserve an extra 15 hours of instructional time.

Expert teachers consistently implement several distinct planning levels—long range, unit, and daily—as an interdependent set of routines (Walsh 1992). These routines help convert long-range plans into daily and weekly schedules, keeping short-term instruction aligned with long-range goals and the overall school calendar (McBer 2000; Ornstein & Lasley 2004).

Summary of Teacher Planning

◆ Planning is based on a plethora of models and a variety of lesson plan formats.

◆ Planning serves a wide array of purposes.

◆ Planning is a continuous process.

◆ Planning is seldom linear.

◆ Planning must be flexible.

Reflective Practice

Donald A. Schön (1995) examined how various professionals—architects, physicians, engineers, and educators—actually practice. He discovered that competent professionals usually know a great deal more than they verbalize. In other words, they have a depth of knowledge; in their professional lives they reflect on that knowledge and then apply it to new or unusual problems. Schön encourages professionals to think, ponder, and reflect about past, present, and future actions as a means of designing productive problem-solving strategies.

Applying Schön's postulates to education has encouraged many educators and educational researchers to promote reflection as a key element in stimulating professional growth and improving professional practice. **Reflection** is an active mental process that master teachers use consistently as they interact with students and the curriculum (see Panasuk & Sullivan 1998; Strong, Silver, & Perini 2001).

Walsh (1992) observed evidence of "reflective dialogue" in the planning behaviors of award-winning teachers. The ones he interviewed stated that they consistently rehearsed classroom scenarios before teaching, frequently talking to themselves about what they wanted to have happen in class. These rehearsals included consideration of the best instructional options and methods for handling anticipated classroom dilemmas, such as a class that doesn't respond as expected to a lesson. Furthermore, these teachers followed each lesson, as soon as possible, with a period of reflection, taking quick notes on what worked well and what didn't.

Treasury of Teaching Materials

Much of planning confidence and expertise stems from two sources that all master teachers possess: (1) file cabinets or computer files full of valuable resources collected over the years and (2) last year's plan book. These two sources constitute part of an experienced teacher's planning edge over new teachers.

Novice teachers cannot compensate for their lack of full file cabinets or huge computer files. Novices who want to become excellent teachers simply have to become savers and collectors (and develop a retrieval system that allows them to find what they have). What should you save? Virtually anything related to your instruction, but especially successful learning activities, tests, quizzes, magazine articles and pictures, bulletin board materials, computer and Internet resources, assignments, study guides—the list is almost endless.

Having last year's plans obviously simplifies this year's planning—much of the groundwork has been done. This is one part of teaching the student teacher usually doesn't see. However, don't be misled into believing that master teachers just reuse their old plans each year. Those plans are only the starting points for current lessons. True professionals are always thinking about and planning how to update content, find more effective instructional methods, and devise better activities to help their students succeed. As three recognized classroom observers stress, it is the lesson that transforms youngsters into students (Mitchell, Ortiz, & Mitchell 1987). Learning is the primary goal of the schools. Your job is to make planning decisions that ensure learning is always intentionally inviting.

Planning is the heart of teaching. To the degree that you can become a successful planner, you will become a successful teacher. Refer to our companion website at www.cengage.com/education/orlich to examine the effect sizes associated with planning per se, as well as various specific planning elements.

Planning is the heart of instruction.

An old unit plan is only the starting point; keep improving, updating.

What the Research Shows

Lest you come away from this chapter unconvinced of the value of planning, let's take a look at some research. Studies of the actual processes that teachers use in planning were conducted primarily in the early 1970s through the 1980s. Christopher M. Clark and Penelope L. Peterson (1986) prepared the high-water mark for the genre. Although it is now dated, their work and that of others led to the set of research-based findings described below. These findings will be useful to you as you begin instructional planning.

1. *Researchers have neither identified nor validated any widely accepted or consistently practical planning model* (see McBer 2000). Plans, planning efforts, and planning methods vary widely among teachers. Planning seems to be influenced most by the selection of learning activities, instructional objectives, content, students' age, available time, and teaching strategies. Of these, *time* and *proven activities* appear to have the greatest influence on the way that teachers plan.

2. *Teachers use a variety of lesson plan formats*. Time is a critical teaching constraint, and all teachers organize blocks of instructional time in lessons

Variability in planning

for years, semesters, months, weeks, and days. Content is also a major consideration, and teachers generally agree on the value of organizing content into coherent segments (unit plans) and subsequently into manageable parts (lesson plans). (See Clark & Peterson 1986; Garmston 1998; Hawbecker et al. 2001; Kagan & Tippins 1992; Price & Nelson 2003; Richardson 2000; Sardo-Brown 1988; Sawyer 2001; Wiggins & McTighe 2005.)

3. *Planning serves as a guide to action.* Plans are written to act as a guide during your instructional interactions. In this regard, plans provide and maintain a sense of direction and instill confidence in your teaching. Of course, weekly or daily lesson plans are typically an administrative requirement in most schools (Johnson 2000).

4. *Teachers tend to carry much of their planning in their minds rather than on paper.* Particularly as they gain experience, teachers may make notes about main ideas, yet they base much of their daily teaching on mental images of how the instruction should best proceed. Thus, in your observations of teachers, you may note large differences in the amount of planning that appears on paper. Until you have several years' experience, we urge you to make written plans; the more you work out your plans on paper, the more effective you will become (Sardo-Brown 1988; Wolcott 1994).

Transition from paper to mental notes.

5. *Teachers rarely plan in the linear model often encouraged in textbooks.* Many years ago, Ralph W. Tyler (1949) suggested a sequential planning process of several steps: (1) specify an objective, (2) select appropriate learning activities, (3) organize the activities, and (4) specify an assessment process. The method has been taught frequently in teacher education programs, but practicing teachers seem to use it infrequently. Instead, teachers mostly use a recursive process that focuses on previous successful activities, perceived student needs, and ongoing curriculum programs (Fisher 2000).

Planning is a recursive process.

6. *The best teachers apply planning flexibly.* In their review, "Excellence in Teaching," Maribeth Gettinger and Karen Stoiber (1999) demonstrate that planning for instruction is the key to excellence. In every model they present, a teacher must first plan, but that plan must be flexible so that it can be adapted to fit the actual teaching moment. We encourage you to exercise flexibility in your delivery of instruction.

Planning should be flexible.

Reflect A Closing Reflection

◆ Which of your strengths will make you a successful planner? What limitations must you work around?

◆ How can you build a resource file when you haven't yet been hired?

◆ To what extent have you had to justify your content selection by specifying a written rationale?

◆ What criteria would you generate to critique your lesson plans in the postlesson evaluation?

◆ Ask your instructor for models of IEPs. Do you observe any commonalities?

Summary Points

1. The preplanning phase is essentially one of teacher reflection.
2. Planning decisions are often influenced by what content is *not* included since there is so much to cover.
3. National and state agencies, textbook publishers, and state education agencies supply more than adequate instructional guides and resources.
4. Long-range planning is simplified by use of a school day activity calendar and by collaborating with teachers, parents, and students.
5. Student readiness is critical for content mastery.
6. Unit planning makes learning manageable since lessons are designed and executed to achieve desired learning outcomes.
7. Learning activities provide students with hands-on experiences.
8. Assessment is essential to determine students' levels of achievement.
9. The three tiers of the RTI model are applicable to most classrooms.
10. Expert teachers and novices take different approaches to planning.

Building a Career Portfolio

Being prepared, which requires planning, is essential as you contemplate job interviews and your first teaching position. Therefore your portfolio should include numerous examples of planning by successful educators. You may get some ideas about planning by reading books or journals, but one of your best sources is the successful teacher, and the administrator who has observed many teachers. Fortunately, educators like to share. Following are several suggestions for starting the planning component of your portfolio.

◆ Visit a nearby school and ask the principal to share selected lesson plans with you so you may identify key elements that you can adapt to your own classroom.

◆ Obtain an actual IEP from a school principal or the director of special education to observe the details needed to comply with federal laws. Are you ready to construct one?

◆ Create a list of quality websites that provide actual models of lesson plans, so that you may include them in your portfolio for future use.

Resources

PRINT

Bateman, B. D. *From Gobbledygook to Clearly Written IEP Goals.* Verona, WI: Attainment Co., 2007.
One of the nation's authorities on IEPs provides a set of IEPs that are easy to read and follow, plus pointed critiques.

Bruer, J. T. "In Search of . . . Brain-Based Education." *Phi Delta Kappan 80*(9) (1999): 648–654.

    The author critiques brain-based education literature and research. He cautions that the area lacks empirical testing.

Glasgow, N. A., & C. D. Hicks. *What Successful Teachers Do: 91 Research-Based Classroom Strategies for New and Veteran Teachers.* Thousand Oaks, CA: Corwin Press, 2003, 210 pp.

    The authors provide a series of tested methods that help make an inclusive classroom a center of multi-methodology.

Irvine, J. J., B. M. Armento, A. E. Causey, J. C. Jones, R. S. Frasher, & M. H. Weinburgh. *Culturally Responsive Teaching: Lesson Planning for Elementary and Middle Grades.* Boston: McGraw-Hill, 2001, 224 pp.

    This team provides content-related lesson plans that are multiculturally oriented.

Skowron, J. *Powerful Lesson Planning Models: The Art of 1,000 Decisions.* Arlington Heights, IL: Skylight, 2001, 163 pp.

    Ideas, examples, and models are provided to aid the reader in developing useful lesson plans.

INTERNET

Go to the website for this book at www.cengage.com/education/orlich to find live links to resources related to this chapter. The following list will direct you to many of the best lesson-planning sites:

◆ "The Educator's Reference Desk," maintained by the Information Institute of Syracuse, contains more than 2,000 lesson plans written by teachers of all grades and subjects.
    http://www.eduref.org/Virtual/Lessons/index.shtml

◆ Yahoo!—an index of websites—has an Education section that contains an extensive listing of sites that sell or supply free of charge a wide variety of instructional materials.
    http://www.yahoo.com/education/K_12/teaching/lesson_plans

◆ The Center for Applied Special Technology (CAST) sponsors a detailed site that stresses Universal Design.
    http://www.cast.org

◆ Peter W. D. Wright and Pam Wright cover the waterfront on all aspects of special education—laws, IEPs, news, and print resources.
    http://www.wrightslaw.com

References

Bateman, B. D., & M. A. Linden. (1998–2000). *Better IEPs* (3rd ed.). Longmont, CO: Sopris West.

Baylor, A., A. Kitsantas, & H. Chung. (2001). "The Instructional Planning Self-Reflective Tool: A Method for Promoting Effective Lesson Planning." *Educational Technology 41*(2): 56–59.

Becker, H. J. (2000, July). *Findings from the Teaching, Learning and Computing Survey: Is Larry Cuban Right?* Revision of a paper written for the January 2000 School Technology Leadership Conference of the Council of the Chief State School Officers, Washington, DC.

Bloom, B. S. (1976). *Human Characteristics and School Learning.* New York: McGraw-Hill.

Brophy, J., & J. Alleman. (1991). "Activities as Instructional Tools: A Framework for Analysis and Evaluation." *Educational Researcher 20*(4): 9–23.

Bryant, C., & R. Bryant. (2000). "Social Studies in the Block Schedule: A Model for Effective Lesson Design." *Social Studies 91*(1): 9–16.

Castanos, J. (1997). "Interdisciplinary Instruction." *Thrust for Educational Leadership 26*(6): 33–38.

Clark, C. M., & P. L. Peterson. (1986). "Teachers' Thought Processes." In M. C. Wittrock, Ed., *Handbook of Research on Teaching* (3rd ed.). New York: Macmillan.

Clement, M. C. (2000). "Just How Do You Teach Someone to Be a Teacher?" *Phi Delta Kappan 82*(4): 308–309.

Ediger, M. (2004). "Psychology of Lesson Plans and Unit Development." *Reading Improvement 41*(4): 197–201.

English, F. W. (1986/1987). "It's Time to Abolish Conventional Curriculum Guides." *Educational Leadership 44*(4): 50–52.

Fisher, D. (2000). "Curriculum and Instruction for All Abilities and Intelligences." *High School Magazine 7*(7): 21–25, 52.

Garmston, R. J. (1998). "Becoming Expert Teachers (Part One)." *Journal of Staff Development 19*(1): 60–63.

Gettinger, M., & K. C. Stoiber. (1999). "Excellence in Teaching. Review of Instructional and Environmental Variables." In Cecil R. Reynolds and Terry B. Gutkin, Eds., *The Handbook of School Psychology* (3rd ed.), pp. 933–958. New York: Wiley.

Guskey, T. R. (2005). "Mapping the Road to Proficiency." *Educational Leadership 63*(3): 32–38.

Hagie, C., R. Halualani, R. Henze, J. O. Osland, C. Peterson, M. Saleem, & S. Wilkenson. (2006). *What Do Expert Teachers of Diverse Learners Know and Do?* San Jose, CA: Center for Faculty Development, San Jose State University.

Hanifi, H., D. Kelly, & Y. Zeegers. (2003). "Planning a Unit of Work: Incorporating Students' Questions." *Investigating 19*(1): 24–29.

Hansen, L., & A. Brown. (1997). *The Benchmarks Project.* Bloomington: Center for Excellence in Education and Indiana University. http://www.logicalcreativity.com/projects/benchmarks.

Hardman, M. L., C. J. Drew, & M. W. Egan. (2008). *Human Exceptionality: School, Community and Family* (9th ed.). Boston: Houghton Mifflin.

Hawbecker, B. W., M. Balong, S. Buckwalter, & S. Runyon. (2001). "Building a Strong BASE of Support for All Students Through Coplanning." *TEACHING Exceptional Children 33*(4): 24–30.

Houghton Mifflin Eduplace. The website for this service is located at http://www.eduplace.com.

House, J. D., R. S. Hurst, & E. J. Keely. (1996). "Relationship Between Learner Attitudes, Prior Achievement, and Performance in a General Education Course: A Multi-Institutional Study." *International Journal of Instructional Media 23*(3): 257–271.

Hurst, B. (2001). "ABCs of Content Area Lesson Planning: Attention, Basics, and Comprehension." *Journal of Adolescent and Adult Literacy 44*(8): 692–693.

Jacobs, H. H., Ed. (2004). *Getting Results with Curriculum Mapping.* Alexandria, VA: Association for Supervision and Curriculum Development.

Johns, P. (2003). "Horizontal and Vertical Line Designs." *Arts & Activities 133*(5): 37.

Johnson, A. P. (2000). "It's Time for Madeline Hunter to Go: A New Look at Lesson Plan Design." *Action in Teacher Education 22*(1): 72–78.

Johnston, J., M. Knight, & L. Miller. (2007). "Finding Time for Teams." *Journal of Staff Development 28*(2): 14–19.

Kagan, D. M., & D. J. Tippins. (1992). "The Evolution of Functional Lesson Plans Among Twelve Elementary and Secondary Student Teachers." *Elementary School Journal 92*(4): 477–489.

Kaplan, S. M. (1979). *Inservice Training Manual: Activities for Development Curriculum for the Gifted/Talented.* Ventura, CA: Ventura County Schools.

Kunkel, C. (2008). "The Power of Key: Celebrating 20 Years of Innovation As a Key Learning Community." *Phi Delta Kappan 89*(3): 204–209.

Little, M. E. (2003). "Successfully Teaching Mathematics: Planning Is the Key." *Educational Forum 67*(3): 276–282.

Lively, T., & G. Emerling. (2005, Jan. 13). "Students Like Bush, Not His Proposal." *The Washington Times*, M-1. http://www.washtimes.com/metro/20050112-101258-9433r.htm.

Martin, P. L. (1995). "Creating Lesson Blocks: A Multi-Discipline Team Effort." *Schools in the Middle 5*(11): 22–24.

Martinello, M. L., & G. E. Cook. (2000). *Interdisciplinary Inquiry in Teaching and Learning* (3rd ed.). Upper Saddle River, NJ: Merrill.

McBer, H. (2000, June). *Research into Teacher Effectiveness.* London: Report by Hay McBer to the Department for Education and Employment.

McDonald, J., & C. Czerniak. (1994). "Developing Interdisciplinary Units: Strategies and Examples." *School Science and Mathematics 94*(1): 5–10.

McNary, S., N. A. Glasgow, & C. D. Hicks. (2005). *What Successful Teachers Do In Inclusive Classrooms: 60 Research-Based Teaching Strategies That Help Special Learners Succeed.* Thousand Oaks, CA: Corwin Press.

Mitchell, D. E., F. I. Ortiz, & T. K. Mitchell. (1987). *Work Orientations and Job Performance: The Cultural Basis of Teaching Rewards and Incentives*. Albany: State University of New York Press.

National Center for History in the Schools. (1995). *National Standards for United States History: Exploring the American Experience, Grades 5–12*. Los Angeles: University of California at Los Angeles.

O'Connor-Petruso, S. A. (2003). "A Model for Implementation." *Learning & Leading with Technology* 30(8): 32–35, 38–41.

Ornstein, A. C., & T. J. Lasley II. (2004). *Strategies for Effective Teaching* (3rd ed.). Boston: McGraw-Hill.

Panasuk, R. M., & M. M. Sullivan. (1998). "Need for Lesson Analysis in Effective Lesson Planning." *Education 118*(3): 330–345.

Pappas, M. L. (2003). "My America in Poetry and Pictures." *School Library Media Activities Monthly* 19(8): 21–24, 26.

Parasad, B., & J. Jones. (2005, February). *Internet Access in U.S. Public Schools and Classrooms: 1994–2003*. (NCES 2005-015). U.S. Department of Education. Washington, DC: National Center for Education Statistics.

Pressman, H., & P. Dublin. (1995). *Accommodating Learning Style Differences in Elementary Classrooms*. New York: Harcourt Brace.

Price, K. M., & K. L. Nelson. (2003). *Daily Planning for Today's Classroom* (2nd ed.). Belmont, CA: Wadsworth.

Richardson, J. (2000). "Learning Benefits Everyone." *Journal of Staff Development 21*(1): 54–59.

Roberts, P. L., & R. D. Kellough. (2004). *A Guide for Developing Interdisciplinary Thematic Units* (3rd ed.). Upper Saddle River, NJ: Merrill.

Rose, D. H., & A. Meyer. (2002). *Teaching Every Student in the Digital Age: Universal Design for Learning*. Alexandria, VA: ASCD.

Rose, D. H., & A. Meyer. (2006). *A Practical Reader in Universal Design for Learning*. Cambridge, MA: Harvard Education Press.

Sardo-Brown, D. S. (1988). "Twelve Middle-School Teachers' Planning." *The Elementary School Journal 89*(1): 69–87.

Sawyer, L. (2001). "Revamping a Teacher Evaluation System." *Educational Leadership 58*(5): 44–47.

Schön, D. A. (1995). *The Reflective Practitioner: How Professionals Think in Action*. Aldershot, England: Arena.

Sizer, T. R. (1996). *Horace's Hope: What Works for the American High School*. Boston: Houghton Mifflin.

Smerdon, B., S. Cronen, L. Lanahan, J. Anderson, N. Iannotti, & J. Angeles. (2000). *Teachers' Tools for the 21st Century: A Report on Teachers' Use of Technology* (NCES 2000-102). Washington, DC: U.S. Department of Education.

Strong, R. W., H. F. Silver, & M. J. Perini. (2001). *Teaching What Matters Most: Standards and Strategies for Raising Student Achievement*. Alexandria, VA: Association for Supervision and Curriculum Development.

Tomlinson, C. A., & J. McTighe. (2006). *Integrating Differentiated Instruction and Understanding By Design: Connecting Content and Kids*. Alexandria, VA: ASCD.

Tyler, R. W. (1949). *Basic Principles of Curriculum and Instruction*. Chicago: University of Chicago Press.

Walsh, F. M. (1992). *Planning Behaviors of Distinguished and Award-Winning High School Teachers*. Unpublished doctoral dissertation, Washington State University, Pullman. Various ideas and materials reprinted by permission of the author.

Washington State Commission on Student Learning. (2007). *Revised Essential Learnings: Reading, Writing, Communication, Mathematics*. Olympia, WA: Commission on Student Learning.

Wiggins, G., & J. McTighe. (2005). *Understanding by Design* (expanded 2nd ed.). Alexandria, VA: Association for Supervision and Curriculum Development.

Wolcott, L. L. (1994). "Understanding How Teachers Plan: Strategies for Successful Instructional Partnerships." *School Library Media Quarterly 22*(3): 161–165.

Yelon, S. L. (1996). *Powerful Principles of Instruction*. White Plains, NY: Longman.

Ysseldyke, J. E., B. Algozzine, & M. L. Thurlow. (2000). *Critical Issues in Special Education* (3rd ed.). Boston: Houghton Mifflin.

Ysseldyke, J. E., & J. Elliott. (1999). "Effective Instructional Practices: Implications for Assessing Educational Environments." In Cecil R. Reynolds and Terry B. Gutkin, Eds., *The Handbook of School Psychology* (3rd ed.), pp. 497–518. New York: Wiley.

Zemelman, S., H. Daniels, & A. Hyde. (1998). *Best Practice: New Standards for Teaching and Learning in America's Schools* (2nd ed.). Portsmouth, NH: Heinemann.

Sequencing and Organizing Instruction

Josh, a second-year humanities teacher at Middlebrook Junior High, was handing back the first-quarter tests to his third-period students, and he complimented Amy on getting an A on her exam.

Amy replied, "I like humanities and find the class very interesting."

"Why is that?" asked Josh

"The class is hard, but it isn't boring," replied Amy. "You challenge us to give our own views but you ask us to back up our answers with supporting information. Every day is different. Sometimes you explain things, but sometimes you give us problems or questions and we have to find the solutions ourselves."

Josh was elated. Well organized by nature, Josh found instructional planning easy. He had worked hard to select the best strategies and techniques to help his students analyze each reading assignment but also to enjoy learning. Amy's comment indicated that he was achieving his instructional goals.

In Chapters 3 and 4, you learned how to use procedures and skills for instructional planning. In this chapter, we will address the transition from planning to teaching. This chapter addresses the following three questions:

◆ How can I select the most appropriate sequencing techniques for my course?

◆ Which model of organization provides the greatest assistance to students in mastering lesson goals and objectives?

◆ How can I ensure that my teaching is enriched by multi-methodology?

SECTION 1 Basic Concepts

What Is Sequencing?

Sequencing is the art of developing a logical plan for instructional activities that will help your students effectively master a body of knowledge or discipline in an organized way. Presenting knowledge in a series of carefully interrelated steps not only helps students to master content but also develops their information-processing skills—that is, their ability to think.

Sequencing has two basic purposes. The first is to isolate either a piece of knowledge (a fact, concept, generalization, or principle) so that students learn and understand its unique characteristics or a thinking process to help students master it under varying conditions. The second is to relate the knowledge or process being taught to a larger organized body of knowledge. The first function—isolating what is being taught—helps make learning more manageable. The second function—relating the information to the bigger picture—makes learning more meaningful.

> Isolate one piece of knowledge; relate it to the big picture.

For example, to teach the concept of a metaphor, you would first teach the characteristics of a metaphor by providing examples. This provides students with a manageable amount of information and a focus for their study. You can then teach a second figure of speech—a simile—in the same way. After the students have mastered both concepts, you can show that similes and metaphors have common characteristics; that is, they are both figures of speech. In this way you relate the lesson content to a larger body of knowledge. This example shows the relationship between instructional sequencing and hierarchies of knowledge. A sequence is an instructional process because it establishes a schedule for learning the various parts of the related content. In a subject area such as mathematics, in which there is an accepted hierarchy of knowledge, the sequence and hierarchy are very similar because the relationships among the content components usually dictate a sequence of learning activities. Students learn to add before learning to multiply. In a subject such as social studies, on the other hand, in which it is difficult to agree on an established hierarchy of information, the sequencing of learning is usually established by either the interest or the experience of the teacher or a curriculum committee. If a **content hierarchy** exists, it influences the instructional sequence. If a content hierarchy does not exist, the sequence of instruction establishes a hierarchy for the student.

The type of hierarchy can vary with subject area.

To teach effectively, you must sequence learning objectives in a way that reflects the relationships between the various components of the curriculum, a practice that is referred to as "bridging." This allows you to identify and teach prerequisite or entry-level skills and competencies at the appropriate stage. For meaningful learning to take place, the sequenced objectives should be communicated to students so they will understand the relationships among the various components of the unit or the overall curriculum. You may want to use graphic organizers, described later in this chapter, to organize and communicate objectives and lesson components to students.

General Principles of Sequencing   Four general principles apply to all kinds of sequencing. The first principle is that you always *begin with a simple step.* This does not mean that you "talk down" to your students. Rather, it means that you structure your lessons so that learners can understand easily identified characteristics of the content. At this step you should provide numerous examples. Using analogies often helps. In a biology class, you could begin by stating, "The circulatory system is similar to a river system in that it carries both food and waste and can be overused and misused." Because your students studied river systems in a previous year, your use of an analogy has provided them with a simple entryway to understanding the circulatory system.

Analogies can help.

The second principle is to *use concrete examples.* This means that you use materials, simulations, models, or artifacts that illustrate the fact, concept, or generalization being taught. Let's stay with the biology class example. You call your students' attention to the circulatory system on the life-size plastic model of the human body at the front of the classroom. You point out major arteries and discuss their similarity to major rivers such as the Mississippi and the Columbia. Then you proceed to identify and name the major arteries and veins, discussing the primary functions of each one.

The third principle is to *add complexity to the lesson.* Sequence the learning experience so that it becomes more and more complex as you progress. You can do this by introducing additional variables, generating new sets of criteria, or establishing relationships between the content of the lesson and other content. For example, you may add the functions of the heart, liver, and other organs of the circulatory system to the discussion. The topic now becomes significantly more complex; as you add the organs one at a time, explaining the functions of each, you may need to go back to the first step (the river–circulatory system analogy) or the second (the plastic human model)—bridging.

Add complexity and abstractions.

Finally, the fourth principle is to *introduce abstractions.* You might want to do this with a question: "When you are sick, why does the doctor start an examination by checking your blood pressure and listening to your heartbeat?"

Again, you may need to go back to previous steps. For example, you might point out that blocking a river tributary produces pressure on the banks and

Key Ideas ➤ **Four Principles of Sequencing**
1. Begin with a simple step.
2. Use concrete examples.
3. Add complexity to the lesson.
4. Introduce abstractions.

that this is similar to what happens when a vein or artery becomes blocked. Or you might note that, by testing water systems for contaminants, you can determine the health of an ecosystem, which is similar to what blood testing does.

The four steps or principles of sequencing are useful in that they provide a logical progression of learning. They are interactive, though, in that you may need to go back to a previous step to help explain the idea currently under discussion.

Although we have divided sequencing into four steps, don't be fooled into thinking too literally that on Monday your lesson should be "simple," on Tuesday it should be "concrete," on Wednesday you should address "complex" issues, on Thursday you should deal with the "abstract" issues, and on Friday you should test. It may take years to apply all four principles in the teaching of certain complex topics—for example, the basic concept of democracy is never completely taught and mastered. The process of teaching the concept of democracy begins at the preschool level and continues throughout the entire educational system, becoming more complex and abstract at each successive level. Or you may use all four principles in a single lesson, as in the example involving the circulatory system. Each discipline or area of the study has similar core facts, concepts, and generalizations that permeate the entire curriculum. What we wish to stress is that understanding the interrelationships of these four principles helps teachers teach. Using this instructional technique will remind you of the sequential nature of learning and thus help you incorporate appropriate learning experiences for each instructional objective. Figure 5.1 provides a visual model of the technique.

- - - - - - - - - - - - - - - -
Not a lockstep process

FIGURE 5.1
A Hierarchy for Student Success

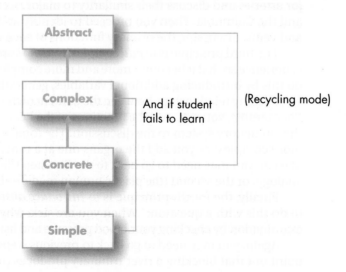

Example: Graphing   To illustrate the long-term nature of sequencing, let's examine a concrete example that was observed in the Pasco, Washington Public Schools by your authors. In the first grade, teachers introduce the concept of graphing. The overall goal is to provide a series of experiences through which the idea of graphing will emerge. The complete sequence of instruction, which includes all types and levels of difficulty of graphs, may take 10 years or more.

The sequence begins with a first-grade science lesson. The children plant bean seeds to study plant growth. The teacher raises the idea of regularly measuring the growth of the plants (say, every Friday). All plants are watered as uniformly as possible. As the seeds germinate, the teacher gives each child a strip of paper. The child places the paper next to the seedling and tears the strip to equal the height of the plant on the prescribed day. (This measuring technique uses a 1:1 scale, or one-to-one correspondence.)

Each child glues his or her strip to a large piece of paper, adding a date label. This process continues each week until the unit has been completed. The teacher asks the children to observe the changes in plant height, which are discussed. Everyone has a concrete graph of the changes over time—a simple histogram. The teacher encourages the class to discuss how they made the histograms and then introduces the concept of one-to-one correspondence.

Continuing the study of graphs at the next grade level, the second-grade teacher also uses histograms but makes them more complex. The teacher shows that if a dot is placed at the top of the piece of paper and scales are made (labeling the axes), all the information will be available in a form that is easier to use. This is reinforced with many examples during the second grade or maybe the third grade.

At the next grade level, the teacher provides other data, such as daily maximum temperatures and, later, minimum temperatures. The graphing concepts thus become more complex and abstract; yet these activities provide a concrete experience that the class shares. A possible culmination of this set of experiences would be to have the children obtain data of their own choosing and make graphs of them, providing foundational knowledge for research projects.

Obviously, not all concepts take the same amount of time to teach. In high school, it often takes only a few days to complete a unit. Still, it is often helpful to sequence lessons from simpler to more complex concepts, even in very short units. Each unit should illustrate the use of the principles described previously. Our main point is that you, the teacher, control the learning environment.

One concept can grow throughout the child's school career.

Reflect

◆ How does sequencing help bring together isolated pieces of information to form an organized body of knowledge?

◆ Why can you sequence the same content in more than one way?

◆ How has sequencing helped your learning processes? Do you remember teachers who were good at sequencing course activities?

◆ What is a concept from your own schooling that you continued to explore over many years? Think of one in any subject area. Make a list of the different ways you learned this concept over the years.

Content Forms

You want your students to understand both content and processes as well as the relationship between the two. **Content** is the information you want them to learn; *processes* are the thinking skills you want them to acquire (see Marzano 2004). For example, in a geography course, you want students to understand that there are different kinds of land forms, such as mountains, plateaus, and valleys, and to recognize the characteristics of each. The processes you want them to acquire will involve map-reading skills, reference skills, and information-gathering and organizing techniques. We focus on your instruction of skills and processes in Part 3, especially in Chapters 7, 8, and 9. In this section, we concentrate on content.

Content = information

Although terms may differ occasionally, educators agree that content exists in three primary forms: facts, concepts, and generalizations (see Figure 5.2).

Facts   The most fundamental piece of information is called a *fact*. A **fact** is a type of content that is singular in occurrence, occurs or exists in the present time, does not help you predict other facts, and is acquired solely through the process of observation. The following are examples of facts.

1. Olympia is the capital city of the state of Washington.
2. President George W. Bush was governor of the state of Texas.
3. The sun set at 4:15 P.M. today.

Because acquiring facts does not lead to predicting other facts, the primary means of learning facts is through memorization and recall. One of the most effective ways of learning facts is verbal repetition. It is also easier to remember facts that are related to other content. A program of studies built

FIGURE 5.2
Hierarchy of Content Forms

Generalizations Statements of relationships between two or more concepts, usually qualified to fit specific conditions. Developed through the processes of observation and inference.

Concepts A class of stimuli having common characteristics. Developed through the processes of observation and inference (categorizing).

Facts Isolated occurrences that can be observed but have no predictive value.

Facts are individual and specific.

on facts is at the lowest level of Bloom's taxonomy, knowledge (see Chapter 3). Facts are fundamental to learning, but learning is limited if teaching does not go beyond facts.

Concepts **Concepts** are expressions, usually consisting of one or two words, or ideas having common characteristics. We defined concepts in Chapter 4 as category words that we use to group objects as ideas. They are the result of the categorization of a number of observations. Forming concepts seems to be a natural process in the human brain. For example, young children form concepts of what cats and dogs are like based on their observations of these familiar animals. Children learn to differentiate dogs and cats because of the distinctive behavior of each species, the sound each produces, the distinctive shape of their heads, and perhaps some other characteristics. They do not rely on a single characteristic, such as size. Thus, for example, even though a particular cat may be larger than a particular dog, a child is able to tell the difference between them.

Concepts group and categorize.

Much of schooling consists of learning concepts. For example, in a beginning class on parts of speech, students learn that a noun is a "person, place, or thing." All concepts have the following five components.

1. *Name.* For example, *noun* is the name, or label, of a concept. When it is used, people who have learned the concept understand what is being communicated. The name is more efficient than a lengthy definition.
2. *Definition.* A definition is a statement about the concept's characteristics. For example, "a noun is a person, place, or thing."
3. *Characteristics.* Characteristics are qualities that must be present for the concept to apply. For example, the characteristics of a noun are "person, place, or thing." Only one of these must apply to a word for it to be considered a noun. For other concepts—for example, democracy—a number of characteristics must be present for the concept to apply.
4. *Examples.* Examples are members of a class of things that show a concept's essential characteristics. *Tom* is an example of a noun; so are *car* and *Iceland.*
5. *Place in a hierarchy.* Most concepts are part of a content hierarchy that gives meaning to the concept and makes it easier to learn. The content hierarchy for *noun* is parts of speech. Related, or coordinate, concepts to *noun* are *verb, adverb,* and *adjective.* Subordinate concepts are *common noun, proper noun,* and *pronoun.* In Section 2 of this chapter, you will learn about concept analysis, an approach for the sequencing of concepts. This approach will teach you to use all five components to develop lessons that will help your students learn and remember concepts.

Concept learning takes place at all grade levels. Birkili (2007) makes the case for a conceptually based curriculum in which facts are placed in a conceptual framework. Such a framework overcomes barriers to understanding threshold concepts and troublesome knowledge in science, accounting, economics and other disciplines at the college level (Meyer & Land 2006).

Generalizations As Chapter 4 explains, a **generalization** is an inferential statement that expresses a relationship between two or more concepts. It applies to more than one event and has predictive and explanatory value.

For example, "People who smoke have a higher incidence of lung cancer than those who don't" is a generalization. It states a relationship between smoking (a concept) and lung cancer (another concept). The statement is predictive and applies to anyone who smokes. A good example of the use of generalizations in teaching is given in James A. Banks's book *Teaching Strategies for Ethnic Studies* (2003). Banks presents the following generalizations about immigration and migration: "In all cultures, individuals and groups have moved to different regions in order to seek better economic, political and social opportunities. However, movements of individuals and groups have been both voluntary and forced" (p. 112).

Given this general statement, students would expect evidence of both forced and voluntary migration, regardless of the country being studied. Therefore, Banks's statement has predictive value and applies to more than one event. The statement also contains many concepts—*cultures; individuals and groups; economic, political, and social opportunities*; and *voluntary and forced*. The statement suggests relationships among these many concepts.

As students proceed from facts to concepts and then to generalizations, the amount of information increases and becomes more complex. Using Bloom's taxonomy, which Chapter 3 explains, facts are at the knowledge level, concepts are at the comprehension level, and generalizations are at the application and analysis levels. Students can recall facts, concepts, and generalizations, but facts and concepts are not adequate for application and analysis because neither has predictive nor explanatory value (Vasilyev 2003).

Facts are often confused with generalizations, but there are three important differences between them:

1. Generalizations are inferences that condense a large amount of data; facts are statements that are singular in occurrence. For example, the statement "Sunset occurs earlier every day between June 21 and December 21 in the Northern Hemisphere" is a generalization. "The sun set at 4:15 P.M. today" is a fact.

2. Facts are statements of events that occurred in the past or exist in the present, whereas generalizations are statements about general trends or patterns. For example, "Governors often choose to run for the U.S. presidency" is a generalization; "Ronald Reagan was governor of California before becoming president of the United States" is a fact.

3. Generalizations can be used to make predictions, whereas facts, because they are singular in occurrence, do not have predictive value. For example, "Studying enhances learning" is a generalization because it makes a prediction. By contrast, "Liza is studying for her calculus test" is a statement of fact because it does not predict Liza's performance.

Now let's look at two modes of presenting cognitive information that influence sequencing of activities within a lesson.

Modes of Presentation: Deductive and Inductive Reasoning

There are two basic modes of thinking: deductive reasoning and inductive reasoning. **Deductive reasoning** moves from the general to the specific; **inductive reasoning** proceeds from the specific to the general.

Generalizations have predictive value.

The primary modes of presentation are based on these modes of thinking. As a teacher, you have options: You can teach students a concept or a generalization by providing them with a definition followed by examples, or you can help students form the concepts or generalizations themselves based on observation or examples you provide. The type of reasoning you select will determine the sequence of lesson activities. The scenarios in the Instructional Strategies box below illustrate the different approaches.

Deductive: concept first; inductive: examples first

INSTRUCTIONAL *Strategies*

Modes of Lesson Presentation

Mode 1: Deductive Reasoning

Mr. Fisher began a lesson on magnetism by giving each student a handout. On the handout was this statement: "Magnets are attracted to some objects and not to others, and the things magnets are attracted to are called metals."

After a brief discussion regarding the concepts in the statement (such as *attraction*), Mr. Fisher asked, "Will a magnet pick up your textbook?"

"No," responded the class.

"Why not?"

"Because it is not a metal."

Mr. Fisher gave each student a magnet and asked the class to use their magnets on objects on their desks. The discussion continued.

Mode 2: Inductive Reasoning

Ms. Shamison wanted her students to understand magnetism. She began the lesson by handing out a magnet and an envelope to each student. In each envelope were objects—paper clips, plastic buttons, an iron nail, a penny, a plastic chip, an aluminum nail, a pencil. She asked the students to observe what happened when the magnet was applied to each object or other objects on their desks. After allowing a brief period of exploring, she called the class to order by saying, "Let's describe some observations you made about the magnet."

After a brief discussion that ranged from color and size of magnets to objects that were picked up by magnets, one of the students said, "It seems that magnets pick up some things but not others."

"Fine," said Ms. Shamison. "Let's organize what we have observed into lists. One list is for the objects that magnets pick up, and the other list is of those objects that magnets do not pick up."

After students made lists and discussed the characteristics of each object, Ms. Shamison asked, "Would someone summarize in statements what we have discovered?"

Angelica raised her hand and said, "We found that magnets pick up things that are called metals and do not pick up things like plastic and wood."

Both Mr. Fisher and Ms. Shamison would use graphic organizers or visuals, such as pictures, drawings, Venn diagrams, and student summaries. This technique keeps the topic in clear focus for the students.

Mr. Fisher and Ms. Shamison were teaching the same content, and both wanted their students to learn the same generalization: "Magnets attract objects made of metal." Additional similarities in their approaches are using magnets and examples and asking questions.

Everyone participates in an active learning environment.

© Ellen Senisi/The Image Works

However, there are major differences. Mr. Fisher initiated the activity with a generalization, whereas Ms. Shamison started the activity by asking students to make observations. The two examples illustrate the essential difference between inductive and deductive reasoning and how this difference influences sequencing within a lesson. They also illustrate that sequencing is influenced by things other than content, because the content was the same in both cases.

If a music teacher has an objective that students understand that the length of the string determines the sound, he or she can share the generalization with students and then have them hear strings of different lengths or play strings of different lengths and have students observe the pattern. In teaching the color wheel in an art class, the teacher can provide the concepts followed by a demonstration with paints or begin by providing paints and letting the students experiment and see if they develop the concepts. In both the inductive and deductive mode, the teacher uses examples as part of the instruction.

Your chosen mode of presentation is often determined by the lesson objectives. If you want your students to understand the process by which a generalization is formed, you may want to use the inductive approach. If your primary concern is only that your students know a particular concept or generalization, you may want to use the deductive approach. The mode of thinking you use is determined by the objective (Broeder & Murre 2000; Holyoak & Morrison 2005). The next section provides more examples of inductive and deductive teaching.

Which to use? Determined by learning objective.

Reflect

◆   What topics that you teach would be best taught by the various modes of instruction?

◆   Think about a movie, TV show, or book that you have seen or read involving detectives or investigators. What mental processes did these professionals use to solve the cases? Was their reasoning inductive or deductive?

SECTION 2 Models of Lesson Organization

Section 1 of this chapter discusses the following components of instructional planning: sequencing, content forms, and modes of presentation. In this section, we describe how these components are integrated into three models of lesson or unit organization: the *task analysis, concept analysis*, and *advance organizer* models.

Each model presents a guideline for sequencing objectives and activities and establishes a hierarchy or relationship of knowledge. Each model has unique characteristics that assist the teacher in selecting a planning model (see Table 5.1). Although each model has intrinsic strengths, no model is inherently superior. The teacher as a decision maker should choose the one that provides the greatest assistance in lesson planning, organizing, and implementing.

Each model of lesson organization has intrinsic strengths.

Task Analysis Model

VIDEO CASE

In the Video Case "Academic Diversity: Differentiated Instruction" on the student website, third-grade teacher Chris Colbath-Hess uses graphic organizers and task analysis in her writer's workshop for a heterogeneous classroom. As you watch the clips and study the artifacts in the case, reflect on the following questions: 1. What makes these approaches suitable for such a wide range of learners? 2. How does task analysis influence the sequencing of learning activities?

Consider the following common scenario: You have taught a lesson, and you assume that your students will be able to answer nearly all the questions you plan to ask on an examination covering that lesson. From all indications, your students enjoyed the lesson, and you anticipate no problems at assessment time. To your dismay, the class performs poorly on the examination. Was the test poorly constructed or was the instruction lacking? An incident similar to this happened to one of America's foremost learning theorists, Robert M. Gagné (Gagné, Wager, Golas, & Keller 2005). The lesson was in subtraction, but the content could have been high school chemistry, college calculus, English, physical education, or any subject at any level. What is important is that Gagné was not satisfied with the results and wanted to determine why his students had not performed as expected.

Task Analysis and Sequencing Gagné began to study the sequence in which his learning activities were planned. He concluded that some instructional

TABLE 5.1	Models of Lesson or Unit Organization
Model	**Primary Characteristics**
Task analysis	Careful sequencing of intermediate and terminal objectives
Concept analysis	Sequencing of concept characteristics or examples that relate to the concept or to a concept hierarchy
Advance organizer	Use of an "identical scaffold" to teach the interrelationships within an organized body of knowledge

- - - - - - - - - - - - - -

Task analysis breaks learning into steps.

elements should have preceded others and that some concepts he had omitted should have been introduced. This initial study led Gagné to rearrange some of the learning sequences and try the lesson again. The result was a dramatic change in student success as measured by test results.

Gagné arranged the concomitant learning experiences in his lesson in a chart (see Figure 5.3). The top of the chart contained the end of the instructional sequence, usually called the *terminal objective*. The terminal objective is what students should achieve after a series of planned instructional encounters (in this case, "subtract whole numbers of any size"). Below the terminal objective he listed the *intermediate objectives*. Until students master the basic skills (the bottom half of the chart), they probably will not

FIGURE 5.3

A Learning Hierarchy for Subtracting Whole Numbers

Source: From *Principles of Instructional Design*, 4th ed., by Robert M. Gagné and Walter W. Wager. Copyright © 1992 Wadsworth, a part of Cengage Learning, Inc. Reproduced by permission. www.cengage.com/permissions.

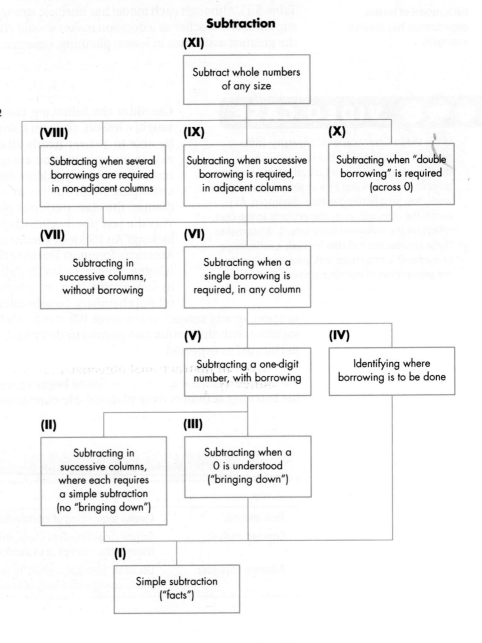

Subtraction

(XI) Subtract whole numbers of any size

(VIII) Subtracting when several borrowings are required in non-adjacent columns

(IX) Subtracting when successive borrowing is required, in adjacent columns

(X) Subtracting when "double borrowing" is required (across 0)

(VII) Subtracting in successive columns, without borrowing

(VI) Subtracting when a single borrowing is required, in any column

(V) Subtracting a one-digit number, with borrowing

(IV) Identifying where borrowing is to be done

(II) Subtracting in successive columns, where each requires a simple subtraction (no "bringing down")

(III) Subtracting when a 0 is understood ("bringing down")

(I) Simple subtraction ("facts")

be able to reach the learning objectives at the higher levels (the top half of the chart). In Figure 5.3, the Roman numerals refer to the order of presentation, and the lines illustrate the relationships between each cell.

Typically, a lesson on subtraction begins with "simple subtraction" (facts). As a teacher, you have two options. You can prepare activities that teach "simple subtraction," or, as we discussed in Chapter 4, you can first identify your students' entry skills with a brief test. The benefit of using a concept hierarchy chart is that, through testing, you can ensure that students have the requisite skills to be successful learners.

Test first to measure entry skills.

To study the effects of a hierarchical structure on learning, Gagné employed the **task analysis model**, which subdivides a lesson's content, concepts, or processes into smaller, sequential steps, beginning with the least complex and progressing to the most complex. This model has long proved valuable in business and industry. Careful sequencing of tasks has been and continues to be a critical element of efficient production in education, as it is in the industrial and technological sectors. You can imagine how chaotic and costly education would be if there were no grade levels and no methods for identifying the difficulty level of university courses. If you think your program of studies seems disorganized, think of the problems you would have if each piece of information you learned were taught in isolation and not as part of a course or if your courses had no titles or identifying numbers. You can arrange almost any set of facts, concepts, or generalizations into the Gagné system.

Organize learning tasks from simplest (subskills) to most complex (terminal objective).

Procedures for Task Analysis The major purpose of task analysis is to discover the interrelationships among subskills and to use this information to plan for effective instruction. **Enabling skills** are the facts, concepts, and processes that students must be taught before they can move on to the most complex skills or the target objectives. It may be unrealistic to assume that you, as a classroom teacher, will have the time or methodological expertise to identify and validate enabling skills empirically with the perceptiveness of Gagné's investigations, but you can effectively and efficiently use task analysis in your own teaching. The following procedures need to be accomplished to analyze learning tasks successfully.

1. **Select an instructional objective that is at the appropriate level of difficulty.** To make this initial determination, the teacher must know the structure of the content area (such as physics, health, education, mathematics, or social studies) and what the learner has already achieved.

   This step may seem obvious, but its importance is often overlooked. For example, teachers sometimes make statements such as "When students are in the ninth grade, they should read *Julius Caesar*" or "Seventh-graders should master percentages." Such curriculum decisions fail to identify where learners are located in the curriculum plan. For example, it makes little sense to teach students how to figure percentages if they do not first understand decimals—regardless of their grade level.

   Therefore, in selecting appropriate learning objectives, you need to identify the general area where your students' knowledge ends. This process is referred to as *diagnostic vigilance*. This is the point at which you should formulate new learning objectives and analyze the subskills that lead to the attainment of these objectives. The technique of diagnostic vigilance allows the teacher to check on whether the original objective is, in fact, at the right level of difficulty.

2. **Identify the enabling skills students need to attain the objective.** For example, in a physical education class, students are to be taught the golf skill of putting. Without regard to sequencing, the teacher lists the skills necessary for putting: gripping the club, maintaining the proper stance, positioning the club face correctly, using the appropriate amount of force, executing the backswing, following through, and mentally visualizing the ball's path.

3. **Subdivide independent and dependent enabling skills and learning sequences.** For any given objective, there are two basic types of enabling skills: independent and dependent. (Sometimes an objective requires both.) Learning these skills can be thought of in terms of sequencing: In an independent sequence, the enabling skills are not incremental. For example, when you learned to tie your shoes, it did not matter whether you started with the right or the left shoe. These activities are independent of each other. In the dependent sequence, on the other hand, accomplishment of one skill is essential before attainment of the next skill in the series. For example, when first learning to hit a baseball in T-ball, the coach demonstrates to the players how to hold the bat. The players learn how to swing followed by learning how to stand while swinging the bat. This practice allows the players to actually hit the ball off the tee. The successful hitting of the ball is dependent on the sequence of skills.

4. **Arrange the independent and dependent sequences in order.** Use this sequence to construct a lesson that will systematically facilitate the learning of the terminal objective. Once you have analyzed the objective and discovered its component parts (independent and dependent enabling skills or learning sequences), these parts will provide an entry point of learning for all students. The enabling skills themselves become objectives that you use to help students learn the terminal objective. As an example, let's return to the putting lesson. The teacher determines that the grip and stance are **independent skills** that can be learned in any order, but they should be mastered before the backswing and follow-through because you need to know how to grip the club and how to stand in order to practice these **dependent skills**. Because the grip and the stance are independent skills, the teacher may decide to teach the grip first because it may be easier to teach the stance when students are holding a golf club.

   It is doubtful that you will be able to identify all the prerequisite enabling skills before implementing a lesson and consistently emphasize the most important ones. As you teach, your judgment will allow you to adjust, to add other skills to the list, and to emphasize certain skills with particular students. Keep notes about such skills in your daily lesson plan book. These notes will be a handy reference for your next class.

5. **Sequence specific tasks for students.** Before you do this step, you must first plan the sequence in which you will conduct the class. As Chapters 3 and 4 explain, there are some tasks that you must accomplish every time you prepare and implement a lesson. You must (1) identify the instructional objectives; (2) plan the appropriate educational activities or experiences;

(3) obtain the materials; (4) plan the strategies that you will employ in the teaching act; (5) evaluate the students; and (6) develop a student assessment—that is, decide how you would improve the lesson. But now you need to establish the sequence or order in which specific dependent tasks will be taught. This sequencing plan ensures student success.

Task analysis is especially useful in planning instruction for children with special needs (Reigeluth & Beatty 2003), integrating topics in a multidisciplinary unit, and designing multicultural activities. As you identify each task, you can analyze it for content that is culturally biased, skills that are difficult for students with special physical or learning needs to accomplish, and skills and knowledge that were not covered previously. You might even be surprised to learn that a task analysis approach can be used to help students write better papers (Bailey 2001). In the same vein, task analysis principles are used for creating lesson plans (see Baylor et al. 2001). To identify commonalities and differences in word identifications between Chinese and Korean students in an English as a Second Language class, task analysis was used (Wang & Koda 2007). Also, task analysis is being used to identify grammatical features that are functional for particular kinds of writing tasks (Schleppegrell & Go 2007).

Task analysis ideal for special needs and ESL classes.

Susan Black (2001) uses an adaptation of task analysis in describing her "backward design" for key curriculum concepts, instructional activities, and planning. When introducing new material, you may find such an analysis beneficial for student understanding.

Example: Density   One of the authors of this text, a science educator, has observed that teachers often have difficulty teaching the concept of density. By observing student errors, he inferred that if the tasks associated with learning the concept of density were identified and structured, some of the problems could be reduced. Table 5.2 lists the various tasks or elements that are prerequisites to mastering the concept of density.

On examining Table 5.2 carefully, are you surprised at the number of operations and prerequisite skills that are needed to learn about density? Several teachers were, and so were we.

TABLE 5.2	Task Analysis for Teaching the Concept of Density
I.	Using the metric system A. Weight B. Linear measurements
II.	Understanding two-dimensional measurements: computing the area of a rectangle and a circle
III.	Computing volumes A. Rectangular objects B. Cylindrical objects C. Irregularly shaped objects 1. Those that float in water 2. Those that sink in water
IV.	Defining and using a "unit standard" A. Linear B. Volumetric
V.	Using mathematics skills A. Division B. Multiplication C. Linear equations ($a = b/c$)
VI.	Knowing that the mass of water in grams approximates the volume of water in cubic centimeters (cc)
VII.	Deriving that density is mass per unit of volume

Once this table was created, it became apparent that it is inappropriate to teach this concept before the seventh grade. Students simply do not have the necessary intellectual background until that time—and some may not have it until one year later.

As researchers and teachers, we often wonder why students cannot learn certain concepts or principles. The truth is that, in many cases, teachers have to revise even the order of the text pages students read so that the material is understandable. To maximize the benefits to the learner, you may have to sketch rough hierarchy charts for every chapter, unit, or module you teach. Thus it is beneficial to set aside a few minutes to prepare a task analysis chart for each new unit you plan.

When you observe student **learning deficits**, you can construct your own hierarchy chart to determine whether key elements of instruction are missing. No doubt other charting modifications can be devised using three techniques. Try your hand at creating such a chart for, say, a concept in English grammar, biology, mathematics, or social studies. We believe that if more teachers used this technique, teaching would improve immeasurably. Both teachers and students would be happier in school—and more successful!

When students can't learn, sequencing may be faulty.

Key Ideas **Analyzing Learning Tasks**

1. Select an appropriately difficult instructional objective.
2. Identify enabling skills.
3. Subdivide independent and dependent skills and sequences.
4. Arrange independent and dependent sequences in order.
5. Sequence specific tasks for students.

Reflect

◆ Examine a complex textbook in your area. To what extent is the content structured hierarchically?

◆ Why would you make the effort to use task analysis? What benefits would you expect to derive from it?

◆ Prepare a chart showing the relationships of various facts, concepts, and generalizations you have learned in previous education courses. Use the concept of dependent and independent sequencing.

Concept Analysis Model

Teaching Concepts   The teaching of concepts encompasses a substantial portion of all instruction. For example, science requires students to understand the concepts of systems, energy, plants, and animals; language arts applies the concepts of communication, paragraphs, parts of speech, and punctuation; mathematics requires students to apply the concepts of sets, commutative property, and inverse operations. A lengthy list could be compiled for every subject area.

When you teach concepts, you must use both sequencing and task analysis. As the example of the magnetism lesson illustrated, you have two sequencing options: (1) start the lesson by describing the concept and follow this with an analysis of characteristics (facts) and a series of illustrations or examples (facts) so that the students gain a thorough understanding of the concept, or (2) provide examples (facts) related to the concept and allow students to discover the concept themselves. As we observed earlier, when you start the lesson by defining the concept, you are teaching deductively; when you begin with examples and expect students to discover the concept, you are teaching inductively. In either instance, a procedure called "concept analysis" is helpful.

Example: Proper Nouns   For example, if you were teaching the concept *proper noun*, it would be helpful to develop a conceptual hierarchy of the content to illustrate the characteristics of the concept (show its uniqueness) and its relationship to the larger body of content covered by the course. An example of this kind of chart is shown in Figure 5.4.

A concept hierarchy provides the teacher with a sequencing technique. To teach the concept *proper noun*, for example, the teacher must demonstrate the characteristics that make a proper noun both "proper" and a "noun." Thus, the teacher provides examples that illustrate the characteristics of a proper noun—in this case, the names of two *persons*, Jim and Mary.

One way to describe the relationship of concepts formed using a concept hierarchy is in terms of *superordinate*, *coordinate*, and *subordinate* concepts. These terms refer not only to the scope of inclusiveness of a concept but also to its relationship to other concepts. For example, the concept of *parts of speech* is inclusive and subsumes the concept of *noun*, which in turn subsumes the concept of *proper*. In this respect, *proper* is a type of *noun*, which is a part of speech. Related concepts such as these form a hierarchy, or ordered arrangement.

In Figure 5.4, the concept *parts of speech* is superordinate to the concepts *noun, verb, adverb,* and *adjective.* The concepts *common, proper,* and *pronoun* are subordinate to the concept *noun.* The connection among the concepts *noun, verb, adverb,* and *adjective* is called a "coordinate relationship."

Describe how concepts relate to one another.

FIGURE 5.4
Concept Analysis

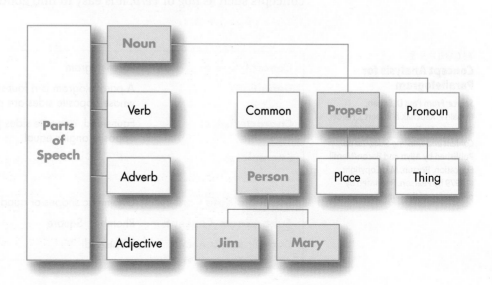

Analyzing Seven Dimensions   In preparing to teach a concept, the teacher must have a thorough understanding of that concept. A **concept analysis** is a thorough examination of the different aspects of a concept, which is described earlier in this chapter, plus the concept hierarchy. A concept analysis includes the following components: (1) concept name, (2) definition, (3) characteristics, (4) exemplars, (5) superordinate concepts, (6) subordinate concepts, and (7) coordinate concepts. Concept analysis is a planning tool that has proved valuable to teachers in structuring their concept-learning activities. Each dimension of concept learning describes a different and unique aspect of the concept. This process not only provides teachers with a thorough understanding of the concept to be taught but also can serve as a plan for instruction. An example of concept analysis for the concept "parallelogram" is provided in Figure 5.5, which shows each step.

In the second phase of teaching a concept, the teacher determines whether the lesson should be taught inductively or deductively. Should the students be given the concept and then be provided with examples of its characteristics, or should they be given examples from which to induce the concept? Whether the lesson is taught inductively or deductively, a thorough analysis of concept characteristics and examples is necessary. The concept analysis hierarchy is an excellent procedure for accomplishing this task.

Select inductive or deductive approach.

The teaching of concepts is often a prerequisite for the teaching of generalizations. For example, a civics teacher might want to use the generalization "Incumbents usually win elections" in a unit on politics. For students to understand this generalization, they must understand the concept *incumbent*. Although incumbents may be older or wealthier or even more experienced than challengers, these are not characteristics of the *concept* of incumbency. If the students don't correctly understand the concept, they will not correctly understand the generalization; they may think incumbents usually win because they are older rather than simply because they are incumbents.

One of the most effective methods for teaching concepts is the use of examples. In planning a lesson, the teacher must come up with enough examples to illustrate all the dominant characteristics adequately. For concrete concepts such as *dog* or *verb*, it is easy to find good examples. For concepts

FIGURE 5.5
Concept Analysis for Parallelogram

Source: From Paul D. Eggen, Donald P. Kauchak & Robert J. Harder, *Strategies for Teachers: Teaching Content and Thinking Skills,* 1st ed. Published by Allyn and Bacon/Merrill Education, Boston, MA. Copyright © 1979 by Pearson. Reprinted by permission of the publisher.

Concept Name:	Parallelogram
Definition:	A parallelogram is a four-sided geometric figure whose opposite sides are parallel.
Characteristics:	Four-sided, opposite sides parallel, opposite angles equal
Exemplars:	
Superordinate Concept:	Geometric shapes or quadrilaterals
Subordinate Concept:	Rhombus, Square
Coordinate Concept:	Trapezoid

such as *anger, justice,* or *poetic*, the teacher must spend considerable time developing good exemplars. Providing examples of coordinate concepts often helps students understand the characteristics of the concept being taught. For example, you might give the examples of *hostility, indignation*, and *wrath* to help students understand the concept *anger*. Negative examples (opposites) can also be used.

Advance Organizer Model

Teaching abstract and complex concepts such as *hate, bigotry, ecosystem, diversity*, and *democracy* can be a great challenge. Often students confuse such concepts. For example, many students believe that *democracy* and *capitalism* are the same concept, not realizing that one is a political concept and the other is an economic concept. The advance organizer model is an effective tool for teaching such concepts. This model is based on an **advance organizer**, which is a statement of those elements that the learner will be required to master in the lesson. It is designed to introduce the material that follows and it must be broad enough to encompass the information. You can use this model to compare *capitalism* to the coordinate concepts *socialism* and *communism*, for example. One of the model's primary purposes is to teach the relationships among such concepts by presenting the "big picture." Sometimes the advance organizer is a study guide, syllabus, or list. Often, it is a visual representation such as a chart.

Begin lessons with the big picture of what students will learn.

The advance organizer model is based on Ausubel's (1968) classic explication of deductive learning. The deductive mode of inquiry includes three basic components: advance organizers, content differentiation, and integration. It requires a body of knowledge that can be organized hierarchically. The purpose of the advance organizer model is to provide students with a structure so that they understand each part of the hierarchy of knowledge in the lesson as well as the relationships among the parts. The model consists of three phases: presenting the advance organizer, content differentiation, and integration.

Presenting the Advance Organizer   As an example of an advance organizer, let's use an English teacher who is starting a unit on metaphors, similes, and personification. This teacher would start the lesson with a *definition of* or *generalization about* figures of speech. The teacher might follow a simple hierarchy chart like the one shown in Figure 5.6.

FIGURE 5.6
Hierarchy Chart for Figures of Speech

If each student understands the advance organizer, it will provide a frame of reference for the lesson so that each part of the lesson can be more easily understood. The organizer enables the learner to relate the lesson materials to previous knowledge. The teacher's task is to develop an abstract statement that encompasses all aspects of the lesson and that the student can relate to previously learned material.

The teacher then has considerable latitude in organizing and developing the lesson. Therefore, two teachers using the same advance organizer may develop and teach the lesson differently. A practical note is helpful here: Record the advance organizer and brief hierarchy chart on a transparency or large sheet of paper. This allows students to refer to it throughout the lesson and thus provides direction and focus (see Forsten, Grant, & Hollas 2003; Lenz & Schumaker 2003).

Content Differentiation   After you have presented the advance organizer and are sure your students understand it, the second phase of the model begins. This phase, content differentiation, is the process by which the content is subdivided into narrower, less inclusive ideas, isolating each fact, concept, or generalization within a hierarchy of knowledge so that it can be learned independently. The English teacher can start a lesson on metaphors with the statement "A metaphor is one kind of figure of speech. The primary characteristics of a metaphor are . . ." The teacher has used a broad, abstract concept (*figure of speech*) and taken from it a narrower, more concrete concept (*metaphor*). Highlighting the unique and discrete characteristics of an element of information makes it easier to understand.

Content differentiation isolates each piece of knowledge.

Integration   The third component of the advance organizer model is **integration**, which is the process of teaching students how main concepts and underlying facts are related or how underlying facts are different or similar. In this phase, you make a deliberate attempt to help students understand similarities and differences among the components of the hierarchy of knowledge and to reconcile real or apparent inconsistencies between the ideas presented. In our English lesson example, the teacher makes certain that students understand the relationship between figures of speech and metaphors (one is a broad category to which the other belongs) and that they comprehend the differences and similarities between metaphors and similes (they are both in the same category). In most hierarchy charts (such as Figure 5.6), broader, more abstract, more inclusive concepts (in this instance, *figures of speech*) are placed above less inclusive, narrower concepts (*metaphors*). *Metaphors, similes,* and *personification* are on the same horizontal level. The terms *vertical integration* and *horizontal integration* describe the way students learn these relationships.

Integration shows relationships.

In summary, the advance organizer model is designed to teach organized bodies of content deductively (based on Ausubel's conception of deductive learning). The advance organizer provides the students with an overview and focus, content differentiation provides items of information that can be more easily understood, and integration provides meaningful learning by helping students understand the relationships among the elements of the content being taught. Ausubel gives you a tool that helps the learner connect the known with the unknown (see Gil-Garcia & Villegas 2003).

Key Ideas

Steps in the Advance Organizer Model

1. *Advance organizer.* Abstract introductory statement related to previously learned material that encompasses all aspects of the lesson. It defines and/or generalizes the information to be learned.

2. *Content differentiation.* Process of subdividing broad ideas into narrower, less inclusive ones.

3. *Integration.* Process of examining similarities and differences among related concepts.

The Steps in Interaction   Although the three components are presented as sequential, in reality they interact with one another (especially content differentiation and integration). If the comparison and differentiation discussion develops students' understanding of a specific concept or generalization, then the teacher should not hesitate to use the two steps concurrently. As with any teaching model, the teacher should use the model and its components in the way that most effectively helps his or her students learn. The model should be applied with flexibility and not become a straitjacket: It serves as a scaffold for learning, bridging the known with what is to be learned.

The three steps can be used flexibly, recursively.

Be careful not to confuse deductive teaching with lecturing. Often, lectures are neither deductive nor inductive. A deductive lesson can contain as much teacher-student or student-student interaction as an inductive lesson does. After presenting the advance organizer, the teacher can hold students responsible for content differentiation and integration by having them provide characteristics and examples and explain relationships (Ausubel 1968). In this instance, the teacher becomes the facilitator of the learning process, in much the same manner as in an inductive lesson. The following box provides a few suggestions for teaching deductive lessons.

Tips for Deductive Lessons

1. Have students verify an understanding of the advance organizer by providing examples, definitions, and characteristics.

2. During the content differentiation phase, involve the students by having them provide examples of the concepts or generalizations being taught.

3. Develop a chart that illustrates both the relationship among ideas and their uniqueness.

For the advance organizer model to work effectively, the teacher must prepare an advance organizer that provides students with an understandable focus for the lesson and a visual representation that illustrates the relationships among the information to be taught. When you bridge previous knowledge and materials to new learning, there are important achievement gains (see Marzano, Pickering, & Pollock 2001, p. 117). Also, advance organizers have been used successfully in a number of subject areas. For example, the use of diagrams as an advance organizer helped students learn bacterial metabolism in a science class (Barbosa, Marques, & Torres 2005); pictures were more effective than text as advanced organizers for learning Chinese in a language class (Wilberschied & Berman 2004); and static visual presentation of content was as effective as animation as an advance organizer (Lin & Dwyer 2004). If you use advance organizers systematically, along with continuous reviews and student summaries, your students will outperform others. Thus, this model is a valuable addition to your knowledge base of teaching.

Benefits of Graphic Organizers   Look back at the beginning of each chapter in this book. We use a graphic organizer called a "concept map" or "concept web." In this chapter alone, we use a variety of **graphic organizers** or, as they are often called, "nonlinguistic representations" to illustrate learning hierarchies, principles of sequencing, the list of items in a task analysis for density, and the concept analysis for parts of speech. As you read the text, you will observe others that we incorporate with the written text. The box below lists several common graphic organizers. Graphic organizers can be extremely helpful at the beginning of the advance organizer process, when you define the material to be learned.

Graphic organizers go beyond words to include shapes, pictures, structures.

Examples of Graphic Organizers

- ◆ Historical time lines
- ◆ Flowcharts
- ◆ Bar graphs
- ◆ Pie graphs
- ◆ Networks
- ◆ Taxonomic keys
- ◆ Tables
- ◆ Continuum scales
- ◆ Family trees
- ◆ Venn diagrams
- ◆ Cyclic diagrams
- ◆ Content outlines

For an example of several different versions of graphic organizers, we suggest the extensive set at Houghton Mifflin Harcourt's eduplace website (http://www .eduplace.com/graphicorganizer/).

Many researchers have verified the effectiveness of graphic organizers for students at all grade levels. The use of concept maps shows promise in determining whether students relate prior knowledge more efficiently and thus expedite current learning (Dochy & Alexander 1995). Concept maps have a long history of helping students absorb content at higher levels, from kindergarten to the university (see Chang, Sung, & Chen 2001; Chase, Franson, & An 2001; Gallavan & Kottler 2007; Stephans & Hermus 2007; Sungur, Tekkaya, & Geban 2001).

Graphic organizers expedite and focus student learning.

Other types of graphic organizers, such as pictures, have enhanced student learning in geography (Fitzhugh 1995) and in science (Tippett 2003). Explicit graphic organizers facilitated information retrieval processes (Dennis 2003). The use of graphic organizers in elementary classrooms helped students to make significant writing progress. Significant student improvements were reported in fourth-grade writing test scores when different forms of concept maps were used when presenting instruction (Hyerle 1995–1996). In learning 32 German-English word pairs, the groups that were given bilingual organizers did better on the exam than the group that received only the list (Bahr & Dansereau 2005). The addition of graphic organizers improved student learning in secondary algebra instruction for students with learning disabilities (Ives 2007). In reading, graphic organizers that reflect text structure were found to be effective (Jiang & Grabe 2007). Using nonlinguistic representations is a must when teaching an inclusive classroom (Baxendell 2003). By using graphic organizers in your teaching, you may help your students reach a level of understanding they would not reach without the organizers (see Calhoun & Haley 2003; Capretz, Ricker, & Sasak 2003).

Each group of students, because its members have different experiences and levels of maturity, provides a different challenge to the teacher. Every discipline has different types of learning problems. Mathematics is very different from social studies or English.

Graphic organizers are *right-brain hemisphere–related*, a topic that is discussed in Section 3 of this chapter. Thus, while you stress left-brain hemisphere content or processes, you reinforce the learning by using techniques that incorporate right-brain hemisphere learning. Graphic organizers provide an instructional double whammy.

Teach your students how to use graphic organizers as they study for your lessons. You can use them as advance organizers, or students can make their own as they work. Their use provides another way to enrich the classroom environment, especially for disabled learners (Eden, Wood, & Stein 2003).

Teach students to use graphic organizers too.

INSTRUCTIONAL
Strategies

Teaching the Concepts of Government

This is a lesson on government and the concepts associated with it. The class has already studied basic forms of government; the current topic is the functions of government. To understand how government functions, the students need to understand the relationship of government to other societal institutions. The teacher might introduce the lesson with the following advance organizer.

> Government is but one of the institutions serving society. The state or government is essential to civilization, yet it cannot do the whole job by itself. Many human needs are met by the home, the church, the press, and private business.

With the presentation of the advance organizer, the teacher is ready to proceed with the content differentiation component of the lesson. He or she makes materials available to students so that they may begin their investigations into human needs that are met by different institutions. First, the teacher and the class prepare a list of different problems that can be studied. As an alternative, they might list steps they could take to identify areas in which various institutions serve society and in which institutional functions overlap. Functions that are not covered by any institution would also be listed. As the students gather material and present it to the class, the teacher leads them in the content differentiation and integration processes. The result is an interactive, deductive lesson.

Because graphic organizers have a positive impact on student achievement, we stress their use. For example, using them along with other interactive teaching methods helps increase reading comprehension (Bowman, Carpenter, & Paone 1998). Likewise, teachers report increased comprehension in K–8 schools when graphic organizers are appropriately used (Culbert et al. 1998). Ron Ritchhart and David Perkins (2008) describe a wide variety of graphic organizers that aid both teaching and learning by making "thinking" visible.

Adapt the instructional planning models presented in this chapter for specific teaching situations. Perhaps the one valid generalization that can be made about planning is that, more often than not, teachers assume students have the prerequisite knowledge when in fact they do not. Some students may have already mastered the intended lesson, whereas other students in the same class do not have the requisite experiences and academic background for success.

TECHNOLOGY *Insight*

Digital Graphic Organizer and Flowchart Tools

Graphic organizers such as diagrams, webs, matrixes, and flowcharts can help you visualize and explain your thoughts as you arrange large amounts of information, which is a critically important part of sequencing and organizing information. Graphic organization software can be a tremendous help in this process. Unlike drawing with pencil-and-paper, computer-based graphic organizers can be easily changed and re-arranged.

Perhaps the most popular education-based graphic organizer software available is Inspiration (a free trial version is available at http://www.inspiration.com/freetrial/index.cfm). A popular Web-based graphic organizer tool is Gliffy (http://www.gliffy.com/), which also offers a free trial.

Reflect

◆ How is the relationship between ideas illustrated by content differentiation and integration?

◆ Think about a time you taught something to a child, either within or apart from your teacher training. Did you teach it inductively or deductively?

◆ Would it be possible to teach the same thing the opposite way? Is there any way to change the experience so that the child is more involved?

◆ What graphic organizers from the list could you use to present concepts in your teaching field?

SECTION 3   Multi-Methodology as an Instructional Process

We begin this section on instructional multi-methodology by briefly introducing three theories that support our thesis of providing an instructionally rich teaching repertoire. The first topic relates to the functions of the right- and left-brain hemispheres in information processing; the second to learning preferences; and the third to multiple intelligences. With those points as your advance organizer, we'll fully develop the idea of multi-methodology.

Hemisphericity: Functions of the Right and Left Brains

Over the past several decades, a major theory about how the brain works, called *hemisphericity*, has given teachers another tool to use in planning instructional experiences. **Hemisphericity** is the study of where in the brain—in the left hemisphere or the right hemisphere—different types of mental functions occur. Research suggests that the right cerebral hemisphere is involved in visual, nonverbal, spatial, divergent, and intuitive thinking. The left cerebral hemisphere is involved in verbal, logical, categorical, detail-oriented, and convergent thinking. The right brain works more with approximations and creativity, whereas the left brain works more with specifics and analysis. For example, the right side of the brain processes the visual information that allows you to recognize a face, but the left side provides the name to go with the face.

Implications for Teaching　The facts that allow us to understand the kinds of functions that occur on each side of the brain are important because they help educators understand that instruction must be planned to enhance the use of both hemispheres. Research conducted over many years has demonstrated that teachers persistently emphasize objectives and instruction that focus on the left side of the brain. The vast majority of objectives focus on the cognitive, analytical, and convergent (i.e., focusing in) functions dominated by the left side of the brain (Caine & Caine 1997; Given 2002; Jensen 2005; Sylwester 2007). Because the literature in most subject areas is cognitive and analytical, even our library collections tend to favor the left brain (Farmer 2004). For example, books are mostly a print medium. However, in science books, the addition of pictures, diagrams, and flowcharts can help one to "see" the content.

Research also tells us that, although each side of the brain tends to emphasize a specific kind of function, the most productive intellectual functioning occurs when both sides of the brain cooperate. Learning exercises that are focused on the left side of the brain (the majority of the learning objectives and instructional experiences we plan for students) are enhanced when the right side of the brain is included in the experience. By largely ignoring the right-side functions of the brain in devising instructional experiences, we have also limited the effectiveness of left-side functions in students' learning. To teach most effectively to either side of the brain, we must balance outcomes and learning experiences to involve *both* sides whenever possible (Baker & Martin 1998; Eden, Wood, & Stein 2003).

Including Creativity in Instructional Plans　It is important to plan learning experiences that use the right side of the brain, but a brief caution applies. Because objectives or outcomes for the right side of the brain emphasize creative functions, the criterion of any outcome for the right side of the brain can be difficult to write. By their nature, the more creative functions of the brain are less measurable in terms of quantity and quality. For example, suppose you assign your students the problem of designing a novel use for plastic soda pop bottles. How do you define an objective for such an assignment? How do you quantify or define creativity? If you remember that effective instruction includes a balance between left- and right-brain emphasis, you will have taken care of most of your problem. A musically inclined student may use the bottles to develop

Left = logical, right = creative

an instrument by filling the bottles with different levels of water or some other material. An art student could construct a sculpture to look like an animal, or a student interested in insects could develop a collection display. One of the benefits of this activity is that fellow students are able to observe creativity in action. Objectives are not presented in isolation; rather, as this chapter shows, they are presented as sequences of expectations that lead to a general outcome. If you write carefully constructed objectives that allow students to master left-brain activities, you can also construct a framework to define and assess right-brain objectives so that they are part of the whole sequence of learning. Such a framework could resemble the Kaplan matrix (see Chapter 4). We offer in the box below a brief sample of objectives that emphasize right-brain functions.

Incorporate both left- and right-brain activities in objectives.

Right-Hemisphere Objectives

1. Using only a pencil and a blank sheet of paper, draw a sketch of a fellow class member that is recognizable by the majority of the class.

2. Presented with 10 objects of different sizes, shapes, and textures, develop a scheme that will enable another person to classify all 10 objects using only the senses.

3. Given a story starter, create a short story in which all the physical elements of the story starter are incorporated into the plot.

4. Using only the three primary colors, create a painting that includes all the elements of the modern style.

5. Using the computer simulation "The Oregon Trail" as a model, construct a simulation for travel from an earth-orbit space station to the moon that adheres to the physical principles regulating movement in an airless and weightless environment.

Do not assume that stressing right-hemisphere activities automatically enhances creativity. No clear evidence supports that a close relationship between creativity and brain hemispheres exists (Hines 1991). Hemispheric differences tend to be relative rather than absolute, and implications for schooling may yet be speculative (Hellige 1988). We strongly suggest that you study Robert Sylwester's *The Adolescent Brain: Reaching for Autonomy* (2007). He provides an excellent overview of how the brain functions.

There is considerable interest in and controversy about brain-based education (Bruer 1999; Weiss 2000; Winters 2001). Experimentation with brain-based strategies shows promise (Erlauer 2003; Myrah & Erlauer 1999). Although neuroscience has much to offer teaching and learning conceptualization, it is rather new, and educators must be cautious about applying lab research prematurely (Jensen 2000). Further, application of these findings takes considerable study and practice, so the topic is an excellent one for your lifelong learning.

Reflect

◆ Prepare a lesson plan that includes right-brain student activities.

◆ Examine a set of textbooks or computer programs for your intended grade level. What hemisphericity traits do you recognize?

◆ Obtain a set of your state's standards for any curricular area. Apply the test of hemisphericity to those standards.

Voices from the Classroom

Lisa K. Cartwright,

Franklin Elementary School,

Pullman, Washington

Employing Multi-Methodology

As a 15-year veteran of the classroom, I find it surprising that good teaching practice is still difficult to come by. With experience, lesson design becomes easier—more creative and flexible. Focus and effort shifts to learning equity; that is, is every child in my classroom able to access the learning and show me that they've done so?

True child-centered teaching creates a learning environment in which each student in a classroom *will* learn and develop, moving, in a sense, from her or his individual Point A to Point B. As the teacher, I provide the learning objectives, and I work toward helping each student attain those Point Bs. Many students will work beyond expectations, but it is my duty to see that all students reach the basic objectives for each and every lesson.

Creating a context within which such learning can take place is more difficult than one would think. Good teaching includes multiple avenues through which children can learn. Multi-methodology, therefore, is critical to the success of a child-centered classroom. I plan lessons with learning preferences, multiple intelligences, and right- and left-brain hemispheres in mind. I want students to be able to show me what they're learning in multiple ways; learning avenues are active, process-oriented, and often technological.

It follows, then, that I also assess using multiple methods. This is the most important component of true child-centered teaching, and the hardest to accomplish. It often means augmenting traditional pencil/paper assessment techniques and allowing children to show what they know in a variety of ways. I use a combination of assessment tools, feeling that this gives me a good snapshot of what each student has learned. In the end, I feel satisfied that, for every child, I have taught and assessed to the best of my ability.

Diversity and Learning Styles

No two people think exactly alike, and it is safe to say that no two people learn in exactly the same way either. Teachers respond to this diversity in a number of ways, one of the most prevalent being grouping (Slavin 2003). At the elementary level, grouping often means dividing classes into subgroups on the basis of students' skills and abilities, particularly in math and reading. At the high school level, grouping often results in tracks, with the curriculum in each track aimed at different educational and vocational goals. But students differ in other, more subtle ways than aptitude and ability. In this section, we consider some factors that may have a positive or negative effect on student learning; then we present a few techniques you can use to accommodate individual learning styles. A major challenge for teachers is to recognize and be sensitive to the wide range of diversity of students within any classroom. In addition to a wide range of ability, students come from families with a wide range of economic resources, varying religious beliefs, and a variety of cultural backgrounds.

Students' cultural backgrounds and experiences influence how they understand new material and how

◀◀ ▶ ▶▶ **VIDEO CASE**

The Video Case "Culturally Responsive Teaching: A Multicultural Lesson for Elementary Students" on the student website shows a literacy specialist working on a writing project in which students describe their cultural origins. As you watch the clips and study the artifacts in the case, reflect on the following questions: 1. How does this project reflect the principles of culturally responsive teaching described here? 2. Dr. Hurley, the literacy specialist, advises new teachers to learn more about the world than they already know. How can you go about acquiring more knowledge of the world and its people?

they respond to, and benefit from, instruction. Differences in background, experience, socioeconomic status, culture, and language all influence learning (Banks & Banks 2004). For example, teachers who move from a rural setting to a big-city school will find that they need to adapt how they teach. A question to first-graders about where milk comes from may elicit one response from rural kids (cows) and a completely different one from suburban or inner-city kids (the store).

Societal differences affect learning.

Educators have recognized the impact of experiential and cultural differences on student success for some time (Cushner, McClelland, & Safford 2003), and most teacher education programs contain courses or units on multiculturalism to help teachers become sensitive to the powerful effect of background experiences (see Knapp & Woolverton 2004 for a detailed discussion). But, more recently, considerable attention has been focused on other, less apparent dimensions of individual differences. Retention of word spelling was higher one week after instruction when teaching style matched the learning style of students (Slack & Norwich 2007).

Researchers in this area have termed this dimension "learning style" and have developed instructional programs to meet the needs of different groups of students. **Learning style** or preference is usually defined as the cognitive, affective, and physiological traits that learners exhibit as they interact in the classroom environment. Students with different learning styles understand problems in different ways, and they tend to try to solve them in different ways.

Different ways of problem solving

Yet not all scholars believe that an understanding of learning styles improves instruction. Some research shows that there is little evidence that understanding one's learning style improves learning (Dembo & Howard 2007).

At this point you might be saying to yourself, "Hey, this is very close to schema theory, which we studied in psychology." In one sense it is. As students of any age or learning style study something, they fit what they learn into a meaningful pattern, or schema. When students are introduced to a new concept, their schema for it might be disorganized, irrational, or just plain wrong. Such a schema obviously will hinder learning. Similarly, in terms of learning styles, students' individual and environmental attributes can help or hinder learning (see Wilson 1996).

Researchers and advocates in the area of learning styles think of these styles as being on the borderline between mental abilities and personality. Learning styles fall between these two areas and are the individual's preferred way to learn new skills, knowledge, or techniques (see Sternberg 1997). The remainder of this chapter illustrates how to accommodate all students by using a diverse array of teaching styles.

Multiple Intelligences

There are at least three key findings about human intelligence that are related to our current discussion. First, intelligence is a dynamic quality not fixed at birth. Second, through appropriate learning experiences, intelligence can be enhanced. Third, intelligence has many different attributes (Gardner 1993). The latter finding is the key element for instructional planning and sequencing;

 VIDEO CASE

Before viewing the Video Case "Multiple Intelligences: Elementary School Instruction" on the student website, make a list of Gardner's eight intelligences on a sheet of paper. Now watch teacher Frederick Park engage students' multiple intelligences in writing about the *Mayflower*. As you watch the clips and study the artifacts in the case, answer the following questions: 1. What examples did you find of each intelligence? 2. Did some of the students exhibit more than one intelligence?

that is, intelligence has multiple facets, rather than being associated only with verbal or quantitative aptitudes. This notion has led to an idea called **multiple intelligences**. The chief proponent of the concept of multiple intelligences is Howard Gardner (1985, 1991, 1999a, 1999b, 2006). Gardner's work is applicable in the school setting because of its ease of use for planning. He identifies eight basic intelligences, but in recent publications he has tentatively suggested that there may be a ninth: existential intelligence. For our discussion we will use the original eight that are listed in the box below.

Intelligence can take many forms.

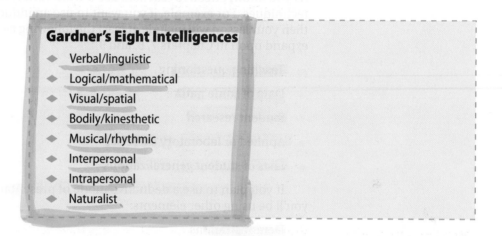

Gardner's Eight Intelligences

- Verbal/linguistic
- Logical/mathematical
- Visual/spatial
- Bodily/kinesthetic
- Musical/rhythmic
- Interpersonal
- Intrapersonal
- Naturalist

Gardner asserts that we all possess these eight intelligences, but schools tend to develop only the first two to any extent. As a consequence, six areas of intelligence are consciously depressed (discriminated against) by schooling. Many teachers find the theory of multiple intelligences appealing because it provides them with a logical system for planning. A pilot study at Glendale Community College incorporated Gardner's multiple intelligences in 10 psychology classes over a two-year period, and the study has been expanded to include other studies (Diaz-Lefebure 2006). Two teachers used multiple intelligence theory to teach little-known facts about slugs with success (Delaney & Shafer 2007). Educators argue that teachers should learn more about Gardner's multiple intelligence theory and use it (Aborn 2006; Beliavsky 2006). Other educators accept and use multiple intelligence theory for research studies (Al-Balushi 2006; Fuhrman & Bunclark 2006; Yuen & Furhrman 2005). The notion of treating these multiple intelligences as learning styles may cause educational psychologists to shudder because there are so many different variables to control.

A common criticism of multiple intelligence theory is that there is no pre-post, longitudinal empirical research to support Gardner's concept of multiple intelligences and it is not consistent with cognitive neuroscience (Waterhouse 2006). Larry Cuban (2004), a scholar of school innovations, notes that multiple intelligence theory usually is not really implemented in classrooms. It is with caution that we close this section because there is a problem finding empirical evidence that clearly substantiates the concept of multiple intelligences. As we noted above these eight items do provide a hint to teachers on how to provide a wide array of activities or formats to conduct

Plan for more than verbal/ linguistic intelligences.

classroom instruction (see Visser, Ashton, & Vernon 2006a, 2006b). We believe it is helpful for teachers to at least make themselves aware of these different intelligences and structure class activities to accommodate some of the intelligences as appropriate to provide multi-methodological experiences for their students (Marzano et al. 2001; Stanford 2003).

Varying Your Teaching Techniques

As you know, effective teachers use a wide variety of teaching methods and techniques. For example, if you want to use an inductive presentation mode, then your lesson will include at least the following elements (which we greatly expand upon in Chapters 7, 8, and 9):

- Teaching questioning
- Data of some nature
- Student research
- Applied or laboratory exercises
- Lists of student generalizations

If you plan to use a deductive mode of presentation for some topic, then you'll be using other elements:

- Demonstrations
- Videos or films
- Student activities
- Guest speakers
- Assigned readings
- Student reports

Obviously, the range of instructional strategies that you can use in the classroom is limitless (Tate 2003). We urge you to start by planning your objectives or *what to teach* and then planning *how to teach it*. By varying your weekly calendar of activities, you will accommodate the spectrum of individual learning differences in your classroom (see Lazear 2003). By using multi-methodology, you will not get stuck in the usual rut. If you have to lecture, then break it up with activities, questions, or student-elicited summaries every 10 minutes. Keep the focus on the content, but vary the pace and the instructional method of the lesson. If you adopt the concept of multi-methodology, you'll have an instructionally rich classroom environment. (See Marzano, Pickering, & Pollock 2001 for a detailed discussion of effect sizes computed for various instructional methods.) Just remember that in your first year of teaching you will have some great days during which the students are engaged and enjoy learning. There will be other days during which you feel students are not learning and seem to be out of touch. It could be that the strategy you selected was not appropriate for learning on that bad day and was very appropriate on the day that was a success. Yet these different days may be caused by conditions such as weather or school activities, such as sports tournaments, over

Break up lecturing with other methods.

VIDEO CASE

You can find a true story about the challenges and excitements of teaching in the Video Case entitled "The First Year of Teaching: One Colleague's Story" on the student website. In this case, watch Will Starner talk about his initial year in the classroom. "I've had a lot of situations that I really didn't know would come up," he says. In the Bonus Video, "Mr. Starner Reflects on the First Year of Teaching," he mentions that he had "all these different theories running through my head," and it felt overwhelming to select the best approach to fit the context. As you watch the clips and study the artifacts in the case, reflect on the following questions: 1. What are the main challenges he identifies? 2. What ways did he find to cope with these difficulties? 3. Discuss your reaction to his candid description of his first year of teaching. 4. What are the attributes that you think make him potentially a very successful teacher?

which you have no control. Your task is find the "key" to turn on those student minds.

Teachers often feel compelled to "cover all the materials," but this is not a function of any style. One young middle school student made a profound observation: "Kids never really get to do anything with new school learning, except just get more of it." Textbooks set the pace for most teachers and learners, the Internet notwithstanding. But you will probably supplement the text with short presentations or demonstrations that provide students with missing skills or background information. One last note: Beverly Hill (2005) observes that with high-stakes testing as the current norm, children who have a learning style or preference that is different from the test formats may be at great risk of failure. She suggests examining the structure of any test so you can help your students succeed.

You have been introduced to instructional sequencing, organizing, and multi-methodology, but to use them appropriately, you will need additional training and classroom experiences in the specifics. Difficult and challenging instructional concepts can be taught and understood if you structure your lessons to be intentionally inviting to learners. Once you are able to sequence major blocks of information while keeping in mind all the differences in your students' learning and abilities, you will be able to implement any planning or learning model. Visit our website at www.cengage.com/education/orlich for data reflecting the instructional effectiveness (effect size) of advance organizers, cues, graphic organizers, and task analysis.

Reflect

A Closing Reflection

◆ Using one of the modes of reasoning (inductive or deductive), outline how you would teach one major concept in your teaching area.

◆ Select one major concept that is not usually taught but that you feel is important. Create a set of advance organizers and a hierarchy chart for it.

◆ How can task analysis be used to plan a daily lesson? Draft a list of steps for a lesson, beginning with a test to measure entry skills.

◆ Design a lesson that incorporates a concept with graphic organizers.

◆ To what extent have you seen or been exposed to the concepts of learning styles, multiple intelligences, and multi-methodology? How has it affected your teaching philosophy so far?

◆ Which of the multiple intelligences on Gardner's list are your strongest? Imagine that you are the teacher of a student very much like you. What activities and approaches would you use for this student?

Summary Points

1. Sequencing instructional activities provides a ladder for student success.
2. Facts, concepts, and generalizations form the basis of most content.
3. Inductive modes of presentation lead the student to generalizations by providing specifics first.
4. Deductive modes of presentation begin with a generalization and follow with specific points.
5. Task analysis allows you to determine what components of more complex instruction are needed for student success.
6. Sequencing isolated tasks provides a meaningful or logical pathway for student success.
7. Hierarchy charts and graphic organizers help teachers plan and students learn.
8. Advance organizers provide students with an instructional map of what is to be learned.
9. Teachers need to plan instruction to incorporate both right- and left-brain activities.
10. Planning, organizing, and sequencing instruction are fluid and flexible processes, not static ones.
11. Graphic organizers are intentionally inviting.
12. Multi-methodology is a planning tool that accommodates individual intelligences and learning styles.

Building a Career Portfolio

◆ As we have noted, it is our desire to provide you with a set of ready-to-adapt strategies as you head for your first real classroom teaching experience. A portfolio that has a "good teaching practices" section will be a valuable tool as you prepare for teaching practicums, student teaching, job interviews, and your first teaching position. Books and journals are good sources, but the best source is a successful teacher. Fortunately, most successful teachers like to share teaching strategies and techniques, and many will also share instructional materials. Listed below are several suggestions on how to get started collecting examples of good teaching practices. Visit three consecutive classes taught by several successful teachers, then answer the following questions.

(a) Is each lesson exactly the same? What are the differences?
(b) Do the teachers use the same strategies and techniques? What are the similarities and differences?
(c) Describe a successful teacher.

◆ Ask your peers to describe their favorite teacher in college, high school, middle school, and elementary school.

(a) Are there common characteristics regardless of grade level or subject?
(b) Was planning an important characteristic?
(c) How important were the strategies and techniques used?

(continued)

◆ Describe your basic teaching model.
  (a) Are you primarily deductive or inductive?
  (b) How important is sequencing?
  (c) How do you accommodate student diversity?
  (d) Do you use task analysis or concept analysis?

Resources

PRINT

Hyerle, D. *A Field Guide to Using Visual Tools.* Alexandria, VA: Association for Supervision and Curriculum Development, 2000, 147 pp.
This small book presents information on and examples of many graphic organizers. It's one for your professional library.

Irvine, J. J., & D. E. York. "Learning Styles and Culturally Diverse Students: A Literature Review." In *Handbook of Research on Multicultural Education.* J. A. Banks and C. A. McGee Banks, Eds. San Francisco: Jossey-Bass, 2001, pp. 484–497.
This singular chapter on the learning styles of culturally diverse students is mandatory reading and discussion by both students and instructors in any instructional methods course. The authors illustrate the complexity of the entire concept of styles and enumerate the "preferences" of African American, Hispanic, and Native American students. There is a note of caution about over-generalizing.

Schwarz, P., & P. Kluth. *You're Welcome: Differential Instruction in the Inclusive Classroom.* Portsmouth, NH: Heinemann, 2007.
Three handbooks are provided, with each containing 10 ideas for understanding and supporting diverse learners. Ideas include classroom structures, instructional strategies, and lesson examples.

Sylwester, R. *The Adolescent Brain: Reaching for Autonomy.* Thousand Oaks, CA: 2007, 176 pp.
With little technical jargon, the author shows how to engage adolescents for more effective personal interactions. He suggests how to mentor this group of students and discusses issues critical to teenagers.

INTERNET

Go to the website for this book at www.cengage.com/education/orlich to find live links to resources related to this chapter.

◆ A comprehensive website about learning styles is offered by the Island Adult Development Association of Victoria, British Columbia, Canada. Included are six broad categories, including multiple intelligences.
  http://www.ldpride.net

◆ Teacher Tap provides an excellent rationale for using graphic organizers. The site provides many examples of using graphic organizers for all grade levels and subject areas.
  eduscapes.com/tap/topic73.htm

◆ Web 2 includes generalizations from research, example activities, recommendations and ideas, and a list of Web 2.0 connections. A great comprehensive overview for advance organizers.
Web2that works.com/index.php

References

Aborn, M. (2006). "An Intelligent Use for Belief." *Education 127*(1): 83–85.

Al-Balushi, S. M. (2006, July). "Enhancing Multiple Intelligences in Children Who Are Blind, A Guide to Improving Curricular Activities." ICEVI World Conference, Kuala Lumpur. ED493 516.

Ausubel, D. P. (1968). *Educational Psychology: A Cognitive View*. New York: Holt, Rinehart & Winston.

Bahr, G. S., & D. F. Dansereau. (2005). "Bilingual Knowledge Maps as a Presentation Format: Delayed Recall and Training Effects." *Journal of Experimental Education 73*(2): 101–118.

Bailey, V. (2001). "The Writing Trek." *TechTrends 45*(2): 14–15.

Baker, J. C., & F. G. Martin. (1998). *A Neural Network Guide to Teaching* (Fastback 431). Bloomington, IN: Phi Delta Kappa Education Foundation.

Banks, J. A. (2003). *Teaching Strategies for Ethnic Studies* (7th ed.). Boston: Allyn and Bacon.

Banks, J. A., & C. A. McGee Banks, Eds. (2004). *Handbook of Research on Multicultural Education* (2nd ed.). San Francisco: Jossey-Bass.

Barbosa, H. R., M. V. Marques, & B. B. Torres. (2005). "Advance Organizer for Teaching Bacterial Metabolism." *Biochemistry and Molecular Biology Education 33*(4): 265–268.

Baxendell, B. W. (2003). "Consistent, Coherent, Creative: The 3 C's of Graphic Organizers." *Teaching Exceptional Children 35*(3): 46–53.

Baylor, A., A. Kitsantas, & H. Chung. (2001). "The Instructional Planning Self-Reflective Tool: A Method for Promoting Effective Lesson Planning." *Educational Technology 41*(2): 56–59.

Beliavsky, N. (2006). "Revisiting Vygotsky and Gardner, Realizing Human Potential." *Journal of Aesthetic Education 40*(2): 1–11.

Birkili, M. (2007). "Making the Case for a Conceptually Based Curriculum in Early Childhood Education." *Early Childhood Education Journal 35*(2): 141–147.

Black, S. (2001). "Stretching Students' Minds." *American School Board Journal 188*(6): 31–33.

Bowman, L. A., J. Carpenter, & R. A. Paone. (1998). *Using Graphic Organizers, Cooperative Learning Groups, and Higher Order Thinking Skills to Improve Reading Comprehension*. Unpublished Action Research Project. Chicago: Saint Xavier University. ED 420 842.

Broeder, P., & J. Murre, Editors. (2000). *Models of Language Acquisition: Inductive and Deductive Approaches*. New York: Oxford.

Bruer, J. T. (1999). "In Search of . . . Brain-Based Education." *Phi Delta Kappan 80*(9): 648–654.

Caine, R. M., & G. Caine. (1997). *Education on the Edge of Possibility*. Alexandria, VA: Association for Supervision and Curriculum Development.

Calhoun, S., & J. Haley. (2003). *Improving Student Writing Through Different Writing Styles*. Chicago: Saint Xavier University and Skylight Professional Development Field-Based Master's Program. ED 473 052.

Capretz, K., B. Ricker, & A. Sasak. (2003). *Improving Organizational Skills Through the Use of Graphic Organizers*. Chicago: Saint Xavier University and Skylight Professional Development, M.A. Research Project. ED 473 056.

Chang, K. E., Y. T. Sung, & S. F. Chen. (2001). "Learning Through Computer-Based Concept Mapping with Scaffolding Aid." *Journal of Computer Assisted Learning 17*(1): 21–33.

Chase, P. A., K. L. Franson, & A. An. (2001). "Discovery Maps: A Student-Centered Approach to Reinforcing the Curriculum." *American Journal of Pharmaceutical Education 65*(1): 74–77.

Cuban, L. (2004). "Assessing the 20-Year Impact of Multiple Intelligences on Schooling." *Teachers College Record 106*(1): 140–146.

Culbert, E., M. Flood, R. Windler, & D. Work. (1998, May). *A Qualitative Investigation of the Use of Graphic Organizers*. Paper presented at the SUNY-Geneseo Annual Reading and Literacy Symposium. Geneseo, NY: State University of New York at Geneseo. ED 418 381.

Cushner, K., A. McClelland, & P. Safford. (2003). *Human Diversity in Education: An Integrative Approach* (4th ed.). New York: McGraw-Hill.

Delaney, C. J., & F. K. Shafer. (2007). "Teaching to Multiple Intelligence by Following a 'Slime Trail.'" *Middle School Journal 39*(1): 38–43.

Dembo, M. H., & K. Howard. (2007). "Advice About the Use of Learning Styles: A Major Myth in Education." *Journal of College Reading and Learning 37*(2): 101–109.

Dennis, S. (2003). *Multipurpose Poetry: Introducing Science Concepts and Increasing Fluency*. Newark, DE: International Reading Association. ED 480 244.

Diaz-Lefebure, R. (2006). "Learning for Understanding: A Faculty Driven Paradigm Shift in Learning Imaginative Teaching and Creative Assessment." *Community College Journal of Research and Practice* 30(2): 135–137.

Dochy, F. J. R., & P. A. Alexander. (1995). "Mapping Prior Knowledge: A Framework for Discussion Among Researchers." *European Journal of Psychology of Education* 10(3): 225–242.

Eden, G. F., F. B. Wood, & J. F. Stein. (2003). "Clock Drawing in Development Dyslexia." *Journal of Learning Disabilities* 36(3): 216–218.

Eggen, P. D., D. P. Kauchak, & R. J. Harder. (1979). *Strategies for Teachers: Information Processing Models in the Classroom.* Englewood Cliffs, NJ: Prentice Hall.

Erlauer, L. (2003). *The Brain-Compatible Classroom: Using What We Know About Learning to Improve Teaching.* Alexandria, VA: Association for Supervision and Curriculum Development.

Farmer, L. S. J. (2004). "Left Brain, Right Brain, Whole Brain." *School Library Media Activities Monthly* 21(2): 27–28.

Fitzhugh, W. P. (1995). "Magazine Geography: Using Magazine Pictures to Enhance Social Studies Instruction." ERIC Document Reproduction Service No. ED 390 784.

Forsten, C., J. Grant, & B. Hollas. (2003). "Reading to Learn: Are Textbooks Too Tough?" *Principal* 83(2): 28–33.

Furhman, A., & K. Bunclark. (2006). "Sex Differences in Parents' Estimates of Their Own and Their Children's Intelligence." *Intelligence* 34(1): 1–14.

Gagné, R. M., W. W. Wager, K. Golas, & J. M Keller. (2005). *Principles of Instructional Design* (5th ed.). Belmont, CA: Wadsworth.

Gallavan, M. P., & E. Kottler. (2007). "Eight Types of Graphic Organizers for Empowering Social Studies Students and Teachers." *Social Studies* 98(3): 117–123.

Gardner, H. (1985). *Frames of Mind: The Theory of Multiple Intelligences.* New York: Basic Books.

Gardner, H. (1991). *The Unschooled Mind: How Children Think and How Schools Should Teach.* New York: Basic Books.

Gardner, H. (1993). *Multiple Intelligences: The Theory in Practice.* New York: Basic Books.

Gardner, H. (1999a). *Intelligence Reframed: Multiple Intelligences for the 21st Century.* New York: Basic Books.

Gardner, H. (1999b) "Who Owns Intelligence?" *The Atlantic Monthly* 283(2): 67–76.

Gardner, H. (2006). *Multiple Intelligences,* New Horizons, New York: Basic Books.

Gil-Garcia, A., & J. Villegas. (2003). *Engaging Minds, Enhancing Comprehension and Constructing Knowledge through Visual Representatons.* Paper presented at a Conference on Word Association for Case Method Research and Application, Bordeaux, France, June 29–July 2, 2003. ED 480 131.

Given, B. K. (2002). *Teaching to the Brain's Natural Learning Systems.* Alexandria, VA: Association for Supervision and Curriculum Development.

Hellige, J. P. (1988). "Split-Brain Controversy." In *Encyclopedia of School Administration and Supervision,* R. A. Gorton, G. T. Schneider, & J. J. Fisher, Eds. Phoenix: Oryx.

Hill, B. (2005, Spring). "Learning Styles and Standardized Test Scores: Is There a Connection?" *The Delta Kappan Bulletin 20:* 27–30.

Hines, T. (1991). "The Myth of Right Hemisphere Creativity." *Journal of Creative Behavior 25:* 223–227.

Holyoak, K. J., & R. G. Morrison, Eds. (2005). *The Cambridge Handbook of Thinking and Reasoning.* New York: Cambridge.

Hyerle, D. (1995–1996). "Thinking Maps: Seeing Is Understanding." *Educational Leadership* 53(4): 85–89.

Ives, B. (2007). "Graphic Organizers Applied to Secondary Algebra Instruction for Students with Learning Disabilities." *Learning Disabilities Research and Practice* 22(2): 110–118.

Jensen, E. (2000). "Brain-Based Learning: A Reality Check." *Educational Leadership* 57(7): 76–80.

Jensen, E. (2005). *Teaching with the Brain in Mind* (2nd ed.). Alexandria, VA: Association for Supervision and Curriculum Development.

Jiang, X., & W. Grabe. (2007). "Graphic Organizers in Reading Instruction Research Findings and Issues." *Reading in a Foreign Language* 19(1): 34–35.

Knapp, M. S., & S. Woolverton. (2004). "Social Class and Schooling." In J. A. Banks & C. A. M. Banks, Eds., *Handbook of Research on Multicultural Education* (2nd ed.), pp. 656–681. San Francisco: Jossey-Bass.

Lazear, D. (2003). "Eight Ways of Teaching: The Artistry of Teaching with Multiple Intelligences" (4th ed.). Glenview, IL: Skylight.

Lenz, K., & J. Schumaker. (2003). *Adapting Language Arts, Social Studies, and Science Materials for the Inclusive Classroom. ERIC/OSEP Digest.* Arlington, VA: ERIC Clearinghouse on Disabilities and Gifted Education. ED 480 433.

Lin, Chih-Lung, & F. M. Dwyer. (2004). "Effect of Varied Animated Enhancement Strategies in Facilitating Achievement of Different Educational Objectives." *International Journal of Instructional Media* 31(2): 185.

Marzano, R. J. (2004). *Building Background Knowledge for Academic Achievement: Research on What Works in Schools.* Alexandria, VA: Association for Supervision and Curriculum Development.

Marzano, R. J., J. S. Norford, D. E. Paynter, D. J. Pickering, & B. B. Gaddy. (2001). *A Handbook for Classroom Instruction That Works*. Alexandria, VA: Association for Supervision and Curriculum Development.

Marzano, R. J., D. J. Pickering, & J. E. Pollock. (2001). *Classroom Instruction That Works: Research-Based Strategies for Increasing Student Achievement*. Alexandria, VA: Association for Supervision and Curriculum Development.

Meyer, J. H. F., & R. Land, Eds. (2006). *Overcoming Barriers to Student Understanding: Threshold Concepts and Troublesome Knowledge*. New York, Routledge.

Myrah, G. E., & L. Erlauer. (1999). "The Benefits of Brain Research: One District's Story." *High School Magazine 7*(1): 34–40.

Reigeluth, C. M., & B. J. Beatty. (2003). "Why Children Are Left Behind and What We Can Do About It." *Educational Technology 43*(5): 24–32.

Ritchhart, R., & D. Perkins. (2008). "Making Thinking Visible." *Educational Leadership 65*(5): 57–61.

Schleppegrell, M. J., & A. L. Go. (2007). "Analyzing the Writing of English Learners: A Functional Approach." *Language Arts 84*(6): 529–538.

Slack, N., & B. Norwich. (2007). "Evaluating the Reliability and Validity of a Learning Styles Inventory: A Classroom-Based Study." *Educational Research 49*(1): 51–63.

Slavin, R. E. (2003). *Educational Psychology: Theory and Practice* (7th ed.). Boston: Allyn and Bacon.

Stanford, P. (2003). "Multiple Intelligence for Every Classroom." *Interaction in School and Clinic 39*(2): 80–85.

Stephans, P., & C. Hermus. (2007). "Making Art Connections with Graphic Organizers." *The Art Education Magazine for Teachers 106*(8): 55.

Sternberg, R. J. (1997). *Thinking Styles*. New York: Cambridge University Press.

Sungur, S., C. Tekkaya, & O. Geban. (2001). "The Contribution of Conceptual Change Texts Accompanied by Concept Mapping to Students' Understanding of the Human Circulatory System." *School Science and Mathematics 101*(2): 91–101.

Sylwester, R. (2007). *The Adolescent Brain: Reaching for Autonomy*. Thousand Oaks, CA: Corwin.

Tate, M. L. (2003). *Worksheets Don't Grow Dendrites*. Thousand Oaks, CA: Corwin.

Tippett, C. (2003). "Demonstrating Understanding in Science: Connection to Learning Styles." *Canadian Children 28*(1): 21–28.

Vasilyev, Y. (2003). "The Network of Concepts and Facts: Forming a System of Conclusions Through Reflection." *Thinking Classroom 4*(2): 29–33.

Visser, B. A., M. C. Ashton, & P. A. Vernon. (2006a). "Beyond g: Putting Multiple Intelligences Theory to the Test." *Intelligence 34*(5): 487–502.

Visser, B. A., M. C. Ashton, & P. A. Vernon. (2006b). "g and the Measurement of Multiple Intelligences: A Response to Gardner." *Intelligence 34*(5): 507–510.

Wang, M., & K. Koda. (2007). "Commonalities and Differences in Word Identification Skills Among Learners of English as a Second Language." *Language Learning 57*(1): 201–222.

Waterhouse, L. (2006). "Inadequate Evidence for Multiple Intelligence, Mozart Effect and Emotional Intelligence Theories." *Educational Psychologist 41*(4): 247–255.

Weiss, R. P. (2000). "Brain-Based Learning." *Training and Development 54*(7): 20–24.

Wilberschied, L., & P. M. Berman. (2004). "Effect of Using Photos from Authentic Comprehension in a FLES Chinese Class." *Foreign Language Annals 37*(4): 534–543.

Wilson, W. J. (1996). *When Work Disappears: The World of the New Urban Poor*. New York: Knopf.

Winters, C. A. (2001, April 13). "Brain-Based Teaching: Fad or Promising Teaching Method." University Park, IL: Governors State University.

Yuen, M., & A. Fuhrman. (2005). "Sex Differences in Self Estimation of Multiple Intelligences Among Hong Kong Chinese Adolescents." *High Ability Studies 16*(2): 187–199.

Instruction as a Dynamic Process in Classrooms

*I*n Parts 1 and 2 we discussed the vitally important, yet somewhat passive, areas of preparation and instructional planning. We describe these subjects as *passive* because the work is often done in isolation, after school, or with colleagues; it may or may not involve interacting with students. Now we present the *dynamic* parts of teaching, where students and teachers interact. In Part 3, we show you how to create an environment for learning.

Chapter 6, "Managing the Classroom," shows you how to keep the classroom ethos positive. Questioning and conducting highly involved recitations are the topics of Chapter 7. Conducting authentic small-group discussions is the principal subject of Chapter 8. In addition, we introduce you to a cooperative learning model that fosters learning for all students in a small-group configuration. Chapter 9 adds the complete inquiry model to your teaching repertoire. Here are methods that will help you teach students how to think. We close Part 3 with Chapter 10, "Classroom Assessment." The strategies described in Chapters 6 through 10 will help you create a classroom that intentionally invites everyone to engage in learning at the highest possible level.

Managing the Classroom

Today's math lesson in Mr. Davis's fourth-grade class involves adding three-digit numbers. All the students are busy writing puzzle problems for each other to solve. As each student comes up with a problem and a solution, Mr. Davis checks it for accuracy, and the student then challenges another student to solve the problem. As the students become increasingly involved in this activity and move around the room to challenge and be challenged, the murmur of activity gradually rises. The steady, loud drone is continually punctuated by cries of "Let me try!" "Did you get it?" "Who wants to try this one?" "Wow! That's not the solution I came up with, but you're right, too!"

What's going on in this classroom?

Some observers might consider this classroom to be out of control. Does Mr. Davis have a classroom management problem in this noisy, active place? Is he using a model of classroom management? Is this a good environment for all learners? Does his approach suit both boys and girls? How would Mr. Davis handle an emergency or an unanticipated interruption such as a fire alarm or a classroom visitor?

In this chapter we will help you assess and learn to apply positive classroom management models and strategies to achieve desirable learning outcomes. As you move through this chapter, think about how you would answer the following questions.

What makes a good environment for all learners?

- How can you manage your classroom so that the learning environment is fair to all your students?
- How important are parents to achieving your goals as a teacher?
- How can you analyze a classroom management technique to determine its impact on student learning?
- How will you establish a classroom environment that rewards appropriate behavior and deters inappropriate behavior?
- How do teacher directions, classroom arrangement, and teacher observation affect student learning and behavior?

SECTION *1* Goals of Classroom Management

The goal of this section is to help you become an informed decision maker about classroom strategies to control and manage the instructional environment.

Prospective teachers tend to focus their preparation on learning and subject matter. As a result, many teachers feel inadequately prepared to maintain order and discipline in the classroom, and even fewer feel competent to address the needs of students from diverse cultural backgrounds (Baker 2005).

Why are classroom management issues so challenging? While the *Davis v. Monroe County School Board* decision and the Columbine High School shootings may or may not be familiar events to you, these two events captured the attention of the educational establishment in our country. In the case of *Davis v. Monroe County School Board*, a Georgia elementary school failed to act to protect a fifth-grade girl whose classmate made unwanted physical contact and sexual remarks. The U.S. Supreme Court ruled in this case that educators who are deliberately indifferent to student-to-student sexual harassment might be liable under a federal anti-bias law (Greenberger 1999). If you, as a teacher, overlook some "children just being children" behavior that others deem harassment, you may be liable.

The 1999 Columbine High School incident, in which two Jefferson County, Colorado, students killed 12 fellow students and a teacher, displayed the gross inadequacies of educational institutions to address planned violence. The U.S. Department of Education's National Center for Education Statistics showed that during the 2005–2006 school year, among students ages 12 to 18, there were about 1.5 million victims of nonfatal crimes at school, including 868,100 thefts and 628,200 violent crimes. Additionally, 25 percent of students reported that drugs were made available to them on school property. In the same year, 28 percent of students ages 12 to 18 reported having been bullied at school during the previous 6 months (National Center for Education Statistics 2007). These are the negatives about U.S. schools. Before we address possible strategies for dealing with these realities, let's review the historical changes that have occurred regarding discipline in schools.

Recent events put classroom management in the news.

Changing Definitions of Discipline

Discipline is usually defined as the preservation of order and the maintenance of control—the two traditional outcomes of classroom management techniques. However, this view of discipline is far too narrow. Teachers must make on-the-spot, split-second decisions and must react spontaneously to solve problems that arise in the classroom. As shown in Figure 6.1, classroom management techniques are determined by *teacher–student–situation* factors. The attitudes students develop in formal classroom settings are influenced by the teacher's classroom management skills. Your ideas about what a classroom should look like and how it should function will determine your classroom's atmosphere. Recall the level of activity and energy in Mr. Davis's classroom.

Classroom climate and student conduct are a teacher's responsibility.

Before the 1950s, the major emphasis of teacher preparation programs was maintaining classroom *control*. Accepted ideas about "mental discipline," physical punishment, order, and obedience provided educators with a consistent frame of reference that was enforced throughout the school. Then, in the 1950s, school administrators began to shift more of the burden for establishing classroom climate and managing student conduct to the individual teacher. While this shift in responsibility was occurring, the results of relevant studies of discipline by social and behavioral scientists began to be applied in the schools. The shift to teacher

FIGURE 6.1

Interaction Among These Three Factors Determines Classroom Order and Learning

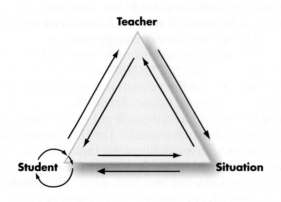

responsibility, combined with social and behavioral research, set the stage for **democratic discipline**.

Two principles are essential for the use of democratic discipline in the classroom:

◆ As the adult member of the class, the teacher must add the rational dimension to the rule-making capacities of the group.

◆ Rules administered by the teacher should reflect the wisdom, fairness, and patience of a judge.

The changes in classrooms were even more dramatic during the 1970s and 1980s. Four changes had a distinct effect on classroom management during that time. First, families became very mobile. It was not uncommon for even rather stable schools to show 25 percent annual student turnover. Such a high degree of turnover had an impact on both the learning environment and the expected patterns of student behavior and classroom systems. Thus, today's classrooms tend to be relatively unstable social systems.

The second phenomenon was acceleration of the decline of the nuclear family. More students now live with single parents than at any other time in history, and this number is increasing. Examining the population of U.S. households with children, the U.S. Census Bureau reported that about one of three children in 2006 was living in a single-parent family (Bergman 2007). Third, many students began to view school as a place to "get through." Social promotion (promoting failing students with their age group) had firmly taken hold; as a result, students felt entitled to advancement. How could teachers motivate students if there was little threat of failure and little reward for achievement?

Fourth, urban schools experienced a distinct set of problems (gangs, violence, high dropout rates, poverty) that were quite different from the problems facing suburban and rural schools. States and school districts could no longer compile a single list of rules and expect it to apply to all schools.

We use the terms *discipline* and **classroom management** throughout this chapter. The box below describes how the two concepts differ operationally. The list for discipline shows reactive teacher behaviors. The list for classroom management shows teacher actions that are proactive. A proactive teacher is in charge of the classroom environment and establishes the climate for instructional activities.

Student behavior is affected by social trends.

INSTRUCTIONAL
Strategies

Discipline Versus Classroom Management:
The Most Common Teacher Strategies

Discipline

Giving in-school suspensions
Sending misbehaving students to the office
Contacting parents
Using a check or demerit system
Taking away privileges
Confiscating a cell phone or other student item

(continued)

INSTRUCTIONAL
Strategies

Discipline Versus Classroom Management: The Most Common Teacher Strategies—Cont'd

Classroom Management

Emphasizing rules at the start of the school year
Planning for smooth transitions; leaving minimal time between activities
Paying attention to the entire class; continuously scanning the group
Pacing activities effectively
Giving clear and concise instructions
Carefully designing the classroom environment
Organizing activities in advance

Source: Based on information from Rita Seedorf. Used with permission.

Understanding the Variables of Classroom Management

Our approach to classroom management is based on a **humanistic orientation** toward the classroom environment, which views students as diverse individuals seeking acceptance and fulfillment. Teachers must be mindful of the fact that young minds and attitudes are shaped by both *overt* and *covert* teacher behaviors. Thus, in this section, we discuss three concepts that are central to the principles of classroom management and represent an important influence on student development: *norms, power,* and *awareness*.

A **norm** is a behavioral rule or pattern accepted by most members of a group. For example, raising one's hand before speaking may be a norm in many classrooms. Norms are usually not recorded the way the laws of a country are. However, there exists in the minds of group members an ideal standard directing how each member ought to behave under specific conditions. This shared standard introduces a high degree of regularity and predictability into their social interactions (see the box below). An observed deviation from the norm usually results in a negative response. It is important to note that norms can change over time. For example, changes in the racial and ethnic makeup of a school or classroom can and should influence prior norms. Also, elementary teachers spend a great deal of their time establishing classroom norms and secondary teachers benefit dramatically from these established behavioral norms.

Norm = accepted standard of behavior

Key Ideas

The Importance of Norms

- Norms are valuable to social relationships and classroom cooperation.
- Norms reduce the necessity for constant teacher enforcement.
- Norms provide for the control of individual and group behavior without anyone overtly exerting power.

By virtue of your role and position in the classroom, you as the teacher have influence, or **power**. Unrestrained use of that power creates insecurities and resistance among students, adversely affecting their learning. Students

Establishing classroom norms is practical for democratic management.
© Randy Faris/Corbis

can retaliate against the teacher (and other students) by forming cliques, creating irritating disturbances, and making threats (see Table 6.1). To be an effective classroom manager, you must learn to exercise the least amount of power necessary to accomplish the desired academic results (see Leriche 1992) and maintain essential classroom norms.

The term **awareness** refers to a teacher's attention to and insight about the classroom environment. A class constantly gives its teacher verbal and non-verbal clues. Children's behaviors offer insights regarding student-to-student interactions (Power 1992). Furthermore, communication occurs both between

TABLE 6.1	Reported Crimes Against Students (2005–2006)	
While reports of crimes against students have dropped nationally, publicity of school crime has increased.		
	Percentages	
Offense Reported	Male	Female
Threatened or injured with a weapon	10	6
Carried a weapon	10	3
In a physical fight	18	9
Injured by bullying	31	18

Source: National Center for Education Statistics, *Indicators of School Crime and Safety 2007* (NCES 2008–021), December 2007.

Awareness = use of eyes and
ears to read students' cues

the teacher and individual students and between the teacher and the class as a whole. The master teacher understands how to read this mixture of communications. Knowing which communications to ignore and which to attend to quickly separates the "pros" from the "rookies." When you are given the opportunity, carefully observe your "master" teacher's verbal and nonverbal communication.

Initially, a teacher must determine how his or her class presents cues. The teacher who simply complains, "My class was particularly lousy today" has not adequately analyzed the information provided by the class. This teacher must define precisely what he or she means by "lousy." Did students recite inappropriately, not pay attention, or not accomplish the work requested? Were they just generally off task? Were they unprepared? Disorderly? The teacher must be able to specify what behaviors were demonstrated (cues). Next, the teacher must be prepared to state what behaviors/outcomes are desired (see Evertson 1995).

For example, the cell phone has become an accessory item to our lives. Students and faculty carry them about like quick-draw pistols—reflexively drawing at the first ring or vibration. Schools and teachers must understand how prevalent cell phones are and the impact they have on attention and learning (DeLisio 2007). The faculty should discuss appropriate and inappropriate uses (both when and where) of cell phones on school grounds. Ideally, all phones, including the teacher's, should be turned off and placed in a secure location during the instructional period.

How would you handle student
cell phones in your class?

Reflect

◆ Research the Supreme Court's *Monroe County* ruling at http://www .washingtonpost.com/wp-srv/national/longterm/supcourt/1998–99/davis .htm. What was the Court's ruling on this case, and do you agree with the ruling? What discipline or classroom management techniques would you use to avoid this situation?

◆ Research violence in schools. Do you agree or disagree that the four national trends discussed on pages 172–175 may contribute to increased incidents of school violence? What might schools and teachers do to reduce these situations?

◆ To what extent do teachers have the responsibility to ensure classroom management under all circumstances, even if the results are contrary to the desires of some in the community?

SECTION 2   The Impact of Society on Your Teaching and Classroom

The classroom is a social and emotional environment as well as a learning environment. As teachers, we need to be certain that all students play an equitable role in academic and nonacademic activities. If boys are asked to go first and girls to follow, if boys lift and girls clean, if seat-work and quiet work predominate, if language over problem solving are accentuated; then we can expect girls and boys to settle into expectations that fail to prepare them for the world outside the classroom. We must be careful not to institutionalize the "glass ceilings" or set differentiated expectations for some students.

The manner in which a teacher engages every student has potential learning and achievement overtones. This means you must consciously address many of your personal attitudes and habits and avoid reinforcing social barriers and stereotypes. Helping every student feel the thrill of success and the value of "belonging" is what effective teaching is all about. And that applies to all students.

In this section, we approach the influences of society on the social and emotional environment of the classroom through two main topics: achieving diversity and cooperation, and fostering parental involvement.

If you look at the characteristics listed in Table 6.2, you will notice several that support the topics we now approach in depth. They are useful in discussing academic and behavioral expectations with parents and can serve as a yardstick for measuring your classroom management success.

A teacher's behaviors can include or exclude students.

Achieving Diversity and Cooperation

When you establish classroom management strategies, remember that students are, for the most part, anxious to make their classrooms cooperative and pleasant places in which to be (Johnson & Johnson 1989). By enlisting students in the formulation of classroom activities and rules (democratic discipline), you help prevent classroom management problems in three ways: (1) you are setting the stage for classroom equity through a process of respect and understanding; (2) students tend to have a greater interest in the maintenance of these rules when they have had a part in generating them; and (3) they have a greater understanding of the need for and the meaning of rules when they help to develop them.

Students who are invested in the rules follow the rules.

TABLE 6.2	Characteristics That Engender Diversity, Cooperation, and Involvement

Academic Characteristics
- ◆ Clear instructional focus
- ◆ High academic time on task
- ◆ Frequent monitoring of student progress
- ◆ High expectations from the school
- ◆ Appropriate award structures
- ◆ Active teaching
- ◆ Few student absences

School Climate Indicators
- ◆ Orderly and safe environment
- ◆ Minimal instructional interruptions
- ◆ Few discipline problems
- ◆ Little time spent on classroom management
- ◆ Friendly ambience
- ◆ No graffiti
- ◆ Frequent contact with parents

Source: Bickel 1999, pp. 959–983; Teddlie & Stringfield 1993.

Gender and Race Issues   Teachers are often unaware that they project a bias toward or against some students because of sex, race, ethnic background, or perceived intelligence. Such bias has resulted in proportionately fewer girls and minorities in science and mathematics classes (see Chang 2003; Graham 2001; Wood 2000). Additionally, low expectations and a lack of role models are considered additional contributors to high dropout rates among boys and minorities (Greene & Winters 2006).

Several studies have shown that teachers interact with boys more than girls in secondary science classes. Researchers discovered that girl-initiated science interactions *declined* during the middle school years, teacher expectations favored boys, and racial minorities tended to be rejected more by teachers (Good & Brophy 2008). These situations are all *disinviting* to female and minority learners. Interestingly enough, both male and female teachers were found to be equally disinviting.

How can we recognize our own "disinviting behaviors" and avoid them in our classrooms? First, you or someone else can chart your interactions with students. Tabulate positive and negative feedback, nonverbal cues, use of male pronouns, and male bias. If bias is apparent, use a list of student names to conduct recitations on a regular schedule. Change your verbal and written communication patterns to use inclusive language. Public condemnations and strong tone are considered "put-downs" in some cultures and should generally be avoided. (In case you need a model, this textbook is written with inclusive, gender-neutral language.) Provide an equal distribution of leadership positions to males, females, minority students, and students with disabilities. In short, become proactive by making the classroom environment equitable to all.

To enhance equity and promote achievement, Sam Kerman (1979) perfected a series of 15 strategies that are collectively labeled TESA, "Teacher Expectations and Student Achievement" (see the box below and Phi Delta Kappa 1993). As you examine these 15 elements, you will see that, in this chapter, we have stressed all but touch. Very young pupils do touch their teachers and vice versa; but we suggest that, beginning at middle school, you should be very cautious with teacher–student physical contact, especially with members of the opposite sex. The best intentions may be misinterpreted and might lead to charges of sexual harassment or physical abuse. Chapter 2 provides additional insights into issues affecting gender and racial equity. The most critical point is to be fair, impartial, and intentionally inviting to every student.

> Is classroom participation important for academic success?

The TESA Program

Teachers who value equity incorporate these strategies in their classrooms.

Response Opportunities

Equitable distribution of participation
Individual attention
Pausing to allow students to think
Asking for clarification
Asking higher-level questions

(continued)

> ## The TESA Program—Cont'd
>
> ### Feedback
>
> Validating correct responses
> Praising participation
> Providing feedback
> Listening to all
> Accepting feelings
>
> ### Personal Regard
>
> Proximity of teacher to student
> Courtesy
> Personal interest and compliments
> Touching (as a positive gesture)
> Desist strategies

Educational Equity and Student Tracking   A great deal has been written for and against student tracking, but the greatest concern deals with expectations of students placed in "lower" tracks. Once a student has been labeled a low performer, that label has a tendency to stick with that student throughout his or her academic career.

Low track = low expectations = sense of failure

Evidence supporting academic tracking at both the elementary and secondary levels, especially over long periods of time, has been inconclusive (Oakes 1992). Teachers have reported, however, that they *dislike* teaching low-ability classes, spend less time preparing for them, and schedule less-interesting or less-challenging activities for them (Good & Brophy 2008). Students in low-track classes are merely kept busy with mundane, irrelevant work. Not surprisingly, students in high-track classes have better attitudes toward school and better work habits, and they assume positions of greater leadership.

We recognize that specific classes will automatically draw motivated students (advanced placement calculus, foreign languages, music theory, and art history are several). Of course, some teachers in these classes may unwittingly discourage some students from participating. Racial or gender inequality in achievement may result from academic tracking (Slavin 1991). It is important that teachers provide their best instructional and management strategies for each class they teach, not just the highly motivated, super achievers.

Fostering Parental Involvement

Do you want to provide a pleasing, enriching, successful classroom experience? The path to such a learning experience is well known: Get parents involved (Bennett 2007). Active parents follow the development of their children, reinforce the expectations of the schools, and monitor student behavior and participation. Getting the parents into the schools is so important that it is the eighth goal in the Goals 2000 Educate America Act of 1994: "Every school

Parents or other significant adults provide positive influences on student behavior.

© Elizabeth Crews

will promote parental involvement and participation to promote social, emotional, and academic growth of children."

It is rare for the parents of problem students to closely follow their children's educational achievement. There are few models parents can follow in deciding just what role they should play in their children's educational career. This lack of direction, coupled with the demands of two-career and single-parent homes, fosters poor parent participation (Amato & Maynard 2007).

Working Parents   Families headed by two working parents now represent the norm. This leaves little time and even less energy for oversight of children's schooling. Today's parents tend not to ask for school reports, monitor class assignments, or attend school activities. If you are a primary teacher, you have a good chance of encouraging parents to build an active school attendance record along with their children. However, you must call, call, call! Don't wait for participation; go out and get it. This is also an opportunity for teachers and schools to take advantage of the Internet. A school website can offer the opportunity for parents and community members to stay in touch with activities and requirements, check school schedules, and monitor their child's progress. If possible, e-mail communication may be a double blessing for busy teachers and parents (quicker access and positive feedback). Teachers should take advantage of such opportunities to relay positive as well as negative occurrences. Such extra work will pay off in fewer classroom disruptions and better achievement over the course of the year.

Be proactive in contacting working parents.

Secondary teachers face too many years of parental inactivity to hope for increased parental participation. Yet the teacher still has an obligation to keep parents informed. There are committed parents who actively pursue a good education along with their children. These parents will demand your attention, and you will need to learn how to provide it. Rejoice in this all-too-rare occurrence. What do parents wish to know? In a national survey (Horace Mann 2001) conducted among teachers in K–12 grades, five questions were asked most often. See the box below.

Questions Most Frequently Asked by Parents

◆ How do my children behave in school?

◆ How do my children interact with their peers?

◆ How important is reading in my child's life?

◆ Can you give me more information about homework assignments?

◆ How hard do my children work at school?

The Single Parent   In urban areas, the single parent is the norm. The *2007 Kids Count* report by the Annie E. Casey Foundation noted that in 2004–2005 the percent of children in single-parent households ranged nationally from 17 to 65 percent by race, with the national average being 30 percent (*2007 Kids Count*, Table 1, p. 29; NCES, No. 2005-312). These parents work double-time to keep up with all the demands of their jobs, parenting, and personal lives. Don't jump to the conclusion that the single parent is always female or young. Many parents share custody of their children, so you may find a different parent present at consecutive school activities. Confusion for you and the student may be a frequent result. To make sure everyone in the family is well informed, be prepared when you meet with each parent to give him or her sufficient background on what you've already discussed with the other parent in earlier meetings. If possible, use e-mail to keep both parents updated. Be sure they know the school and district's website address if it exists.

VIDEO CASE

In the Video Case entitled "Students with Special Needs: The Importance of Home-School Partnerships" on the student website, you will observe middle school teacher Sophia Boyer working with parents of two students with special needs. As you watch the clips and study the artifacts in the case, reflect on the following questions: 1. What strategies does Sophia offer for establishing effective relationships with parents? 2. What other ideas do you have for ways to begin home-school partnerships?

Extended Families   Many children are being raised today by members of their extended family. This might be a grandmother, uncle, sister, or cousin. Don't ask questions; just build a relationship with any "parental" figure who supports the child. *Concern* is the operative word here. If they are involved and concerned, then they are the parent and should be treated the same way you treat other parents.

Meeting Effectively with Parents   Most schools have some type of parent orientation night. This is a good time to meet as many parents as show up. In Chapter 10, we discuss a technique of having the student provide the parents with his or her work. If some problem seems to be chronic, initiate a parent conference. Of course, a working single parent will not be meeting with you during school hours, so some accommodations need to be made, such as communication by telephone, letter, or e-mail.

INSTRUCTIONAL *Strategies*

Conducting a Teacher-Parent Conference

Here are some tips for preparing for your conference and making sure it runs smoothly.

- ◆ First, review school and district policies on parent conferences. Seek input from master teachers and school counselors on approaches to behavioral and academic issues that are relevant.
- ◆ Provide adequate notification to the parent (or parents) of the time, location, and purpose of the conference. If possible, provide written examples of the academic problems you wish to discuss.
- ◆ Follow this conference process: (1) issues, (2) goals, (3) possible approaches, (4) parental input, and (5) agreement. Explain the five-step process before you begin.
- ◆ Encourage questions. Emphasize that you are both working toward a common purpose, the student's welfare.
- ◆ Before moving ahead with any plan or procedure, ensure that the parent understands the issues. Achieve agreement through consensus. Do not take any additional step until mutual commitment to a desired outcome is clear.
- ◆ Document the conference's outcomes and next steps and allow the parent to review the document and sign off on it. Discuss this last step with school administrators if you are concerned about possible repercussions such as a lawsuit or complaint.

Voices from the Classroom

Kevin Post

Manhattan Beach Middle School

Handling Plagiarism

I was grading a group of recent student essays from my eighth-grade English class about the novel *Animal Farm*. As I read one particular student essay I came across a questionable passage. The wording was that of a professional writer, and I knew it was not characteristic of a student. I then wondered: "Cliff's Notes? Spark's Notes? The Internet?" Whatever the source, it didn't matter. After 20-plus years of teaching, the language always jumps off the page.

I was always careful to discuss plagiarism during the orientation to the class and frequently mentioned it before each essay assignment. I also recognized that the Internet made the temptation to copy just too easy.

I had spelled out the consequences for plagiarism. According to the disciplinary matrix, as the teacher I was to meet with the student's parents following a meeting with the student. As I picked up the phone to call the parents, I wondered if the parents would be defensive or accept their child's lapse in judgment.

Reflect

- Do you feel there is a difference between cheating on a test and cheating on a homework assignment?
- How would you prepare for and manage the parent conference?
- What do you think will be the easiest and most enjoyable aspect of meeting with parents?
- What will be the most difficult?
- Discuss parent meetings and conferences with your mentors. Talk about good and bad experiences and what they learned from each.

SECTION 3   Classroom Management Models

As you strive to maximize learning time for your students, you must choose from among a large number of classroom management strategies. We have arranged these strategies along a continuum ranging from those that rely on self-discipline to those that involve imposing discipline on your students (see Figure 6.2). *Self-discipline* implies voluntary adherence to norms that promote students' self-interest and protect the welfare of others. *Imposed discipline* suggests a student code of conduct prescribed by the teacher in the best interests of individual students and the class as a whole. Between self-discipline and imposed discipline there are numerous choices.

Students can follow an example or set the example.

To provide you with an overview of selected classroom management models, we will discuss three theories that lean toward self-discipline: Maslow's hierarchy of needs; moral reasoning and character development; and reality therapy. On the imposed-discipline side, we will discuss desist strategies, assertive discipline, and behavior modification. Reality therapy, desist strategies, and behavior modification are highlighted because they are generic (that is, other systems have been developed from them).

Models of Student Self-Discipline

Self-discipline strategies are based on the premise that the students' self-discipline depends heavily on effective teacher-student and student-student relationships. Advocates of self-discipline as a classroom management strategy argue that to facilitate learning, teachers need to increase their

FIGURE 6.2

A Continuum of Classroom Management Models

Watch the Video Case entitled "Cardinal Rules for Classroom Management: Perspectives from an Urban Elementary School" on the student website. Observe Benvinda Timas's strategies for classroom management as she teaches a math lesson. As you watch the clips and study the artifacts in the case, reflect on the following questions: 1. How is Benvinda proactive in her approach? 2. How does Benvinda position herself in relation to the students and why?

involvement. Involvement requires that teachers demonstrate genuineness, empathy toward the student, and acceptance and trust of the student.

While success is attained with involvement, teacher involvement also means working with individual students on a one-to-one level to address behavioral or academic problems. While remaining in the "teacher role," the teacher helps the student make plans, carry them out, revise them, and strive continually for success. Involvement means that the teacher helps the student become more responsible for his or her behavior by having the student constantly state what he or she is doing. Involvement also means meeting with parents or guardians, if possible, and seeking their cooperation. Furthermore, it means meeting with other teachers to discuss the needs of certain students.

Additionally, self-discipline requires a positive perspective and *positive expectations* on the part of the teacher. Through positive feedback, self-discipline is expected and achieved by students (Cotton 2001). With these prerequisites in mind, let us examine classroom management strategies that focus on self-discipline.

Maslow's Hierarchy of Needs   Abraham H. Maslow's humanistic approach (1968) has had a major impact on educational theory and classroom management for decades. Maslow's *hierarchy of needs* theory (see Figure 6.3) assumes that an individual's behavior at any time is determined by his or her needs. For example, a hungry student will have a hard time focusing on learning new skills. Maslow's theory suggests that a teacher determine what need might be causing a behavior problem and then address that need. Naturally, teachers would prefer self-esteem and self-actualization to direct student behavior, for then students could be truly self-regulated and teachers would not have to spend time managing the classroom.

FIGURE 6.3

Maslow's Hierarchy of Needs

A well-managed classroom allows the students to focus on personal growth, not on safety and belonging.

Tran-
scendence:
Helping others
find self-fulfillment

Self-actualization:
Self-fulfillment, realizing
one's potential

Aesthetic needs: Symmetry,
order, and beauty

Cognitive needs: Knowing,
understanding, and exploring

Esteem needs: Achieving, gaining
approval and recognition

Belongingness/love needs: Affiliating with
others and being accepted

Safety/security needs: Safeguarding one's existence

Physiological needs: Hunger, thirst, bodily comforts, etc.

To use Maslow's ideas, you must truly believe in your students. Students need to be shown that they are valued and respected and play important roles in the class. Structure, routines, and consistency are all hallmarks of this strategy. You help all students to develop a positive, constructive self-image. The classroom environment must be structured to be supportive. Even when someone is "in trouble," it is always the act that is corrected, not the person. Teachers stress the intrinsic value of each student and attempt to motivate all students to do the best they possibly can. Implementing Maslow's system requires a long-term commitment to classroom management and routines consistent with students' self-actualization.

Focus on the behavior, not the person.

Moral Reasoning and Character Development   Many recent calls for educational reform have come from parents and community leaders who believe that the schools have ignored their responsibility to build the character and moral values of students. Researchers have also argued that the schools should focus more on students' moral reasoning and character development (Noddings 2002; Ryan & Bohlin 1999; Simon 2002). Others argue that the public schools have no role in character development and moral education, and that they should concentrate exclusively on developing students' cognitive skills. We believe that the process of schooling necessarily affects the way children think about issues of right and wrong, so it is important to purposefully address those issues.

A model for providing a moral education was developed by Lawrence Kohlberg (1975; Power, Higgins, & Kohlberg 1989). His model presents "moral dilemmas" in which students are faced with a personal choice. One such dilemma might be a group of students who are aware that a friend has a weapon in his locker and has recently threatened another student. What action should the group take? How would the students feel if someone were injured or killed by the weapon? Such an exercise forces students to work through their values and develop and apply their moral compasses.

For such an exercise, the class is divided into groups for discussion. Kohlberg believes that these discussions will help students raise their consciousness and develop a better understanding of the motivations of others. He stresses that the classroom should be a "just community" in which a democratic society is the model. Obviously, the dilemmas posed must be appropriate for the maturity of the class members. (See also Etzioni 1997; Myers 2001.)

There is a need for a great deal of consensus surrounding moral development and positive classroom environments. The Josephson Institute of Ethics (2008), a nonprofit foundation, is a strong advocate of ethics and character development in schools, government agencies, and the business sector. The institute stresses "six pillars" of character:

1. Trustworthiness
2. Respect
3. Responsibility
4. Fairness
5. Caring
6. Citizenship

If the schools are to be reformed, they must reclaim their traditional responsibility to pass on to students the best of our culture's values. With this in mind, the Boston University Center for the Advancement of Ethics and

Character (2008) wrote a Character Education Manifesto for U.S. schoolchildren. The following statements are adapted from its seven guiding principles.

1. Education is a moral enterprise that should guide students to know and pursue what is good and worthwhile.
2. Schools have an obligation to foster in their students personal and civic virtues such as integrity, courage, responsibility, diligence, and respect for the dignity of all people.
3. Character education is about developing virtues—habits and dispositions—that lead students to become responsible and mature adults.
4. All adults in a school must embody and reflect the moral authority that has been invested in them by parents and the community.
5. Schools must become communities of virtue in which responsibility and kindness are modeled, taught, expected, celebrated, and continually practiced.
6. Teachers and students must draw from the human community's reservoir of moral wisdom, much of which exists in our great stories, works of art, literature, history, and biographies.
7. Young people need to realize that forging their own character is an essential and demanding life task.

Character education is a fundamental dimension of good teaching, notes the home page on the Boston University Center website (2008). For an elaborating discussion on this entire subject, see Sizer & Sizer 1999; Soder, Goodlad, & McMannon 2002.

Reality Therapy   In an approach called **reality therapy**, individuals take responsibility for solving their own problems. Reality therapy requires positive, genuine, human involvement that allows people to recognize their own reality and to begin to reshape their own behaviors to meet selected needs without any threats or implied punishments.

Students own their failures and their successes.

The main premise is that an individual must acknowledge his or her own failures and be personally responsible for becoming successful. Toward this end, teachers must avoid labeling inappropriate behaviors with tags such as *disadvantaged, dysfunctional,* or *disabled.* Another premise is that examination of family or personal histories is not essential for change to occur.

Seven key principles form the basis for reality therapy:

Principle 1: Demonstrate Human Involvement   In the classroom setting, this means devising a structure that facilitates teacher–student and student–student involvement. Classroom management problems can then be solved in ways that express care and concern on the part of the teacher, with direct student involvement. Thus, small-group instruction on self-regulated learning is very much in concert with reality therapy.

Principle 2: Focus on Current Behavior   Although reality therapy does not deny emotions and their importance, its success depends on focusing on current behaviors—on what the student is doing *now.* Thus, the teacher should ask a misbehaving student what he or she is doing. Rather than recall previous behavior ("Well, that's the seventh time today that you've interrupted without raising your hand"), the teacher should ask, "What are you doing?" Note that the emphasis is on the pronoun (*you*). There should be no misunderstanding concerning who is responsible for the misbehavior.

Principle 3: Examine Current Inappropriate Behavior   This means that the student who constantly misbehaves must be made to discuss his or her behavior and come to the conclusion that another type of behavior would be more appropriate. The teacher does not evaluate or label behaviors as good or bad, but simply indicates whether behaviors are appropriate or inappropriate in the classroom.

Principle 4: Create a Plan for Change   The student, with the help of the teacher, develops a plan to help meet his or her personal or educational goals. This plan becomes a contract between the student and the teacher. For example, a student who never studies should not be expected to begin studying two hours a night. Fifteen-minute sessions a few times a week would be more appropriate. Be certain that remedial plans are realistic for the particular student.

Principle 5: Require Evidence of Student Commitment   After a reasonable plan has been devised, it must be carried out. Typically, the student prepares a plan in writing and signs it as a means of increasing personal motivation to maintain and fulfill the plan. This kind of commitment intensifies and accelerates the student's behavioral change.

Principle 6: Reevaluate the Plan   It is essential that both the teacher and the student be willing to reexamine the plan and renew or change it if it is in some way inappropriate. This does not mean that the teacher excuses the student's failure. When failure occurs, it must be mutually recognized that the responsibility lies with the student, either for not having fulfilled the plan or for not having planned appropriately in the first place.

The best goals and plans are constantly examined and modified.

Principle 7: Remove Punishment   William Glasser (1972, 1998) believes that punishment hinders the personal involvement that is essential between the teacher and the student. The purpose of punishment is to change an individual's behavior through fear or pain. Rather than punishment, Glasser suggests using a program of positive feedback to achieve success. In the reality therapy model, the teacher's praise of student success increases the involvement between the teacher and student and leads to more responsible student behaviors.

Key Ideas   **Principles of Reality Therapy**

◆ Teacher–student and student–student involvement is essential.

◆ The focus is on current student behavior.

◆ The student examines and evaluates his or her behavior.

◆ The student designs a plan for change.

◆ The student makes a commitment to change.

◆ The student owns the success or failure of the plan.

◆ A program of positive reinforcement is essential.

Reality Therapy and the Entire Class   Reality therapy may also be applied to an entire class through classroom meetings (Styles 2002). A social problem-solving meeting involves a group discussion of classroom problems with the goal of reaching a mutually agreed-upon solution (see the Instructional Strategies box below). Such a meeting may be an extremely useful first step in resolving a seemingly intractable classroom-wide problem. Teachers can use many individual and group techniques in implementing a program of reality therapy. However, one requirement is essential to all of these techniques: teacher involvement. This takes training, patience, and, above all, perseverance.

INSTRUCTIONAL
Strategies

Elements of Social Problem-Solving Meetings

1. All group and individual problems in the class are eligible for discussion.
2. The session focuses on solving the problem, not finding fault or specifying punishment.
3. Meetings are conducted with all individuals positioned in a tight circle to foster interaction.

If you are philosophically against punishment, reality therapy may be a classroom management strategy that you should explore further. Please glance through the reference section at the end of this chapter for further reading on this strategy.

Models of Teacher-Focused Discipline

Imposed-discipline systems are based on the teacher's recognized authority to set standards within the classroom and to dictate appropriate classroom behaviors and consequences of misbehavior. A teacher's authority derives from both state and local laws and societal expectations. When a teacher's responsibility is challenged, the teacher has the authority to use rewards or punishments to maintain classroom order and achieve educational goals.

In the following discussion, we describe three imposed-discipline strategies: *desist strategies*, *assertive discipline*, and *behavior modification*. Each of these strategies uses a variety of methods to exercise the teacher's authority within the classroom.

Desist Strategies   Of the imposed-discipline strategies we discuss here, the desist strategy is the most traditional. The term is derived from "desist techniques" suggested by Jacob S. Kounin and Paul V. Gump (1959). The **desist strategy** is a means of systematically communicating the teacher's desire for a student's behavior to stop or change. The communication may be accomplished by a command such as "Stop that!" or by a glance or movement (Lasley et al. 1989). Numerous other terms have been used to describe such use of teacher authority in the classroom. However, because desist strategy is the "granddaddy" of imposed-discipline approaches, we begin with it. In your personal experience, your parents' authority and discipline most likely were examples of desist strategies.

Basics   Desist strategies offer a systematic framework for applying the teacher's authority to maintain group norms. The technique of desist strategies involves two basic concepts. First, there are three levels of force—low, moderate, and high. Second, there are two types of communication of teacher desires—public and private.

In dealing with classroom discipline, it is usually best to use a low rather than a high level of force, and it is always better to use a private than a public form of communication. Occasionally, however, a situation calls for a high-level, public display of force. A classroom fight is one example. In the vast majority of cases, though, you will find it best to use private displays and low levels of force to handle "normal" discipline problems. Desist strategies are further explained in Tables 6.3 and 6.4.

The concept of the desist strategy is summarized by two principles first presented by Carl J. Wallen in 1968:

1. If a classroom activity is about to occur and you have not previously established standards of student behavior and your expectations, specify these expectations and behavioral standards before you begin the activity.
2. If, in a continuing activity, a student or group of students behaves in a manner contrary to specific expectations, use a desist strategy aimed at reaching the level of expectations while causing the least possible disruption to the classroom setting.

It is important that you specify the appropriate behavior for a particular activity. During a test, for example, you may decide that students should not speak out unless they raise their hands and are called on. During small-group

In most cases, it's better to correct a student's behavior in private.

TABLE 6.3   Desist Strategies

In general, the teacher should rely on low levels of force and private communications.

Level of Force	Definition	Desist Strategy
Low	Nonverbal, a signal or movement	Glancing at child, shaking head, moving over to child unobtrusively in the instructional activity
Moderate	Verbal, conversational, no coercion	Appealing to a child to act reasonably, removing disturbing objects, commanding the child to stop
High	Verbal and nonverbal, changed voice pitch, may use coercion	Raising voice and commanding child to stop, removing the child from group, threatening, punishing, physically restraining the child

Type of Communication	Definition	Desist Strategy
Public	Intended to be noticed by most of the children in a class	Acting and/or speaking in a way that commands attention
Private	Intended to be noticed only by small groups of children	Using unobtrusive actions or moving close to a child when speaking

Source: From Wallen 1968, Appendix A, p. 15.

TABLE 6.4	Desist Strategies: Combining Force and Communication	
Force Level	**Private Communication**	**Public Communication**
1. Glance (low level)	Teacher shakes head so only one or two other children notice the action.	Teacher shakes head dramatically so most of class notices the action.
2. Appeal (moderate level)	Teacher moves close to child, asks child to act reasonably, and uses voice and manner so only one or two other children notice the action.	Teacher asks children to act reasonably, in a manner that most of the class notices.
3. Threat (high level)	Teacher moves close to child, tells what will happen if misbehavior continues, and uses voice and manner so only one or two other children notice.	Teacher tells what will happen if misbehavior continues, uses a loud and commanding voice that most of the class notices.

Source: From Wallen 1968, Appendix A, pp. 15–16.

activities, students may be permitted to speak quietly. Your verbal statement of the appropriate behavior is the expected norm.

Punishments   In contrast to reality therapy, desist strategies allow some form of punishment to be administered to non-responsive students. Punishment entails consequences that reduce the future rate of undesirable behavior (Skinner 1953, 1974). *Loss of privilege* is the most common form (for example, loss of recess, sports pass, or an assembly).

George Sugai emphasizes, however, that "we also know that increasing the intensity of sanctions and excluding students for rule violations are insufficient solutions. Problem behavior often increases when only punitive discipline practices are used" (1996, p. 10).

Punishment: a consequence that reduces undesirable behavior.

Observations About Desist Strategies   We should not leave the topic of desist strategies without including a short summary of one of the more important works on the topic. Kounin's classic study (1970) reported that more than half (55.2 percent) of perceived student misbehavior can be categorized as talking or other noisy behaviors. Off-task behaviors—for example, gum chewing—accounted for 17.2 percent of the total, and all other deviations from accepted norms—being late, not having homework, moving about the room without permission—accounted for the remainder (27.6 percent). According to Kounin's categories, the bulk of student misbehaviors would be regarded as low-level discipline problems.

Yet, when teachers were given the options of punishing, providing a suitable desist, or prescribing another form of productive activity in reaction to these misbehaviors, over half opted for high-level, public desists. The most interesting, or perhaps sad, finding in Kounin's study is that, in 92 percent of the cases, the teachers could give no reason for perceiving student behavior as being bad. Furthermore, in 95.6 percent of the cases, the teacher never provided the class with any knowledge of expected standards. This, of course, is an indictment of the teacher, not the students.

In another study, Kounin (1970) noted the effects on the class of the way in which teachers either punished students or provided desists when a student or group misbehaved. After observing students in kindergarten through college, he collected data based on experimental conditions to show that the way the teacher provided a desist had, in fact, an accompanying effect on all of the class members. Kounin called this the *ripple effect*. As the students in a class observe the teacher confronting a student for apparent misbehavior, all other class members tend to be adversely affected as well. Kounin reported that the angry desist did not motivate the other students to behave better or to attend to the task; rather, it made them anxious, restless, and uninvolved.

Reflect — The use of punishment as a classroom management tool is controversial. Are there any circumstances in which proponents of desist strategies and assertive discipline might agree on the use of punishment as appropriate? Do you believe there are any circumstances in which punishment is permissible in our schools?

Assertive Discipline   A structured approach called **assertive discipline** is designed to assist teachers in running an organized, teacher-in-charge class-room environment. Lee and Marlene Canter (1992) created the original asser-tive discipline program after working with numerous school systems. Using their research and observation, together with behavior management theory, they developed an approach to help teachers become the stewards of their classrooms, while positively influencing their students' behavior.

Assertive discipline is a form of behavior management.

A Discipline Plan   At the core of assertive discipline is a *classroom discipline plan*, a lesson plan that allows the teacher to detail classroom rules and the corresponding behaviors that are expected from students. Additionally, the lesson details what can be expected from the teacher in return. The aim of the plan is to have a fair and consistent way to establish a safe, orderly, positive classroom in which teachers teach and students learn. A discipline plan has the following three parts.

1. **Classroom rules.** The assertive teacher has clearly stated classroom rules and provides firm, clear, concise directions to students who are in need of behavior management. Effective rules are limited in number (five at most), are observable (not vague), apply at all times of day, apply to behavior only and not to academics, and are written or chosen with student participation.
2. **Positive recognition.** During this phase of the lesson, the teacher focuses on building positive teacher–student relationships and emphasizing the importance of cooperative behaviors for everyone. As discussed in the upcoming section on behavior modification, positive recognition can take many forms and should be appropriate for the age and the subject being taught. It may include giving frequent praise, sending positive notes home to parents, or motivating students with special privileges.
3. **Consequences.** When disruptive behavior occurs, the teacher must be prepared to deal with it calmly and quickly. Consequences should be organized in a hierarchy from the first time a student breaks a rule until the fifth time. A warning is the most common first consequence. Contacting parents and making administrative referrals should appear near the end of the hierarchy. The hierarchy should include a "severe clause" for severe misbehavior such as a fight or bullying.

Assertive discipline underscores the belief that teachers can mold a student's ability to control his or her behavior through a program of positive recognition and consequences.

Behavior Modification   The process of changing behavior by rewarding desired actions and ignoring or punishing undesired actions is called **behavior modification**. It is a set of strategies you can use in establishing effective classroom management. The classroom teacher can select components of the behavioral approach while retaining a humanistic approach to learning and students. The basic steps in the technique are discussed below (adapted from Salvia, Ysseldyke, & Bolt 2007).

Phase 1: Charting Baseline Behaviors   During the baseline period, the teacher observes and records instances of the target behavior (the behavior to be changed). This phase provides evidence of whether the problem actually exists. Systematic observation may reveal that a student who has been labeled "disruptive" does not exhibit disruptive behavior more often than his peers. All data are recorded and tallied so that an established rate of occurrence may be determined. (See Figure 6.4, which illustrates one example of charting.)

Phase 2: Intervention or Experimentation   The chart serves as a baseline in choosing an appropriate strategy and determining its effectiveness. For example, if the behavior occurs only two or three times during silent reading, you may select ways to increase the student's ability to read silently. Structure the day so that during these periods you are positioned near the student to

FIGURE 6.4

Charting an Effective Behavior Modification Strategy for "Turning in Homework"

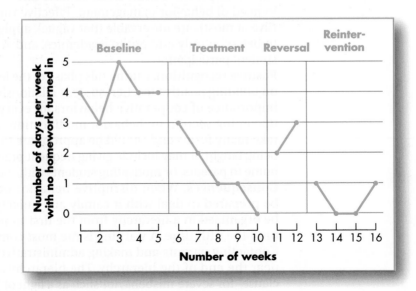

INSTRUCTIONAL
Strategies

Recording Classroom Behaviors: Make It Simple

Systematic observation: Incorporate the simple steps suggested below when charting in your classroom:

◆ Create a seating chart with students identified.

◆ Create a shorthand code for behaviors you wish to record:

"O" Off-Task
"P" Classroom Participation
"I" Inappropriate Behavior

◆ Record the behaviors across at least three instructional periods.

◆ Analyze resulting data for trends. (For example: Is there a relationship between "off-task" and "classroom participation"? Could you change this outcome by redirecting questions to nonparticipating students?)

administer verbal praise when the appropriate behavior (silent reading) occurs. If, after a few days of your increased attention, there is a decrease in the number of times the student talks to neighbors during a silent reading period, you can assume that the strategy is having a positive effect. In most cases, you will try to reinforce an appropriate behavior while ignoring or not responding to inappropriate ones.

Sometimes verbal reinforcers are adequate to modify the student's behavior. You may need to experiment to determine the set of reinforcers that changes the student's behavior with the least effort. In some cases, you need visible or material reinforcers such as stars on the student's papers, the student's name on the class "honor list," tokens, pencils, or special privileges. Whatever the reward, it is absolutely imperative that it follow the appropriate behavior immediately.

Reinforcement is defined as consequences that increase the future rate of a behavior. The use of reinforcers, or rewards that encourage students to repeat positive behaviors, is a critical component of behavior modification (see the box below). If you use the same set of reinforcers over an extended time, you may find that they lose their impact. After studying this problem, Roger Addison and Donald T. Tosti (1979) compiled a system and a list of reinforcers that can be applied with various motivational strategies in an educational environment.

Sample Reinforcers for Classroom Situations

◆ Recognition

◆ Tangible rewards (e.g., school supplies)

◆ Classroom learning activities

◆ Classroom and school responsibilities

◆ Status indicators

◆ Incentive feedback

◆ Personal activities

(continued)

Sample Reinforcers for Classroom Situations—Cont'd

- ◆ Social activities
- ◆ Relief from restrictive policies or procedures (for example, freedom to move around the classroom)
- ◆ Relief from restrictive classroom environments (for example, work independently or in small groups)

Reinforcers are very personal; a teacher may have to try various reinforcers with a specific student before finding the most powerful one (Addison & Tosti 1979, McElroy 2000). Obviously, there is no one universal reinforcer. Several of the above activities have been classified as being aspects of *student recognition programs*. Such programs emphasize student success. Recognition helps create a positive climate and makes schooling intentionally inviting.

Select reinforcers to fit the student.

Phase 3: Reversal to Baseline Conditions   For most teachers, no further class manipulation is necessary once the appropriate reward or reinforcer is determined. However, to follow the behavior modification paradigm completely, you should return from the phase 2 conditions to those classroom conditions that were present during the original baseline period. Teachers often resist this requirement because it means returning to the original conditions that seemingly prompted the undesired behavior.

As in phases 1 and 2, in phase 3 data are consistently tabulated so that the behavioral patterns are quickly discernible. Phase 3 usually is conducted only long enough to effect a reversal of behavior to the baseline type. When you have again observed such behavior, go on to phase 4.

Phase 4: Reinstating the Intervention Conditions   The final stage reinstates the conditions used during phase 2. If the intervention caused a change in behaviors during the second phase, it should do so again at this time. But if there is no change toward the desired behaviors, then you were just lucky in phase 2 and you will have to start all over again. Now you can understand why teachers dislike phase 3.

General Principles for Using Classroom Management Strategies

1. *Accentuate the positive.* Schools have been criticized for being too "unpleasant" and teachers for being far too negative toward students. To change this image, the teacher must praise students, even if it is for the most inconsequential matter. Admittedly, it may be difficult to praise a student who continually disrupts the class, but it has been frequently demonstrated that simply admonishing a student will not reduce the inappropriate behavior. Praising some positive aspect of the student's behavior is more likely to bring about change (see Ellett 1993).

Finding something to praise is not always easy.

How does the teacher use different forms of praise or social reinforcement? There are verbal, nonverbal, and tactile reinforcers. Several examples of positive verbal and nonverbal praise are listed in the box on page 195. We comment on tactile reinforcers in the next section.

2. *Identify productive behavior for the class.* Praise provides reinforcement not only for the student to whom it is directed but also for the entire class. Praise provides students with an explicit model of what you expect of them. To be sure, public praise can be embarrassing as well as reinforcing; therefore, you must learn what technique works best for each student—and hence for the whole class.

3. *Start small.* In most cases, students view major changes in behavior as unachievable. If a student hands in about 25 percent of the required homework assignments, there is little chance that reinforcement will result in 100 percent completion right away. However, you can still establish a definite contingency schedule by making a behavioral contract with the student. The student may complete two of five assignments in the first week. If so, move up the requirement to three of five assignments for the next week. Remember that the student probably did not reach the present level of academic deficiency in one step. Therefore, do not expect to remedy the problem in one great leap. Take small initial steps by increasing the quantity or the quality until the student reaches the agreed-upon criterion. This requires you to be patient and to give constant positive feedback to the student.

4. *Be consistent.* As you begin to use behavior modification in the classroom, whether on an individual or a group basis, keep your own behavior consistent and predictable. If you remain consistent in your responses to student stimuli, then you can better predict the reactions of class members. For example, ask that every student always raise his or her hand and wait to be called on to answer a question, and always wait until students do so before calling on them.

INSTRUCTIONAL *Strategies*

Examples of Verbal and Nonverbal Praise

Verbal Praise

All right	Great	Dynamite	Very interesting
Fantastic	Nice work	Keep it up	Wonderful
Splendid	Terrific	Cool	Fabulous
Awesome	Clever	A winner	Marvelous
Neat	Ideal	Excellent	Yes
Super	Good job	Lovely	Wow
Beautiful			

Nonverbal Praise

Laughing	Thumbs-up signal
Pointing with a smile	Moving toward student
Smiling	Nodding approval
Looking with interest	Raising the eyebrows
High-five	

Key Ideas

Basic Steps in Behavior Modification

1. Collect baseline information to verify the problem behavior.
2. Use a strategy to bring about a change in the behavior.
3. Revert to the baseline problem by discontinuing the selected strategy.
4. Once again, reintroduce the change strategy.

Reflect

Select your favorite classroom management model and provide a brief explanation for its selection and several steps for implementing it in your classroom.

SECTION 4   Managing Classroom Routines

Chart behaviors to support a hunch!

Classroom management models provide a strategy for managing instructional and behavioral interactions in the classroom (see Table 6.5). We focus here on the three key elements master teachers use to effectively establish classroom management rules and routines (see the box below).

Three Key Elements of Effective Classroom Management

1. Planning and preparing a classroom
2. Selecting and establishing usable rules
3. Keeping student records

VIDEO CASE

Find out which strategies work best for seasoned teachers in the Video Case entitled "Classroom Management: Best Practices" on the student website. As you watch the clips and study the artifacts in the case, answer these questions: 1. Which of their techniques echo what you're learning in this chapter? 2. Which are different? The bonus video gives tips for managing a technology-based lesson.

Planning and Preparing Your Classroom

Planning is a top priority for effective time management. Detailed planning is initially time consuming, but teachers who make explicit plans are better organized and progress faster in achieving educational goals (Walsh 1992). Teachers who plan and communicate their expectations to their students promote a positive academic environment. Thus, teachers with an effective plan know what, to whom, and how they will teach; they have materials ready for their students; they plan for smooth transitions between classes and activities; and they have additional activities ready for students who finish early (Starr 2005).

Master teachers have evolved their planning and preparation strategies over a number of years. It may appear at first haphazard to you, but in reality their approach has evolved through successes and failures. Do not make the mistake of believing planning is a quick, one-time effort.

TABLE 6.5	Sources of Problems in Classroom Management

If you observe several of these problems in a classroom, you likely will find lower student achievement and poor student morale.

Motivation Problems

Insufficient activity for students
Student apathy
Difficulty getting students involved
Negative student attitudes
Daydreaming
Lack of student success
Negative teacher attitudes

What comes first: poor rules, unclear directions, or the misbehavior?

Instructional Problems

Lack of variety in instructional techniques
Inadequately communicated goals and objectives
Bad pacing (too fast or too slow)
Lack of prerequisite skills, causing student failure
Student distress or anger over evaluations
Students not following directions
Failure to complete all assignments

Procedural Problems

Unclear assignments
Moving the class to a different room
Lack of a systematic routine for procedural activities
Failing to reserve a special room or space for an activity
Forgetting to check out projector or AV equipment
Failing to preview media, resulting in presentation of inappropriate material
Not having the necessary materials in the classroom
Failure to plan discussion groups in advance

Disruptive Problems

Excessive talking at beginning of class
Note passing
Cheating
Stealing
Vandalism
Attention seeking
Arriving late for class
Racial tensions
Teacher making value judgments about students' dress, home life, or parents
Teacher making unenforceable threats
Students using obscene language or gestures

Well-prepared teachers keep lessons moving at a brisk pace but do not ignore students who are having difficulties. They do not allow interruptions during a lesson, and they stress the importance of every lesson. They make a practice of critiquing their day's work. They jot a few notes into their lesson planning books to act as tips for future lessons. Their lesson plans are very brief and conceptual in nature, but they do carry out formal planning (see Martella & Nelson 2003).

Well-prepared teachers critique each day's lesson.

Selecting and Establishing Classroom Rules

The purpose of establishing rules is to enhance students' academic and social achievement (see Marzano, Marzano, & Pickering 2003). Teachers who are effective managers explain the importance and need for each rule, teach students how to follow rules and procedures, and begin with the rules that are of the most immediate importance. (How do I get permission to leave the room? How do I ask a question?) They state rules clearly and enforce them consistently. On-again, off-again enforcement contributes to student behavior problems.

Rules must be introduced, reinforced, and applied consistently.

Effective teachers also make rules that are not related to discipline. These cover classroom routines for distributing materials, transitioning to new activities, starting and ending class, obtaining permission to leave the classroom, and accomplishing tasks such as sharpening pencils (norms). Simplicity is the hallmark of effective rules (Kentucky Department of Education 2008). If your rules are complicated, you will not be able to enforce them, and students will become confused. Thus simplicity will allow you to easily explain and enforce your rules.

Characteristics of Effective Classroom Rules
The effective teacher has clearly stated classroom rules and provides firm, clear, concise reinforcement of these rules when it is appropriate. Effective rules:

◆ are limited in number

◆ are observable (not vague)

◆ apply at all times of day in all school locations

◆ apply to behavior only and not to academics

◆ are selected with democratic student participation

Reflect   To what extent do you believe that the gender of the teacher or the student influences the selection of classroom rules? Provide an example.

Maintaining Student Records Efficiently

Every teacher faces the tasks of recording grades, taking attendance, keeping track of students' class participation, recording disciplinary actions, and documenting other aspects of classroom life. For legality, fairness, and consistency, you need to develop a comprehensive and systematic approach to record keeping.

Good records are essential to fair grading.

Records management is an extremely important part of maintaining a fair and equitable grading system. After you have established reasonable guidelines for standards, quality, late work, missed assignments, bonus work, makeup tests, and class participation, you must be prepared to track each student's performance in each area reliably and consistently.

In addition, you should maintain objective anecdotal records (short objective notes about student actions) to document classroom incidents such as fights, inappropriate behavior, and cheating. Of course, you should also record acts of courage, ingenuity, and creativity. If you notice a rapid change in a student's dress, friends, language, or attitude, you should note the change and closely monitor it. Such behavioral change frequently indicates abuse of some nature (physical, gang, or drug). Record these acts when they happen. This record will provide you with a chronicle that may provide evidence to support or confront a student at some later date.

SECTION 5 Managing the Classroom Environment

Every day in each class you will find yourself facing a group of students anticipating your every action and remark. Some students are eager to learn and others are not so eager. In prior chapters you have been presented with strategies for managing the academic objectives for your classroom; now you will need to face the practical realities of teaching: managing the space, the interactions among students and yourself and all outside influences that frequently occur and influence learning outcomes. You are the teacher and you are in charge. Now we will discuss five essential ingredients for successfully managing the flow of your instructional day.

Elements for Managing the Flow of Classroom Instruction

1. Getting off to a good start
2. Giving effective directions
3. Monitoring the classroom environment
4. Managing classroom interruptions
5. Managing abusive student attitudes and behaviors

Getting Off to a Good Start

Effective classroom managers discuss classroom procedures with their students at the beginning of the school year and provide opportunities for students to practice the procedures to ensure understanding (Lombardi 1992; Tauber 2007). During the first few days of school, your students will require frequent feedback. State your expectations often and give students positive or corrective responses. By the end of the third or fourth week of school, you can

Simplicity is the hallmark of effective rules.

© Ellen Senisi/The Image Works

anticipate that transitions will be smoother and shorter and that reminders to your students on class routines can be greatly reduced (Evertson, Emmer, & Worsham 2006). It is much easier to be firm and precise in the beginning and then relax as you observe that students have adopted your rules. It is almost impossible to gain control once chaos takes over.

The first day of school is a testing period. Students will test your rules, your determination to apply them fairly, and your commitment to maintaining them. Proper management is essential for learning and for student safety. Apply your rules immediately, fairly and with determination. Introduce, explain, reinforce, and repeat. The first day is also the best time to initiate routines. This is the day to establish a positive, caring, and businesslike environment.

Giving Effective Directions

Giving directions is a core skill (Anderson 2002). Whether the directions concern instruction or classroom procedures, give them clearly and succinctly. Even more importantly, their tone must be positive. Directions such as "Stop that" or "Cut that out" given to disruptive students omit the most important part: What is the student to do after he or she stops the disruptive behavior? Provide the student with a constructive alternative. For example, you might suggest that the student return to work, or you might provide some instructionally related activity to replace the disruptive behavior. For example, you might say, "Sam, let's turn to page 72 in your book and complete the questions about today's reading. I will review your answers in 10 minutes."

Positive correcting: State the desired behavior.

INSTRUCTIONAL
Strategies

Steps for Effective Directions

1. Give the directions.
   - ◆ Get the class's attention.
   - ◆ Deliver the directions in brief steps (both orally and in writing).
   - ◆ Explain expectations—what students will produce and when.
   - ◆ Ask a student to restate the directions and expectations.
   - ◆ Repeat the directions.
2. Follow up the directions.
   - ◆ Closely monitor selected individuals until it is clear that the directions are understood and being applied.
   - ◆ If the class or an individual student is having a problem, point out a positive example as an alternative to the problem.

Monitoring the Classroom Environment

Effective teachers monitor student behavior in the classroom. They make each student responsible for some work during the learning activity and then watch to see that it is actually accomplished. These teachers are strong student motivators (Wood 2001).

Room Arrangement   The arrangement of the room is an important part of a monitoring strategy (AFT 2008). An orderly arrangement of desks and tables in a classroom contributes to a smooth, businesslike atmosphere that promotes effective use of instructional time. Two criteria for effective room arrangement are (1) your ability to see all students at all times and (2) the circulation patterns that you establish. It is important to be able to monitor all students from your desk and from all other areas where you are likely to be. Simply being visually close to a student can prevent many problems. This is your greatest deterrent against harassing and bullying behavior.

Sightline to all students prevents problems.

   If the physical aspects of your classroom permit the rearranging of student seats, you might consider various small-group arrangements: circles, U shapes, or 50-50 splits. Often, a change in perspective results from rearranging the classroom and may energize the students with a different perspective on the material and learning.

Questioning   Another effective monitoring strategy is questioning (see Chapter 7). During learning activities, effective teachers ask questions and then look around the room before calling on a student. They call on volunteers as well as others and seem to get around to everyone, but not in a predictable manner. Effective teachers intersperse calls for group answers with solicitations of individual responses and occasionally throw out challenging statements such as "I don't think anyone can get this!" Finally, effective teachers monitor their classes by asking students to react to the answers of others. Such monitoring strategies promote a smooth-flowing, highly interactive learning environment with a high percentage of on-task student behavior.

Observing   Effective teachers constantly observe the activities of their students. This requires always placing yourself in a position to observe and be observed. If your students know you are watching how they behave and interact, you will prevent many problems. This might be called "classroom management by walking around." This concept is highly espoused in business management, but we believe it was first employed by classroom teachers. Walking around your classroom allows you to check on those students who may be having difficulty with the small group or individual seat-work and deter misbehavior by proximity to students contemplating mischief. It is important for academic achievement to catch problems early on in the lesson and correct student misunderstanding.

A watchful eye is a deterrent to bad behavior.

Managing Classroom Interruptions

Teachers spend a tremendous amount of time planning instruction: preparing lesson plans, selecting support materials, creating student activities, designing tests, and so on. Yet all too often the anticipated instructional period is drastically reduced by interruptions. Lost time! Studies have demonstrated that frequently 30 percent or more of the instructional day is lost to anticipated and unanticipated interruptions. These interruptions range from student misbehavior to announcements over the intercom. (We heard of one example of 30 such announcements in one day!) Whatever its cause, lost time has a negative impact on student academic achievement and contributes to student behavior problems (see Ysseldyke & Elliott 1999).

Interruptions steal time from teaching and learning.

The ability to manage most interruptions is fully within a teacher's control (Leonard 1999). You simply need to anticipate and plan for them. You must plan for transitions in instruction (anticipated interruptions), and you must establish firm expectations regarding student behavior to reduce the instructional impact of unanticipated interruptions. Table 6.6 lists some examples of anticipated and unanticipated interruptions.

TABLE 6.6	The Best Teachers are Prepared for Interruptions
Anticipated Interruptions	
Transitions between and during instructional episodes	
Equipment setup and breakdown	
Materials distribution/collection	
Changing from teacher- to student-centered activity	
Beginning/end of class or school day	
Unanticipated Interruptions	
Student illness	
Visitors	
Announcements/messages	
Student behavioral problems	
Equipment malfunctions	
Fire alarms/classroom evacuations	
Materials shortages	

Anticipated Interruptions Twenty-one percent of class time is spent on transitions (Gump 1982, Smith 1985)—ending one activity and beginning another. Effective teachers prepare their students for transitions (Cotton 2001) by using advance cues ("In five minutes we're going to start our math quiz!"). Besides making smooth transitions from one activity to the next, they are especially careful not to end one activity and begin a second and then return to the first. Abrupt endings to activities set the stage for numerous behavior problems. To become more efficient, give signals, set time limits, and provide very clear instructions—even modeling them as needed (Gump 1982).

Gaps in teacher directions before and after an instructional episode or interruption are a frequent cause of both classroom management problems and lost instructional opportunities. Frequently teachers get caught up in the physical requirements of lesson setup or breakdown, materials handling, and student assessment. While the teacher is focusing on these tasks, the class is left idle, which often leads to problems! Thus, teachers must develop strategies for managing prelesson transitions, transitions that occur during a lesson, and postlesson transitions. Among other strategies, teachers should plan to use "fillers"—student activities or routines that fill the gaps created by transitions between instructional episodes and administrative activities.

1. *Prelesson transitions.* Delegate administrative tasks to students whenever possible. Whenever possible, a routine should be established and followed for managing attendance, announcements, materials distribution and collection, and special activities. For example, you could create a routine in which homework is checked by a peer or teacher's aide and deposited in student files. Rotate the students selected for such administrative support activities. Many teachers use the first few minutes of class and the last few minutes to encourage creative thinking activities, which are repeated each day. Puzzles, thought problems, computer games, or related art and media projects that can be quickly started and stopped are good fillers. Naturally, it is important to assign some value to these activities in terms of student grades (see Scofield 2000–2001 for ideas).

2. *Transitions that occur during a lesson.* Students rarely complete an activity in a uniform time span. A prepared teacher recognizes the likelihood of this and prepares supplementary activities or additional resources for the fast workers. Many teachers use peer tutor strategies or have fast finishers assist with administrative tasks (such as correcting tests) or prepare for the next instructional episode. The transition from a regular to a supplementary activity must be carefully thought out and the procedures explained to the class in advance. If you develop activities that can be used on a regular basis, be sure to state your expectations for their use clearly and then reinforce appropriate student behaviors.

3. *Postlesson transitions.* Teacher control of the classroom can easily break down at the end of an instructional episode, due to the many details a teacher must attend to before the class moves on. Frequently you will be involved with materials collection, equipment management, individual student assignments, or administrative chores. Prepare for such demands

Be prepared: Expect interruptions and plan for them.

Quick learners can be effective peer tutors during transitions.

by developing routine student activities. Create a routine for the last five minutes of each class period or instructional episode. The routine will give you time to shift from one class or activity to the next. The ending activity should be self-paced and self-instructional for the students. The teacher should merely announce the beginning of the "curtain" (ending) activity, and everyone should know what to do. For such curtain activities, avoid student movement, materials distribution, and teaming. The activities should focus on the individual and provide an opportunity for relaxed exploration. Reading, writing, drawing, student planning, or journal writing are appropriate for the closing minutes. Avoid the rigorous, the active, the involved. *Slow things down. Your students need a breather before moving on to the next instructional episode,* just as you do.

Unanticipated Interruptions   During the course of a typical day, many unanticipated events occur. These events may be initiated by students, school personnel, visitors, or others. They include fire alarms, intercom announcements, broken equipment, problems with the school building, messages from the office, and untold other attention breaks. You can anticipate that such events will occur each day; however, you cannot anticipate when they will occur or how long they will last. For example, loss of electrical power is always an interesting instructional interruption with which to cope. All you can do is prepare yourself and your classes for such eventualities. During the initial weeks of the school year, you should explain your expectations for how the class is to deal with unanticipated interruptions. Provide specific instructions concerning what students should do in an emergency (fire, injury, chemical spill, accident, electrical failure, earthquake). How should students behave for a visitor (parent, student, other)? How will the class manage itself if your attention is required to resolve another issue or if you must leave the room? You may want to simulate these events. The expected behaviors should become part of your classroom's norms.

Visitor Simulation   An expected guest enters your classroom for a brief period of observation. You introduce the guest and explain what is taking place in your class. You suggest a good vantage point for observation before you go on with the day's lesson. After a reasonable time you stop the lesson and involve the class in a discussion of the issues and student behaviors surrounding the visit and the guest. After the discussion, you ask the guest to provide input and suggestions for a better environment for guests.

When explaining your expectations for interruptions and transitions, be sure to provide a detailed explanation of the importance of good behavior and ongoing academic effort. All too frequently, a teacher will establish a set of classroom rules but fail to explain their importance to classroom citizenship and learning.

The specific way you approach planning for interruptions obviously will vary according to your students' maturity levels. Individual planning can help reduce the time loss caused by anticipated interruptions; however, many unanticipated interruptions are school-wide or otherwise beyond the teacher's control (intercom messages, inappropriate classroom visitors). The teachers in a school must band together to address such interruptions and suggest ways to stop or greatly reduce them.

Explain the rule and its importance.

Reflect What impact do unanticipated interruptions have on a teacher and her/his lesson plan?

Managing Abusive Student Attitudes and Behaviors

Alcohol, drugs, harassment, bullying, and cyber-bullying are a few of the abusive and destructive student behaviors teachers may encounter. With instruction being our primary focus, we often miss the signals of these problems in our classes. Parents and school personnel at Columbine High School denied there were any prior indicators of the murderous events that later unfolded. However, a Governor's report clearly underscored the many signals that were available to anyone choosing to pay attention (The Report of Governor Bill Owens 2001). It is very important for every teacher to be aware of the classroom and school environment and to work at ensuring that it is safe and inclusive.

Child Abuse Every school has a strict written policy outlining the steps to be taken if child abuse is suspected by a teacher or reported to school personnel. These policies have been developed in conjunction with the courts to protect our most vulnerable citizens. A teacher has little recourse but to follow such policies exactly. Most school districts will provide an orientation to all new teachers regarding the policy and procedure for handling such cases and will expect all personnel to follow the guidelines rigorously. States such as Washington have laws requiring all school personnel to report suspected child abuse. Discuss this point with your principal on the first day of school!

Most schools have specific, directive policies for reporting child abuse.

Alcohol and Drug Abuse In today's schools, you almost certainly will come in contact with possible drug and alcohol use among your students. According to the University of Michigan News and Information Services (2006), 66.5 percent of high school seniors used alcohol in the previous 12 months and 31.5 percent used marijuana. High use of prescription drugs (21.3 percent) was also tabulated. An article in *Time* magazine by Ken Thomas (2008) made a special note of the increasing dropout rate in our nation's largest school districts. These are the same districts that face an epidemic of alcohol and drug use in their schools. Without help, the young people indulging in alcohol and drugs will drop out of school and be likely to face a life of unemployment and poverty.

As a teacher, you are responsible for encouraging students to understand and value our system of government and laws. Your role demands that you exhibit high ethical standards because the community has given you charge of its youth. Furthermore, professional ethics preclude your support of student use of alcohol or illegal drugs. On a personal level, we must do a better job of listening to and making time for our students. Plan regularly for after-school conference time to talk with your students. Encourage those you feel are at risk to drop by for a chat. Encourage at-risk students to

◀◀ ▶ ▶▶ VIDEO CASE

Peer pressure is often cited as a cause of drug and alcohol use in students. Watch the Video Case entitled "Social and Emotional Development: The Influence of Peer Groups" and the bonus segment "A Real Story About Bullying" on the student website. 1. How does teacher Voncille Ross help her students process these everyday pressures? 2. How would you react if this were your class?

Teacher attitudes should reflect the importance of laws.

become involved in after-school activities. Too frequently, children are raising themselves and are alone after school when the riskiest behaviors, including drug and alcohol use, sexual activity, and criminal activities, surface. The box below lists several early warning signs of alcohol and drug abuse.

Early Warning Signs of Alcohol or Drug Abuse

◆ *Sudden behavioral changes.* Homework is lost, is not turned in, is copied, or declines in quality.

◆ *Attitude changes.* Comments are made to hurt others' feelings, or an "I-don't-care" demeanor emerges.

◆ *School problems.* Grades decline, difficulties with other teachers and school personnel appear, fights and arguments occur.

◆ *Changes in social relationships.* Student abandons old friends, becomes involved with a different social group.

◆ *Self-destructive behavior.* Student develops injuries from "falls" or "fights" that he or she has difficulty recounting.

◆ *Avoidance.* Student withdraws or refuses to communicate, spends an inappropriate amount of time in isolation.

All teachers must be cautious in handling students suspected of drug or alcohol abuse. An accusation may lead to a lawsuit by the student or his or her parents. Our advice is to check with school administrators on the accepted protocol for dealing with such problems (Zabel & Zabel 1996). Managing alcohol and drug problems not only is critical to learning, it is essential for the health and well-being of your class, school, and community.

Bullying, Cyber-Bullying, and Harassment   In 2005, students ages 12 through 18 were asked if they had been bullied (that is, picked on or made to do things they did not want to do) at school. About 9 percent of the students reported they had been bullied, with females as likely as males to report being bullied (National Center for Education Statistics 2007). Bullying contributes to a climate of fear and intimidation in schools. "Bullying is one of the most serious and yet under-rated problems in school today," said Ronald Stephens, executive director of the National School Safety Center, a California nonprofit group that researches school crime and violence (Wicker 1999).

Educators are redefining school violence to include all the time-honored tools of the schoolyard bully—ridicule and jokes, mean tricks, and exclusion. Bullying is a power issue (Jacobson, 2007). While much of the bad behavior occurs in bathrooms, hallways, playgrounds, and classrooms, it is quickly finding a home on digital media (see the Technology Insight box on Cyber-Bullying on page 208). Many kids try bullying strategies at some time, but a few use them regularly. Whereas boys typically use physical tactics, girls often bully with insults and by ostracizing and gossiping about others. In her book *Odd Girl Out*, Rachel Simmons (2002) discusses this covert aggression shown by girls against other girls. In addition, Emily White (2002) writes how labels and rumors about other girls' alleged sex lives create social ostracism and isolation. Elementary school bullies generally pick targets of their own gender, but as early as the fifth grade, bullies begin to target the opposite sex. Young bullies, left unchecked, are likely to move on to sexual harassment or physical violence when they get older. Children who seem friendless are such magnets for bullying that even one friend can make a difference. As a teacher, you need to be aware of even the subtlest social manifestations of bullying (see Garbarino & deLara 2003).

Girls and boys differ in how they bully.

Teacher intervention must be consistent, thoughtful, and skilled (see below). Teachers should establish classroom rules regarding bullying and harassment and enforce them. Inappropriate behavior should draw consequences that are administered immediately and calmly. Remove the bullying child from the environment and instruct the child privately of the resulting consequences. No matter what caused the behavior, seek assistance from your school's administrators, counselors, psychologist, and other teachers to reinforce the consequences. Remember, the bully is frequently a victim in other circumstances.

INSTRUCTIONAL *Strategies*

Strategies for Overcoming Bullying

◆ Tell students that standing up to meanness takes more courage than fighting.

◆ Put up banners with antibullying slogans.

◆ Urge bystanders to speak up in defense of the victim, tell a teacher, and be sure not to encourage bullying behavior.

◆ Intervene when bullying or teasing behavior is observed.

◆ Have zero tolerance for unwanted touching, verbal comments, name-calling, sexual rumors, and rude gestures, jokes, or cartoons.

◆ Assign older students to be "book-buddies" with new kids and with those students who demonstrate tendencies to be isolated during student activities.

◆ Organize breakfast clubs for new students to help them build friendships and support networks.

The effectiveness of any classroom management strategy depends on how much time, energy, and confidence you invest in it. A possible pitfall is moving quickly from one technique to another without expending the necessary time and energy to make any strategy succeed. Such efforts are likely to be counterproductive, thus confusing the student and making management problems more severe. The final selection and implementation of any one strategy or combination of strategies rest solely with you, but the ultimate criterion is student success.

Only you can transform the classroom into an interesting and positive learning environment. Structure that environment so that everyone is highly motivated to learn. It is the very least that you can do—or perhaps the very most!

Reflect

◆ If you observed a case of bullying *off* the school campus, should you take action? How might other adults/parents respond?

◆ If you suspected the use of an illegal substance by a student and you believed harm was resulting, what action would (or must) you take?

TECHNOLOGY
Insight

Cyber-Bullying in Schools

"Cyber-bullying" occurs when a preteen or teen is threatened, harassed, humiliated, or otherwise targeted by another preteen or teen using the Internet, interactive and digital technologies, or mobile phones. When schools use disciplinary actions toward a student for cyber-bullying actions that took place off-campus and outside of school hours, they may be sued for exceeding their authority and violating the student's freedom of speech. Here are a few suggestions for dealing proactively with cyber-bullying situations:

◆ *Sponsor cyber-bullying awareness events:* Schools can be very effective brokers in working with parents to stop and remedy cyber-bullying situations (www.cyberbullying.org). They can educate their students on cyber-ethics and the law. (A provision can be added to the school's acceptable use policy reserving the right to discipline students for actions taken off-campus if they are intended to adversely affect the safety and well-being of student(s) in or out of school. This makes it a contractual issue between the student, parents, and school.

◆ *Provide "walled garden" DSN environments:* Schools have an obligation to prepare their students for the digital world. A large part of the digital world for preteens and teens is the world of digital social networking (DSN). The general perception that all DSN takes place in what is essentially an uncontrolled environment is incorrect. "Walled garden" DSN environments do exist and some are available free to educators, students and parents. These environments permit adults to moderate interactions between students and help them learn the appropriate uses of digital applications. The free DSN site provided by The Oracle Foundation through Think.com (http://www.think.com) is an example of a "walled garden" DSN environment. In the "walled garden" environment, a student has the opportunity to learn about the digital world in a social networking environment safe from potential harassment.

For further information on cyber-bullying awareness strategies, visit http://www.cyberbullying.org

Reflect

A Closing Reflection

◆ How will you establish a classroom environment that rewards appropriate behavior and deters inappropriate behavior?

◆ How can you evaluate a management strategy's potential impact on learning in your classroom?

◆ What "yardsticks" will you use to judge the effectiveness of your classroom management philosophy during your first week in front of a class?

Summary Points

1. A positive classroom management model is based on adherence to norms and your awareness of and insight into the classroom environment.

2. Parental involvement aids in achieving learning expectations and reinforcing classroom norms and behaviors.

3. Classroom management models based on student self-discipline, which include the hierarchy of needs, moral reasoning, and teacher effectiveness training, stress student personal responsibility.

4. Classroom management models based on teacher discipline, such as desist strategies, assertive discipline, and behavior modification, stress teacher authority and control.

5. The application of behavior modification strategies in the classroom requires the identification of positive student behavior and consistent use of rewards.

6. A positive environment is based on creating a plan, establishing rules, getting off to a good start, providing clear directions, observing student behavior, managing interruptions, and maintaining records.

7. A positive environment adapts the classroom environment to the individual needs of the students and inhibits abusive behaviors.

8. Teachers must learn to recognize the signs of child abuse, drug and alcohol abuse, and bullying (including cyber-bullying) in order to deter abusive behavior and maximize learning outcomes.

Building a Career Portfolio

As you continue to assemble your career portfolio, we strongly suggest that you include a set of personally tested classroom management strategies. You might begin with the following items and ideas.

- Collect a set of school district classroom management or discipline policies. (e.g., child abuse policies, alcohol and drug policies, website postings).

- Interview a master teacher or two to learn what classroom management strategies and rules they use.

- Examine your state educational codes to locate regulations for classroom management and discipline.

- List three or four rules you will introduce in your classroom on the first day of school.

Resources

PRINT

Algozzine, B., & P. Kay (Eds). *Preventing Problem Behaviors: A Handbook of Successful Prevention Strategies.* Thousand Oaks, CA: Corwin, 2002, 247 pp. This compilation of papers is provided under the auspices of the Council for Exceptional Children and covers a wide array of problems and solutions.

Brainard, E. "Classroom Management: Seventy-Three Suggestions for Secondary School Teachers." *Clearing House 74*(4) (2001): 207–210. If you are looking for just one quick reference, this is it. The author provides extensive checklists on (1) relating to students positively, (2) preventing misbehavior, (3) handling discipline, and (4) providing classroom leadership.

Charles, C. M. *Building Classroom Discipline* (9th ed.). Boston: Allyn and Bacon, 2008, 336 pp.
   The author analyzes 17 different models of school discipline. Case studies and historical precedents are included.

Daniels, V. I. "How to Manage Disruptive Behavior in Inclusive Classrooms." *Teaching Exceptional Children 30*(4) (1998): 26–31.
   This short article provides helpful tools for teachers with mainstreamed students or inclusive classrooms.

Evertson, C. M., & C. S. Weinstein (Eds). *Handbook of Classroom Management: Research, Practice and Contemporary Issues.* Mahwah, NJ: Lawrence Erlbaum Associates, 2006.
   This tome provides an extensive historical perspective on classroom management practices and research in the United States.

Rigby, K. *Stop the Bullying: A Handbook for Teachers.* Portland, ME: Stenhouse, 2001, 64 pp.
   In just 64 pages, the author provides a practical and research-based guide for action.

The Journal of Moral Education
   For detailed discussions focused on moral and character education, refer to current issues of this journal.

INTERNET

Go to the website for this book at www.cengage.com/education/orlich to find live links to resources related to this chapter.

◆ The website of the Boston University Center for the Advancement of Ethics and Character is rich with information related to moral and character education.
   http://www.bu.edu/education/caec

◆ The Josephson Institute of Ethics organized "Character Counts," a coalition of schools, communities, and organizations to advance character education.
   http://www.charactercounts.org

◆ The following sites provide a rich dialogue about assertive discipline strategies, resources, and programs.
   http://www.honorlevel.com/
   http://www.humboldt.edu/~tha1/canter.html
   http://www.adprima.com/assertive.htm

◆ Alfie Kohn examines the negative aspects of assertive discipline and similar approaches in *Education Week.* A copy of the article is available online at
   http://www.alfiekohn.org/teaching/edweek/discipline.htm

◆ The following sites are useful for developing strategies for the safe use of technology in the classroom.
   http://www.think.com
   http://www.isafe.org
   www.cyberbullying.org

◆ This site is an excellent first visit when developing personal strategies for developing classroom rules.
http://www.education-world.com

References

Addison, R., & D. T. Tosti. (1979). "Taxonomy of Educational Reinforcement." *Educational Technology 19*: 24–25.

Amato, P. R., & R. A. Maynard. (2007, Fall). "Decreasing Nonmarital Births and Strengthening Marriage to Reduce Poverty." *The Future of Children 17*(2): 117–141.

American Federation of Teachers (AFT). (2008). "Classroom Management: Effective Classroom Arrangement". http://www.aft.org/teachers/jft/management.htm.

Anderson, S. C. (2002). *Learning for All: Giving Effective Directions and the Peg System of Memorization. ERIC Digest.* Eugene, OR: ERIC Clearinghouse on Educational Management. ED 478 384.

Baker, P. H. (2005). "Managing Student Behavior: How Ready Are Teachers to Meet the Challenge?" *American Secondary Education 33*(3): 51–64.

Bennett, S. (2007, March 5). "A Parent's Perspective: How (and Why) to Turn the Parent-Teacher 'Partnership' into a Two-Way Relationship." *Teachers College Record.*

Bergman, M. (2007). "Single-Parent Households Showed Little Variation Since 1994." U.S. Census Bureau News. Released August 09, 2007. http://www.census.gov/apsd/techdoc/cps/cpsmar06.pdf.

Bickel, W. E. (1999). "The Implications of the Effective Schools Literature for School Restructuring." In C. R. Reynolds & T. B. Gutkin, Eds., *The Handbook of School Psychology* (3rd ed.), pp. 959–983. New York: Wiley.

Boston University Center for the Advancement of Ethics and Character. (2008). http://www.bu.edu/education/cace/.

Canter, L., & M. Canter. (1992). *Lee Canter's Assertive Discipline: Positive Behavior Management for Today's Classroom.* Santa Monica: Lee Canter & Associates.

Chang, J. C. (2003). "Women and Minorities in the Science, Mathematics and Engineering Pipeline" http://www.ericdigests.org/2003-2/women.html.

Cotton, K. (2001). "Schoolwide and Classroom Discipline." School Improvement Research Series (SIRS). Northwest Regional Educational Laboratory. http://www.nwrel.org/sepd/sirs/5/cu9.html.

DeLisio, E. R. (2007). "Crafting a Workable Cell Phone Policy in Front of the Class." *Education World 2007.* www.EducationWorld.com.

Ellett, L. (1993). "Instructional Practices in Mainstreamed Secondary Classrooms." *Journal of Learning Disabilities 26*(1): 57–64.

Etzioni, A. (1997). *The New Golden Rule: Morality and Community in a Democratic Society.* New York: Basic.

Evertson, C. M. (1995). "Classroom Rules and Routines." In L. W. Anderson, Ed., *International Encyclopedia of Teaching and Teacher Education* (2nd ed.), pp. 215–219. Tarrytown, NY: Elsevier Science.

Evertson, C. M., E. T. Emmer, & M. E. Worsham. (2006). *Classroom Management for Elementary Teachers* (7th ed.). Boston: Allyn and Bacon.

Garbarino, J., & E. deLara. (2003). "Words Can Hurt Forever." *Educational Leadership 60*(6): 18–21.

Glasser, W. (1972). "Reality Therapy: An Anti-Failure Approach." *Impact 2*: 6–9.

Glasser, W. (1998). *Choice Theory in the Classroom* (Rev. ed.). New York: HarperPerennial.

Good, T. L., & J. E. Brophy. (2008). *Looking in Classrooms, My Lab School Edition* (10th ed.). Boston: Allyn and Bacon.

Graham, M. (2001). "Increasing Participation of Female Students in Physical Science Class." Chicago: St. Xavier University, MA Action Research Project. ED 455 121.

Greene, J. P., & M. A. Winters. (2006). "Leaving Boys Behind: Public High School Graduation Rates." http://www.manhattan-institute.org/html/cr_48.htm.

Greenberger, R. S. (1999, May 25). "Justice Rules on School Bias and Land Use." *Wall Street Journal*, p. A3.

Gump, P. V. (1982). "School Settings and Their Keeping." In D. Duke, Ed., *Helping Teachers Manage Classrooms.* Alexandria, VA: Association for Supervision and Curriculum Development.

Horace Mann Educator Corporation. (2001). *Educator Survey, 2000–01.* Springfield, IL: Horace Mann Educator Corporation.

Jacobson, R. B. (2007). "School Bullying and Current Educational Practice: Re-Imagining Theories of Educational Transformation." *Teachers College Record 109*(8): 1931–1956.

Johnson, D. W., & R. T. Johnson. (1989). *Cooperation and Competition: Theory and Research.* Edina, MN: Interaction.

Josephson Institute of Ethics. (2008). *Character Counts!* Marina del Rey, CA: Josephson Institute of Ethics. http://www.charactercounts.org.

Kentucky Department of Education. (2008). "Establishing Classroom Rules." http://www.kde.state.ky.us/KDE/Instructional+Resources/Career+and+TechnicalEducationEstablishing+Classroom+Rules.htm.

Kerman, S. (1979). "Teacher Expectations and Student Achievement." *Phi Delta Kappan 60*(10): 716–718.

Kohlberg, L. (1975). "The Cognitive-Developmental Approach to Moral Education." *Phi Delta Kappan 56:* 670–677.

Kounin, J. S. (1970). *Discipline and Group Management in Classrooms.* New York: Holt, Rinehart and Winston.

Kounin, J. S., & P. V. Gump. (1959). "The Ripple Effect in Discipline." *Educational Digest 24:* 43–45.

Lasley, T. J., et al. (1989). "Activities and Desists Used by More and Less Effective Classroom Managers." http://www.eric.ed.gov/ ERICWebPortal/recordDetail?accno=Ed315162.

Leonard, L. J. (1999). "Towards Maximizing Instructional Time: The Nature and Extent of Externally-Imposed Classroom Interruptions." *Journal of School Leadership 9*(5): 454–474.

Leriche, L. (1992). "The Sociology of Classroom Discipline." *The High School Journal 75*(2): 77–89.

Lombardi, T. P. (1992). *Learning Strategies for Problem Learners* (Fastback No. 345). Bloomington, IN: Phi Delta Kappa Educational Foundation.

Martella, R. C., & R. J. Nelson. (2003). "Managing Classroom Behavior." *Journal of Direct Instruction 3*(2): 139–165.

Marzano, R. J., J. S. Marzano, & D. J. Pickering. (2003). *Classroom Management That Works: Research-Based Strategies for Every Teacher.* Alexandria: VA: Association for Supervision and Curriculum Development.

Maslow, A. H. (1968). *Motivation and Personality.* New York: Van Nostrand.

McElroy, C. (2000). "Middle School Programs That Work." *Phi Delta Kappan 82*(4): 277–292.

Myers, R. E. (2001). "Taking a Common-Sense Approach to Moral Education." *Clearing House 74*(4): 219–220.

National Center for Education Statistics (2005). "Indicators of School Crime and Safety 2005." NCES 2005-312. http://nces.ed.gov/programs?crimeindicators.

National Center for Education Statistics. (2007, December). "Indicators of School Crime and Safety 2007." NCES 2008-021. http://nces.ed.gov/programs/crimeindicators/crimeindicators2007/#top.

Noddings, N. (2002). *Educating Moral People: A Caring Alternative to Character Education.* New York: Teachers College Press.

Oakes, J. (1992). "Can Tracking Research Inform Practice? Technical, Normative and Political Considerations." *Educational Researcher:* 12–21.

Phi Delta Kappa. (1993). *TE&SA: Teaching Expectations and Student Achievement.* Bloomington, IN: Phi Delta Kappa.

Power, B. M. (1992). "Rules Made to Be Broken: Literacy and Play in a Fourth-Grade Setting." *Journal of Education 174*(1): 70–86.

Power, F. C., A. Higgins, and L. Kohlberg. (1989). *Lawrence Kohlberg's Approach to Moral Education.* New York: Columbia University Press.

The Report of Governor Bill Owens: Columbine Review Commission. (2001). http://www.state.co.us/columbine/columbine20Report.

Ryan, K., & K. E. Bohlin. (1999). *Building Character in Schools: Practical Ways to Bring Moral Instruction to Life.* San Francisco: Jossey-Bass.

Salvia, J., J. E. Ysseldyke, & S. Bolt. (2007). *Assessment in Special and Inclusive Education* (10th ed.). Boston: Houghton Mifflin.

Scofield, R. T., Ed. (2000–2001). *School-Age Notes, 2000–2001.* ED 455 000.

Simmons, R. (2002). *Odd Girl Out: The Hidden Culture of Aggression in Girls.* New York: Harcourt Brace.

Simon, K. G. (2002). *Moral Questions in the Classroom: How to Get Kids to Think Deeply About Real Life and Their Schoolwork.* New Haven, CT: Yale University Press.

Sizer, T. R., & N. F. Sizer. (1999). "Grappling." *Phi Delta Kappan 81*(3): 184–190.

Skinner, B. F. (1953). *Science and Human Behavior.* New York: Macmillan.

Skinner, B. F. (1974). *About Behaviorism.* New York: Knopf.

Slavin, R. E. (1991). "Are Cooperative Learning and 'Untracking' Harmful to the Gifted?" *Educational Leadership 48*(6): 68–71.

Smith, H. A. (1985). "The Marking of Transitions by More and Less Effective Teachers." *Theory Into Practice 24*(1), 57–62.

Soder, R., J. I. Goodlad, and T. J. McMannon, Eds. (2002). *Developing Democratic Character in the Young.* San Francisco: Jossey-Bass.

Starr, L. (2005). "Planning for Your First Day at School." www.EducationWorld.com.

Styles, D. (2002). "Class Meetings: A Democratic Approach to Classroom Management." www.EducationWorld.com.

Sugai, G. (1996). "UO and Public Schools Design Just-In-Time Learning Approaches to Find Solutions to Rising Student Discipline Problems." *Education Matters 3*(1): 10–11.

Tauber, R. T. (2007). *Classroom Management: Sound Theory and Effective Practice* (4th ed.). Portsmouth, NH: Praeger/Greenwood.

Teddlie, C., & S. Stringfield. (1993). *Schools Make a Difference.* New York: Teachers College Press.

Thomas, K., & Associated Press. (2008, April 1). "Low Graduation Rates in US Cities." http://www.time.com/time/nation/ article/0.8599,1726797.00.html.

2007 Kids Count Data Book Online. Baltimore: Annie Casey Foundation, Table 1, p. 29. http://www.aecf.org/kidscount/sld/auxiliary/race_child.jsp.

University of Michigan News and Information Services. (2006). "Reported Drug and Alcohol Use by High School Seniors, 2006." http://www.ojp.gov/bjs/dcf/ du.htm.

Wallen, C. J. (1968). "Establishing Teaching Principles in the Area of Classroom Management." In *Low Cost Instruction Simulation Materials for Teacher Education.* Monmouth, OR: Teaching Research. (U.S. Department of Health, Education and Welfare, Office of Education, Bureau of Research.)

Walsh, F. M. (1992). *Planning Behaviors of Distinguished and Award-Winning High School Teachers.* Unpublished doctoral dissertation, Washington State University, Pullman.

White, E. (2002). *Fast Girls: Teenage Tribes and the Myth of the Slut.* New York: Scribner's.

Wicker, C. (1999, April 4). "Educators Work to Rid Schools of Bullying Behavior." *The Salt Lake Tribune,* p. A14.

Wood, J. (2000). "The Girls Have It!" *Instructor 109*(6): 31–35.

Wood, M. M. (2001). "Preventing School Failure: A Teacher's Current Conundrum." *Preventing School Failure 45*(2): 52–57.

Ysseldyke, J., & J. Elliott. (1999). "Effective Instructional Practices: Implications for Assessing Educational Environments." In C. R. Reynolds & T. B. Gutkin, Eds., *The Handbook of School Psychology* (3rd ed.), pp. 497–518. New York: Wiley.

Zabel, R. H., & M. K. Zabel. (1996). *Classroom Management in Context: Orchestrating Positive Learning Environments.* Boston: Houghton Mifflin.

The Process of Classroom Questioning

Your mentor has scheduled you to observe another teacher, Diane Cole, because she is a master of the questioning technique. You are very interested because you read a recent report noting that teachers could ask between 300 and 400 questions a day. Diane begins her class with a series of questions and, in a businesslike manner, calls on a number of students for responses. She calls on as many as four students to respond to the same question. The students respond eagerly. Their responses are lengthy and thoughtful, and they seem to be carrying on the recitation among themselves with few verbal cues from the teacher.

"Wow," you say to yourself, "I'd like to know how to use this technique. I'm glad my mentor suggested this classroom for my observation."

The entire process of questioning is an organized activity. Questioning also requires planning so that as the students begin to mature, you begin to use a variety of questions that coincide with the six levels of Bloom's cognitive taxonomy.

In this chapter, we describe the skills you will need to become a master questioner. As you read, think about how you would answer the following questions:

◆ Why is questioning so important for student learning?
◆ How can I ask a variety of questions during a recitation period?
◆ How can I use a positive and respectful approach to questioning?
◆ What techniques should I use to conduct effective recitations?
◆ What are some common problems when conducting recitation sessions?

SECTION *1* The Importance of Questioning

Next to lecturing and small-group work, the teaching method most often employed in U.S. schools (and, for that matter, around the world) may well be the asking of questions. Questioning plays a critical role in teaching. Teachers must be knowledgeable in the process of *framing questions* so that they can guide student thought processes in the most skillful and meaningful manner. This implies that teachers must design questions that will help students attain the specific goals (that is, objectives or outcomes) of a particular lesson. Although written questions in textbooks and examinations contribute to the learning process, most classroom questions are verbal and teacher formulated. Questions can be critical elements for teachers to use to stimulate student thinking (see Harvey & Goudvis, 2007; Marzano 2007; Walsh & Sattes, 2005).

Research on Questioning

Classroom questions and the process of teacher questioning have been studied for nearly a hundred years. Rather than listing these studies, we summarize the key findings and conclusions in the box on page 216.

Teachers ask a plethora of questions, but on average they do not systematically organize or classify the ways in which they ask classroom questions. In this chapter, we provide empirically tested and validated techniques that are easy to use and, more important, that invigorate classroom recitation. **Recitation** is a learning technique in which the teacher calls on different students to answer factual or knowledge-based questions that limit students to one "correct" response. In keeping with our concept of multi-methodology, you will learn about several models to use when you conduct questioning or recitation sessions.

Research Findings on Questioning

◆ Questioning tends to be a universal teaching strategy.

◆ A broad range of questioning options is open to you.

◆ Being systematic in the use and development of questioning tends to improve student learning.

◆ By classifying questions according to a particular system, you may determine the cognitive or affective level at which your class is working and make adjustments as needed.

◆ Through systematic questioning, you may determine students' entry skill and knowledge levels for specific content areas.

◆ Questions should be developed logically and sequentially.

◆ Students should be encouraged to ask questions.

◆ A written plan with key questions provides lesson structure and direction.

◆ Questions should be adapted to students' levels of ability.

◆ Questioning techniques that encourage the widest spectrum of student participation should be used.

◆ Statements rather than questions should also be used to promote student reactions.

◆ No single questioning strategy is applicable to all teaching situations.

An Overview of Questioning Techniques

Teachers use recitation and question-answer periods for a variety of reasons. One key purpose is to determine what students have remembered or achieved as a consequence of some assignment. In this regard, you are conducting a brief *formative evaluation*—a topic to which we devote an entire section in Chapter 10. This evaluation tells you what points everyone knows and, equally important, which students do not know or have misunderstood some element or concept. With this feedback, you can take corrective action immediately. Although formative checks tend to focus on low-level questions with factual answers, they can lead to higher-level questions that use skills in the top four categories in the cognitive taxonomy. George W. Gagnon (2001) illustrates how a teacher can bridge concepts and enhance student understanding with well-chosen questions. *Bridging* means that you or the students connect previously learned material to the new topic or concept being taught. Prompts such as "Think back to yesterday's assignment" and "How might we approach this problem from what we know?" help students to bridge.

Why use questioning?

Edit Yerushalmi and Corina Polingher (2006) observed that students often tend to repeat mistakes, even after classroom discussions of the errors. They suggest assigning those written statements as homework so the students analyze their errors and then discuss the analyses in a subsequent class session. This strategy applies formative evaluation and helps promote student understanding.

Merely asking questions does not cause students to think. If you ask a low-level question, then you can expect a low-level response (see Dillon 1982a, 1982b). But your higher-level questions *invite* and encourage higher levels of critical thinking in students. Higher-level or critical thinking skills imply that there is more to learning than just knowing facts. Students can be taught how to analyze situations, make comparisons, draw conclusions, and then make inferences. Judging or evaluating information also promotes higher-level thinking (see Paul & Elder, 2008). Furthermore, it appears that if teachers systematically raise the level of their questioning, students raise the level of their responses correspondingly (Filippone 1998). This requires a carefully planned questioning strategy that may span several weeks of instruction (van Zee & Minstrell 1997). Asking higher-level questions also requires an adjustment in your attitude toward your students. As a teacher, you hold high expectations for your students. Your attitude should be *Yes, you can!*

Through appropriate questioning, student curiosity is fostered (Arnone, 2003). Curiosity is an *affective* dimension of learning, which means that it deals with the emotions and with motivation. The influence of emotions cannot be discounted in student performance. As we develop this chapter, you will observe how the art of questioning subtly encourages student curiosity, creativity, and reflectivity (see Lampert 2006).

As an alternative to asking questions, making *declarative statements* can also stimulate student responses, curiosity, and thinking. This technique elicits longer and more complex student responses. There is some evidence that students' verbal responses are of higher quality when they respond to statements rather than to questions alone (Dillon 1990). For example, a teacher might say, "It really doesn't matter what tense you use when writing." That statement predictably will evoke a wide range of student responses. Another example might be the statement, "Laboratory-based science instruction helps students to learn." Keep such statements short (about one sentence) and, when appropriate, seek comments from students. Using declarative statements requires some practice. One useful application of this technique is examining the complaints listed in the Declaration of Independence. The statements can become sources for student questioning and subsequent discussion (see "Declare the Causes," 2001). Microteaching—teaching a single concept to a small group of peers—and peer coaching are ideal ways to practice the declarative statement technique (see Glickman 2002; L'Anson, Rodrigues, & Wilson 2003; McKenzie 2007).

Using Students' Questions and Summarizations

Even when using higher-level questions, it is important not to let yourself dominate the scene. Orient your class toward giving students a chance to express their opinions and ideas and to originate questions of their own. Some evidence shows that teachers tend to do most of the talking and questioning. Disturbingly few students ask questions during recitations, "nor are they encouraged to do so" (Swift, Gooding, & Swift 1995, p. 1). What an example of being intentionally disinviting! This is particularly unfortunate because encouraging student questions leads to higher-level questions, stimulates more students to interact, provides positive cognitive effects, and promotes analytic reasoning (see Gall & Artero-Boname 1995; Koegel et al. 1998).

Teachers' expectation helps students reach for higher levels.

"Questions" also can be phrased as declarative statements.

Don't dominate verbal interactions.

Teachers need to try hard not to dominate classroom verbal interactions and thereby cause class members to become passive and dependent on the teacher. Student passivity hardly fosters ingenuity, creativity, or critical thinking—traits we all consider desirable. Nor is passive student behavior appropriate for a constructivist method of teaching. Instead, the classroom should be highly interactive, which creates an atmosphere affirming that what is taking place is of significance for students (Wells & Arauz 2006).

One way to ensure that you will not dominate a discussion or recitation is to end appropriate sections of all lessons with student summaries. According to research, this is one of the nine most effective teaching strategies (Wormeli 2004). This simple technique shifts the burden of reflecting and interpreting directly to the students and provides another form of formative evaluation.

> Encourage students to ask questions and to summarize.

Aiming for Critical and Higher-Level Thinking

If you want to stimulate critical thinking among your students, take a look at the way you use textbooks. Be aware of the advantages and disadvantages of your textbook materials. To involve students more, you may have to supplement the materials provided by the publisher. For example, you might teach lessons with focused questions that require students to compare or contrast items, persuade others, determine cause and effect, or even question the textual presentation. These processes are crucial to developing thinking skills (see Carpenter 2003). You can use questions to diagnose student progress, determine entry-level competence, prescribe additional study, and enrich an area (Gibson 1998).

> Systems for categorizing classroom questions

Lelia Christenbury and Patricia P. Kelly (1983) have discussed seven different taxonomies or hierarchies of learning that can be used in formulating questions. One of these is Bloom's cognitive taxonomy, and three others are also "sequential hierarchies" with stages similar to his. Thus, for our purposes and for the sake of uniformity, we will simply rely on using Bloom's (1956) cognitive taxonomy as a means for classifying questions and their responses. Refer to Chapter 3 to review the six categories.

Voices from the Classroom

Jack Guske

Washtucna, Washington High School

Using Thought-Provoking Questions

Being a social science teacher in a small rural high school means that I am truly the school's history department. Much of my instructional time is used to plan questions that help my students to "think." My definition of thinking is that a student "digs" into the material and seeks information that goes beyond the facts. For example, when we discuss World War II, I ask the students questions such as: (1) Why did the Japanese attack Pearl Harbor? (2) Why did President Truman order the atomic bomb to be dropped? (3) What lessons can we learn from this war?

Note that these questions require students to reflect on motives, goals, policy, and other issues that tend not to be asked or discussed in the typical history class.

When we study the U.S. Constitution, questions about the Bill of Rights help students reach levels of understanding that many members of our adult population do not have. One higher-level question about the Second Amendment is "What have been some unintended consequences of this amendment?" I often ask, "What rights do students have due to the First Amendment?" These questions cause my students to reflect—and that is a part of thinking.

Higher-level questions do not *guarantee* higher-level responses; they only open a very important door to critical thinking for your students. Keep in mind the "if-then" strategy: *If you want to encourage a response at a particular level of thinking, then you must frame the question at the appropriate intellectual level.* This strategy requires concomitant and continuous decision making and evaluation. It can be applied to *all* levels of instruction and with *all* types of students.

Use a questioning hierarchy as a plan for your recitations and discussion. This will allow you to structure facts, concepts, and generalizations within a framework for thinking—the hierarchy becomes a visible blueprint for action (see Buehl 2001). Note that a questioning hierarchy can also be used to plan declarative statements and to structure them in a hierarchical manner to elicit higher-level student responses. You'll find yourself asking fewer questions (see Barnette et al. 1995). Refer to Chapter 4, in which the Kaplan matrix illustrates a series of statements arranged in the hierarchy of Bloom's taxonomy. Your questions can be tailored after that model.

Key Ideas

Ways to Develop Higher-Level Thinking

- ◆ Ask higher-level questions.
- ◆ Don't rely too heavily on a textbook.
- ◆ Frame questions appropriately.
- ◆ Use a questioning hierarchy.
- ◆ Encourage students to interact verbally in class.

Questioning is a highly interpersonal and interactive teaching strategy.

© David Grossman/The Image Works

Reflect
- ◆ To what extent have you heard students summarizing lessons in your classroom observations? Was this technique effective?
- ◆ In one of your methods classes, practice making declarative statements rather than asking questions. Do you receive a different reaction with this technique?

SECTION 2   Questioning Strategies

Four distinct questioning strategies.

In this part of the chapter, we describe four basic questioning strategies: *convergent, divergent, evaluative,* and *reflective* questioning. If you assign particular importance to the different types of questions you ask, then you will need a method for verifying that you are indeed using the desired questioning patterns. The classification scheme we present here will help you conduct goal-specific recitation periods.

Convergent Strategy

Convergent questions lead to a common set of responses.

The convergent questioning strategy focuses on a narrow objective. When using a convergent strategy, you encourage student responses that converge, or focus, on a central theme. **Convergent questions** typically elicit short responses from students and focus on the lower levels of thinking—that is, the knowledge or comprehension levels. This does not mean that using a convergent technique is bad per se. In many situations, you will decide that your students need to demonstrate their knowledge of facts and specifics; in such cases, lower-level questioning strategies are appropriate. Remember that the appropriateness of any questioning strategy must be judged solely on the basis of its ability to fulfill your predetermined objectives (see Crespo 2002).

So when might convergent questioning be the appropriate choice? If you use an inductive teaching style (proceeding from a set of specific data to a student-derived conclusion), then you will use a large proportion of convergent-type questions. Or you may wish to use short-response questions as rapid-fire warmup exercises (for example, when you are building vocabulary skills). Teachers in foreign language classes may use a convergent, rapid-fire pattern to help develop students' oral, vocabulary, and spelling skills. This technique also allows all students to participate. The same method may be used by a science teacher to build technical vocabulary. Thus, a biology teacher may wish to use a convergent technique for the first few minutes of class to maximize participation and to generate constructive verbal motivation among the students.

The convergent technique is an ideal application of "teacher-directed instruction," or *direct instruction*, in which all students in class respond in unison to teacher-asked questions. Everyone gets to participate. A convergent questioning pattern is not an appropriate means of stimulating thought-provoking responses or classroom discussions; rather, it focuses on factual knowledge (see Rowe 1996).

The box on page 221 includes examples of convergent questions. Note that these questions all meet two criteria: (1) they limit student responses to a narrow spectrum of possible options, and (2) they are more recall-oriented than analytical.

Examples of Convergent Questions

◆ In what works did Robert Browning use the dramatic monologue as a form for his poems?

◆ Under what conditions will water boil at less than 100°C?

◆ What helps bread dough rise?

◆ What rights are ensured by the First Amendment?

◆ Why do relatively few people live in the deserts of any country?

◆ Where and when was Fort Ticonderoga built?

◆ What's 5 to the third power?

Divergent Strategy

Divergent questions are the opposite of convergent questions. Rather than seeking a single focus a divergent questioning strategy is designed to evoke a wide range of student responses. Divergent questions also elicit longer student responses. The divergent technique is ideal for building the confidence of students with learning difficulties because divergent questions do not always have right or wrong answers (see Beamon 1997).

Divergent questions lead to an array of responses.

Eliciting Multiple Responses   If you want to elicit multiple responses, use a multiple-response questioning technique. After asking a question, call on three or four students and then assume a passive role in the ensuing discussion. Such a technique teaches students to conduct a classroom recitation themselves. It is a rather sophisticated teaching strategy when used properly. The multiple-response technique also sharpens students' listening skills.

Accepting Diverse Responses   If encouraging creative responses to questions and novel solutions to problems is your goal, then the divergent method is also appropriate. Remember, though, that if you elicit diverse responses from students, you have a professional obligation to listen respectfully to them. To reinforce appropriate response behavior, you must demonstrate a high degree of acceptance for the responses of each student (van Zee & Minstrell 1997). This means that you may not use subtle put-down tactics, regardless of how outlandish a student's point of view may seem (or how different from what you expected). Again, this is a great technique for students with some learning difficulties because they get to become stars in the classroom.

Many responses to a single question.

Preparing Yourself and the Students   When you begin to use divergent questions, you will find it helpful to write out the questions ahead of time. Then examine them to ensure that they are clearly stated and convey the precise meanings you intend. You probably will find your initial class experience with divergent questions difficult or even disappointing, usually because students are not yet oriented toward giving longer or higher-level responses (see Savage 1998).

It takes a good deal of reshaping of student behavior patterns to elicit higher-level student thinking and responses. From grade school through high school, over thousands of classroom hours, students have been conditioned to give short, low-level responses. When you begin to ask divergent questions, you must let your students know that the level of questions is changing and that you want the level of their responses also to change, quite drastically. You will soon find that students' responses will demonstrate higher-level thinking—application, analysis, and synthesis. They may even be prepared to conduct discussions themselves and to give longer and more diverse written responses (see Epstein 2003).

When you inform the students about your change in questioning strategy, you should also inform them that you expect multiple responses, with each student taking cues from other students' responses. For example, you might begin by stating, "Today, we are going to change how we recite. I am going to call on three of you, and after each of you has responded, I'll ask three more of you to react to your classmates' responses. Ready?" This means that, as a general rule, you do not repeat student responses to other class members, except when a student speaks too quickly or softly to be heard or when a statement needs some clarification. The rationale for not repeating responses is that, if students know that the teacher will repeat the previous response, they become conditioned to listening only for the teacher's repetition instead of paying close attention to their fellow student's original words.

When using the divergent strategy, allow all students to present their responses without your interference. This has a positive effect on the class. Teachers tend to interrupt before students have fully explained their positions. When the teacher avoids interrupting, students realize that their responses are important and that they must be responsive to one another. As a result, the class's attending behavior improves. It does little good for a teacher continually to remind students that they are not paying attention; such negative comments only make a class less attentive. By encouraging students to listen to one another, you encourage them to participate in a dynamic fashion. You also encourage peer reinforcement of positive, constructive classroom behavior.

To get the best results, your emphasis must be on systematic development of questions over an extended time, with well-conceived, appropriate learning objectives (see Streifer 2001). Do not expect overnight miracles. It takes weeks, even months, to incorporate these techniques into the usual repertoire of teaching strategies.

Use of divergent questions requires you to help students locate different sources of information so that they can share a variety of viewpoints in class. The box below lists examples of divergent questions. Note that we have adapted a few of these from the previous list of convergent questions.

Examples of Divergent Questions

◆ What type of social and cultural development might have taken place if Christopher Columbus had landed on Manhattan Island on October 12, 1492?

◆ What would happen in a school if it had no computers or Internet connection?

◆ Explain the attitude that the Romantic poets had toward nature.

◆ What do you think are effective methods for creating a sustainable environment?

◆ What kinds of evidence would you seek if you were an opponent of global warming?

◆ Why was Fort Ticonderoga built where it was on Lake Champlain?

◆ Under what conditions are First Amendment rights abridged?

Evaluative Strategy

The third questioning strategy is based on the divergent strategy, but with one added component—evaluation. The basic difference between a divergent question and an **evaluative question** is that the evaluative question has a built-in set of **evaluative criteria**. For example, an evaluative question might ask why something is good or bad, why something is important, or why one theory explains the facts better than another. When you frame an evaluative question, emphasize the specific criteria on which students should base their judgments. As with divergent questions, you should accept all student responses to evaluative questions.

Helps students generate criteria for making judgments.

A major component of the teacher's role in the evaluative strategy is to help students develop a logical basis for establishing evaluative criteria. To illustrate this, we'll give you a classic example. You ask a question, and a student presents a response. You next ask, "Why?" and the student replies, "Because." You should recognize immediately from this response that the student does not understand how to frame a logical, consistent set of evaluative criteria. Again, you must never use sarcasm or any other disparaging approach; instead, reinforce the student in an environment conducive to the development of logical evaluative criteria. For example, you might suggest a number of criteria: "What happens when someone is convicted of a crime? What about situations of national emergency?" Provide a specific set of criteria from which students may develop their own criteria. Some students might be intimidated if you ask "Why?" It has been suggested that instead of asking why, ask *what*. For example, in an art class discussing backgrounds, the teacher might ask, "What type of background did Charles M. Russell usually use?" This would be more appropriate than, "Why did Charlie Russell use this background?" This is a subtle form of shifting the burden of proof from the student to the topic (see Dana et al. 1992). As an introduction to the evaluative technique, you might try a joint writing session in which the teacher and small groups of students collaboratively list criteria. Then, as you pose evaluative questions and students make responses, you and the students can classify the evaluative responses along a continuum ranging from "inappropriate" or "illogical" to "appropriate" or "logically developed." An alternative method would be to have the class develop a set of evaluative rubrics such as those shown in Table 10.1 (see page 348) (Eppink 2002; Jackson & Larkin 2002). Note that we have been using the term *responses*, not *answers. Answers* carry the connotation of being final or complete. To be sure, convergent questioning patterns may elicit such answers, but when you ask divergent and evaluative questions, students will not be giving you definitive or absolute answers. They will be providing responses that tend to be relative, tentative, or less than certain (see Martinello 1998).

Usually no definitive, final answer

Most student responses to evaluative questions will demonstrate a broad range of thought when rated on a set of evaluative criteria. You can classify them according to their logical development, internal consistency, and validity. Again, we suggest that you accept all student responses. When apparent logical inconsistencies develop, don't rush to bring them up. Discuss them *after* the student has had an opportunity to participate in classroom discourse.

The box below provides examples of evaluative questions. Some of the questions we previously designated as divergent have been converted now into evaluative questions. Remember that most evaluative questions are also divergent. The one characteristic that separates divergent questions from evaluative ones is that the latter rely on established judgmental criteria.

Evaluative Questions

◆ Why is the world a better (or worse) place because of computers and the Internet?

◆ Why will the federal position on welfare reform affect social and moral attitudes and behaviors?

◆ What reasons could be given to switch to hybrid automobiles?

◆ What evidence is there that the federal system of interstate highways harmed our city environments?

◆ Defend (or criticize) oil drilling in the Alaskan tundra.

◆ Why is global warming a critical issue?

◆ What made the location of Fort Ticonderoga critical to early colonial development?

Reflective Strategy

The newest addition to the list of questioning techniques is the *reflective* questioning strategy. This strategy draws its historical perspective from the classical Socratic method of questioning (Elder & Richard 1998). Reflective questions stimulate a wide range of student responses, as do divergent questions. Reflective questions also have an evaluative element. The major difference between this strategy and the other three techniques is that the goal of the **reflective question** is to require your students to develop higher-order thinking: to elicit motives, make inferences, speculate on causes, consider impact, and contemplate outcomes. Rather than asking a student a "why" or "what" question, as with the evaluative strategy, you are trying to encourage the student to ponder, to think of implications, to search for unintended consequences (see Moutray, Pollard, & McGinley 2001; York-Barr et al. 2001). The box on page 225 lists the types of thought processes that can be stimulated through reflective questions.

Probes for implications

TECHNOLOGY
Insight

Web 2.0: Using the Internet for Creative Communication

Within the past few years the Web has become considerably easier to use as a medium for responsive communication. As such, you may choose to use components of blogs and Wikis for student-led questioning sessions. A few years ago, the Web was a place where pages and sites required considerable skill to produce, and communication was mostly in the form of passively perusing and reading the work of others. Today the Web is a place where people can easily respond to each other. This new interactivity is sometimes referred to as the "Read/Write Web" (Richardson 2006) or "Web 2.0" (O'Reilly 2007).

(continued)

Web 2.0: Using the Internet for Creative Communication—Cont'd

Popular methods of reading and writing using the Web include *Wikis, social spaces,* and *blogs.* As mentioned in Chapter 1, **Wikis** are Web pages or sites that can be modified by anyone who visits the site. Wikipedia (www.wikipedia.com) is perhaps the most famous example of a Wiki. Social spaces are sites that allow people to establish a public profile and to send and receive messages from other members of the social space. MySpace (www.myspace.com) and Facebook (www.facebook.com) are two of the most popular social spaces. A **blog** is a kind of online journal ("blog" is short for "Web log"). The person operating the blog may post message topics and messages for others to read and respond to. Of these three online communication tools, blogging is perhaps the easiest and safest method for school-age children. Blog software designed specifically for schools and school-age students is available at http://www.gaggle.com and http://www.schoolblogs.net (Green, Brown, & Robinson, 2008).

Stimulating Thinking Process with Reflective Questions

- ◆ Seeking motives
- ◆ Expanding a vision
- ◆ Listing implications
- ◆ Searching for unintended consequences
- ◆ Identifying issues
- ◆ Analyzing persuasive techniques
- ◆ Making unique interpretations
- ◆ Inferring values
- ◆ Challenging assumptions
- ◆ Seeking meanings

The process initiated by reflective questions can also be called *critical* or *analytical thinking.* A teacher doesn't bring students to this stage of intellectual development without carefully shaping the classroom environment and instructing the students as to what the process entails. Jim Minstrell (van Zee & Minstrell 1997) uses a technique that he calls the "reflective bounce." He bounces questions from the student back to the same student and others so that the student needs to provide an expanded version of a previous response, adding another dimension. In civics, a student might ask, "I wonder why 'Deep Throat' waited so long to be identified?" As teacher, you would "bounce" that question back to the originating student and then to another. The box on page 226 includes a few examples of additional reflective questions. Jamie A. McKenzie (2005) has developed a very useful Questioning Toolkit in which he discusses 17 types of questions. The following five exemplify reflective questions: *hypothetical, irreverent, probing, provocative,* and *unanswerable.*

Maureen Boyd and Don Rubin (2006) collected data on the power of "*contingent*" questions. They observed that English-language learners (ELL) reacted very positively to *authentic* questions. These appear to be reflective questions that are based on common experiences or on common thematic assignments. By focusing on key points, this type of questioning led to extended and thoughtful student responses. We suggest using contingent questions for students with special needs.

Using reflective questions requires even more planning than using convergent or divergent ones. We recommend that you write out a cluster of several reflective questions that would be relevant to the content being taught and learned. In some cases, the reflective strategy approaches a constructivist perspective; that is, the students must construct their own meanings to the questions. You might also organize student teams to write a few reflective questions. This approach gives you double value: Students work cooperatively, and they have to think.

Contingent and authentic questions help ELL students.

Reflective Questions

◆ What are some twenty-first-century implications of Manifest Destiny?

◆ What issues are unresolved by having security persons in our high school?

◆ What rationale is given to support interscholastic activities?

◆ What problems might you anticipate if algebra were to be made a required course for all eighth-graders?

◆ What values can we infer are important in our school by examining its entry showcase?

◆ What assumptions did we make when we constructed the interstate highway system?

◆ What impact have personal computers made on our school courses?

◆ What metaphors do teachers use when describing school, and what do they imply?

◆ What impact did Fort Ticonderoga have when state boundary lines were drawn?

Reflect

◆ How can you provide students with content knowledge so that they can respond to evaluative and reflective questions?

◆ What question have you been asked by a friend or classmate lately that elicited the longest, most thoughtful response? Which of the four question categories did it fall into?

◆ Reflect on the techniques discussed here and identify the content areas for which they are most appropriate. List five ideas for using questions in your content area.

SECTION *3* Appropriate Questioning Behaviors

To develop a repertoire of questioning skills, you must be aware of a wide spectrum of techniques for eliciting appropriate responses from students. The questioning skills that follow address specific kinds of problems that may arise in any class using questioning strategies.

Using Questioning Positively

The questioning in a recitation period, a tutorial period, or an inductive session (described in Chapter 5) is always based on the assumption that some meaningful or purposeful learning activity will take place, allowing the student to gain another learning experience. For this to happen, questions must be asked in a positive, reinforcing manner—that is, in such a way that the student will enjoy learning and responding. All students should receive positive reinforcement from the questions being asked as well as for the responses elicited. Thus, questions should *never* be used for punitive purposes. The teacher who asks a question to punish a student is turning a positive learning situation into a negatively reinforcing one. The result is that the teacher not only "turns off" the learner but also shuts down the learning process. It is extremely important to avoid doing this, especially when working with young students or those who have learning disabilities.

Questioning should enhance student enjoyment.

Framing Questions and Using Wait Times

The basic rule for asking questions is to proceed in three steps: *ask the question, pause*, and *then call on a student.*

A, P, C: Ask, pause, then call on.

This rule is grounded in the psychological rationale that when you ask a question and follow it with a short pause, all students will attend to the communication. The nonverbal message—the pause—communicates that any student in the class may be selected for a response, so the attention level of the class remains high. If you do the opposite and call on a particular student before you ask a question, all the other students may ignore the question.

To be an effective questioner, you must be able to pose clear, concise, succinct questions. Avoid using "uhs," false starts, uncertain pauses, and ineffective transitions between topics. All such verbal behaviors by teachers ultimately cause student uncertainty (see Gettinger & Stoiber 1999). Thus, the complete technique of **framing** a question entails asking a clear, succinct question, pausing, and then calling on a student. You can use this technique even when you intend to select several students to respond. Furthermore, once you and the students have mastered this technique, you can modify the third element to a nonverbal action of simply pointing or nodding to a student for a response. This technique becomes easy with a little practice.

Benefits of Wait Time

For the Teacher

◆ Less teacher talking
◆ Less repetition of questions
◆ Fewer questions per period
◆ More questions with multiple responses
◆ Fewer lower-level questions
◆ More probing
◆ Less repetition of students' responses

(continued)

Benefits of Wait Time—Cont'd

◆ More application-level questions

◆ Less disciplinary action

For the Students

◆ Longer responses

◆ More student discourse and questions

◆ Fewer nonresponding students

◆ More student involvement in lessons

◆ Increased complexity of answers and improved reasoning

◆ More responses from slower students

◆ More peer interaction and fewer peer interruptions

◆ Less confusion

◆ More confidence

◆ Higher achievement

Source: (Tobin 1987)

Wait Time 1   The time between when you first ask a question and when you call on a student is called **wait time 1**. Why wait at all? There are several reasons to use the pause. First, it gives students a chance to think about their responses to the question. This is especially important when you ask higher-level questions (Van Es 2006). Additionally, English-language learners or students with special needs will have some time to ponder the question so that they may respond appropriately.

Second, this pause gives you time to read students' nonverbal cues. With some practice, you can readily observe nonverbal signals indicating pleasure, apprehension, fright, excitement, joy, or shame. As you become more sensitive to humanitarian considerations in the classroom, this dimension of teaching becomes very important to gauging your students' well-being. It also allows you to pick up on how prepared the students are or how well they understand the material.

Waiting gives a window into nonverbal cues.

Wait Time 2   After the student has given a first answer to your question, wait again. **Wait time 2,** the pause after the student you have called upon has responded, is equally important because it gives the student additional time to think or allows other students to respond as well (Rowe 1969, 1980). If the teacher waits a while to respond after the initial student response, students will continue to respond—without prompting. Figure 7.1 on page 229 illustrates the use of wait time.

The effectiveness of wait time—even up to five seconds—has been well documented (see Gilbertson & Bluck 2006; Stahl 1994). The box on pages 227–228 lists the benefits to both teachers and students. However, many teachers are impatient with students when asking questions (Rowe 1969, 1974, 1978). Studies show that the wait time between asking a question and either answering it for the student or calling on another student is often less than one second! Is it any wonder, then, that some students dread being called on? They fear that being called on will bring impatience from the teacher and that they will be "in hot

FIGURE 7.1

Wait Times 1 and 2

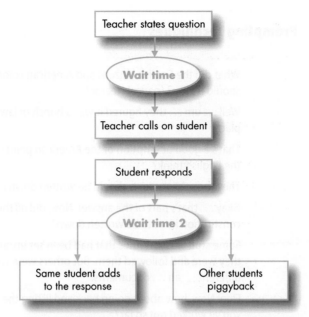

water" again. It's important to note that while wait time has no effect on student responses to lower-level questions (Riley 1986), it has a significant effect on responses to higher-level questions. Lack of wait time with higher-level questions can cause students to give low-level responses (Gipperlich 2006).

Remember that classroom silence is not all bad—even when you are asking questions (see Sangster 2007). So make the decision to wait—not only once, but twice, even three times, if students are interacting. With practice, you'll develop *the art of staying silent.*

Using Positive Prompting Techniques

Once you have asked a question and called on a student to respond, the student may not answer the question the way you want him or her to, or he or she may not answer at all. When this happens, you should prompt the student. You may do this by clarifying the question, by eliciting a fuller response, or by eliciting additional responses from the student to allow you to verify whether he or she comprehends the material (Dann et al. 1995). As you develop prompting skills, you can follow many rules. However, to simplify matters, keep one rule foremost in mind: *Prompt in a positive manner.*

You may have to prompt a student many times during a questioning session to evoke a more complete or logical response. Always provide positive reinforcement so that the student will be encouraged to complete an incomplete response or revise an incorrect one. In many cases, a student will answer with a *partially* correct response. When you hear such a response, immediately begin to prompt the student so that the response can be completed, made more logical, reexamined, or stated more appropriately.

The Instructional Strategies box on page 230 illustrates two possible prompting techniques. Observe that, in the first example, the teacher tries to focus the student's ideas. In the second example, the student's response is recast to answer the question that was asked. In both cases, the teacher is trying to use some aspect of the student's responses to keep the episode positive.

Value partially correct responses.

INSTRUCTIONAL
Strategies

Prompting Techniques

Example 1

TEACHER: What did the English citizens and American colonists think a constitution should be like? (pause) Hector?

HECTOR: Well . . . um . . . they figured it was a bunch of laws all written down in one place.

TEACHER: That's a good description of the American point of view. Now . . . what did the English think?

HECTOR: They thought the laws should be written down in different places . . . sort of.

TEACHER: Okay . . . that's part of the answer. Now, did *all* the laws for the English constitution have to be written down?

HECTOR: Some stuff was just rules that had been set up, and everybody knew what they were and followed them. But others were written down in many different . . . ah . . . documents.

TEACHER: Fine! Now, how about going back and listing the main points on what you've worked out so far?

Example 2

TEACHER: Class, now let's examine the data that we collected on our experiment on absorption and radiation. What differences did you observe between the covered and uncovered shiny pans? (3- to 5-second pause) Angela?

ANGELA: The water in the covered pan had a temperature of 96 degrees.

TEACHER: At what point in the experiment was that temperature measured?

ANGELA: After the pan had been covered for 10 minutes.

TEACHER: What was the temperature of the water when you took the first reading?

The teacher prompts the student in a nonthreatening or neutral verbal tone (including all the nonverbal cues mentioned in Chapter 6). The episode continues until the student provides all the necessary information for an appropriate closure.

Handling Incorrect Responses

No matter how skillful a teacher is at motivating students, providing adequate and relevant instructional materials, and asking high-quality questions, one continual problem will detract from both the intellectual and the interpersonal aspects of classroom questioning sessions—incorrect student responses.

As we discussed previously, you may use prompting techniques when students' responses are partially correct or stated incompletely. Prompting is an easy technique because you can reinforce the positive aspect of a student's response while ignoring the negative or incomplete component. However, when a student gives a totally incorrect response, a more complex interpersonal situation arises. First, it's hard to reinforce positively in such a case. But comments such as "No," "You are *way* off," or "That is

Avoid negative responses.

incorrect" should be avoided because they all act as negative reinforcers and may reduce that student's desire to participate in a verbal classroom interaction. This is critical, especially with students whose first language is not English.

Second, if you respond negatively to an incorrect student response, there is a high probability that a **ripple effect** will occur (Kounin 1970). This effect describes the way in which students who are not themselves the target of a teacher's negative behavior are still negatively affected by what the teacher says or does in correcting another class member. Therefore, when a student gives an incorrect response, try to move to a neutral prompting technique rather than responding with "No, that is not at all correct."

How should you do this? Because this method is designed to stress the positive, you might first analyze the student's verbal response to determine whether any portion of it can be classified as valid, appropriate, or correct. After you make this split-second decision, you then provide positive reinforcement or praise for the correct portion of the response. For example, if you ask a general mathematics question and the student gives a totally incorrect answer, then you might state, "Your response is close to the answer, so do some recalculating." "Could you tell us how you arrived at your answer?" or "Could you rethink your solution and take another try at it?" These responses are *neutral*, not negative.

Another strategy is to rephrase the question, to remove from the student the onus for incorrectly answering the original question. You can carefully lead the student to a correct response with a set of convergent questions.

Always avoid being sarcastic or punishing. A put-down strategy provides negative reinforcers and ultimately has unpleasant residual effects because it causes students to ignore opportunities to respond verbally. A primary goal of schooling is to provide a positive and stimulating environment in which learning can take place. But learning can be blocked by insults and negative teacher responses. The student learns nothing by humiliation—except to despise the teacher and to hate school. Verbal abuse is never an appropriate or professional response.

When carrying out this strategy, you must be careful that nonverbal cues—such as frowning—do not show that you are upset or angered by the incorrect response. You must maintain congruency between your verbal and nonverbal behaviors when handling incorrect responses. (See Chapter 6 for a list of positive verbal and nonverbal responses.)

Another strategy for helping a student correct a response is to immediately assess the type and level of question you asked and then ask the student a similar, but less difficult, question, without making any other comments. Always react flexibly; give students the opportunity to show that they know *some* answer.

Interpersonal relationships between teachers and students are delicate and take time to build. After you have assessed each student's personality type, you may find that it is appropriate to use some negative as well as positive reinforcers with certain students. It is not uncommon for better students to clown or joke with the teacher or to kid the teacher. When you see such situations developing, you can predict fairly accurately how a specific student will react, and you can then humor that student. For example, if a top-performing

---

Reward partially correct answers; if you can't be positive, be neutral.

Teacher put-downs cause students to hate school.

student gives a response that you consider "off the wall," then you might comment, "Are you putting me on?" and then smile or laugh. This diffuses those tense moments.

The Instructional Strategies box below illustrates a number of ways to handle incorrect responses. Note that in these examples, the teacher's response does not criticize the student. We hope you will create an atmosphere in your classes that is supportive—one in which students can react freely without the fear of being wrong. (See McTighe & Lyman 1988 for a series of "tools" that help students respond.)

INSTRUCTIONAL *Strategies* ►

Handling Incorrect Responses

Example 1

TEACHER: What relationships did we find between the hypotenuse and sides of a right triangle? (pause) Sarah?

SARAH: Well, we did some squaring of a side. I forgot.

TEACHER: Okay. Now think of the model that the class constructed. Can you visualize it in your mind? What did those constructions look like?

Example 2

TEACHER: What was one of the military reforms instituted by Senator Harry Truman? (pause) Joe?

JOE: Didn't he want to stop building forts?

TEACHER: What was it about building the forts that he challenged?

JOE: Was it something about costs and waste?

TEACHER: You're on the right track now. What were some of the wasteful practices that he uncovered?

Reflect

◆ Recall your own experiences as a student. To what extent did your teachers employ the positive behaviors discussed here?

◆ With a group of peers, act out a role-playing exercise in which you take turns responding to incorrect or completely illogical student responses. Do you find it difficult to prompt positively? Why?

SECTION 4 How Questioning Can Create a Dynamic Learning Environment

In Section 3 of this chapter, we discussed some prompting techniques you can use to help your students become more successful. Now let's focus on how you can increase student verbal interaction and reduce yours. The goal is for your students to go home tired from thinking and working—and for you to go home refreshed.

Promoting Multiple Responses

As noted earlier, teachers typically conduct recitation periods by sequential questioning: They ask one student to respond, then another student to respond, and so on. For the most part, the teacher does the talking. Few students, if any, listen carefully to their peers' responses because at any one time there is a closed communication circuit between two individuals: the teacher and one student. We recommend that you avoid this closed technique and instead use **multiple-response questions**, which are questions to which at least three or four students respond. The key to increasing the number of students who respond to each question is to emphasize divergent and evaluative questions. These types of questions allow for many different responses. In the multiple-response technique, you ask a question, pause, and then call on three or four students to respond.

Of course, before you use the multiple-response technique, you must carefully explain it to the class. Also caution students that you will not repeat any student responses. Thus, students must listen carefully to their peers' responses so that they will not repeat them.

The multiple-response strategy also allows the teacher to speak less. It is difficult for you to be an empirical observer of student behavior, direct a question-and-answer period, manage the classroom, and plan for appropriate questions—all at the same time. You cannot listen and talk simultaneously. But if you use divergent or evaluative questions coupled with the multiple-response strategy, you will have time to analyze the responses that are being given. In short, you will be able to make a qualitative evaluation of each student's response.

Shifts more activity to the students

You can modify this technique by subdividing the class into teams of three, four, or five students to add the motivating factors of small-group solidarity and identification. Once the groups are formed, you ask a divergent or evaluative question of the class. Each group discusses it, and then a spokesperson responds. This situation increases student-to-student verbal interaction. (You can further facilitate students' interaction by rearranging their desks.) Any competition that develops within the class will be peer oriented rather than between teacher and student. Friendly intraclassroom competition can be established by incorporating some type of game into the lesson (see MacKenzie 2001).

By using historical picture books, Kay A. Chick (2006) has been able to motivate students to reflect and collaborate and explore alternative viewpoints. She notes that at-risk students participate fully in the lesson. We suggest using pictures to develop student skills in asking questions.

Teachers tend to be parsimonious with rewards. But by using this variation of the multiple-response strategy, you can reward one group for providing the most novel responses, another for the best responses obtained from an encyclopedia, another for the best nonverbal responses (pictures, cartoons, posters), and another for the best multimedia presentation. Motivational strategies like these help to make the classroom an enjoyable, creative, and interesting place. The Instructional Strategies box on page 235 illustrates the multiple-response technique. Notice how the teacher frames a question and then calls on three or four students to answer it.

When you use the multiple-response technique, you also build other communication skills in students. For example, when you start using this technique, you can ask students to write one-sentence summaries of each response given by their peers. Think of the implications of this simple teaching technique for improving listening skills; structuring logical discussions; identifying the main points in an oral discourse; enabling students to classify arguments, positions, or statements systematically; and learning to outline. Because questioning is such a widely used communication technique in the classroom, it follows that teachers should maximize the usefulness of questioning so that it improves other cognitive skills and processes as well. As with using reflective questions, we strongly recommend that you write out in advance questions that have multiple responses. By composing them ahead of time, you can phrase them in a manner that is clear and understandable for all students (Kindem 2006). Writing divergent, evaluative, reflective, and multiple-response questions helps you, as teacher, master the techniques.

Builds numerous communication skills

The multiple-response strategy allows for longer student responses, greater depth in student statements, and greater challenges for all students. It is a logical precursor to student-conducted **discussions** (see Chin 2007). Student discussions are extremely difficult to conduct effectively because many students do not demonstrate the behaviors or skills needed. By using multiple-response questions, you can subtly condition students to accept more responsibility for listening to one another and to modify their responses based on previous ones, paving the way for student-led discussion. We recommend, however, that such discussions be postponed until the multiple-response technique is mastered by teachers and students alike.

The multiple-response technique shifts more activity to the students.

INSTRUCTIONAL
Strategies

The Multiple-Response Technique

TEACHER: Today I'm going to use a new technique that we'll continue using from here on. I'll ask you a question, pause for a few seconds, and then call on three or four of you for responses. Listen carefully, because I won't repeat the question. Furthermore, listen to your classmates as they respond, because I will not repeat any of their responses either. Any questions? Okay? Where might Christopher Columbus have landed if he had set sail from London and headed due west? (pause) Lisa, Raphael, Randy, Tommie.

LISA: He'd have landed in Canada.

TEACHER: (Smiles and points, without comment, to Raphael.)

RAPHAEL: I think he would miss Canada and land near Boston, because the Pilgrims landed in that area.

TEACHER: (Nods head and points to Randy, without verbal comment.)

RANDY: You're both off. He'd have been blown to Greenland.

TOMMIE: That would not happen, either. Christopher Columbus would have been blown by the Gulf Stream winds right back to England.

TEACHER: Those are all interesting ideas. Class, let's check the direction of the Gulf Stream and the air currents. Helen, will you please get the big map of ocean and air currents from the closet and give us a reading?

HELEN: Okay.

Conducting Review Sessions

How can you review previously taught concepts using questioning strategies? One successful method is to reintroduce previously discussed concepts in the context of newly presented material. For example, if you are teaching a unit on transportation and you wish to review the topic of railroads, which has already been covered, you could compare the placement of airports and bus stations with that of railroad stations as part of a discussion on transportation infrastructures. Through questioning, you could elicit from students the fact that most railroad terminals, like airports, were initially built at the edges of cities. Students would then have the opportunity to demonstrate their comprehension of city growth, noting that transportation terminals became engulfed as cities expanded and that this, in turn, caused a set of problems unique to cities and the transportation industry.

What we are suggesting, as a viable alternative to separate, discrete review sessions, is continual review. Such review may be conducted at any level of Bloom's taxonomy. As students begin to relate previously learned skills or concepts to new ones, they may begin to perceive the relationships between old and new material. If you wish to use the true basic liberal arts approach, then you should relate the ideas of one discipline to those of other disciplines. But instead of *telling* students about subtle interdisciplinary relationships, you can direct them to the library or the Internet so that they may discover them on their own and report them to the class. This is particularly useful for

Build in continual review.

those students who are always finished with their work and have "nothing to do"—except disrupt the class. (See Gagliardi 1996 for other examples.)

To use the **concept review questioning technique**, you must always be on the alert for instances that will allow you to establish meaningful relationships, reinforce previously learned concepts, or synthesize students' knowledge, and thereby create added motivation for the class. More importantly, you will be using the technique of "ideational scaffolding," or "bridging," that is, diagramming a concept map on the chalkboard and showing how other ideas or concepts are related to it.

The Instructional Strategies box on pages 237–238 illustrates the concept review questioning technique. The class is a group of new teachers studying the affective domain.

Encouraging Nonvolunteers

In most situations, you will not have much problem encouraging students to respond to questions. To be sure, if you kept careful records of which students respond to questions, you would find that a few students dominate recitation sessions. Furthermore, observation of any class tends to show that there are several students who do not volunteer responses, often because the teacher calls on students who are quick to respond. If your goal is to encourage verbal responses, then you must encourage nonvolunteers to respond. Such encouragement is most difficult at the beginning of a new term, when you are relatively new to the students. As you become more knowledgeable about your students' interests, it becomes easier to prompt nonvolunteers because you can ask questions that reflect their individual areas of interest. What, then, are some helpful strategies to motivate nonvolunteers to respond during questioning sessions?

1. Maintain a highly positive attitude toward nonvolunteering students. Allow them to respond appropriately or correctly each time they are called on. In other words, ask nonvolunteers questions that they will be likely to answer successfully. Once the student has responded appropriately, give generous positive feedback to encourage him or her to continue responding. Ask questions that require short responses *but lead to other questions that require longer responses*. Thus you will progress from a convergent frame of reference to a more divergent one. You may even begin by using easy evaluative questions because most students respond readily to questions that concern judgment, standards, or opinions.

2. Attempt to determine why each nonvolunteer remains quiet. Is the student merely shy, or is there a language disability? We do not mean that you should play the role of an amateur psychologist, but you should determine whether a specific student manifests a speech deficit and, if necessary, make an appropriate referral.

3. Occasionally make a game out of questioning. For example, place each student's name on a card and draw cards at random to select respondents. Or, if certain students always raise their hands when you ask a question, you can politely ask these students to "hold all hands for the next three minutes" so that other students have an opportunity to respond. In this way you can shape the behavior of those students who are already adequately reinforced through verbal participation to allow other students to respond.

4. There is nothing wrong with giving each nonvolunteering student a card with a question on it the day before the intended oral recitation period. Quietly hand these students their cards and tell them they may review the assignment so that they can summarize their responses for the next class period. This method begins to build a trusting relationship between teacher and student.

Provide prompts to encourage shy students.

Implicit in this technique is the task of systematically recording who is volunteering responses in class recitations, and in what class situations. If time permits, it would even be desirable to keep a daily record of each student's verbal activity. You could appoint one member of the class to keep such a tally each day. At the end of a week, you will begin to see patterns for each student.

Calling on nonvolunteers should never be a punishment. Schooling ought to be a positive, enjoyable experience that makes students *want* to learn. As a general rule, the most effective way to encourage nonvolunteers to participate is to treat each student sincerely and as a human being. Many nonvolunteers have learned—sometimes painfully—that it does not pay to say anything in class because the teacher will put them down or make a joke at their expense. Be considerate and encouraging at all times.

INSTRUCTIONAL *Strategies*

Concept Review Questioning Technique

TEACHER: How does the taxonomy of the cognitive domain, which we studied last month, differ from the taxonomy of the affective domain? (pause) Kevin?

KEVIN: The cognitive domain is concerned with the intellectual aspects of learning, while the affective domain is more concerned with emotional outcomes.

TEACHER: Good. Can you list some examples of these "emotional outcomes"? (pause) Nicole?

NICOLE: Attitudes and values?

TEACHER: Fine. Now, going back to my original question, how are the two taxonomies similar? (pause) Amanda?

AMANDA: Well, because they both are called taxonomies, they both are classification systems, and both are hierarchical in nature.

TEACHER: Excellent. What do we mean by "hierarchical" in nature? (pause) Kevin?

KEVIN: I think it means that each category builds on the ones below it.

TEACHER: Okay, could you give us an example of another kind of taxonomy that would illustrate your point?

KEVIN: Sure, the taxonomy of the animal kingdom. Each phylum supposedly is related in some evolutionary fashion to the one below it.

TEACHER: Good. Does everyone see how that example applies to Bloom's taxonomy? Okay, let's take a second now and try to relate the module on the taxonomy to previous modules. In other words, how could we use the taxonomy with some of the other ideas we've talked about? (pregnant silence, which does not last for long) Let me try to be more specific. How could the taxonomy be used in constructing better lesson plans? (pause) Jim? Nicole?

(continued)

INSTRUCTIONAL
Strategies

Concept Review Questioning Technique—Cont'd

JIM: You can use the taxonomy to look at your performance objective and see if your procedure correlates with the terminal behavior.

NICOLE: (with emotion) You could also use the taxonomy to kind of judge whether the lesson is worth doing at all.

TEACHER: How do you mean, Nicole?

NICOLE: Well, if the lesson consists of nothing more than transmitting a lot of facts, maybe the teacher should ask if these facts are ever going to be used again in one of the higher categories. And if the facts are important, there are more effective ways of having the students master them than by recitation.

TEACHER: Good. Anything else? (pause) How about the discussion module? Can you make any connections with the taxonomy? (pause) Allan?

ALLAN: Kind of going along with what we said about lesson plans, the taxonomy might give teachers some new ideas about discussion topics.

TEACHER: Could you elaborate?

ALLAN: Well, sometimes it's easy to get in a rut. Though teachers aren't likely to use discussions with performance objectives at the knowledge level, they may not be aware of the full range of possibilities open for discussion topics.

TEACHER: Excellent. Anyone else?

TINA: Also, the taxonomy might be useful in analyzing why discussions bog down.

TEACHER: In what respect?

TINA: If the students are attempting thought processes at the higher levels and don't have the background at the lower levels, there's likely to be a lot of confusion because the students don't "know" or "comprehend" what they're talking about.

Developing Students' Questioning Skills

The techniques discussed so far all are oriented toward improving your questioning skills. But there is great value in attempting to teach students how to frame *their own* questions.

For the most part, unfortunately, teachers neither encourage nor teach their students to ask questions. Some teachers are even upset when students do ask questions (see Commeyras 1995). However, if you, as an educator, desire to encourage critical or reflective thinking, or thinking of any sort, then you must develop your students' skill at framing questions (Ciardiello 1993). One technique is to play a game of Twenty Questions. In Twenty Questions, participants ask questions in order to identify something. The teacher thinks of some problem, concept, place, or historical figure, and students attempt to discover it through questioning. For example (if it is a place), "Does it still exist under its original name?" "Does it have a democratic form of government?" The teacher can respond with only yes or no answers. Initially you will conduct the session, but as students master the technique and develop their

Twenty Questions.

questioning skills, you can let them conduct the entire session. This will leave you free to analyze their interactions.

Another technique is to demonstrate some phenomenon and have the students raise questions about what is happening. Here the teacher plays a passive role while the students actively generate questions that the teacher must answer. For example, when teaching about the transfer of energy, a teacher might have a tray of marbles in a row. The teacher rolls one marble into the rest, and only one marble rolls from the other end. Students begin asking the teacher about possible explanations. The teacher provides only a yes or no response to each question. This technique causes other students to continue asking questions until the concept of momentum and transfer of energy has been correctly described by the students (see Suchmann's classic, 1966).

When this technique is first used, students tend not to ask the teacher logical questions because much of schooling requires little logic, causing initial results to be discouraging. However, the teacher should review each lesson and then give students precise and detailed directions on how to improve their questioning logic. As one alternative, if it will not be too slow, the teacher may write each student's question on a chalkboard or transparency. This will allow students to accumulate information and skills gradually and in a systematic manner. (See Chahrour 1994 for an extension of this technique.)

Of course, to develop effective questioning skills, it is imperative that students have the ability to formulate questions that address a specific point, not some vague one. The teacher can demonstrate how to develop this ability by moving from a general point of reference to a specific one. (In other words, use a deductive logic questioning process, and encourage students to do the same.)

Model effective questioning for students.

A third method of developing students' questioning skills is to have them prepare study or recitation questions ahead of time about the subject being studied. Select a few students each day to prepare a series of questions for their peers. You might even share with students a few of the questioning techniques discussed here, such as following Bloom's taxonomy. To be sure, most students will be oriented only toward their knowledge level because that is what is reinforced the most in their schooling. But a skillful teacher will continually reinforce those questions that are aimed at higher-level thinking skills and will ultimately help students prepare appropriate higher-level questions.

As you begin to encourage class members to ask questions of one another, you will see a subtle shift of responsibility away from the teacher and toward the students (Rallis et al. 1995). This shift implies that responsibility is a learned behavior. As a teacher, you owe it to your students to help them become articulate and thinking individuals. You have a splendid opportunity to do so when you transfer more responsibility for classroom questioning to them (see Richetti & Sheerin 1999). Additionally, you will be creating the conditions necessary for student-initiated learning (Callison 1997; Commeyras & Sumner 1996).

After conducting extensive research, Cynthia T. Richetti and Benjamin B. Tregoe (2001) identified five reasons why students should develop their own questions. These reasons are listed in the following box.

Reasons to Develop Student Questioning

◆ Increases motivation to learn.

◆ Improves comprehension and retention.

◆ Encourages creativity and innovation.

◆ Teaches how to think and learn.

◆ Provides a basis for problem solving and decision making.

Make every effort to encourage students to ask questions.

Like all new methods, this one must be explained carefully to students and then practiced for a few class periods. Then, once a week or more often, students can conduct questioning sessions on their own. This method is a prerequisite experience to student-led discussions. If you teach children with learning disabilities or exceptional children, they can display their responses (and questions) on cards (Heward 1996).

A novel technique for creating a more interactive questioning session is to have the students question the author of the texts they have read for class. Isabel L. Beck and Margaret McKeown (2002) illustrate how you can encourage students to do this, just as if the author of the text were standing in the classroom. Students are shown how to initiate queries in three forms:

1. What is the author trying to say?
2. What did the author say to make you think that?
3. What do you think the author means?

These queries are then followed with other student questions as they construct the author's meaning (see Kucan & Beck 1997). This technique is handy when you study complex topics or when the textbook is difficult to comprehend. Now you have one more way to create an active learning environment in what is traditionally a dull one!

You and the class may generate a set of criteria on which to base student-framed questions. The criteria may also be applied to a broader context. Students can be requested to evaluate the kinds of questions that are asked on various television quiz shows as a means of improving their own skills in data collection and interpretation.

Think-Pair-Share   Let us close this section with one more student-oriented method of encouraging students to respond to teacher questions. Frank Lyman (1981) described this method as having three steps:

Step 1: Think. You ask a question to the whole class and allow them a short time to "think" about the response.

Step 2: Pair. Designate partners (desk mates, buddies) to pair up and discuss the best answers, or even the most novel possibilities. In some cases you could even have them write their team responses.

Step 3: Share. You now call on the pairs to share their thinking with the class. Responses can be recorded on the chalkboard.

The Think-Pair-Share method is another means by which ELL students or those with special needs can participate meaningfully in the recitation session. Also keep in mind that assistive technology is available to aid handicapped students. We encourage you to check on these technologies with your principal.

All the teachers we have worked with have been pleased with the results of the techniques described here. More important, they were amazed at how much they had underestimated their students' potential. We are not suggesting that these techniques are simple to implement; they take much work and planning. But the attendant rewards make both teaching and learning more worthwhile.

Include student-led questioning periods as part of your unit plans.

Reflect

◆ With a small group of your peers, discuss which of these questioning techniques you are likely to try during your first year on the job. Do you have other ideas as well? Try them out on your peers.

◆ What fears, concerns, or reservations do you have about allowing students to take more responsibility for the questioning and discussing that takes place in the classroom? How can you overcome these concerns?

SECTION 5 Common Challenges of Questioning

Avoiding Teacher Idiosyncrasies

Up to this point, we have been discussing only those teacher behaviors associated with questioning that are positive and encouraging. We hope we haven't made you think that you need only a few tricks and a smile to achieve instant success. Unfortunately, inappropriate teacher behaviors specific to each teacher can interfere with smooth verbal interaction in the classroom. These behaviors, or **idiosyncrasies**, include repeating the question, repeating all student responses, answering the question yourself, not allowing a student to complete a long response, not attending to the responding student, and always selecting the same student respondents. How and why to avoid these pitfalls are discussed next.

Be vigilant about recognizing and eradicating possibly harmful habits.

◆ *Repeating the question.* This habit conditions students to catch the "replay" of the question instead of attending to it the first time, either cognitively or intuitively. It also causes a loss of valuable time and does not help the teacher efficiently manage the classroom. Repeating a question is sometimes appropriate: when the class is in a very large room with poor acoustics, when the question is multifaceted, when the question was not adequately framed the first time (often a difficulty for beginning teachers), or when the question is being dictated for the class to write down. In most cases, though, avoid repeating a question.

◆ *Repeating students' responses.* An equally distracting and time-wasting habit is repeating all or nearly all of your students' verbal responses. If you are sensitive to the need to build positive student self-images, you will not want to be the center of verbal interaction: You will keep the focus on the responding student. After all, if it is important to call on a student and require a response, then it ought to be equally important to listen to that response.

Make an exception for large-group sessions held in rooms with poor seating arrangements and for students with very soft voices. But if students are to develop prediscussion behaviors, then they must learn to take cues from one another.

◆ *Answering the question yourself.* Have you ever observed or participated in a class in which the teacher carefully framed a question, paused, called on a student, and then answered the question him- or herself? This idiosyncrasy deflates student morale.

◆ *Not allowing a student to complete a long response.* One very distracting, inappropriate, and rude teacher idiosyncrasy is to ask a question and then interrupt the student by completing the response or by adding personal comments. Such interruptions discourage participation and do not allow students to develop logical response systems.

◆ *Not attending to the responding student.* When you call on a student, show that you are attending to (that is, listening to) him or her. You must model good listening habits for your students.

◆ *Exhibiting favoritism.* One frequently heard student complaint is that "my teacher never calls on me" or that "the teacher has a few pets who are always being called on." These statements typify the frustrations of students who recognize partiality when they see it.

Equity is the goal.

Many teachers exhibit strong biases against students who are struggling academically. The box below lists a few of the *intentionally disinviting* teacher behaviors exhibited toward these students.

It is tempting to call on students who often volunteer and who will give you the "right" answer, so that you will appear to be an effective teacher. But if you wish to encourage all of your students to be winners, then you must accord them an equal opportunity to respond. A quick way to determine whether you show bias is to ask a different student each day to list the number of times that you call on each student. A quick tally at the end of the week will provide the data you need. If students are hesitant about responding, then you must gear your questions to their needs and abilities so that they too can enjoy the feeling of success and positive reinforcement.

How Teachers Treat Low Achievers

◆ Giving them less time to answer a question.

◆ Giving them answers, or calling on others rather than trying to improve the low achievers' responses by giving clues or repeating or rephrasing questions.

◆ Reinforcing inappropriately by rewarding their inappropriate behavior or incorrect answers.

◆ Criticizing them more often for failure.

◆ Praising them for success less frequently than high achievers.

◆ Failing to give feedback to their public responses.

◆ Paying less attention to them or interacting with them less frequently.

◆ Calling on them less often to respond to questions or asking them easier, nonanalytical questions.

(continued)

How Teachers Treat Low Achievers—Cont'd

◆ Seating them at a distance from the teacher.

◆ Using less eye contact and other nonverbal means of communicating attention and responsiveness (such as leaning forward and nodding) in interactions with them.

Source: Good, Thomas L., and Jere E. Brophy. *Looking in Classrooms,* 10th ed. Published by Allyn and Bacon, Boston, MA. Copyright © 2008 by Pearson Education. Adapted by permission of the publisher.

Reflect

A Closing Reflection

◆ Describe the questioning techniques you have observed in your teacher education courses. How do they compare to the techniques described here?

◆ Arrange to microteach lessons to practice the art of questioning. What do you discover about the art of questioning?

◆ What kinds of lessons lend themselves to convergent, divergent, evaluative, and reflective questions?

◆ Why is it useful to apply a taxonomy to your questions?

◆ Examine the effects on students of wait time 1 and wait time 2 in your classes by collecting data on student responses. What is the effect of wait time on higher-level responses?

◆ Review a few studies involving teacher responses to incorrect student answers. Do you find any conclusions that differ from what you read in this chapter?

◆ List some of your own ideas about ways to attain instructional equity in questioning.

Summary Points

1. The convergent strategy elicits short or even one-word responses.
2. The divergent strategy elicits varied student responses.
3. The evaluative strategy elicits a divergent response plus a rationale.
4. The reflective strategy helps students actively develop a concept.
5. Hierarchies or taxonomies may be used to categorize questions.
6. Students need to be encouraged to ask questions in class and summarize lessons.
7. Using wait time is a powerful technique to aid student learning.
8. Teachers need to develop skills in prompting, handling incorrect responses, prompting multiple responses, framing review questions, and encouraging nonvolunteers to participate.
9. Positive responses to incorrect answers encourage continued student participation.
10. Stress the positive and avoid sarcasm, cynicism, and idiosyncrasies that interfere with student learning.
11. Provide opportunities for equity in responding.

***Building a
Career Portfolio***

As you begin looking forward to the first day of teaching your own classes, you might think about what you need to know to successfully conduct questioning sessions. In your career portfolio, be sure to include the following items:

◆ an outline of questioning procedures and a few written questions that you know you'll have to ask, based on your teaching specialty;

◆ an outline of this chapter that pulls out various ways to frame questions;

◆ finally, be sure to create a few higher-level and thought-provoking questions for your teaching specialty.

Resources

PRINT

Below are four carefully selected resources that will provide you with an expanded knowledge base about the art of questioning.

Buehl, D. *Classroom Strategies for Interactive Learning* (2nd ed.). Newark, DE: International Reading Association, 2001, 170 pp.
This book provides 45 skill-building strategies for learning middle through high school content.

Cotton, K. *Classroom Questioning.* Portland, OR: NWREL, Close-Up #5, 2001, 16 pp.
In a few pages, Kathleen Cotton distills the essence of classroom questioning. This is an excellent resource for your portfolio.

McKenzie, J. A. *Learning to Question to Wonder to Learn.* Bellingham, WA: FNO Press, 2005, 180 pp.
This may be one of the most comprehensive books written about the processes of questioning. The "Questioning Toolbox" cleverly addresses the scope of the technique.

Wormeli, R. *Summarizing in Any Subject: 50 Techniques to Improve Student Learning.* Alexandria, VA: Association for Supervision and Curriculum Development, 2004, 226 pp.
Here is a practical handbook that illustrates how summarization strategies can be easily implemented to improve student comprehension.

INTERNET

Go to the website for this book at www.cengage.com/education/orlich to find live links to resources related to this chapter.

◆ Jamie McKenzie provides a treasury of question-related material at **http://www.fno.org**

◆ The following URL provides leads into several different topics associated with questioning. You will find "Topical Syntheses" or research findings, "Close-Ups" on specific techniques, and "Snapshots" describing effective schooling practices.
http://www.nwrel.org/scpd/sirs/

References

Arnone, M. P. (2003). *Using Instructional Design Strategies to Foster Curiosity. ERIC Digest*. Syracuse, NY: ERIC Clearinghouse on Information and Technology. ED 479 842.

Barnette, J. J., S. Orletsky, B. Sattes, & J. Walsh. (1995). *Wait-Time: Effective and Trainable*. Paper presented at the annual meeting of the American Educational Research Association, San Francisco, April 18–22, 1995. ED 383 706.

Beamon, G. W. (1997). *Sparking the Thinking of Students, Ages 10–14: Strategies for Teachers*. Thousand Oaks, CA: Corwin.

Beck, I. L, & M. G. McKeown. (2002). "Questioning the Author: Making Sense of Social Studies." *Educational Leadership* 60(3): 44–47.

Bloom, B. S., Ed. (1956). *Taxonomy of Educational Objectives. Handbook I: Cognitive Domain*. New York: McKay.

Boyd, M., & D. Rubin. (2006). "How Contingent Questioning Promotes Extended Student Talk: A Function of Display Questions." *Journal of Literacy Research* 38(2): 141–169.

Buehl, D., (2001). *Classroom Strategies for Interactive Learning*. Newark, DE: International Reading Association.

Callison, D. (1997). "Key Term: Questioning." *School Library Media Activities Monthly* 13(6): 30–32.

Carpenter, L. P. (2003). "A Teaching Note: Getting Started in a Course on Historical Method." *Teaching History: A Journal of Methods* 28(1): 37–42.

Chahrour, J. (1994). "Perfecting the Question." *Science Scope* 18(2): 8–11.

Chick, K. A. (2006). "Fostering Student Collaboration Through the Use of Historical Picture Books." *The Social Studies* 97(4): 152–157.

Chin, C. (2007). "Teacher Questioning in Science Classrooms: Approaches That Stimulate Productive Thinking." *Journal of Research in Science Teaching* 44(6): 815–843.

Christenbury, L., & P. P. Kelly. (1983). *Questioning: A Critical Path to Critical Thinking*. Urbana, IL: ERIC Clearinghouse on Reading and Communications Skills and the National Council of Teachers of English.

Ciardiello, A. V. (1993). "Training Students to Ask Reflective Questions." *The Clearing House* 66(5): 312–314.

Commeyras, M. (1995). "What Can We Learn from Students' Questions?" *Theory into Practice* 34(2): 101–106.

Commeyras, M., & G. Sumner. (1996). *Questions Children Want to Discuss About Literature: What Teachers and Students Learned in a Second-Grade Classroom*. Athens, GA: National Reading Research Center. ED 390 031.

Crespo, S. (2002). "Praising and Correcting: Prospective Teachers Investigate Their Teacherly Talk." *Teaching and Teacher Education* 18(6): 739–758.

Dana, N. F., K. L. Kelsay, D. Thomas, & D. J. Tippins. (1992). *Qualitative Interviewing and the Art of Questioning: Promises, Possibilities, Problems and Pitfalls*. Paper presented at the Qualitative Research in Education Conference, Athens, GA, January 1992. ED 343 308.

Dann, E., et al. (1995). "Unconsciously Learning Something: A Focus on Teacher Questioning." Paper presented at the Annual Meeting of the North American Chapter of the International Group for the Psychology of Mathematics Education. Columbus, OH: October 21–24, 1995. ED 389 618.

"Declare the Causes: The Declaration of Independence—Understanding Its Structure and Origin." (2001). Washington, DC: National Endowment for the Humanities, EDSITE. ED 455 517.

Dillon, J. T. (1982a). "Cognitive Correspondence Between Question/Statement and Response." *American Educational Research Journal* 19: 540–551.

Dillon, J. T. (1982b). "Do Your Questions Promote or Prevent Thinking?" *Learning* 11: 56–57, 59.

Dillon, J. T. (1990). *The Practice of Questioning*. London: Routledge.

Elder, L., & P. Richard. (1998). "The Role of Socratic Questioning in Thinking, Teaching and Learning." *Clearing House* 71(5): 297–301.

Eppink, J. A. (2002). "Student-Created Rubrics: An Idea that Works." *Teaching Music* 9(4): 28–32.

Epstein, A. S. (2003). "How Planning and Reflection Develop Young Children's Thinking Skills." *Young Children* 58(5): 28–36.

Filippone, M. (1998). *Questioning at the Elementary Level*. M.A. Research Project. Union, NJ: Kean University.

Gagliardi, C. (1996). "Changing the Rules (Teaching Idea)." *English Journal 85*(3): 86–90.

Gagnon, G. W. (2001). *Designing for Learning: Six Elements in Constructivist Classrooms*. Thousand Oaks, CA: Corwin.

Gall, M. D., & M. T. Artero-Boname. (1995). "Questioning." In L. W. Anderson, Ed., *International Encyclopedia of Teaching and Teacher Education* (2nd ed.), pp. 242–248. Tarrytown, NY: Elsevier Science.

Gettinger, M., & K. C. Stoiber. (1999). "Excellence in Teaching: Review of Instructional and Environmental Variables." In C. R. Reynolds & T. B. Gutkin, Eds., *The Handbook of School Psychology* (3rd ed.), pp. 933–958. New York: Wiley.

Gibson, J. (1998, Jan.–Feb.). "Any Questions, Any Answers?" *Primary Science Review 51:* 20–21.

Gilbertson, D., & J. Bluck. (2006). "Improving Responsiveness to Intervention for English Language Learners: A Comparison of Instruction Pace on Letter Naming Rates." *Journal of Behavioral Education 15*(3): 131–147.

Gipperlich, W. R. (2006). "Effects of Increased Wait-Time on Student Participation." M. Ed. Thesis. Cedar Rapids, IA: Graceland University, 51 pp.

Glickman, C. D. (2002). *Leadership for Learning: How to Help Teachers Succeed*. Alexandria, VA: Association for Supervision and Curriculum Development.

Good, T. L., & J. E. Brophy. (2008). *Looking in Classrooms, MyLabSchool Edition* (10th ed.). Boston: Allyn and Bacon.

Green, D., A. Brown, & L. Robinson. (2008). *Making the Most of the Web in Your Classroom: A Teacher's Guide to Blogs, Podcasts, Wikis, Pages, and Sites*. Thousand Oaks, CA: Corwin Press.

Harvey, S., & A. Goudvis. (2007). *Strategies that Work: Teaching Comprehension for Understanding and Engagement*. Markham, Ontario: Pembroke Publishers.

Heward, W. L. (1996). "Everyone Participates in This Class: Using Response Cards to Increase Active Student Response." *Teaching Exceptional Children 28*(2): 4–10.

Jackson, C. W., & M. J. Larkin. (2002). "Rubric: Teaching Students to Use Grading Rubrics." *TEACHING Exceptional Children 35*(1): 40–45.

Kindem, C. J. (2006). "Promoting Higher-Order Thinking Through Questioning Techniques." St. Paul, MN: M.A. Thesis, Hamline University, 66 pp.

Koegel, L. K., S. M. Carmarata, M. Valdez-Menchaca, & R. L. Koegel. (1998). "Setting Generalization of Question-Asking by Children with Autism." *American Journal on Mental Retardation 102*(4): 346–357.

Kounin, J. S. (1970). *Discipline and Group Management in Classrooms*. New York: Holt, Rinehart & Winston.

Kucan, L., & I. L. Beck. (1997). "Thinking Aloud and Reading Comprehension Research: Inquiry, Instruction and Social Interaction." *Review of Educational Research 67*(3): 271–299.

Lampert, N. (2006). "Enhancing Critical Thinking with Aesthetic, Critical, and Creative Inquiry." *Art Education 59*(5): 46–50.

L'Anson, J., S. Rodrigues, & G. Wilson. (2003). "Mirrors, Reflections and Refractions: The Contribution of Microteaching to Reflective Practice." *European Journal of Teacher Education 26*(2): 189–199.

Lyman, F. T. (1981). "The Responsive Classroom Discussion: The inclusion of all Students." In A. Anderson, Ed., *Mainstreaming Digest:* 109–113.

MacKenzie, A. H. (2001). "Brain Busters, Mind Games, and Science Chats." *Science Scope 24*(6): 54–58.

Martinello, M. L. (1998). "Learning to Question for Inquiry." *Educational Forum 62*(2): 164–171.

Marzano, R. J. (2007). *The Art and Science of Teaching: A Comprehensive Framework for Effective Instruction*. Alexandria, VA: ASCD.

McKenzie, J. A. (2005). *Learning to Question to Wonder to Learn*. Bellingham, WA: FNO Press.

McKenzie, J. (2007). *Leading Questions: Managing Complexity in the Public and Private Sectors*. Seattle: FNO Press.

McTighe, J., & F. T. Lyman, Jr. (1988). "Cueing Thinking in the Classroom: The Promise of Theory-Embedded Tools." *Educational Leadership 45*(7): 18–24.

Moutray, C. L., J. A. Pollard, & J. McGinley. (2001). "Students Explore Text, Themselves, and Life through Reader Response." *Middle School Journal 35*(5): 30–34.

O'Reilly, T. (2007). "What Is Web 2.0: Design Patterns and Business Models for the Next Generation of Software." *Communications & Strategies, No. 1*, p. 17.

Paul, R., & L. Elder. (2008). *The Miniature Guide to Critical Thinking Concepts and Tools*. Dillon Beach, CA: Foundation for Critical Thinking.

Rallis, S. F., G. B. Rossman, J. M. Phlegar, & A. Abeille. (1995). *Dynamic Teachers: Leaders of Change*. Thousand Oaks, CA: Corwin.

Richardson, W. (2006). *Blogs, Wikis, Podcasts, and Other Powerful Web Tools for Classrooms*. Thousand Oaks, CA: Corwin Press.

Richetti, C., & J. Sheerin. (1999). "Helping Students Ask the Right Questions." *Educational Leadership 57*(3): 58–62.

Richetti, C. T., & B. B. Tregoe. (2001). *Analytical Processes for School Leaders*. Alexandria, VA: Association for Supervision and Curriculum Development.

Riley, J. P., II. (1986). "The Effects of Teachers' Wait-Time and Knowledge Comprehension Questioning on Science Achievement." *Journal of Research in Science Teaching 23:* 335–342.

Rowe, M. B. (1969). "Science, Silence and Sanctions." *Science and Children 6*(6): 11–13.

Rowe, M. B. (1974). "Wait-Time and Rewards as Instructional Variables, Their Influence on Language, Logic and Fate Control. Part I: Fate Control." *Journal of Research in Science Teaching 11:* 81–94.

Rowe, M. B. (1978). "Wait, Wait, Wait." *Science and Mathematics 78:* 207–216.

Rowe, M. B. (1980). "Pausing Principles and Their Effects on Reasoning in Science." *New Directions for Community Colleges 31:* 27–34.

Rowe, M. B. (1996). "Science, Silence, and Sanctions." *Science and Children 34*(1): 35–37.

Sangster, M. (2007, Sept.). "Reflecting on Pace." *Mathematics Teaching 204:* 34–36.

Savage, L. B. (1998). "Eliciting Critical Thinking Skills Through Questioning." *Clearing House 71*(5): 291–293.

Stahl, R. J. (1994, May). *Using "Think-Time" and "Wait-Time" Skillfully in the Classroom. ERIC Digest.* Bloomington, IN: ERIC Clearinghouse for Social Studies/Social Science Education. ED 370 885.

Streifer, P. A. (2001). "The 'Drill Down' Process." *School Administrator 58*(4): 16–19.

Suchmann, J. R. (1966). *Inquiry Development Program in Physical Science.* Chicago: Science Research Associates.

Swift, J. N., C. T. Gooding, & P. R. Swift. (1995). "Using Research to Improve the Quality of Classroom Discussions." *Research Matters . . . to the Science Teacher*, No. 9601. Cincinnati: The National Association for Research in Science Teaching.

Tobin, K. (1987). "The Role of Wait-Time in Higher Cognitive Level Learning." *Review of Educational Research 57:* 69–95.

Van Es, J. M. (2006). "Encouraging Reflective Thinking in the High School Classroom: Effective Use of Questioning and Wait-Time Strategies." Sioux Center, IA. M. Ed. Thesis, Dordt College, 52 pp.

van Zee, E., & J. Minstrell. (1997). "Using Questions to Guide Student Thinking." *Journal of the Learning Sciences 6*(2): 227–269.

Walsh, J. A., & B. D. Sattes. (2005). *Quality Questioning: Research-Based Practice to Engage Every Learner.* Thousand Oaks, CA: Corwin Press.

Wells, G., & R. M. Arauz. (2006). "Dialogue in the Classroom." *Journal of the Learning Sciences 15*(3): 379–428.

Wormeli, R. (2004). *Summarization in Any Subject: 50 Techniques to Improve Student Learning.* Alexandria, VA: Association for Supervision and Curriculum Development.

Yerushalmi, E., & C. Polingher. (2006). "Guiding Students to Learn From Mistakes." *Physics Education 41*(6): 532–538.

York-Barr, J., W. A. Sommers, G. S. Ghere, & J. Montie. (2001). *Reflective Practice to Improve Schools: An Action Guide for Educators.* Thousand Oaks, CA: Corwin.

Small-Group Discussions and Cooperative Learning

Pete Gordon wanted to observe a class that had student-to-student interaction. When he mentioned this to his faculty advisor, Pete was invited to observe a teacher at the Lincoln Middle School. He was greeted by the principal and was given permission to sit in on two classes.

The topic of class discussion focused on recycling. Pete observed that students' desks were arranged in circular groups, with eight students to a group. A buzz of meaningful noise emanated from the room. The teachers walked about the room, sitting in with each group for a few minutes but not participating verbally. After the discussion period was over, students begin to give reports to the class. Students then prepared summary statements on sheets of newsprint, and there was more interaction among them.

As the lesson ended, Pete was impressed with the level of responsibility and control the students exhibited, as well as with the amount of real learning they had achieved. He wondered how he could organize similar work groups in his future classrooms.

Using small groups is one of the best ways to promote student autonomy, cooperation, and learning in your classroom. This chapter shows you how to organize discussion, small-group, and cooperative learning experiences for your students. As you read, think about the following questions:

◆ How can I organize my class for small-group discussions?

◆ What kinds of small groups can be organized, and how can I use them in my classroom?

◆ How can I use cooperative learning in my classroom?

SECTION 1 Organizing and Initiating Discussion Groups

A major tenet of the constructivist philosophy of education is the importance of an active learning environment. If every student were always active in the classroom, however, chaos would soon reign. Accordingly, the most effective way to implement active learning is to organize the class into small groups of students who can work harmoniously together, foster their own learning strategies, and create an atmosphere in which information sharing can take place.

VIDEO CASE

Joshua Lawrence uses both traditional and online discussion formats to teach the Greek myth "The Judgment of Paris," as shown in the video "Middle-School Reading Instruction: Integrating Technology" on the student website. As you watch the clips and study the artifacts in the case, reflect on the following questions: (1) What traditional discussion techniques translate well to an online environment? (2) How does Joshua interact with the students in his class?

The Discussion Method Defined

What exactly do we mean by a "discussion" in the context of schooling? As we said in an earlier chapter, discussion is a teaching technique that involves an exchange of ideas, with active learning and participation by all concerned.

The discussion method requires the teacher to develop a viewpoint and to tolerate and facilitate the exchange of a wide range of ideas. Discussion is an active process of student–teacher involvement in the classroom environment (see Gauthier 2001). Discussion allows a student to discover and state a personal opinion or perspective, not merely repeat what the teacher or text has already presented. Janet I. Angelis (2003) observed that achievement gains in middle school

---

Discussion is a purposeful learning exchange, *not* a recitation.

---

literacy could be attributed to well-planned classroom discussions. In discussion groups, students are active learners (Bond 2001).

For example, a previously tracked Advanced Placement high school English class was opened to all interested students. The teacher changed her technique to use small groups, tutoring, and role playing (all discussed later). These processes gave students more responsibility for learning and created an opportunity for some to experience learning that had previously been denied to them (Cone 1992). This is an example of being intentionally inviting.

Besides promoting meaningful personal interaction, discussion promotes a variety of learning, including content, skills, attitudes, and processes. It is an appropriate way to improve the thinking and speaking skills of students. Discussions can also be a means of enhancing students' analytical skills (Furinghetti, Federica, & Domingo 2001; George & Becker 2003; Rex 2001). Discussion techniques lead to greater student engagement and reflection in language arts as well as the content areas (Spiegel 2005). If you desire to have different students doing different tasks or activities at the same time, all leading to meaningful goals, then discussions are suitable. If you want to practice indirect control of learning, then discussion is the technique to use.

Before we discuss the specific links between classroom discussion and the use of small groups, we focus on a fundamental skill that you and your students must develop to participate in successful discussions.

Teaching Good Listening Skills

All discussions involve verbal interaction. This means that without good listeners, a meaningful discussion cannot take place. Being a good listener is partly a matter of positive attitude and partly a matter of listening skill, so you and your students have two things to practice. From our work with students and others (see Carico 2001), we have gathered tips that can help you become systematic and thorough in fostering listening in the classroom.

Listening can be taught by modeling.

---

1. Begin by modeling excellent listening habits for your students. Observe yourself: Do you lean forward, make eye contact, and show interest in students? Or do you fidget, look away, show boredom, or walk around the classroom? The former behaviors are indicators of listening, while the latter indicate that you couldn't care less. You must give your students nonverbal feedback when they talk to you. Your nonverbal posture is the only way they can determine if you really heard and understood what they said. Also observe whether you reinforce students for listening to one another (Smith 2003).

2. Support your modeling with sound instructional practices. First, use short and simple directions. Children in the early grades can usually remember only one or two directions. Even older students become confused if you give long directions or a series of directions at a time. (Write detailed sets of directions on paper and hand them out to students.) Second, do not keep repeating and explaining the directions. Expect students to listen the first time. Third, to help students develop into listeners, check to see that background noises, such as talking and equipment noises, are kept to a minimum (see Owca, Pawlak, & Pronobis 2003).

When students know that there are concrete reasons for listening, they will improve. If you give them practical listening experience, some of what they learn will show up in their discussion activities. Honing students' listening skills will improve their academic achievement in all subject areas. Carl Glickman (1998) suggests that teachers also develop these skills.

Listening is a learned behavior, and the teacher's attitude illustrates to the student that listening is important (Gehring et al. 2003; Mosher 2001). The Instructional Strategies box below describes a number of additional techniques that have helped students develop their listening skills.

INSTRUCTIONAL
Strategies

Tips for Teaching Listening

◆ Deliver a short, well-organized lecture and have the class outline it. Review the content to identify main topics and main points.

◆ Ask a question. Have students paraphrase the question and recite these paraphrases in class.

◆ Conduct oral tests frequently.

◆ Limit or avoid repetition of directions, questions, and comments.

◆ Allow students to conduct recitations.

◆ Have students summarize television programs they have seen.

◆ List good listening habits on the blackboard (at the end of each class, each student could list one good listening habit).

◆ Post a bulletin board display related to listening skills.

◆ Appoint a class recorder to provide a summary of recitation or discussion activities.

◆ Appoint one or two students to listen for any grammatical errors spoken in a class.

◆ Ask a student to paraphrase instructions, directions, or a student's previous response to a question.

Lecturing   Before we move into discussions, let us briefly address the "lecture." No doubt you have listened to some outstanding lectures during your educational journey, and we are willing to speculate that you've heard some awful ones. To deliver a first-rate lecture, first you need a clear objective. In most cases, at the K–12 level, that means you might only speak for 10 to 15 minutes. Then you initiate a recitation session using the wait-time questioning model. Second, use some type of advance organizer-outline on chalkboard, whiteboard, or overhead projector. Third, seek feedback from your students. Fourth, reflect back on what was previously discussed and what is forthcoming. This adds the element of "bridging"—that is, connecting the known with the unknown. Fifth, evaluate the effort. Sixth, keep in mind that a lecture should be a synthesis of information or an expanded explanation with examples, not just a repeat of material from the textbook (see Aarabi 2007 for details).

Key Elements of Small-Group Discussions

Because they encourage interaction among students, small-group settings are particularly appropriate for exchanging ideas and focusing on processes—in short, they are ideal for classroom discussion. This section explains what is involved in conducting successful **small-group discussions**: verbal exchanges of ideas and information in groups of four to eight students. But first, we will put this topic in a context for you and describe how long a time period you may typically expect this process to take. As you'll see, it doesn't happen overnight! (See Evans 2001 for additional insights and experiences.)

It takes time to develop the skills that *both teachers and students* must master before implementing student-led discussion techniques effectively. Our work with teachers shows that it takes approximately eight weeks to practice all of the discussion elements (although it can be done in as little as four weeks). However, the first steps using discussions are based on the divergent and reflective questioning strategies we considered in Chapter 7; thus, the needed skills must be identified, and they must be practiced repeatedly so that students will understand the routines and support one another's learning. By having students perform the process, the teacher can better discover problems and effectively resolve them.

Let's look at four key elements of organizing small groups in your classroom: goals and objectives, ideal group size, room arrangement, and choice of topics and applications.

Goals and Objectives   Small groups can learn from activities as diverse as making time lines, observing courts in session, or taking field trips to museums. The value is in the experience. In fact, small-group learning is especially suited to activities like these, in which the most important learning outcome is the process itself rather than its end result. For such outcomes, teachers write **process objectives**, which require the learner to participate in some technique, interaction, or strategy. Whereas performance objectives, discussed in Chapter 3, indicate a specific desired achievement, process objectives usually call for the gradual and more openly defined development of skills and attitudes.

The first task in planning a successful process-oriented learning activity is to develop a set of long-range priorities or goals. From these you will derive process objectives, which will help you to focus individual lessons. Each process objective in turn will require carefully planned learning experiences and ample time for student practice. A teacher who wishes to develop students' writing skills, for example, must give them guidance, feedback, *and* repeated opportunities to practice their writing. The same applies to building students' discussion skills. Students need practice and cumulative experience within a carefully planned framework to gain the skills necessary to be successful in these areas (see Tate 2003).

Ideal Group Size   In this chapter, we make a distinction between small-group discussions and whole-class recitations. Group size is an important variable that influences learner participation. There is no absolute minimum or maximum number of persons that must be included in a small group to ensure a successful discussion. Small groups can number anywhere from three to fifteen participants (Miller 1986). Some suggest that two to five is the ideal size (Cohen, Lotan, & Holthuis 1997; Schmuck & Schmuck 2001); others assert that six is the maximum (Johnson, Johnson, & Holubec 1994, 1998). Our own observations suggest that the optimal group size is from six to eight students.

Discussion techniques may take eight weeks to develop.

Integrate process skills into your unit plans.

Students can learn the skills to work in harmony toward achieving meaningful goals.

© Bob Daemmrich/The Image Works

When four or fewer individuals are involved in a discussion group, the participants might pair off rather than interact with all members. (For studies on group size, see McCann et al. 2005; McCann et al. 2006; Pendergrass 1973; Wells 2001.)

Group size affects participation.

However, William W. Wilen (2004) does make a case for whole-class discussion. He notes that in these large groups the teacher's primary function is to attempt to involve all students in the interaction. (Review the Think, Pair, Share "tool" discussed in Chapter 7 for involving students.)

Room Arrangement   Probably the optimal physical arrangement for small-group discussion consists of several discussion centers located within a large room. You can partially isolate the centers from the rest of the room with bookshelves or folding room dividers. A simpler way is to turn student desks so that participants face one another and are not distracted by activities in the rest of the room. Students will normally block out noise from the other groups if each circle is enclosed so that students make eye contact only with members of the same group. By converting the room into "centers," you can conduct several types of activities simultaneously without disruptions.

Rooms can easily be rearranged to promote discussion.

Choice of Topics and Applications   Discussion topics may arise from ongoing classwork, or they may follow students' interest in a selected area. The usefulness of the discussion depends in large part on group members' ability and willingness to define the problem to be solved.

Discussions can be held on appropriate subject matter in any classroom and among students of any age or developmental level. The topic chosen should be pertinent to classroom studies and be able to hold students' interest. The issue being discussed should be sufficiently difficult to sustain interest and require serious, creative thinking. In short, the topic must have relevance to those discussing it. Sufficient information should be available to class members, either in print or via the Internet, to keep the discussion going. Controversial issues and moral dilemmas are excellent topics for small-group discussions (see Soja & Huerta 2001 for a clever model).

Students need to learn how to express their ideas and to incorporate discussion skills effectively. For example, the National Council of Teachers of Mathematics published a series of case studies and questions that are appropriate for children in grades K–5 (Bush, Dworkin, & Spencer 2001). This resource provides mind-stretching experiences for young pupils. Within the same discipline, Susan H. Chapin, Catherine O'Connor, and Nancy Caravan Anderson (2003) illustrate specific discussion ideas that promote mathematical reasoning and understanding. Math does not have to be just a pencil-and-paper activity. Reflection comes from interaction.

Introducing a new topic is appropriate for small groups, as is seeking alternative solutions to problems or respecting the viewpoints of others on controversial issues (see also Scotty-Ryan 1998).

What kinds of sharing experiences do you want your students to have? Perhaps you will focus immediately on multicultural experiences—on sharing customs related to dress, games and recreation, family activities, and religion. Or you might think about the need for students to display and share their unique talents, or the benefits of sharing the experiences of students who are socioeconomically impoverished or who have disabilities (see Sapon-Shevin 2001). By using pictures of the Seven Wonders of the World, children from all walks of life can be involved in discussions. For example, when viewing the Great Pyramids of Egypt the focus question could be "How could they build these huge structures?" Asking open-ended questions allows for all kinds of responses. The key is to involve everyone.

Learning how to conduct small-group activities is important because you are likely to teach in a school where mainstreaming or school policy mandates the placement of students with disabilities within regular class settings (see Chapter 1). Or perhaps you will be involved with gifted and talented classes. Regardless of the setting, you will be faced with the challenge of providing a nongender-biased, multiculturally oriented education for your students. Becoming adept at handling small-group discussions will help you meet these challenges (see Adler & Rougle 2005).

Group discussions can occur as early as kindergarten.

Discussions promote instructional equity: Everyone participates.

Reflect

◆ How might process skills and content work together when you create a small-group discussion project for your class?

◆ What are some ethical or moral dilemmas that you might present for small-group discussion in the grade you plan to teach?

◆ What are the most effective room arrangements for facilitating student interactions when conducting discussions? Can you think of arrangements other than the ones we've discussed so far? Draw a sketch of a possible classroom arrangement.

Basic Small-Group Concepts

As you initiate small-group discussions, you need to understand four basic concepts: process, roles, leadership, and cohesion.

Key Ideas ▶ **The Four Basic Concepts Related to Small-Group Methods**

◆ *Process:* The interactions that take place within the group

◆ *Roles:* Each group member's specific responsibilities within the group

◆ *Leadership:* The capacity to guide and direct others in a group setting

◆ *Cohesion:* Group members' support for one another

Process and Interaction As we have already discussed in earlier sections of this chapter, the essence of process in small-group discussion is verbal interaction. Communication processes are most vital for successful discussion. Students must be taught and encouraged to listen to what each person is saying and to respond appropriately. Involvement by everyone is part of the process.

Roles and Responsibilities Every member of a discussion group has a **role**. Group members may be assigned roles by the teacher or by the group as it matures. Each role has specific privileges, obligations, responsibilities, and powers. As the teacher, your own role is best described by the term *facilitator*. A **facilitator** gives students the skills, materials, and opportunities they need to direct their own learning experiences. As facilitator, you need to walk around the class, listening, observing, and encouraging every student to participate (see Ngeow & Kong 2003). In most discussion groups, other roles typically include a leader and a recorder, for example, and additional roles are assigned as needed. All class members must be rotated through the roles so that everyone gets experience as the leader and in the other roles. It is your responsibility to provide all students with the opportunity to participate in a variety of roles (see Schmuck & Schmuck 2001). Roles are discussed in more depth in Section 3 of this chapter.

Rotate students through leader and other roles.

Leadership The single most important role in a small group is that of the leader. The leader is the person in authority—the spokesperson for the group. Leadership is a learned quality. So, as teacher, you have to model how a leader opens the discussion, calls on participants, clarifies statements, and seeks everyone's comments. Leaders have to be taught how to plan the discussion, organize the group for maximum efficiency, direct the discussion, and coordinate different individual assignments.

When you begin to use small-group discussions, you may choose the initial student leaders on the basis of leadership abilities already observed in class situations. Attributes that enhance leadership ability may include personal popularity, academic standing, temperament or sociability, thinking ability, and speaking ability.

Ideally, leadership develops through experience, but it is wise to discuss with the class early in the semester what qualities a leader must have to help the group work together. At first, appoint leaders. As new leaders emerge, they should then be rotated in. It is your responsibility to help students develop the desired leadership behaviors and competencies. For example, leaders will need time to learn how to ask questions, how to report a summary, how to involve nonvolunteers, and how to restrain dominating volunteers without using aversive techniques. Ultimately, every class member should have an opportunity to develop those skills and be a leader. You must emphasize the main functions of the small-group leader and provide the leaders with special training (see Miles 1998). Leader functions are summarized in the box below.

Key Ideas **Functions of the Discussion Leader**

◆ *Initiating:* Getting the group going and keeping it moving when it becomes bogged down or goes off on a dead-end tangent (for example, by clarifying certain statements or asking questions that call for more than a yes or no answer).

◆ *Regulating:* Influencing the pace of the discussion (by summarizing or pointing out time limits).

◆ *Informing:* Bringing new information to the group (but not by lecturing).

◆ *Supporting:* Making it easier for members to contribute (by harmonizing opposing viewpoints, voicing group feelings, varying members' places in the group, and helping group members get acquainted).

◆ *Evaluating:* Helping the group evaluate process goals (by testing for consensus or noting the group's progress in some area).

Cohesion: The "We" Attitude   The final concept is group **cohesion**—the tendency of a group to stick together and support its members. A cohesive group displays a "we" attitude: The members support one another and show pride in belonging. The tone the teacher sets is all-important here. In fact, possibly the most important criterion for predicting your ability to facilitate small-group discussions is your own set of attitudes and feelings. Mastering small-group discussion methods requires an appreciation of the atmosphere or emotional setting of the classroom. As the teacher, you must believe that students can accept responsibility and that your actions are closely related to the manner in which the students respond. Groups can take on names of favorite sports teams or favorite animals. In addition, roles such as recorder and evaluator help groups to be more cohesive.

Attitude begins with teacher's belief.

Evaluation in Small-Group Settings: Providing Positive Feedback

Why use positive feedback in a small-group setting? First, as we have already seen in Chapter 7, positive feedback increases responses. Many students do not respond because they are afraid of giving an incorrect reply and receiving a negative teacher reaction. If they give a partially correct response, some positive feedback from you usually will motivate students to try again (see Chapters 7 and 10). This feedback can also come from the group leader. To many students, especially at the middle and secondary levels, peer approval or feedback is even more important than teacher approval.

Second, students need to learn to cooperate with and support others. Students *can* and *will* learn to give positive feedback to one another, but only if you are not the only one giving feedback. Gradually shift the responsibility for providing feedback to the group. This helps to promote activity and harmony within the group while giving students practice with the valuable leadership skill of providing feedback to others (see Weissglass 1996).

Evaluative processes should provide feedback concerning group members' progress in discussion skills and processes, and they should inform the teacher about how the group is progressing in relation to process objectives and group goals. You (or the group leader) and each student need to assess individual group members' progress. Evaluation should be nonthreatening and varied, and it should be based on specific learning objectives. Students need to know, before the discussion or group project, the criteria on which they will be evaluated (see Beach, Appleman, Hynds, & Wilhelm 2006).

Figures 8.1 and 8.2 show forms we've used when collecting feedback in discussions. The process is cyclical. You collect, tabulate, and summarize the

---

Base evaluation on learning objectives.

FIGURE 8.1

Personal Data Check Instrument

PERSONAL DATA CHECK

Name_____

Directions: Keep track of the number of times that you participate orally in the small-group activity. Then insert the total number in the place provided in Item 1. After the discussion is over, place an X next to the statement that best describes your response to each question.

1. Tally the number of times that you participated verbally in the small-group discussion.

_____ Your tally

2. To what extent did you participate in the discussion?

_____ (a) I really dominated it.
_____ (b) I participated as much as the others did.
_____ (c) I didn't participate as much as I would have liked.

3. To what extent would you like to contribute more (or less) to the group discussion?

_____ (a) I'd like to contribute more.
_____ (b) I'm contributing just about the amount I'd like.
_____ (c) I'd like to contribute less.

4. How would you rate the extent to which your group encourages all of its members to participate fully?

_____ (a) The group encourages everyone to participate fully.
_____ (b) The group could encourage its members to participate more.
_____ (c) The group discourages individuals from participating.

Modify the form to match your process objectives.

FIGURE 8.2

FIGURE 8.2

**Discussion Evaluation
Form: Individual
Participant Rating**

DISCUSSION EVALUATION FORM

Group _____

Your Name _____

Directions: Place an X next to the response that best describes how you felt.

1. **Do you think that your time was being well used in the discussion
   group?**

   _____ (a) Not at all

   _____ (b) About right

2. **Was there sufficient discussion between you and your group members?**

   _____ (a) Not at all

   _____ (b) About right

3. **Was the discussion in your small group informative enough?**

   _____ (a) Not at all

   _____ (b) About right

Suggestions or comments _____

_____

_____

---

*A simple form like this provides data from which improvements can be
made.*

data and then share the results with the entire class for its collective reaction.
Remember that it takes planning, time, and experience to develop smoothly
functioning small groups in any setting.

Benefits of Small-Group Discussions

Small-group discussions have been proven to be beneficial to students, particularly if the groups are involved in tasks requiring higher-level thinking,
decision making, problem solving, or positive social behaviors and attitudes.
One summary of several research studies noted significant gains by students
who worked collaboratively in groups (Fillmore & Meyer 1992).

Moreover, small-group discussions may be a way to rekindle the enthusiasm of your turned-off students. Because small-group learning requires varied activities and interactions, it gives students more chances for success. For
example, a student who is a flop at initiating discussion but is highly percep-
tive may be called on for analysis or to craft a compromise. The class member who is a poor reader has a chance to excel in reporting or visualizing. (See
Berne & Clark 2006.)

The now classic HumRRO study noted five benefits to the learners associated with discussion (Olmstead 1970). These are listed in the box at the top of
page 259.

The Key Ideas box on page 259 summarizes some of the important points
we have covered about small groups so far.

More chances for students
to prove themselves

Learner Benefits from Discussion

◆ Increased depth of understanding and grasp of course content

◆ Enhanced motivation and greater involvement with the course

◆ Positive attitudes toward later use of material presented in the course

◆ Problem-solving skills specific to content of the course

◆ Practice in the application of concepts and information to practical problems

Key Ideas

Attributes of Discussion Formats

◆ Active learning can be implemented in small groups of students (preferably six to eight).

◆ Achieving process objectives requires active student involvement and interaction.

◆ Discussions are highly interactive, not teacher-led recitations.

◆ Discussions cannot be used for any topic—they are selectively incorporated into teaching units.

◆ A positive classroom environment is essential for collaborative work.

◆ Everybody in a discussion group is assigned some responsibility.

Reflect

◆ How does your role as small-group facilitator differ from your traditional role as teacher?

◆ Parents are often concerned that small-group learning destroys individual initiative. How would you address this issue?

◆ Plan a unit that could be taught using discussions. How does the plan differ from one you might write if you were using other techniques?

◆ How might you plan to include all students in a discussion?

SECTION 2   Six Basic Small-Group Discussion Types

In this part of the chapter, we present six basic types of small-group discussion: brainstorming, tutorials, task-directed, role playing, simulations, and inquiry-centered. From this list, you should be able to find at least one type of discussion that will fit your instructional and process objectives at any given time.

One method for classifying (and remembering) discussion types is to use the variable of control or domination. When implementing small-group discussions, you must decide on the proper amount of teacher control for the activity: You can dominate the activities of the groups almost totally, you can act in an egalitarian manner, or you can choose not to participate at all. Likewise, you must decide how much control you want the group leaders to exert within their groups. Table 8.1 illustrates the basic types of discussion groups we have identified, viewed along a continuum from greater control (at the top) to lesser control (at the bottom).

How much control do you want?

In addition to deciding on the proper amount of control, there are two other important decisions you must make when choosing a discussion type for a particular situation: the desired or anticipated process or skill to be learned and the desired or anticipated product of the discussion. Group work always

TABLE 8.1	A Taxonomy of Discussion Groups		
Type of Discussion	General Instructional Purposes	Orientation	Knowledge, Skills and Control Continuum
Brainstorming	Creativity Stimulation Idea generation Role building Listening	Process	Lowest need of discussion skills and moderate probability for teacher control
Tutorial	Individual skills Questioning Basic competencies	Process and product	
Task group	Delegation of responsibility Initiative Achievement Planning skills Group learning Affective consequences Reflection Evaluation	Product and process	
Role playing	Evaluation Reflective thinking Values analysis Situation presentation	Process	
Simulation	Inquiry Decision making Application of skills	Process and product	
Inquiry group	Analysis Synthesis Evaluation Student initiative	Process	Highest need of discussion skills and lowest probability for teacher control

has a goal, such as the completion of a given task. This goal is the *product*. How the members interact with one another during the discussion is the *process*. These two objectives must be taught to students. With this point in mind, let's explore each type of discussion in detail.

Brainstorming

Brainstorming is a simple and effective skill-building technique to use when a high level of creativity is desired. The entire class can participate in a brainstorming activity, but the shorter the time available for discussion, the smaller should be the number of participants (which should, in any case, be between five and fifteen persons).

The leader begins the brainstorming session by briefly stating the problem under consideration. The problem may be as simple as "What topics would the group like to consider this semester?" or as complex as "How can the school lunchroom be arranged to maximize efficiency?" Every school subject has some elements that require students to do some freewheeling thinking. This is when you want to use a brainstorming group.

After the topic has been stated and before interaction starts, it is crucial to select a method for recording the discussion. It can be taped, or one or two students who write quickly can serve as recorders. The leader should stress to the group that *all* ideas need to be expressed. All group participants need to realize that achieving the highest possible *quantity* of suggestions is paramount. Refer to Chapter 5 to review the topic of graphic organizing because it is an effective way to display and organize participants' suggestions.

There are some very important rules to follow for brainstorming sessions. The box below summarizes them. All students should be oriented to the rules ahead of time, and the student leader should enforce them.

Brainstorming is an initiating process; it must be followed by some other activity. For example, the group might use the ideas generated in the brainstorming session as the basis for another type of discussion. After the brainstorming session, the ideas should be categorized and evaluated, and as many as possible should be used by students in follow-up activities. The group may arrange the elements in priority order; for example, members may evaluate the suggested topics according to their importance for future study.

A structure for freewheeling thinking

Rules for Brainstorming

◆ All ideas, except for obvious jokes, should be acknowledged and recorded.

◆ No criticism is to be made of any suggestion.

◆ Members should build on one another's ideas. In the final analysis, no idea belongs to any individual, so encourage "piggybacking."

◆ The leader should solicit ideas or opinions from silent members and then give them positive reinforcement.

◆ Quality is less important than quantity, but this does not relieve group members of the need to think creatively and intelligently.

Tutorial

The **tutorial discussion group** is most frequently used to help students who have difficulties learning or processing information at a satisfactory rate. The group is very small (usually four or fewer) and focuses on a narrow range of materials. Teachers of subjects such as reading, mathematics, home economics, art, and business often use the tutorial group for remedial instruction. In the social studies, language arts, math, and sciences, the tutorial group is often used to help students grasp a concept, again with the purpose of remedying a learning difficulty (see Berry 2002). Physical education and primary grade teachers employ a tutorial mode frequently in the area of motor development. It is an excellent way to facilitate student handling of manipulatives, allowing the teacher to evaluate students' motor skills and helping students understand the relationships between movement and body functions (see Davies 1999). Peer tutoring is an excellent technique for *inclusive* class use (see Bond & Castagnera 2003; Kennedy 2003).

The tutorial leader performs three major functions: questioning the students to pinpoint the exact problem that has blocked learning, providing feedback or skills to facilitate learning, and encouraging students to ask questions and to seek answers among themselves. It has been demonstrated that students often learn as well from one another as they do from the teacher (Cracolice & Deming 2001). We caution, however, that before you use student tutors, you must be satisfied that each potential student tutor has mastered the necessary competencies—such as the skills of questioning, giving positive reinforcement, and analyzing work tasks.

Many school districts currently use student tutors and are finding them to be invaluable resources for the classroom teacher. Although this technique is most often used for remedial work, the tutorial discussion group is also an excellent method by which to encourage independent projects or advanced learning (see Mastropieri et al. 2001). Many gifted students find it a challenge to explain their projects to other students.

The person who leads the tutorial discussion needs to develop the skills of giving feedback and encouragement. The leader must also keep the group moving toward its goal, accept feedback from students who learn slowly, and prod group members who do not contribute. It may be helpful to give your student leaders a brief review of the questioning techniques covered in Chapter 7. (See also Berry 2002 for details on developing a tutoring program.)

Tutoring that combines feedback and formative evaluation is such a powerful instructional technique that tutored students can gain 98 percent more than students in conventional classes, as measured by achievement tests (Bloom 1984; Walberg 1999). This critical finding validates the instructional efficacy of the tutorial group. No other instructional variable—homework, advance organizers, conventional classes—surpasses tutoring in increasing achievement.

We have been discussing the use of adults, peers, or older students as tutors. It is also possible to prepare a tutorial in advance, on which a student may work privately and individually as a form of programmed instruction. Printed workbooks are available that use the elements of programmed instruction to help teach a wide variety of subject matter. Programmed instruction also is available in the form of computer software that can be used for drill, practice,

Peers, older students, adults, and computer software can all be tutors.

or remediation (see Grabe & Grabe 2007 for details). Computer software has the advantage of being completely reusable (printed workbooks often required students to fill in blanks), and if well designed, software may be perceived by the student as something that behaves very much like a live tutor.

Task-Directed Discussion

One of the least complex types of small groups used for discussion is the **task group**. Each student in a task group can make significant contributions to the discussion. A prerequisite to using task groups is to delineate specific tasks for all group members. A task group has clearly defined goals and clearly identified individual assignments and roles—for example, recorder, library researcher, artist, leader, and evaluator. It may be beneficial for you to establish a work schedule for the groups and a way to internally monitor participants' achievements and, initially, even to provide all the learning resources that are necessary to accomplish the identified tasks (see Choe & Drennan 2001 for an example using the "jigsaw" technique).

Establish goals, individual tasks, schedules.

The *Jigsaw* technique is a method in which each member of the small group is given a specific piece of textual information. Each group member must then contribute to the group so that the entire textual content can be learned by all. Thus, each member must help the others to learn (see Opitz & Ford 2008 for details).

Task groups tend to begin as teacher-dominated groups, as the teacher usually selects the tasks and assigns each group member to a specific role. You will find that this type of group is especially efficient for helping students learn to interact positively in small work groups. You may also observe how selected students work with one another and how responsibly they tend to accomplish the assigned task. The *reflective questioning strategy* that we introduced in Chapter 7 is an ideal technique to use with task groups. Each team would be given the challenge to generate one reflective question on which the class could ponder—individually or in small groups.

VIDEO CASE

Find out more about using task groups by watching the Video Case "Cooperative Learning in the Elementary Grades: Jigsaw Model" on the student website. As you watch the clips and study the artifacts in the case, reflect on the following questions. (1) How much teacher control is evident at each stage of learning about the Greek Olympics? (2) How much student control?

We must end with a cautionary note. Even though you give a specific assignment to each task group member, do not assume that he or she will completely finish it. Students must ultimately learn to accept responsibility, but it is your job to help them set appropriate goals, to motivate students, and to monitor each student's activities to help all students achieve their assigned goals (see Anderson 2001).

Role Playing

Role playing is a process-oriented group technique in which students act out or simulate a real-life situation. It may involve almost any number of participants, although seven to ten is ideal. To use this type of group, you should be well acquainted with role-playing techniques. Students will also need some coaching to use the technique effectively. The box on page 264 lists the basic elements of role playing.

Thorough preparation will help students enjoy the process and experience of role playing. A key point to emphasize with your class is that they should *not be overly concerned* about interactions that might, in other situations, be perceived as personal attacks. It is especially important for participants to understand the difference between regular acting and psychodrama. Role players and all students who participate in the follow-up discussion should abstain from psychoanalyzing anyone or pretending that they are psychologists. In role playing, as we are using the term, the emphasis is not on the psyche of any participant, but on reenacting or dramatizing a situation and demonstrating how different characters would react in that situation.

Each role-playing group discussion is a unique experience, but there are some common criteria on which you can base your evaluation of a group's effort: Did students who are usually quiet take an active part? Did the role playing lead to a better understanding of the topic being investigated? Was the situation resolved (if the topic of study involved a problem)? Did the participants take their roles seriously? Did they avoid making self-serving comments during the discussion phase?

Role playing can be used with students of all grade levels and all levels of academic achievement, and it can be used to investigate almost any situation or topic (see McCormick 1998). In a unit on environmental problems, for example, students can be assigned specific roles to play as they explore the complexities of scientific or mathematical issues (see Mesmer 2003; Resnick & Wilensky 1998). The U.S. Constitution is a great topic for role-playing groups, especially the First Amendment and how it affects schooling (Vessels 1996). A complete lesson plan that uses the stated grievances in the Declaration of Independence can be easily adapted for role playing and other discussion techniques (see "Declare the Causes" 2001). Role playing can also be effective in developing students' social skills (van Ments 1999). Role-playing groups can help teachers assess students' competency levels, especially in literature classes (Peterson & Belizaire 2006). Your own creativity and that of your students are the only limits to using role playing as a powerful learning and evaluation tool.

Not an opportunity to psychoanalyze

Role playing allows for some drama in the classroom.

Steps of Role Playing

◆ *Briefing students:* Explaining the topic and establishing the situation in understandable terms for each student

◆ *Conducting the drama:* Behaving as an actor in the described situation

◆ *Debriefing:* Analyzing how the roles were played and identifying what concepts were learned

Simulation

A **simulation** is a representation or re-creation of a real object, problem, event, or situation. Although it mirrors reality, a simulation removes the possibility of injury or risk to the participants. The learner is nevertheless an active participant, engaged in demonstrating a behavior or previously acquired skills or knowledge. Interactive simulations may be special cases of role playing. Simulations can be used to motivate students, provide information, enhance conceptual development, change attitudes, assess performance, and provide interdisciplinary activities (see Alsup & Altmyer 2002; Lauer 2003; McGee, Corriss, & Shia 2001; Verker 2003).

Although simulation groups have long been used in the military, in business, in medicine, and in administrative planning, their introduction into the schools is a more recent event. But we should remember that teachers have for years used play stores and student councils as instructional devices to reflect selected dimensions of reality. Some goals of instructional simulation are listed in the box on page 266.

Simulation exercises should be selected for specific learning objectives for which they are appropriate. Usually you cannot achieve all of the goals listed in the box with a single simulation. All simulation exercises should stimulate participants to learn more through independent study or research. Furthermore, as students engage in relevant simulation exercises, they may begin to perceive that knowledge learned in one context can become valuable in different situations. One paper-and-pencil example compares the United States and Europe. Five data sets are provided by which to make comparisons— climatic, economic, political, demographic, and quality of life. Thinking, analyzing, and communication skills are stressed (Richburg & Nelson 1991).

Select simulations to suit learning objectives.

Voices from the Classroom

Dennis Griner

Garfield-Palouse High School

Palouse, Washington

A Simulation for Teaching Economics

I use a stock-exchange simulation learned at a summer economics institute to introduce the Stock Market Crash and the Great Depression to my U.S. History classes. First, I create a trading floor by spreading the chairs apart and making space in the center of the room. I divide the class and designate half as buyers and half as sellers. Each student picks up an order form. The buyer order form lists the maximum price buyers are to pay per share of stock, and the seller form lists the minimum amount sellers are to accept.

The simulation begins when a bell rings to open trading. Students buy or sell their stock by shouting out the price they are willing to pay or accept. Once they agree, both buyer and seller come to the recorder (me or a designated student) to record the sale on the "big board," which can be a chalkboard, overhead, or interactive white board. After ten minutes, I ring the bell to signify the end of a trading day. Students use a buy/sell sheet created in Excel to record their goals and transactions.

While they complete their sheets to determine how much money they made or lost for the day, the recorder averages the overall price using the information on the big board. If the activity is used over a three-day period, students will see the average price of the stock rise and fall.

Students tell me how much they enjoy this simulation. As an introductory exercise, it involves students at all levels of academic ability in a positive learning activity. The simulation introduces the ideas of stock, stock trading, profit and loss, market fluctuations, daily averages, and other basic concepts. It also establishes a common knowledge base for later discussion of margin buying, margin calls, stock pools, speculative buying, and the Dow Jones Industrial Average.

In our use of simulations, we have observed that students become immersed in the activities almost immediately. Simulations are great icebreakers for diverse groups of students. There is also an element of risk taking for all participants. Even though there is no penalty for "wrong" answers, participants tend to view simulations in a serious, personal way, especially those that require decisions. For example, whereas middle and high school students *simulate* investment decisions as illustrated in the Voices from the Classroom box, the D. A. Davidson Company of Great Falls, Montana, provides cash grants to several universities in the Northwest to help students learn about stock investing. In these instances, participants are actually making (or losing) real money. The step from simulated classroom learning to real capitalism is just one grade level away (Davidson 2008). Jane Lopus and Dennis Placone (2002) identify a website for stock market simulations. Simulations seem to be applied more easily to the study of issues than processes. The simulation encourages students to express, in their own words, the basic arguments for the various sides of an issue (see Boston 1998).

Applications include practice with investments.

Two easy-to-use computer-aided simulations include "The Oregon Trail" and "Sim City." Perhaps one of the better applications of computer technology is the use of simulations. A computer simulation can be "played" by just one student or by a small group of students if the classroom has networking capabilities. One student could even play a simulation with students in several different classrooms.

While on the topic of simulations, it is important to note that networked computer communication offers one more dimension for human interaction. The Internet allows students to participate in discussions locally, regionally, or internationally. Students may interact with others synchronously (in real time) by participating in chat rooms (examples include ICQ, Netmeeting, and AOL Instant Messenger). They may also interact **asynchronously** by reading and replying to short messages that are part of a larger, continuous discussion (examples include threaded discussions on sites, blackboard.com, e-mail list-servs, and usenet groups) but not in a scheduled class period.

Whether simulations will work for you depends on your goals and objectives. If you want to teach processes associated with decision making, then simulations provide alternatives to the usual classroom routines. Simulations are also appropriate if you wish to promote human interaction. If you want to provide experiences that students may not get from the routine application of learning skills or principles, then simulations can achieve this end. With some ingenuity, knowledge of your subject, initiative, and imagination, you, too, can design an effective small-group simulation (Brown 1999).

Goals of Simulation

◆ Develop changes in students' attitudes.

◆ Change specific behaviors.

◆ Prepare participants for assuming new roles in the future.

◆ Help individuals understand their current roles.

◆ Increase students' ability to apply principles.

◆ Reduce complex problems or situations to manageable elements.

◆ Illustrate roles that may affect students' lives but that they may never assume.

◆ Motivate learners.

◆ Develop analytical processes.

◆ Sensitize individuals to other persons' life roles.

In the video case entitled "Integrating Technology to Improve Student Learning: A High School Science Simulation" on the student website, observe teacher Ken Bateman as he interacts with his students during the "Dragon" simulation. As you watch the clips and study the artifacts in the case, reflect on the following questions: (1) How is the simulation being utilized? (2) What type of learning is taking place?

Emphasis on questions

Inquiry-Centered Discussion

If you wish to emphasize problem solving, then you will find the *inquiry discussion group* extremely valuable. Any number of students may participate in the discussion group, but six students per team is ideal. The purposes of an **inquiry discussion group** are to stimulate scientific thinking, develop problem-solving skills, and foster the acquisition of new facts through a process of discovery and analysis (Sparapani 1998). The teacher may be the leader of this type of group. If, however, you have a student who has demonstrated good questioning skills and understands the concept under consideration, then allow that student to be the leader.

Inquiry groups are used to stimulate students to become skillful askers of questions. They also allow students to test the validity of hypotheses, determining by direct experience whether they are valid. Inquiry groups are most appropriate for disciplines that lend themselves to problem solving—science and social science (George & Becker 2003; Yell 1998).

Before you introduce the inquiry-group technique, your students should have mastered the skills of observing and inferring. You can encourage these behaviors by having students ask questions based on selected observations of phenomena, by having them collect data, and by having them summarize and draw conclusions. After you and the students have identified the problems to be explored, subdivide the class into small inquiry groups to complete the investigation of each problem. In the box below are several suggestions for inquiry-group topics.

Selected Topics for Inquiry Groups

- ◆ How are the commercials on television presented to the viewers—that is, what graphical representations deliver the message?
- ◆ What major issues or topics dominate newspaper headlines right now?
- ◆ How much food is consumed or wasted in the school lunchroom?
- ◆ Which school intersections carry the heaviest traffic when students arrive at school or leave?
- ◆ What themes are most often repeated by persons seeking political offices?

To make the inquiry-group exercise most meaningful, plan an activity that has some degree of authenticity. For example, the inquiry-group technique can be used effectively when students are studying about the general subject of human and civil rights. A group can role-play an episode in which a civil right has been violated and then, through inquiry discussion, isolate specific aspects of the violation or solve the problem in other ways. Student hypotheses should be testable; for this reason, situations that affect students directly are excellent sources of material. For example, an inquiry group could study a specific area in which students' rights are seen as jeopardized.

How to evaluate an inquiry group is fairly obvious. What you need to know, and what students need to know, is how well they ask questions. Were they able to ask higher-order questions that could lead to hypothesis making and testing? Of course, you also will want to know whether they learned the concept being discussed. How the students ask questions may be tabulated by listing higher-order questions, lower-order questions (refer to Chapter 7), formal statements of hypotheses, and miscellaneous statements. We suggest that the evaluation be accomplished simply. See the Instructional Strategies box below for suggestions.

Plan to evaluate every discussion.

INSTRUCTIONAL *Strategies*

Three Ways to Evaluate an Inquiry Group

1. Maintain a continuous checklist as each participant comments during the discussion (similar to taking minutes at a meeting).

2. Videotape the discussion and evaluate student performance during playback. Examine questioning skills and accuracy of information exchange.

3. Invite a colleague or train a student to tabulate selected behaviors during the discussion sessions.

Reflect

◆ What means would you use to evaluate students' performance during a simulation experience?

◆ What situations might you suggest as role plays in the grade you plan to teach? What kinds of role plays would you avoid? Why?

◆ Under what circumstances might you employ any of these discussion groups when teaching?

SECTION 3   Cooperative Learning

So far we have described a variety of tested discussion methods. The purpose of all these methods is to involve students actively in thoughtful verbal exchanges. Cooperative learning has much in common with the methods already discussed. **Cooperative learning** is learning based on a small-group approach to teaching that holds students accountable for both individual and group achievement. The practice is a very "hot topic." During the first decade of the twenty-first century more than 3,000 citations related to cooperative learning were listed in the online ERIC service. Arthur K. Ellis (2005, pp. 173–182) discusses in detail the various models associated with this technique and provides a set of empirical findings to substantiate its use. (See the box on page 289 for a summary.)

Empirical Support for Cooperative Learning

- ◆ Teacher preparation for using the model is a prerequisite to success.
- ◆ Group and individual accountability are essential to enhance student achievement.
- ◆ Clearly defined group goals are necessary for student achievement.
- ◆ Positive achievement results have been found for nearly all grade levels and subjects.
- ◆ Positive attitudinal attributes are associated with cooperative learning.
- ◆ Cooperative learning aids in student problem solving.

Students accountable for their own and group's achievement

Five characteristics of cooperative learning are shown in the Key Ideas box below (Johnson & Johnson 2004).

Key Ideas → **Characteristics of Cooperative Learning**

- ◆ Uses small groups of three or four students (microgroups).
- ◆ Focuses on tasks to be accomplished.
- ◆ Requires group cooperation and interaction.
- ◆ Mandates individual responsibility to learn.
- ◆ Supports division of labor.

Rationales for Cooperative Learning

Cooperative learning takes many forms within classrooms. Its essential characteristic is that it fosters positive interdependence by teaching students to work and learn together in a small-group setting. Traditional cooperative learning groups consist of three to four students who work on an assignment or project together in such a way that each group member contributes to the learning process and then learns all the basic concepts being taught. Cooperative learning provides unique learning experiences for students and offers an alternative to competitive models of education. It is especially beneficial to students who learn best through social or group learning processes (including a large number of students of color who come from cultures where learning often takes place in social contexts). It offers opportunities for students to learn through speaking and listening processes (oral language) as well as through reading and writing processes (written language).

Cooperative learning offers many benefits: For students, it improves both academic learning and social skills; for teachers, it is an aid to classroom management and instruction (see Cohen, Brody, & Sapon-Shevin 2004; Evertson, Emmer, & Worsham 2006). Cooperative learning enhances students' enthusiasm for learning and their determination to achieve academic success (Mueller & Fleming 2001; Roman 2007). It has been shown to increase the academic achievement of students of all ability levels (Stevens & Slavin 1995a, 1995b;

Yamarik 2007) in reading, writing, mathematical computation and application, comprehension, critical thinking, and physical education (Bramlett 1994; Dyson & Grineski 2001; Hart 1993; Megnin 1995; Nattiv 1994; Stevens & Slavin 1995a; Webb, Trooper, & Fall 1995). Time on task and engagement increase in cooperative learning settings because each student is a necessary part of the whole group's success (Mulryan 1995).

Cooperative learning is great for social studies classes (Chick 2006; Morton 1998). For learning groups to be effective, students must learn to honor and respect one another's differences, to support one another through learning processes, to communicate effectively with one another, and to come to a consensus or understanding when needed. Thus, cooperative learning provides valuable training in skills needed to become effective citizens, to engage in group problem solving, and to attain and keep employment. It has also been shown to improve interpersonal relations and strengthen conflict resolution skills (Gillies & Ashman 2003; Megnin 1995; Zhang 1994; Zuckerman 1994). It improves students' emotional well-being, self-esteem, coping skills, and attitudes toward schoolwork (Patrick 1994; Patterson 1994). Students engaged in cooperative learning experiences have been able to identify an increase in their own knowledge and self-esteem, trust of peers, problem-solving and communication skills (see Elliott, Busse, & Shapiro 1999), and technology proficiency (McGrath 1998).

African American, Hispanic, and Native American children often learn by socializing with their extended family and community members. Many cultures also have strong oral traditions that foster creativity, storytelling, and kinesthetic expression of language in students, skills that go unrecognized in school settings where students are expected to work primarily as individuals producing written work. Although most cultures value cooperation, group loyalty, and caring for extended family and community members, these values may clash with the values of individual accomplishment, competition, productivity, and efficiency that are dominant in U.S. schools and workplaces. Cooperative learning has been specifically shown to increase school success for Hispanic students (Losey 1995). Cooperative and social learning is also the preferred learning style for many students of European descent. Obviously, students still learn by studying on their own. But some learn better in settings in which they can share ideas, ask questions, and receive feedback.

Cooperative learning experiences have also been shown to improve the relationships among diverse students, when teachers are careful to construct groups of students from various cultures (see Allison & Rehm 2007; Gallego & Cole 2001) and levels of physical need and ability (Stevens & Slavin 1995b).

Cooperative learning benefits you as a teacher in terms of classroom management and instruction. When you teach the whole class and students are not allowed to interact or assist one another, it is up to you to provide individualized assistance to students who have not understood a given concept, have difficulty following directions, lack skills needed to begin a task, or have trouble following classroom routines. Much valuable student learning time is lost when students must wait for the teacher to circulate through the classroom. The overall model of cooperative learning is also useful in classes where there are English-language learners (McCafferty, Jacobs, & Iddings 2006). And there is no question that you will have students diagnosed with attention deficit hyperactivity disorder (ADHD). Working in collaborative groups can help these students achieve academic success (Simplicio 2007).

Promotes citizenship, social skills.

Taps into diverse cultural values.

Frees the teacher, increases learning time.

Cooperative learning provides exciting learning opportunities across content areas. Students can work in cooperative groups to research topics, write reports, and plan and implement class discussions, debates, and panels. Students can also use cooperative groups to read materials, write summaries, find specific information, and answer questions. They can work together to study for tests, memorize information, and articulate concepts. Students can receive feedback and editing assistance from peers. They can engage in hands-on projects, experiments, and practical applications. They can design and implement school and community service projects. (For more examples, see Coelho 1998; Johnson & Johnson 1996; Lord 2001; Marzano, Pickering, & Pollock 2005; Slavin 1995; Webb, Trooper, & Fall 1995).

You can increase student learning time and reduce your own stress level and workload by teaching students to help one another with learning and organizational tasks and to monitor one another's progress. This allows you to become a facilitator of learning and encourages students to become responsible for their own learning and that of their peers. Some other benefits of cooperative learning are listed in the box below.

Cooperative learning works well in multicultural classrooms.

Cooperative learning enhances students' academic, management, and social skills.

Benefits of Cooperative Learning

- ◆ Improves comprehension of basic academic content
- ◆ Reinforces social skills
- ◆ Allows student decision making
- ◆ Creates active learning environment
- ◆ Boosts student self-esteem
- ◆ Celebrates diverse learning styles
- ◆ Promotes student responsibility
- ◆ Focuses on success for everyone

Features of Cooperative Learning

Traditional models of cooperative learning share five distinct features (Jacobs, Power, & Loh 2002; Johnson & Johnson 2004): positive interdependence, face-to-face interaction, individual accountability, development of social skills, and group evaluation.

Positive Interdependence In traditional classrooms where competition is emphasized, students experience **negative interdependence**—a management system that encourages competing with one another for educational resources and academic recognition. Competition encourages better students to hoard knowledge and to celebrate their successes at the expense of other students. In cooperative learning classrooms, students work together to ensure the success of each student. **Positive interdependence** is a management system that encourages students to work together and teaches students that school life for each one of them is enhanced when everyone succeeds.

Face-to-Face Interaction In cooperative learning situations, students interact, assist one another with learning tasks, and promote one another's success.

The small-group setting allows students to work directly with one another, to share opinions and ideas, to come to common understandings, and to work as a team to ensure each member's success and acceptance.

Individual Accountability   In cooperative learning settings, each student is held accountable for his or her own academic progress and task completion, apart from the accomplishments of the group as a whole. In traditional models of cooperative learning, individuals are asked to sign statements describing their contribution to a particular project. Individuals may also be held accountable by means of grades based on their academic achievement and social skills and by evaluations conducted by the teacher, their peers, or themselves.

Development of Social Skills   Cooperative learning offers students a chance to develop the interpersonal skills needed to succeed at school, at work, and within the community. Primary among these skills are effective communication, understanding and appreciation of others, decision making, problem solving, conflict resolution, and compromise. As the teacher, you must actively teach and monitor the use of social skills. You need to actively teach social skills on a daily basis, ask students to practice those skills within their cooperative groups, and have students provide feedback on group interactions and social processes (Abruscato 1994; Kagan 1999; Wolford, Heward, & Alber 2001).

Group Evaluation   Groups of students need to evaluate and discuss how well they are meeting their goals, what actions help their group, and what actions seem to hurt group interactions. They may articulate these evaluations during class discussion or provide the teacher with written progress reports. Students should also have a way of alerting the teacher to group problems. As a teacher, you should develop plans for engaging students in problem solving and conflict resolution.

Initiating Cooperative Learning in the Classroom

Providing cooperative learning opportunities is not simply a matter of placing students in groups and assigning tasks. Teachers must carefully select student groups, plan cooperative learning activities, set both academic and social goals for group work, and monitor individual student progress and group learning and social processes. It will take you about one year or longer to master the model (see Ishler, Johnson, & Johnson 1998).

Patience is required.

Selecting Student Groups   Several details should be considered when you form cooperative learning groups. Groups may be formed on the basis of academic skill level, interests, personality characteristics, social skills, or a combination of these factors. Groups usually contain students of varying ability levels who support one another in multiple ways. Traditionally, cooperative learning groups have been set up to contain one above-average, two average, and one below-average student. One difficulty with this is that it blatantly categorizes students when all students have areas of greater and lesser ability. In addition, it ignores the importance of considering the whole student. It ignores the fact that coping and social skills affect students' academic performance and that performance can vary from day to day based on emotional factors.

Avoid blatant ability placements.

You might also form groups and have them pursue different activities based on students' interests. One group might paint pictures while others plan a play, develop a presentation, conduct experiments, or work as a group of reporters. In science, each group might decide to spearhead a different project to increase environmental awareness. In home management, each group might create a different portion of a family budget. In art, each group might design a different project to beautify the city or town. Note how the above activities are applications of multiple intelligences, which are highlighted in Chapter 5.

Multiple-intelligence activities come into play.

It is essential to group students carefully whenever cooperative learning groups are first formed, so that student experiences can be positive and reinforcing. As the year progresses and students become accustomed to working together, group membership should become less of a factor in success. Students should try as many roles as possible. In this way, they are allowed to share their strengths, learn new skills from peers, and then apply them in a small-group setting.

Cooperative learning groups often remain together for two to six weeks; at that time, group membership changes to allow students to experience cooperation and caring with other peers. How long students should stay in a group depends on the characteristics of the students in the class and the nature of the tasks or projects on which they are working.

You may assign a specific role to each group member. Typical roles might include group leader (facilitates group discussion and makes sure group sets goals and works to meet them), monitor (monitors time on task and ensures that everyone gets an equal opportunity to participate), resource manager (gathers and organizes materials), recorder (keeps a written or taped record of group activities), and reporter (shares group findings and plans in whole-class discussions). Assigning roles allows teachers to influence the workings of the group, to capitalize on student strengths, and to encourage students to take risks by assuming new roles. On the other hand, group roles often evolve, with students falling into natural roles. Although this may create spontaneous and natural interactions, it may also lock students into negative roles based on behaviors and social status. Keep in mind that it will take from three to nine weeks of experience before a class begins to maximize the benefits of cooperative learning.

Planning Activities   Many types of learning can take place in cooperative settings. Learning activities may allow for both individual and collaborative work, or for small-group interaction followed by whole-class discussion and analysis (see Zuckerman, Chudinova, & Khavkin 1998). For example, students might read a history text and articles as individuals, then convene in small groups to review the materials and discuss the causes of the Great Depression, and then share their findings with the whole class to generate a comprehensive list of causes. Later, students might be asked to write individual essays to show their understanding of the causes of the Great Depression.

Setting Academic and Social Goals   You must carefully set academic and social goals for cooperative groups, and articulate these goals to students on a daily to weekly basis. Especially when first using cooperative learning, students will need specific training and monitoring. Seasoned teachers suggest that it is essential to teach social skills within the classroom and to model these before cooperative groups begin their work. As with other kinds of group work, it is important to help students develop communication skills. It has been reported that students with poor communication skills benefit less from cooperative learning (Kramarski & Mevarech 2003). In addition, it is helpful to emphasize one or two social skills each day or week and to remind students to practice them within their group. Examples of such skills are listed in the box below.

Key Ideas

Key Social Skills

- ◆ Knowing how to brainstorm with others
- ◆ Making sure each person has an equal opportunity to participate
- ◆ Solving problems cooperatively
- ◆ Knowing what to do when one group member fails to contribute
- ◆ Knowing how to handle conflict with other group members
- ◆ Choosing roles

Academic as well as social learning must be subdivided into meaningful tasks and goals. A teacher who wants students to choose a project, do research, write a report, and present the results to the class must teach students how to set group goals, brainstorm options, choose a viable topic, assign tasks to group members, find and access resources, write a meaningful and well-organized exposition, and execute effective oral presentations.

Track subordinate objectives for academic and social skills.

TECHNOLOGY
Insight

Multimedia Production and Cooperative Learning

Multimedia projects tend to generate excitement among students. Learners of all ages have found multimedia production projects to be satisfying and fun (Green & Brown, 2002). Presentations created using software such as PowerPoint or Windows Media Maker or the creation of class Web pages can be wonderful learning experiences that encourage students to work cooperatively in small and large groups.

Green and Brown (2002) have developed guidelines for planning a cooperative learning activity involving a multimedia project:

1. Set clear objectives for the group(s). Be specific about what the group must complete. Be sure to focus on the content of the presentation. For example, instead of saying "You are going to make a PowerPoint presentation about George Washington Carver," state "Your group is going to make a presentation on the contributions George Washington Carver made to science and society." This will help students avoid the pitfall of creating a presentation that is all "flash" with no substance.

2. Have individuals in the group take specific roles. The group can act as a production team, with individuals taking responsibility for various aspects of the production. Roles include writer, fact-checker, graphics designer, tester (the person who makes sure the product works the way it is supposed to), and production manager.

(continued)

Multimedia Production and Cooperative Learning—Cont'd

3. Plan opportunities for group members to talk about their experiences with students outside their own group. Meetings could be role-based: Have all the writers meet to discuss their experiences, and have the production managers meet to talk. It is important that students get to see and hear about how other groups go about solving problems similar to those of their own group.

4. Monitor the group(s) carefully. Students are learning how to work together in a novel situation. Make sure that no single student or subgroup is taking over the entire project. Make sure students are resolving their differences in a productive manner.

5. Find ways to offer positive feedback to groups that are performing well. Look for opportunities to recognize and celebrate students' development of new abilities and their successful resolution of problems.

Cooperative activities and multimedia projects both take a little extra time; be sure to plan for this in advance. Also, plan to show off a little! Invite parents, friends, and administrators to see what your class has created, and give students an opportunity to be recognized for their work.

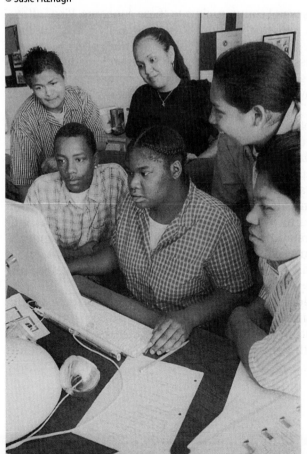

Students doing online research for an oral history project.

© Susie Fitzhugh

◀◀ ▶ ▶▶ VIDEO CASE

Gretchen Brion-Meisels teaches a unit on Costa Rica that culminates in a student PowerPoint presentation in the Video Case "Multimedia Literacy: Integrating Technology into the Middle School Classroom" on the student website. How does she apply the jigsaw approach to this group project?

Monitoring and Evaluating Individual and Group Progress

It is essential to monitor and evaluate the progress of individual students and working groups as a whole. You need to assess both (1) the academic progress, social functioning, and emotional well-being of individual students, and (2) the productivity and social functioning of the working groups. Individual academic progress may be measured by assessing the portion of the group project completed by a given student or by giving students individual assessments apart from their group work. Individual social functioning and emotional well-being may be assessed through teacher observation and group or self-evaluations that give feedback on how members are functioning within the group. Evaluations of group productivity may be made by assessing time logs, progress reports, and final group projects. Assessment of group social functioning may be made by teacher observations, conferencing with groups, group self-evaluations, or requests for teacher assistance (see Johnson & Johnson 2004).

Cooperative learning supports the process of *authentic assessment,* in which students produce summative essays, creative works, and projects that allow them to use critical thinking, application, synthesis, analysis, and evaluation skills (Crotty 1994). Students might write essays, photo journals, or editorials; design public information pamphlets, posters, videos, or home pages; create works of visual or performing art; or design and implement community service projects (see Tate 2003).

VIDEO CASE

View the Video Case "Cooperative Learning: High School History Lesson" on the student website, along with the bonus material. As you watch the clips and study the artifacts in the case, reflect on the following questions: (1) How does teacher Sarabinh Levy-Brightman form and monitor the groups in her class? (2) How do the students relate to each other?

Methods for gauging individual and group progress.

Cooperative groups should be presented with real challenges.

Criticisms of Cooperative Learning

Several criticisms have been leveled at the concept of grouping together students of varying abilities. Advocates for gifted children believe that heterogeneous grouping may hold back those with the greatest academic talent. Advocates for students with learning difficulties state that children with disabilities may not get a chance to improve their reading, writing, and math skills when they receive so much assistance from peers. Research tends to refute this, showing significant academic gains for students who are gifted and students with learning disabilities in cooperative settings (Johnson & Johnson 1992; Slavin 1990; Stevens & Slavin 1995a, 1995b).

In addition, there are several counterpoints to these concerns. First, *all* students have areas of lesser and greater abilities. Academically gifted students, for instance, may lack essential social skills, feel separate from peers because of unique abilities, or fear class presentations, while students with reading disabilities may have outstanding oral language and listening comprehension skills. Cooperative learning allows students to share their diverse talents and learn new skills.

Second, cooperative learning provides benefits to students beyond academics, including the teaching of social skills essential to working in families, schools, communities, and workplaces. All students benefit from learning cooperative processes and social skills (see Baloche 1998; Gabriele & Montecinos 2001).

Third, the *type* of task assigned influences whether all students will benefit from a cooperative learning situation. Tasks that focus on finding information generally do not provide much benefit to gifted students, but if the assignment also involves understanding essential concepts, exploring new meanings, thinking critically, and synthesizing information, each group member can provide ideas that will contribute to emergent, constructivist learning (see Kagan 1994; Vermette 1998).

Fourth, whether students benefit from group work seems to be a function of the classroom climate, which must be one of support, trust, and caring. Of greatest concern is whether students are building a sense of efficacy and self-esteem, both prerequisites to continued, successful academic learning.

Do only typical students benefit?

Research shows gains for all.

Last, cooperative learning groups should not remain static, nor should they always be based on heterogeneous grouping. Certainly, gifted students need opportunities to work, think, and learn together, and students with special needs need time to work together on essential reading, writing, and mathematics skills.

Another frequently heard criticism of traditional models of cooperative learning concerns the practice of rating, grading, or rewarding students on the basis of group accomplishment. Parents have cited instances where one student did his or her part of the group work but received a low grade because some other student in the group failed to follow through. Such a system seems to foster an atmosphere of blame. In addition, awarding privileges on the basis of group performance once again sets up a competitive process, subtly undermining the ethic of cooperation and success for all (Kagan 1996). However, a teacher may assign both a group and an individual grade by using specific assessment criteria for each. And although some students do need extrinsic rewards for work they accomplish, most can learn to appreciate the intrinsic benefits derived from group work. You can learn of the effect size and instructional benefits that students may derive from different discussion techniques at our student website at www.cengage.com/education/orlich.

Reflect — A Closing Reflection

- Parents are often concerned that cooperative learning destroys individual initiative. How would you address this issue?
- Plan a unit that could be taught using cooperative learning. How does the plan differ from one you might write if you were using other techniques?
- List the factors that will support your attempts to use small-group discussions and those that will hinder you.

Summary Points

1. Using small-group discussions can promote student autonomy, cooperation, and learning.
2. Small-group discussions and cooperative learning are ideal for accomplishing process objectives.
3. The ideal size for a small group is six to eight students.
4. Students learn and gain experience by functioning in various roles within the group.
5. The six basic small-group discussion techniques are brainstorming, tutorials, task-directed, role playing, simulations, and inquiry-centered.
6. Cooperative learning requires much time, organization, and structure, but it is an ideal way to focus group work on specific tasks and to mandate individual responsibility.
7. Cooperative learning requires positive interdependence, face-to-face interaction, individual accountability, student involvement, and good listening skills.
8. Collect feedback to analyze small-group efforts.

Building a Career Portfolio

As you prepare for your first teaching job, you may need a few items to help you conduct authentic classroom discussions. We offer the following suggestions for inclusion in your career portfolio.

◆ Duplicate sets of evaluation criteria and rubrics by which to evaluate your initial classroom discussion efforts. Figures 8.1 and 8.2 would be a good start.

◆ Begin to construct a list of possible topics in your teaching specialty that would lend themselves to rich discussion.

◆ Try using a discussion format in just one of your initial classes. From this trial run, you can then make adjustments for other classes.

◆ Publish your results or experiences in one of the appropriate journals or post your paper with ERIC. And please, feel free to contact the authors of this text to let us know how it goes!

Resources

PRINT

We have listed some references below that will expand your knowledge of cooperative learning, simulations, and discussions.

Chapin, S. H., C. O'Connor, & N. C. Anderson. *Classroom Discussions: Using Math Talk to Help Students Learn, Grades 1-6.* Sausalito, CA: Math Solutions Publications, 2003, 232 pp.
The authors present five discussion strategies to help students develop connections among mathematical concepts. Math need not be solely a recitation activity.

Jacobs, G. M., M. A. Power, & W. I. Loh. *The Teacher's Sourcebook for Cooperative Learning: Practical Techniques, Basic Principles, and Frequently Asked Questions.* Thousand Oaks, CA: Corwin, 2002, 168 pp.
Here is a very helpful compendium for anyone using cooperative learning.

Johnson, D. W., & R. T. Johnson. *Assessing Students in Groups: Promoting Group Responsibility and Individual Accountability.* Thousand Oaks, CA: Corwin, 2004, 206 pp.
This handbook is must reading for any teacher who wants a practical lesson on initiating and maintaining cooperative learning, along with ways to ensure fairness when assessing students.

Jones, K. *Simulations: A Handbook for Teachers and Trainers* (3rd ed.). East Brunswick, NJ: Nichols, 1995, 145 pp.
This revised and improved handbook is a minilibrary for anyone who wants to use or design simulations in the classroom.

Kagan, S. *Cooperative Learning.* San Clemente, CA: Kagan, 1994.
One could consider this classic work to be a definitive statement on the topic.

Lord, T. R. "101 Reasons for Using Cooperative Learning in Biology Teaching." *American Biology Teacher* 63(1)(2001): 30–38.
Drop the word *biology* from the title of this must-read article and you have a memo that can be sent home to parents concerned about this technique. Includes a one-page list of 101 referenced findings that summarizes the research on cooperative learning.

Race, P., & S. Brown. *500 Tips for Tutors* (2nd ed.). London: Routledge Falmer, 2005, 136 pp.
If you want a quick orientation to the processes of tutoring, this book provides it.

van Ments, M. *The Effective Use of Role-Play: Practical Techniques for Improving Learning* (2nd ed.). London: Kogan Page, 1999, 196 pp.
The entire spectrum of role playing is presented in an easy-to-adopt format.

INTERNET

Go to the website for this book at www.cengage.com/education/orlich to find live links to resources related to this chapter.

◆ Roger T. Johnson and David W. Johnson direct the Cooperative Learning Center at the University of Minnesota's Cooperative Learning and Assessment Resources:
http://www.co-operation.org/pages/assess.html

◆ The Center publishes *The Newsletter of the Cooperation Learning Institute:*
www.co-operation.org

◆ Kennesaw State University's Introduction to Cooperative Learning:
http://edtech.kennesaw.edu/intech/cooperativelearning.htm

◆ New Horizons for Learning provides an overview of Cooperative Learning at
http://www.newhorizons.org/strategies/cooperative/front_cooperative.htm

References

Aarabi, P. (2007). *The Art of Lecturing*. New York: Cambridge University Press.

Abruscato, J. (1994). "Boost Your Students' Social Skills with This 9-Step Plan." *Learning* 22(5): 60–61, 66.

Adler, M., & E. Rougle. (2005). *Building Literacy Through Classroom Discussion*. New York: Scholastic.

Allison, B. N., & M. L. Rehm. (2007). "Effective Teaching Strategies for Middle School Learners in Multicultural, Multilingual Classrooms." *Middle School Journal* 39(2): 12–18.

Alsup J. K., & D. J. Altmyer. (2002). "Bullish on Mathematics: Using Stock Market Simulations to Enhance Learning." *Mathematics Teaching in the Middle School* 8(2): 112–117.

Anderson, R. P. (2001). "Team Disease Presentations: A Cooperative Learning Activity for Large Classrooms." *American Biology Teacher* 63(1): 40–43.

Angelis, J. I. (2003). "Conversation in the Middle School Classroom: Developing Reading, Writing, and Other Language Abilities." *Middle School Journal* 34(3): 57–61.

Baloche, L. A. (1998). *The Cooperative Classroom: Empowering Learning*. Upper Saddle River, NJ: Prentice Hall.

Beach, R. W., D. Appleman, S. Hynds, & J. Wilhelm. (2006). *Teaching Literature to Adolescents*. Mahwah, NJ: Lawrence Erlbaum Associates.

Berne, J., & K. F. Clark. (2006). "Comprehension Strategy Use During Peer-Led Discussions of Text: Ninth Graders Tackle "The Lottery." *Journal of Adolescent & Adult Literacy* 49(8): 674–686.

Berry, J. D. (2002). *Success . . . One Child at a Time*. Tampa, FL: Plan for Social Excellence. ED 466 308.

Bloom, B. S. (1984). "The 2 Sigma Problem: The Search for Methods of Group Instruction as Effective as One-to-One Tutoring." *Educational Researcher* 13(6): 4–16.

Bond, R. J., & E. Castagnera. (2003). "Supporting One Another: Peer Tutoring in an Inclusive San Diego High School." In D. Fisher & N. Frey, Eds., *Inclusive Urban Schools*, pp. 119–142. Baltimore: Brookes.

Bond, T. F. (2001). "Giving Them Free Rein: Connections in Student-Led Book Groups." *Reading Teacher* 54(6): 574–584.

Boston, J. (1998). "Using Simulations." *Social Studies Review* 37(2): 31–32.

Bramlett, R. K. (1994). "Implementing Cooperative Learning: A Field Study Evaluating Issues for School-Based Consultants." *Journal of School Psychology* 32(1): 67–84.

Brown, A. (1999). "Simulated Classrooms and Artificial Students: The Potential Effects of New Technologies on Teacher Education." *Journal of Research on Computing in Education* 3(2): 307–318.

Bush, W. S., L. Dworkin, & D. B. Spencer, Eds. (2001). *Mathematics Assessment Cases and Discussion Questions for Grades K–5 Set*. Reston, VA: National Council of Teachers of Mathematics.

Carico, K. M. (2001). "Negotiating Meaning in Classroom Literature Discussions." *Journal of Adolescent and Adult Literacy* 44(6): 510–518.

Chapin, S. H., C. O'Connor, & N. C. Anderson. (2003). *Classroom Discussions: Using Math Talk to Help Students Learn, Grades 1–6*. Sausalito, CA: Math Solutions Publications.

Chick, K. A. (2006). "Fostering Student Collaboration Through the Use of Historical Picture Books." *Social Studies* 97(4): 152–157.

Choe, S. W. T., & P. M. Drennan. (2001). "Analyzing Scientific Literature Using a Jigsaw Group Activity: Piecing Together Student Discussions on Environmental Research." *Journal of College Sciences Teaching* 30(5): 328–330.

Coelho, E. (1998). *All Sides of the Issue: Activities for Cooperative Jigsaw Groups*. San Francisco: Alta Book Center.

Cohen, E. G., C. M. Brody, & M. Sapon-Shevin, Eds. (2004). *Teaching Cooperative Learning: The Challenge for Teacher Education*. Albany: State University of New York Press.

Cohen, E. G., R. A. Lotan, & N. C. Holthuis. (1997). "Organizing the Classroom for Learning." In E. G. Cohen & R. A. Lotan, Eds., *Working for Equity in Heterogeneous Classrooms: Sociological Theory in Practice*, pp. 31–43. New York: Teachers College Press.

Cone, J. K. (1992). "Untracking Advanced Placement English: Creating Opportunity Is Not Enough." *Phi Delta Kappan* 73: 712–717.

Cracolice, M. S., & J. C. Deming. (2001). "Peer-Led Team Learning." *Science Teacher* 68(1): 20–24.

Crotty, E. (1994). "The Role of Cooperative Learning in an Authentic Performance Assessment Approach." *Social Science Record* 31(1): 38–41.

Davidson, I. B. (2008, May 2). Personal communication.

Davies, P. (1999). *70 Activities for Tutor Groups*. Brookfield, VT: Gower.

"Declare the Causes: The Declaration of Independence—Understanding Its Structure and Origin." (2001). Washington, DC: National Endowment for the Humanities. (*Note:* Collective author of annotated lesson plan.) ED 455 517.

Dyson, B., & S. Grineski. (2001). "Using Cooperative Learning Structures in Physical Education." *Journal of Physical Education, Recreation & Dance* 72(2): 28–31.

Elliott, S. M., R. T. Busse, & E. S. Shapiro. (1999). "Intervention Techniques for Academic Performance Problems." In C. R. Reynolds & T. B. Gutkin, Eds., *The Handbook of School Psychology* (2nd ed.), pp. 664–685. New York: Wiley.

Ellis, A. K. (2005). *Research on Educational Innovations* (4th ed.). Larchmont, NY: Eye on Education.

Evans, K. S. (2001). *Literature Discussion Group in the Intermediate Grades: Dilemmas and Possibilities*. Newark, DE: International Reading Association.

Evertson, C. M., E. T. Emmer, & M. E. Worsham. (2006). *Classroom Management for Elementary Teachers*. Boston: Pearson/A&B.

Fillmore, L. W., & L. M. Meyer. (1992). "The Curriculum and Linguistic Minorities." In Philip W. Jackson, Ed., *Handbook of Research on Curriculum*. New York: Macmillan.

Furinghetti, F. O. Federica, & P. Domingo. (2001). "Students Approaching Proof Through Conjectures: Snapshots in a Classroom." *International Journal of Mathematical Education in Science and Technology* 32(3): 319–335.

Gabriele, A. J., & C. Montecinos. (2001). "Collaborating with a Skilled Peer: The Influence of Achievement Goals and Perceptions of Partners. Competence on the Participation and Learning of Low-Achieving

Students." *Journal of Experimental Education* 69(2): 152–178.

Gallego, M. A., & M. Cole. (2001). "Classroom Culture and Culture in the Classroom." In V. Richardson, Ed., *Handbook on Research on Teaching* (4th ed.), pp. 951–997. Washington, DC: American Education Research Association.

Gauthier, L. R. (2001). "Coop-Dis-Q: A Reading Comprehension Strategy." *Intervention in School and Clinic* 36(4): 217–220.

Gehring, T., K. McGuire, K. A. Parr, & D. Wiles. (2003). *Improving Language Arts Skills through Use of Modeling and Grade Appropriate Comprehension Activities.* Chicago: Saint Xavier University and Skylight Professional Development Field-Based Master's Program. ED 479 375.

George, L. A., & W. G. Becker. (2003). "Investigating the Urban Heat Island Effect with a Collaborative Inquiry Project." *Journal of Geoscience Education* 51(2): 237–243.

Gillies, R. M., & A. F. Ashman, Eds. (2003). *Cooperative Learning: The Social and Intellectual Outcomes of Learning in Groups.* New York: Routledge Falmer.

Glickman, C. D. (1998). *Revolutionizing America's Schools.* San Francisco: Jossey-Bass.

Grabe, M., & C. Grabe. (2007). *Integrating Technology for Meaningful Learning* (5th ed.). Boston: Houghton Mifflin.

Green, T., & A. Brown. (2002). *Multimedia Projects in the Classroom: A Guide to Development and Evaluation.* Thousand Oaks, CA: Corwin.

Hart, L. D. (1993). "Some Factors That Impede or Enhance Performance in Mathematical Problem Solving." *Journal for Research in Mathematics Education* 24(2): 167–171.

Ishler, A. L., R. T. Johnson, & D. W. Johnson. (1998). "Long-Term Effectiveness of a Statewide Staff Development Program or Cooperative Learning." *Teaching and Teacher Education* 14(3): 273–281.

Jacobs, G. M., M. A. Power, & W. I. Loh. (2002). *The Teacher's Sourcebook for Cooperative Learning: Practical Techniques, Basic Principles, and Frequently Asked Questions.* Thousand Oaks, CA: Corwin.

Johnson, D. W., & R. T. Johnson. (1992). "What to Say to Advocates for the Gifted." *Educational Leadership* 50(2): 44–47.

Johnson, D. W., & R. T. Johnson. (1996). "Cooperative Learning and Traditional American Values: An Appreciation." *NASSP Bulletin* 80(579): 63–65.

Johnson, D. W., & R. T. Johnson. (2004). *Assessing Students in Groups: Promoting Group Responsibility and Individual Accountability.* Thousand Oaks, CA: Corwin.

Johnson, D. W., R. T. Johnson, & E. J. Holubec. (1994). *The New Circles of Learning: Cooperation in the Classroom and School.* Alexandria, VA: Association for Supervision and Curriculum Development.

Johnson, D. W., R. T. Johnson, & E. J. Holubec. (1998). *Cooperation in the Classroom* (7th ed.). Edina, MN: Interaction.

Kagan, S. (1994). *Cooperative Learning.* San Clemente, CA: Kagan.

Kagan, S. (1996). "Avoiding the Group-Grades Trap." *Learning* 24(4): 56–58.

Kagan, S. (1999). *Building Character Through Cooperative Learning.* Port Chester, NY: National Professional Resources. Videocassette.

Kennedy, C. H. (2003). "Commentary. Peer-to-Peer Relationships as a Foundation for Inclusive Education." In D. Fisher & N. Frey, Eds., *Inclusive Urban Schools* (pp. 143–149). Baltimore: Brookes.

Kramarski, B., & Z. R. Mevarech. (2003). "Enhancing Mathematical Reasoning in the Classroom: The Effects of Cooperative Learning and Metacognitive Training." *American Educational Research Journal* 40(1): 281–310.

Lauer, T. E. (2003). "Conceptualizing Ecology: A Learning Cycle Approach." *American Biology Teacher* 65(7): 518–522.

Lopus, J. & D. Placone. (2002). "Online Stock Market Games for High Schools." *Journal of Economic Education* 33(2): 192.

Lord, T. R. (2001). "101 Reasons for Using Cooperative Learning in Biology Teaching." *American Biology Teacher* 63(1): 30–38.

Losey, K. M. (1995). "Mexican-American Students and Classroom Interaction: An Overview and Critique." *Review of Educational Research* 65(3): 283–318.

Marzano, R. J., D. J. Pickering, & J. E. Pollock. (2005). *Classroom Instruction That Works: Research-Based Strategies for Increasing Student Achievement.* Upper Saddle River, NJ: Pearson, Merrill Prentice Hall.

Mastropieri, M. A., et al. (2001). "Can Middle School Students with Serious Reading Difficulties Help Each Other and Learn Anything?" *Learning Disabilities: Research and Practice* 16(1): 18–27.

McCann, T. M., et al., Eds. (2005). *Reflective Teaching, Reflective Learning: How to Develop Critically Engaged Readers, Writers, and Speakers.* Portsmouth, NH: Heinemann.

McCann, T. M., et al., Eds. (2006). *Talking in Class: Using Discussion to Enhance Teaching and Learning.* Urbana, IL: National Council of Teachers of English.

McCafferty, S. G., G. M. Jacobs, & A. C. DaSiva Iddings, Eds. (2006). *Cooperative Learning and Second Language Teaching.* New York: Cambridge University Press.

McCormick, K. (1998). *Plays to Ponder for Grades 6–8: Prompting Classroom Discussion Through Dramatic Play*. Torrance, CA: Good Apple.

McGee, S., D. Corriss, & R. Shia. (2001). "Using Simulations to Improve Cognitive Reasoning." Paper presented at the annual meeting of the American Educational Research Association, Seattle, April, 10–14, 2001. ED 470 975.

McGrath, B. (1998). "Partners in Learning: Twelve Ways Technology Changes the Teacher-Student Relationship." *T.H.E. Journal* 25(9): 58–61.

Megnin, J. K. (1995). "Combining Memory and Creativity in Teaching Math." *Teaching PreK–8* 25(6): 48–49.

Mesmer, K. (2003). "Hire a Scientist." *Science Scope* 25(6): 42–44.

Miles, M. B. (1998). *Learning to Work in Groups* (2nd ed.). Troy, NY: Educator's International Press.

Miller, D. P. (1986). *Introduction to Small Group Discussion*. Urbana, IL: ERIC/RCS and SCA. DRS ED 278 037.

Morton, T. (1998). *Cooperative Learning and Social Studies: Towards Excellence and Equity*. San Clemente, CA: Kagan.

Mosher, R. S. (2001). "Silence, Listening, Teaching, and the Space of What Is Not." *Language Arts* 78(4): 366–370.

Mueller, A., & T. Fleming. (2001). "Cooperative Learning: Listening to How Children Work at School." *Journal of Educational Research* 94(5): 259–265.

Mulryan, C. M. (1995). "Fifth and Sixth Graders' Involvement and Participation in Cooperative Small Groups in Mathematics." *Elementary School Journal* 95(4): 297–310.

Nattiv, A. (1994). "Helping Behaviors and Math Achievement Gain of Students Using Cooperative Learning." *Elementary School Journal* 94(3): 285–297.

Ngeow, K., & Y. Kong. (2003). *Learning through Discussion: Designing Tasks for Critical Inquiry and Reflective Learning. ERIC Digest*. Bloomington, IN: ERIC Clearinghouse on Reading, English, and Communication. ED 477 611.

Olmstead, J. A. (1970). *Theory and State of the Art of Small Group Methods of Instruction*. Alexandria, VA: Human Resources Research Organization.

Opitz, M. F., & M. P. Ford. (2008). *Do-able Differentiation: Varying Groups, Texts and Supports to Reach Readers*. Portsmouth, NH: Heinemann.

Owca, S., E. Pawlak, & M. Pronobis. (2003). *Improving Student Academic Success through the Promotion of Listening Skills*. Chicago: Saint Xavier University and Pearson Skylight Field-Based Masters Program. ED 478 233.

Patrick, J. (1994). "Direct Teaching of Collaborative Skills in a Cooperative Learning Environment." *Teaching and Change* 1(2): 170–181.

Patterson, V. E. (1994). "Introducing Co-Operative Learning at Princess Elizabeth Elementary School." *Education Canada* 34(2): 36–41.

Pendergrass, R. A. (1973). *An Analysis of the Verbal Interaction of Small Group Discussion Members in Secondary Social Studies Classes*. Pullman, WA: Unpublished Doctoral Dissertation.

Peterson, S., & M. Belizaire. (2006). "Another Look at Roles in Literature Circles." *Middle School Journal* 37(4): 37–43.

Resnick, M., & U. Wilensky. (1998). "Diving into Complexity: Developing Probabilistic Decentralized Thinking Through Role-Playing Activities." *Journal of the Learning Sciences* 7(2): 153–172.

Rex, L. A. (2001). "The Remaking of a High School Reader." *Reading Research Quarterly* 36(3): 288–314.

Richburg, R. W., & B. J. Nelson. (1991). "Where in Western Europe Would You Like to Live?" *The Social Studies* 82(3): 97–106.

Roman, H. T. (2007). "Putting Student Enthusiasm to Work." *The Technology Teacher* 66(5): 14–16.

Sapon-Shevin, M. (2001). "Schools Fit for All." *Educational Leadership* 58(4): 34–39.

Schmuck, R. A., & P. A. Schmuck. (2001). *Group Processes in the Classroom* (8th ed.). New York: McGraw-Hill.

Scotty-Ryan, D. L. (1998). *An Investigative Study of How Cooperative Learning Can Benefit High-Achieving Students*. M.S. thesis, State University of New York at Brockport.

Simplicio, J. S. C. (2007). "Achieving Higher Levels of Success for A.D.H.D. Students Working in Collaborative Groups." *Journal of Instructional Psychology* 34(3): 140–141.

Slavin, R. E. (1990). *Cooperative Learning: Theory, Research and Practice*. Englewood Cliffs, NJ: Prentice Hall.

Slavin, R. E. (1995). *Cooperative Learning: Theory, Research and Practice* (2nd ed.). Boston: Allyn and Bacon.

Smith, C. B. (2003). *Skills Students Use When Speaking and Listening: ERIC Topical Bibliography and Commentary*. Bloomington, IN: ERIC Clearinghouse on Reading, English, and Communication. ED 480 895.

Soja, C. M., & D. Huerta. (2001). "Debating Whether Dinosaurs Should Be 'Cloned' from Ancient DNA to Promote Cooperative Learning in an Introductory Evolution Course." *Journal of Geoscience Education* 49(2): 150–157.

Sparapani, E. F. (1998). "Encouraging Thinking in High School and Middle School: Constraints and Possibilities." *Clearing House* 71(5): 274–276.

Spiegel, D. L. (2005). *Classroom Discussion: Strategies for Engaging All Students, Building Higher-Level*

Thinking Skills, and Strengthening Reading and Writing Across the Curriculum. New York: Scholastic.

Stevens, R. J., & R. E. Slavin. (1995a). "The Cooperative Elementary School: Effects on Students' Achievement, Attitudes and Social Relations." *American Educational Research Journal* 32(2): 321–351.

Stevens, R. J., & R. E. Slavin. (1995b). "Effects of a Cooperative Learning Approach in Reading and Writing on Academically Handicapped and Non-Handicapped Students." *Elementary School Journal* 95(3): 241–262.

Tate, M. L. (2003). *Worksheets Don't Grow Dendrites: 20 Instructional Strategies That Engage the Brain.* Thousand Oaks, CA: Corwin.

van Ments, M. (1999). *The Effective Use of Role-Play: Practical Techniques for Improving Learning* (2nd ed.). London: Kogan Page.

Verker, K. W. (2003). "Simulations: Interdisciplinary Instruction at its Best." *Hispania* 86(2): 322–325.

Vermette, P. J. (1998). *Making Cooperative Learning Work: Student Teams in K–12 Classrooms.* Upper Saddle River, NJ: Merrill.

Vessels, G. (1996). "The First Amendment and Character Education." *Update on Law-Related Education* 20(1): 26–28.

Walberg, H. J. (1999). "Productive Teaching." In H. C. Waxman & H. J. Walberg, Eds., *New Directions for Teaching Practice and Research.* Berkeley, CA: McCutchan.

Webb, N. M., J. Trooper, & R. Fall. (1995). "Constructive Activity and Learning in Collaborative Small Groups." *Journal of Educational Psychology* 87(3): 406–423.

Weissglass, J. (1996). "Transforming Schools into Caring Learning Communities." *Journal for a Just and Caring Education* 2(2): 175–189.

Wells, G., Ed. (2001). *Action, Talk and Text: Learning and Teaching Through Inquiry.* New York: Teachers College Press.

Wilen, W. W. (2004). "Encouraging Reticent Students' Participation in Classroom Discussions." *Social Education* 68(1): 51–60.

Wolford, P. L., W. L. Heward, & S. R. Alber. (2001). "Teaching Middle School Students with Learning Disabilities to Recruit Peer Assistance During Cooperative Learning Group Activities." *Learning Disabilities: Research and Practice* 16(3): 161–173.

Yamarik, S. (2007). "Does Cooperative Learning Improve Student Learning Outcomes?" *Journal of Economic Education* 38(3): 259–277.

Yell, M. M. (1998). "The Time Before History: Thinking Like an Archaeologist." *Social Education* 62(1): 27–31.

Zhang, Q. (1994). "An Intervention Model of Constructive Conflict Resolution and Cooperative Learning." *Journal of Social Issues* 50(1): 99–116.

Zuckerman, G. A. (1994). "A Pilot Study of a Ten-Day Course in Cooperative Learning for Beginning Russian First Graders." *Elementary School Journal* 94(4): 405–420.

Zuckerman, G. A., E. V. Chudinova, & E. E. Khavkin. (1998). "Inquiry as a Pivotal Element of Knowledge Acquisition Within the Vogotskian Paradigm: Building a Science Curriculum for the Elementary School." *Cognition and Instruction* 16(2): 201–233.

Inquiry Teaching and Higher-Level Thinking

Sean Redd's social studies class is the designated site for your in-school observations. As you approach the room, you hear the buzz of meaningful noise. Students are working in small groups of three to five; a few students are at the computer center, which is neatly arranged in the far corner of the room; and the teacher is helping a small group of students with learning disabilities align their data on a large poster. The walls of the room are covered with the students' work. Their projects resemble the posters at a professional convention.

A student invites you to work with the group. You observe the division of labor among the students. After about 30 minutes, Sean calls everyone together, and the recorders from three groups give short oral reports to the class. Students question the presenters, and a lively verbal interaction occurs. The teacher then writes a few specific assignments on the chalkboard, and students begin individual seat-work.

"Wow," you say to yourself, "I wonder if I can pull this style off?"

Traditionally, teachers present knowledge to students, who passively absorb it, and this pattern becomes both the means and the end of education. Is it any wonder, then, that students get bored? As an alternative to routine lectures and recitations, we offer an instructional strategy that seems innovative but actually is centuries old. The generic term for the strategy is **inquiry teaching**, an investigative learning process that asks students to pose questions, analyze data, and develop conclusions or generalizations. It can also be referred to as *discovery, problem solving, reflective thinking,* and *inductive teaching,* among other terms. It is associated with teaching techniques and methods that have one thing in common: encouraging higher-level thinking. In this chapter, we discuss these techniques and describe their major characteristics. After you finish studying this chapter, you'll be able to answer the following questions:

- Can we really teach kids how to think?
- What is inquiry teaching?
- How can I use it in my classroom?
- What techniques are associated with inquiry teaching?

SECTION *1* Helping Students Become Better Thinkers

Although few people would disagree that educating students to become good learners and responsible citizens means that they must also be good thinkers, the road toward that goal is not automatic. Helping students reach that goal takes time, knowledge, awareness, and planning on the part of the teacher. We use this first section to examine three key aspects of the effective teaching of thinking skills. First, we explore the concept of thinking itself; then we examine just how successful our schools have been thus far in encouraging the development of thinking skills; and finally we present our own framework for how this essential goal might be better accomplished.

Defining Thinking (and Higher-Level Thinking)

What do we mean by *thinking*? The word is a construct, a label we apply to processes we can observe only indirectly through actions or products. In other words, when someone behaves in a careful, prudent manner, we infer that the behavior resulted from deliberate thought. When we observe an example of complex problem solving—space flight, for instance—we infer the incredible amounts of reasoning that were necessary.

Attempts to define thinking—beyond such synonyms as *reasoning* or *forming an idea*—become clouded by differences of psychological position. Despite the lack of consensus on the definition of thinking, we can still characterize it and suggest ways to make it more effective.

We propose that thinking is a combination of knowledge, skills or processes, and attitudes. Knowledge is involved, of course, because thinking requires an object. One must think about *something*. The more knowledge one has in any area, the more effectively one can think about it (Noddings 2008; Shayer & Adey 2002; Sternberg & Spear-Swerling 1996).

Effective thinking also requires particular attitudes, such as a disposition to perceive and relate to one's surroundings in particular ways. Some people, for instance, are curious about their environment; others are not. Attitude, which is an affective trait, determines in part *what* we think about and *in what ways* we think about it (see the box below).

Pulling together all of this information, we arrive at the following definition: **Thinking** is a complex act comprising attitudes, knowledge, and skills that allows the individual to shape his or her environment more effectively than by intuition alone. Teaching students how to think is a journey, not an event.

> **Attitudes That Promote Effective Thinking**
>
> ◆ Willingness to suspend judgment until sufficient evidence is presented
> ◆ Tolerance for ambiguity
> ◆ A tendency to question rather than simply accept authority
> ◆ Willingness to believe credible evidence

Now let us focus on higher-level thinking skills. Think back to our discussion of Bloom's cognitive taxonomy (Chapter 3). Recall that two of Bloom's higher levels are analysis and synthesis. **Higher-level thinking** skills, also known as critical thinking, consist of the application of these two levels, plus evaluation—that is, determining value. Critical thinking is a multistage construction of meaning. It is rational and logical and results in high levels of student achievement (see Marzano, Pickering, & Pollock 2001; Walberg 1999). Carol B. MacKnight (2000) provides an interesting and practical use of online questions that can also enhance critical thinking by utilizing several techniques that have already been presented in previous chapters of this book. She suggests maintaining a focused discussion, seeking implications or consequences, and clarifying issues. To learn critical thinking skills, your students need to practice the skills listed in the box on page 287.

Combination of knowledge, skills, and attitudes

Thinking is a multifaceted process, not a singular one.

> ## Elements of Critical Thinking
> - Identifying issues
> - Identifying relationships between elements
> - Deducing implications
> - Inferring motives
> - Combining independent elements to create new patterns of thought (creativity)
> - Making original interpretations (creativity)

How Successful Have We Been at Teaching Thinking?

National Data It is one thing to identify and define thinking and higher-level thinking skills; it is quite another to successfully teach them to students. The single best source for standardized and nationally collected data on this topic comes from the National Assessment of Educational Progress (NAEP). Since 1969, the NAEP has intermittently tested 9-, 13-, and 17-year-olds (grades 4, 8, and 12) in civics, science, mathematics, reading, and writing.

We recognize that fourth-graders may not be far enough along in their cognitive development to process formal thinking questions (see Table 2.1, page 33), which are posed at the three upper levels of Bloom's taxonomy and the NAEP levels. Fourth-graders do well at the two lower cognitive levels, which correspond developmentally to the concrete operations levels. Eighth- and twelfth-graders truly shine at the first two levels.

Data reported in the latest *Digest of Education Statistics 2005* (U.S. Department of Education 2006) showed a long-term trend in achievement in reading for American students aged 9 and 13 (grades 4 and 8), but for 17-year-olds (grade 12) scores were stable. Similar findings were reported for mathematics.

International Comparisons Internationally, it must be noted that the United States was ranked the number one nation in global competitiveness (World Economic Forum, 2008). We note this ranking because the 1984 *Nation at Risk* report implied that due to poor schools our nation's economic ranking and competitiveness were in jeopardy.

The *Progress in International Reading Literacy Study* (PIRLS), which surveyed 35 countries, found that only Sweden outperformed the Netherlands and the United States in reading literacy (Mullis et al. 2003).

David C. Berliner (2004) summarizes the findings this way: "The fundamental premise underlying the legislation known as the No Child Left Behind Act (NCLB) is that the public schools of the United States are failing. But that

Findings challenge NCLB.

is a half-truth at best" (p. 167).

Here's more good news. On July 11, 2001, the College Board announced, "A new study of the TIMSS International Study Center shows that Advanced Placement students [in the United States] who score three or higher [on a five-point scale] on physics and calculus AP Exams outperform physics and advanced math students from the United States and other countries in mathematics and science achievement" (*College Board News* 2001). Lee Jones, executive director of the College Board's Advanced Placement Program, stated,

"These results demonstrate that students who do well on the AP Calculus and Physics Exams are indeed at the top of the world in academic achievement."

So teachers must be doing something right. We'll spend some time in the following discussion examining what you as a teacher can and should do "right" as you approach the teaching of thinking skills. (See Orlich 2000, 2002, 2003 for a critical analysis and interesting perspective about the issue of developmentally inappropriate tests.)

Structuring Instruction for Success in Teaching Thinking

First, what does it mean to teach thinking? Nearly all writers agree on the generic aspects of thinking highlighted in the box below (Lyons & LaBoskey 2002; Wallace & Bentley 2002; Weinbaum et al. 2004). These five skills are core skills. To build these skills requires careful teacher planning, appropriate sequencing, and a continuous building of cognitive and attitudinal factors.

> ### Core Skills of Thinking
> ◆ Perception of a problem or issue
> ◆ Ability to gather relevant information
> ◆ Competence in organizing data
> ◆ Analysis of data patterns, inferences, sources of errors
> ◆ Communication of the results

Three aspects of thinking can be identified and taught to students—knowledge, skills, and attitudes. The assumption, of course, is that students will think more effectively as a result of learning these three aspects—that they will be able to relate to and alter their environment better than they otherwise would. Considerable empirical evidence supports this view (see Selwyn & Maher 2003; Wakefield 1996). In fact, we would go as far as saying that helping students identify and use these skills must be a basic part of instruction in *all* classes if students are to benefit from schooling.

Teach knowledge, skills, attitudes.

So, more specifically, what do we mean when we say you can help students become more effective thinkers? Do teachers need to add a new course in thinking to the curriculum? Do teachers need to teach a new content area or a new group of process skills?

The answer isn't simple. Instead, we believe that teachers need to take a threefold approach to the teaching of thinking, especially the teaching of higher-level or critical thinking.

First, you need to develop an overall awareness—a kind of infusion of the need to focus on thinking in all classes at all times. In other words, you must systematically and continually instruct students in ways that will encourage them to think more effectively. Thinking must be taught across all subjects and all grade levels. Teachers must stress meaningfulness, but children must be taught how to understand and think (see Jones 2003 for a rich resource). For example, you might have the students ask one *reflective question* (Chapter 7) after they read a given passage. Or, after you have introduced concepts, such as *infer, classify, hypothesize*, you might challenge the class to use those process skills in some pending assignment. By continuously reviewing thinking skills, you establish a base of knowledge and an attitude of inquiry (see Shayer & Adey 2002).

Second, it appears that the adoption of an inquiry-based teaching strategy will greatly facilitate your teaching of thinking skills (Yager 2007). At the core of this approach is an emphasis on student exploration and understanding.

Third, you should know how to use specific methods and teaching techniques that are themselves offshoots or "relatives" of the inquiry model; we present a number of these at the end of the chapter (Martin-Hansen 2002).

You should always bear in mind that the teacher is the most important factor in thinking instruction (Shayer & Adey 2002). Prepared texts, workbooks, preplanned programs, and drill exercises may be useful instructional aids, but by themselves they are insufficient to induce thinking abilities. Empirical research on commercially marketed thinking skills programs is sketchy; mainly anecdotal. However, by using some of the techniques that we describe, students will gain those skills (Ellis 2005.) The most effective instruction emanates from a teacher who is knowledgeable about both subject matter and thinking processes, who continually demonstrates the skills and attitudes involved in thinking, and who demands systematic, rigorous thought from students—both in speaking and in writing. In this regard, it is the teacher who can add the dimension of meaning. Make your students think about what meaning they might derive from school subjects. It is up to you to provide the bases for meaning when new topics and concepts are introduced. For example, Jacqueline N. Glasgow (2001) shows how easy it is to use political issues, such as social justice, to develop students' critical thinking skills.

In addition to the thinking skills and traits listed, R. Bruce Williams (2007) provides five additional criteria for designing instruction that enhances student thinking.

Teacher adds meaning to the materials.

1. Relevance
2. Richness
3. Relatedness
4. Rigor
5. Recursiveness

Finally, reflect on how you can incorporate the concept of multi-methodology into the entire realm of inquiry and critical thinking. There is really no limit to the number of ways that you may approach these powerful teaching strategies (see Miri, Ben-Chaim, & Zoller 2007).

Reflect

◆ What topics or units in your teaching field would be appropriate for stressing thinking processes?

◆ Examine your state's and school district's NAEP data for selected subjects. What can you conclude about the level of thinking skills shown?

◆ How can you structure classroom questions to stimulate the development of students' thinking skills?

SECTION 2   Inquiry Teaching

In this section, we first present several underlying bases for inquiry-based teaching and take a brief look at its relationship to the constructivist philosophy. We then explore in detail how two different instructional models based on the inquiry strategy can be used in your classroom.

The Basic Elements of Inquiry Teaching

Theoretical Bases of Inquiry Methods   All inquiry methods are predicated on specific assumptions about both learning and learners. The box below provides a synthesis of the views on the subject by several scholars (Bigge & Shermis 2004; Holcomb 2004; Joyce & Calhoun 1998; van Zee et al. 2001).

Basic Tenets of Inquiry Teaching

◆ Inquiry methods require the learner to develop various processes associated with inquiry.

◆ Teachers and principals must support the concept of inquiry teaching and learn how to adapt their own teaching and administrative styles to the concept.

◆ Students at all ages and levels have a genuine interest in discovering something new or in providing solutions or alternatives to unsolved questions or problems.

◆ The solutions, alternatives, or responses provided by learners are not found in textbooks. Students use reference materials and textbooks during inquiry lessons just as scientists and professionals use books, articles, and references to conduct their work.

◆ The objective of inquiry teaching is often a *process*. In many instances, the end product of an inquiry activity is relatively unimportant compared to the processes used to create it.

◆ All conclusions must be considered relative or tentative, not final. Students must learn to modify their conclusions as new data are discovered.

◆ Inquiry learning cannot be gauged by the clock. In the real world, when people think or create, it is not usually done in 50-minute increments.

◆ Learners are responsible for planning, conducting, and evaluating their own efforts. It is essential that the teacher play only a *supportive* role, not an active one (that is, the teacher should not do the work for the students).

◆ Students have to be taught the processes associated with inquiry learning in a systematic manner. Every time a "teachable moment" arrives, the teacher should capitalize on it to further the building of inquiry processes.

◆ Inquiry learning complicates and expands the teacher's work, owing to the many interactions that may emanate from inquiry teaching and learning.

◆ Administrative support is needed since critical thinking requires students to be just that—critical.

Inquiry teaching requires a high degree of interaction among the learners, the teacher, the materials, the content, and the environment. Perhaps the most crucial aspect of the inquiry method is that it allows both student and teacher to become persistent askers, seekers, interrogators, questioners, and ponderers. The end result occurs when your students pose the question every Nobel Prize winner has asked: "I wonder what would happen if . . . ?" It is through inquiry that new knowledge is discovered. It is by becoming involved in the process that students become historians, scientists, economists, artists, businesspersons, poets, writers, or researchers—even if only for an hour or two, in your class.

Recall that in Chapter 7 we urged you to develop the question-asking skills of all students. In this chapter, we take questioning a step further, for it plays a crucial role in both the teaching and learning acts associated with the inquiry mode of learning. The investigative processes of inquiry learning involve the student not only in formulating questions but also in limiting them, selecting the best means of answering them, and conducting study.

Teacher and students as seekers, askers

Basic Inquiry Processes   The basic processes of inquiry learning are listed in the box below somewhat in order of complexity.

Note that each **inquiry process** requires progressive intellectual development and that as this development takes place for one process, it spurs development on other processes. Development of observing, classifying, and measuring skills, for example, speeds development of inferring skills.

These processes are found in every learning episode that involves inquiry. Inquiry is not simply asking questions; it is a process for conducting a thorough investigation, and as such, it applies to all domains of knowledge.

Each inquiry process—that is, the 13 processes in the box below—must be carefully developed and systematically practiced. This means that you must decide how much of *each lesson* will be devoted to building cognitive skills and how much to mastering processes—just as you did when you planned small-group discussions (see Chapter 8).

Inquiry Processes

1. *Observing.* Identifying objects, object properties, and changes in various systems; making controlled observations; ordering series of observations
2. *Classifying.* Making simple and complex classifications; tabulating and coding observations
3. *Inferring.* Drawing conclusions based on observations; constructing situations to test these conclusions

(continued)

Inquiry Processes—Cont'd

4. *Using numbers.* Identifying sets and their members and then progressing to higher mathematical processes

5. *Measuring.* Identifying and ordering lengths and then areas, volumes, weights, temperatures, and speeds

6. *Using space–time relationships.* Identifying movement and direction; learning rules governing changes in position

7. *Communicating.* Constructing graphs and diagrams to describe simple and then more complex phenomena; presenting written and oral reports

8. *Predicting.* Interpolating and extrapolating from data; formulating methods for testing predictions

9. *Making operational definitions.* Distinguishing between operational and nonoperational definitions; constructing operational definitions for new problems

10. *Formulating hypotheses.* Distinguishing hypotheses from inferences, observations, and predictions; constructing and testing hypotheses

11. *Interpreting data.* Describing data and inferences based on them; constructing equations to represent data; relating data to hypotheses; making generalizations supported by experimental findings

12. *Controlling variables.* Identifying independent and dependent variables; conducting experiments; describing how variables are controlled

13. *Experimenting.* Interpreting accounts of scientific experiments; stating problems; constructing hypotheses; conducting experimental procedures

Constructivism and Inquiry Teaching   In Chapter 2, we introduced the topic of constructivism. In our opinion, there is a close match between the philosophy of constructivism and the inquiry model of learning (see Ishii 2003).

Being "constructive" means that your students apply the 13 process skills just presented. You, as the teacher, must invite students to learn through inquiry, and you must direct them to the proper tools. In Chapter 8, we referred to a cooperative lesson in world geography in which students compared the United States and Europe (see Richburg & Nelson 1991). Although the exercise was created for cooperative learning groups, it is precisely the kind of experience that can be adapted for inquiry and constructivist teaching. The exercise encourages active learning: Students must synthesize data, classify information, make inferences, communicate individual findings to the rest of the class, and evaluate their ideas or conclusions.

Inquiry as constructivism and active learning

It is important to recognize that constructivism is not an instructional model, such as direct instruction; nor is it a specific learning method. Constructivism is a theoretical model about how learners come to know (Airasian & Walsh 1997). We also caution that, unlike inquiry methods that have been used in the sciences for centuries, constructivism does not entail a set of procedural steps.

Inquiry teaching takes time and much teacher energy. In our experience, we have never seen inquiry-oriented teachers sitting at their desks—they are on the go, and so are their students. Constructivist teachers behave the same way. We recognize that there are differences in social interpretations of the two approaches, but that is a topic for another book. Virginia Richardson (2003) provides a critical analysis of constructivist pedagogy showing its many interpretations and practices. See the box below for a synthesized set of commonalities between constructivist and inquiry-oriented teachers.

Points of Agreement Between the Constructivist and Inquiry-Oriented Approaches

◆ The focus is on the student.

◆ The pace of instruction is flexible, not fixed.

◆ Students are encouraged to search for implications.

◆ Students are encouraged to generate multiple conclusions.

◆ Students must justify their methods for problem solving.

◆ Neither constructivism nor inquiry sees itself as the sole learning model for all content.

◆ Nature provides the objects, and humans classify them.

Reflect

◆ Locate a book about the constructivist teaching philosophy. Compare the list in the box on page 290, on the basic tenets of inquiry teaching, to lists developed by constructivist writers. What do you find?

◆ Show the list of 13 processes to peers who are studying art, history, or literature. Ask them to relate those processes to their respective disciplines.

Inductive Instructional Models

We have established the basics of inquiry as a teaching strategy. Now let's look at models of **empirical epistemology**: gaining knowledge through observation or experiment. In Chapter 5, we introduced inductive teaching. Remember that induction is a thought process wherein the individual observes selected events, processes, or objects and then constructs a particular pattern of concepts or relationships based on these limited experiences. **Inductive inquiry** is a teaching method in which teachers ask students to infer a conclusion, generalization, or pattern of relationships from a set of data or facts. Inductive inquiry may be approached in at least two different ways: guided and unguided. If you provide the specifics—that is, the data or facts—but want the students to make the generalizations, then you are conducting **guided inductive inquiry** (Tamir 1995). If you allow students to discover the specifics themselves before they make generalizations, the process is **unguided inductive inquiry**. In most cases, you will begin with guided experiences. This way you will know there is a fixed number of generalizations or conclusions that can reasonably be inferred, and you can then help students make them from the data provided. The guided method provides an easy transition from expository teaching to less expository teaching. You may also find that some writers or groups classify the process as (a) directed inquiry, (b) guided inquiry,

Guided (you provide the specifics) or unguided.

and (c) full inquiry. We use four divisions—the first two, problem solving and discovery—for ease of applying each and for making clearer distinctions.

Inductive inquiry is appropriate at all levels of instruction, from pre-school to university graduate schools. At any level, the processes of observing, making inferences, classifying, formulating hypotheses, and predicting are all sharpened (or reinforced) by the students' experiences (see Haury 2002).

Guided Inductive Inquiry   Pictures are usually the easiest way to introduce the concept of inductive inquiry. For young children, show different pictures of the same scene to the class. Ask the children to tell what they see in the pictures and to describe patterns they observe. Have them state these patterns as generalizations. Ask questions that require students to do some generalizing themselves, such as "What could cause this type of track in the snow?" or "Where have we seen this before?"

Distinguish clearly between statements based on observations and those based on inferences. Begin the lesson by explaining and demonstrating the difference between observations and inferences. As the children respond to your questions, ask, "Is that an inference or an observation?"

The process of inductive thinking is developed gradually. As the lesson progresses, prepare a simple chart or list on the blackboard of students' observations and inferences. Students' understanding of each process will gradually develop from studying these examples. This strategy has been applied even to students who were challenged to describe combinations of pizza toppings and then construct a math theorem that could predict the number given the ingredients (see Nord, Malm, & Nord 2002).

At all levels, ask students to list their observations and, beside them, their inferences or generalizations. The Instructional Strategies box below lists the steps to be used in arriving at generalizations through guided inductive inquiry (see Jeong, Songer, & Lee, 2007).

INSTRUCTIONAL *Strategies*

Steps for Guided Inductive Inquiry

1. Decide on the generalization(s) students should make during a particular unit of study.

2. Organize the learning activities and materials in a manner that exposes the strands or parts of the generalization(s) to students.

3. Ask students to write a summary of the content that will form the basis of the generalization(s).

4. Ask students to identify sequences or patterns of events, objects, or other data in the content.

5. Ask students to summarize these sequences or patterns in one sentence.

6. Ask students to offer proof that their statement is, in fact, a generalization by applying it to other events, objects, or data.

Source: Adapted from Brandsford, J. D, et al., Eds., *How People Learn: Brain, Mind, Experience and School* (Expanded Edition). Washington, DC: National Academy Press, 2000, *passim;* and Jeong, Songer, & Lee, 2007.

Time Requirements   The first time you use any type of inquiry activity in your classes, plan to spend at least twice as much class time on each lesson as you normally would. This time is spent on in-depth analyses of the content by the students. Inquiry methods demand greater interaction between the learner and the learning materials, as well as greater interaction between the teacher and the students (see Boss 2003).

At the same time, be prepared to reduce the amount of content you will cover because you will use more time developing process skills and less time covering facts. *You cannot maximize thinking skills and simultaneously maximize content coverage.* If you wish to build higher-order thinking skills, you must reduce some of the content and substitute processes instead (see Eylon & Linn 1988). By doing so, you will provide important instructional experiences that the student can apply across all disciplines.

Reflect

◆ Search the literature or the Internet for two types of inductive inquiry experiences that you can use in your teaching.

◆ Examine a textbook published in the past three years. What inquiry exercises or experiences do the authors provide?

◆ Explain this quote: "When you teach with the inquiry model, you teach less, but your students learn more."

Steps in Guided Inductive Inquiry   Figure 9.1 shows six major steps in the inquiry system it illustrates: (1) identifying the problem, (2) developing tentative research hypotheses or objectives, (3) collecting data and testing the tentative answers, (4) interpreting the data, (5) developing tentative conclusions or generalizations, and (6) testing, applying, and revising the conclusions. This model can be adapted to other inquiry models, such as problem solving (discussed later). These steps form the basis of what is called "the scientific method." (Strictly speaking, our models are adaptations of the Hypothetico-Deductive Model described by Sir Karl R. Popper, 1975.)

Inquiry learning cannot be rushed.

You will usually follow these steps for introductory guided inductive lessons. Recall that the process objectives are to observe, to infer, and to communicate. The problem, in this case, is to find a meaningful pattern in an array of events or objects. All inferences must be supported by some evidence—that is, observations or data. The latter may be obtained from some standard reference source such as the *Statistical Abstract of the United States,* almanacs, yearbooks, reports, or encyclopedias. The data become the focal point of the inquiry session and thus serve as a common experience for the entire class (see Holcomb 2004; Orlich 1989). Guided inductive inquiry includes the seven characteristics listed in the box below.

Students must find the pattern.

Characteristics of Guided Inductive Inquiry Model

1. Learners progress from specific observations to inferences or generalizations.

2. The objective is to learn (or reinforce) the process of examining events or objects and then arriving at an appropriate generalization from the observations.

(continued)

Characteristics of Guided Inductive Inquiry Model—Cont'd

3. The teacher controls the specifics of the lesson—the events, data, materials, or objects—and thus acts as the class leader.

4. Each student reacts to the specifics and attempts to structure a meaningful pattern based on his or her observations and those of others in the class.

5. The classroom is to be considered a learning laboratory.

6. Usually, a fixed number of generalizations will be elicited from the learners.

7. The teacher encourages each student to communicate his or her generalizations to the class so that others may benefit from them.

At this point, you may be thinking, "This certainly sounds like constructivism to me." For the most part, you would be correct. Constructivism is based on the idea that learners construct knowledge from their own thoughts, activities, and experience. What learners understand may be quite different from what the teacher understands. By scheduling time for children to ask

FIGURE 9.1

A Genweral Model of Inquiry

Identifying a problem	A. Being aware of something
Preparing a statement of research objectives	A. Proposing testable hypotheses
Collecting data	A. Gathering evidence B. Conducting an experiment C. Surveying a sample
Interpreting data	A. Making meaningful statements supported by data B. Testing hypotheses
Developing tentative conclusions	A. Establishing relationships or patterns B. Specifying generalizations
Replication	A. Obtaining new data B. Revising original conclusions

questions and share their observations with one another, you will help them construct a more empirical sense of reality. By using inquiry, you challenge the student to ask questions and seek solutions (see Patrick 2003b). Further, this model can be of great help to English-language learners (ELL) in expanding both their vocabulary and basic knowledge. Involvement in the learning experience is the key.

Examples of Guided Inductive Inquiry   An example of guided inductive inquiry is presented in the Instructional Strategies box below. This example is a clever guided inquiry exercise that allows students to learn about paper towel strength from their own observations. This activity demonstrates how easy it is to adapt elements of guided inductive inquiry to consumer issues. Sharon Brendzel (2002) provides sample questions, topics for discussion, and methods to determine absorbency in a classic guided inductive experience.

INSTRUCTIONAL *Strategies*

Adapting Guided Inductive Inquiry to Consumer Issues: Best Deal in Paper Towels

- ◆ Provide sheets of different brands of paper towels.
- ◆ Ask students to design an absorbency test.
- ◆ Students work in small inquiry groups.
- ◆ Students reach conclusions based on data.
- ◆ Students share results.

The Role of Questioning Within Guided Inductive Inquiry   We have noted that teacher questioning plays an important role in inquiry methods because the purpose of inquiry is to pursue an investigation. The teacher thus becomes a question asker, not a question answerer. Teachers who are masters of guided induction inquiry state that they spend their time interacting with students but provide very few answers (see Phillips & Germann 2002).

What kinds of questions should a teacher ask? The boxes on page 298 list relevant question stems or lead-in questions for teachers who want to have a more inquiry-oriented class environment (Orlich & Migaki 1981). These question stems are suitable for use in social studies, literature, science, and mathematics—any class in which the teacher wants to stress the process of inquiry. Note that the first box is oriented to dynamic situations. These stems are probably best classified as prompting questions, similar to those described in Chapter 7. If you are examining more static living or nonliving objects, the stems shown in the second box will prove very useful. Again, note that these prompting questions help the student to examine all kinds of interrelationships—one of the desired goals of inquiry teaching and constructivism.

Questions can be adapted to all subject areas.

Question Stems: Dynamic Subjects

◆ What is happening?

◆ What has happened?

◆ What do you think will happen now?

◆ How did this happen?

◆ Why did this happen?

◆ What caused this to happen?

◆ What took place before this happened?

◆ Where have you seen something like this happen?

◆ When have you seen something like this happen?

◆ How could you make this happen?

◆ How does this compare with what you saw or did?

◆ How can you do this more easily?

◆ How can you do this more quickly?

Source: Orlich, D. C. and J. M. Migaki, "What Is Your IQQ—Individual Questioning Quotient?," *Science and Children*, Vol. 18, 1981, pp. 20–21. Copyright 1981 by the National Science Teachers Association. Reproduced with permission of the National Science Teachers Association via the Copyright Clearance Center.

Question Stems: Static Subjects

◆ What kind of object is it?

◆ What is it called?

◆ Where is it found?

◆ What does it look like?

◆ Have you ever seen anything like it? Where? When?

◆ How is it like other things?

◆ How can you recognize or identify it?

◆ How did it get its name?

◆ What can you do with it?

◆ What is it made of?

◆ How was it made?

◆ What is its purpose?

◆ How does it work or operate?

◆ What other names does it have?

◆ How is it different from other things?

Source: Orlich, D. C. and J. M. Migaki, "What Is Your IQQ—Individual Questioning Quotient?," *Science and Children*, Vol. 18, 1981, pp. 20–21. Copyright 1981 by the National Science Teachers Association. Reproduced with permission of the National Science Teachers Association via the Copyright Clearance Center.

TABLE 9.1	Guided Inductive Inquiry: Social Studies Lessons		
Grade Level	Materials	Questions	Processes
2	Magazine pictures of houses from around the world	What traits can you identify in these pictures?	Observing, Inferring, Communicating
7	Pamphlets and posters about World War II	What explicit messages are communicated by these materials?	Inferring, Hypothesizing
10	Political cartoons	What are the key ideas and meanings conveyed by these cartoons? What is their context? What biases do they reveal?	Inferring, Hypothesizing, Making contextual references
12	A controversial court decision	What actions caused this case? What do you think will happen next? Have we studied any events similar to those in this case?	Analyzing, Predicting, Comparing

Table 9.1 provides examples of guided inductive inquiry in social studies at four different grade levels. The examples for grades 2, 7, and 10 are static, but think about how they could be connected to dynamic lessons. For grade 12 U.S. government classes, the examination of current events provides an easy application of dynamic inquiry teaching episodes. Be advised that several of the examples shown in Table 9.1 are very similar to actual test items used in the NAEP 1994 U.S. History Assessment (Beatty et al. 1996). The authors of that report also state, "The NAEP 1994 U.S. History Assessment was rigorous; many tasks demanded knowledge of complex events and concepts and *abilities to analyze and interpret*" (p. 74, emphasis added).

Reflect

◆ Think of a lesson with which you are familiar and create a guided inductive inquiry experience for teaching it.

◆ How can you restructure curriculum materials to make them more inquiry oriented for your students?

◆ How is thinking enhanced by guided inductive inquiry experiences?

Unguided Inductive Inquiry As we have seen, during guided inductive inquiry, you, the teacher, play the key role in asking questions, prompting responses, and structuring the materials and situations. Again, using guided inductive inquiry is an excellent way to begin the shift from expository or deductive teaching to teaching that is less structured and more open to alternative solutions. Once the class has mastered the techniques of guided inductive inquiry, you can introduce or allow for student-initiated situations that enable the students to take more responsibility for examining data, objects, and events. Because the teacher's role is minimized, the students' activity increases. The Key Ideas box on page 300 summarizes the major elements of unguided inductive inquiry.

More student-initiated than teacher-initiated.

Key Ideas   **Elements of Unguided Inductive Inquiry**

1. Learners progress from making specific observations to making inferences or generalizations.

2. The objective is to learn (or reinforce) the processes of examining events, objects, and data and then to arrive at appropriate sets of generalizations.

3. The teacher may control only the materials provided or encourage student-initiated materials. He or she poses a question, such as "What can you generalize from . . . ?" or "Tell me everything that you can about X after examining these . . . "

4. The students, using the materials provided and without further teacher guidance, ask all the questions that come to mind.

5. The materials are essential to making the classroom a laboratory.

6. Meaningful patterns are generated by students through individual observations and inferences and through interactions with other students.

7. The teacher does not limit the generalizations students make.

8. The teacher encourages all students to communicate their generalizations so that all may benefit from each individual's unique inferences.

Teacher clarifies but does not provide inference.

Inquiry techniques lead to student excitement when discovering concepts not found in a textbook.

© Bob Daemmrich/The Image Works

When you begin to use unguided inductive inquiry, a new set of teacher behaviors must come into play. You must now begin to act as the **classroom clarifier**, guiding students to develop logical thinking skills. As students start to make their generalizations, gross errors in student logic are bound to appear: Students will make generalizations that are too broad, infer single cause-and-effect relationships where there are several, and perceive cause-and-effect relationships where none exist. When such errors occur, you must patiently question the learner in a *nonthreatening* manner to verify the conclusion or generalizations. If errors exist in the student's logic or inferences, point them out. But you should *not* tell the student what the correct inference is, for this would defeat the purpose of any inquiry episode. These types of errors might appear in guided inquiry, but in that model the teacher is controlling the flow of information and can be more subtly directive through questioning (see Hoge 2003). There is much less direct teacher probing in unguided inquiry.

We suggest that you have students work alone during initial unguided inductive experiences. When students work alone, they tend to do most of the work themselves. When they work in pairs or triads without training as discussed in Chapter 8, one in the group usually takes the leadership role and dominates the group's thinking, so that there are really only one participant and two observers. When students demonstrate the necessary aptitude to use the inductive method successfully in an unguided fashion, you can assign small groups to work together. These characteristics are all a part of what is commonly labeled **problem-based learning** (PBL). The essence of PBL is that students generate problems to be examined, or problems are derived cooperatively with the teacher. Problems can be solved by small groups, the whole class, or by individuals. The Intel and Westinghouse student awards programs are predicated on PBL projects.

Techniques for Unguided Inductive Inquiry What are some tested ideas that can be used as prototypes for teachers wishing to incorporate appropriate inductive, unguided learning experiences into an ongoing lesson? Table 9.2 gives a few ideas that are expanded into a matrix of student tasks.

	Reflect	◆ Examine both the guided and the unguided inductive instructional models. What areas are common to both? What areas are different?

◆ Use the Internet to conduct a search of the ERIC database for ideas on using newspapers as sources of material in inductive inquiry lessons.

◆ How can lessons and activities in art, physical education, social studies, and literature be made more inductive for learners?

TABLE 9.2	**Unguided Inductive Inquiry: A Matrix of Tasks**				

Content Area	Lesson Goal	Material	Student Questions	Student Summaries, Patterns, Inferences	Student Generalizations
Social studies	To understand regional difference in the U.S. culture	Recycled telephone books	"How many different churches are there in Boston, Tulsa, Nashville, Salt Lake City?"	1. Lists from Yellow Pages. 2. Lists of different denominations. 3. Percentages computed. 4. Inferences listed.	Students list and discuss generalizations
History, Art	To interpret a classic artwork	Bayeux tapestry, encyclopedias	"What events are shown?" "What order is there to the tapestry layout?"	1. Events listed. 2. Scenes counted and classified into categories. 3. Types of persons indentified. 4. Chronology determined.	1. Students interpret major themes. 2. Students draw conclusions. 3. Class discusses historical events. 4. Class compares means of communication.
Science	To learn about weather patterns	Recycled newspapers, TV news	"How do weather systems usually hit the United States?" "What effect does the jet stream have on weather systems?"	1. Maps constructed showing major fronts. 2. Patterns listed. 3. Data collected north and south of jet stream paths.	1. Students chart weather patterns. 2. Class analyzes patterns. 3. Students make conclusions and present them to class.

SECTION 3   Methods for Developing Higher-Level Thinking Skills

By now you should realize that, as a classroom teacher, you can never be too aware of thinking skills. Encouragement of your students' active observation and exploration should be infused throughout your teaching so that you are not merely transmitting information, but also enhancing thinking abilities. You have been introduced to the basic elements of inquiry teaching and can now play a direct (guided inquiry) or indirect (unguided inquiry) role in classroom inquiry experiences. Within these overall contexts of teaching from an inquiry-based point of view, you also should know about several variations on the theme—that is, specific teaching approaches and techniques that are either directly related to or are themselves considered inquiry methods. The three approaches we focus on here have proven effective across many subject areas. They are problem solving, discovery learning, and techniques that emphasize higher-level critical thinking skills. We conclude by taking a brief look at classroom assessment, which we cover in depth in the next chapter.

Problem Solving

Problem-solving models of instruction are based on the ideas of John Dewey (1916, 1938). Among his major educational contributions was his advocacy of a curriculum *based on problems.* He defined a problem as anything that gives rise to doubt and uncertainty. Dewey held that a problem, to be an appropriate topic of study, had to meet two rigorous criteria: It had to be important to the culture, and it had to be important and relevant to the student.

Dewey's definition of problem.

Many curriculum projects developed between 1958 and 1970 in science, mathematics, and social studies were based on Dewey's problem-solving approach. In addition, most contemporary curricula and a large majority of textbooks suggest "problems" to be solved by students. Some of the curricula that you may encounter will stress elements of inquiry, discovery, or problem solving. Contemporary curricula, especially interdisciplinary ones such as environmental studies, rely heavily on the two criteria Dewey first suggested. If you assign research reports to your students, you are using elements of problem-solving instruction or problem-based learning.

This technique, like any inquiry method, requires careful planning and systematic skill building. Implicit within the problem-solving framework is the concept of **experience**, or the idea that the totality of events and activities that students carry out under the school's direction as part of the planned learning processes will produce certain desirable traits or behaviors that will better enable them to function in our culture. Furthermore, the experiences provided by the schools should articulate the content and the process of knowing. Both knowing *what is known* and knowing *how to know* are important objectives for the learner (see Martinez 1998).

Problem solving through experience.

This description shows that problem solving contains many elements of the constructivist model. As we use it here, **problem solving** refers to an inquiry learning process in which students seek answers to a question relevant to themselves and their culture. The constructivist philosophy requires the learner to be actively engaged in the learning process. Through the interaction of all those elements, the learner makes sense out of something. You, as the teacher, help by providing the environment that allows the student to participate and interact in regular classroom activities or on the Web (see Gordon et al. 2001; Kirk & Orr 2003; Munson et al. 2003).

The Teacher's Role   As the clarifier or definer, your role is to help the learners define precisely what is being studied or solved. Problem-solving methodologies focus on systematic investigation: Students set up the problem, clarify the issues, propose ways to obtain needed information, and then test or evaluate their conclusions. In most cases, learners will establish written hypotheses for testing. Students need your continual monitoring. In a problem-solving model, you must continually receive progress reports from students engaged in the investigative process.

Remember clarifying role

Students are not simply allowed to follow their whims. Problem solving requires building close relationships between students and teacher (see Delisle 1997; Verduin 1996). It also involves systematic investigation of the problem and the proposing of concrete solutions.

Voices from the Classroom

Sandy Shutey
Butte High School
Butte, Montana

Inviting Real Problems for Students

With the major emphasis for hands-on, minds-on science today, it often leaves one mentally fatigued while trying to come up with activities or problems. By providing activities first, then following-up with reinforcing concepts, students have to really begin to understand the concepts, not simply memorize them. This method of teaching is more demanding of both student and teacher.

February is "engineering month," and the local electrical engineers love to come to our physics classes. They encourage science and engineering fields while doing a fun electrical project. Teachers often use hands-on activities to develop vocabulary and math skills. However, most teachers do not have actual field experiences as engineers. Thus, having engineers in the classroom adds a dimension of excitement, fun, and authenticity to the instruction.

The Institute of Electrical and Electronics Engineers, Inc. (IEEE) is the world's leading professional association for the advancement of technology. The IEEE society brings four engineers into my classroom. Along with the information on building an AM radio, they bring AM radio kits, soldering guns, wires, and all the material needed to make a radio. In class, the students build the radio and then are given a week to write a technical paper which the engineers assess. The students "package" their radio in some unusual form, which in the past included toy lawn mowers, stuffed toys, assorted balls, telephones, hats, and even tools. Prizes for design and writing are given at a pizza party sponsored by the IEEE.

Each year, the engineers bring something new to the classroom, starting with crystal radios, then AM radios, and next year a new project seems to be coming to life from questions that the students have raised.

Steps in Solving Problems   Problem solving implies a degree of freedom (to explore a problem) and responsibility (to arrive at a possible solution). One tackles a problem to achieve objectives, not simply to use the process of inquiry per se. The steps listed in the Instructional Strategies box on page 304 compose the problem-solving technique, although students may not follow them in strict linear fashion. Compare the steps to those of the inquiry model in Figure 9.1.

Student freedom and responsibility

INSTRUCTIONAL *Strategies*

Steps for Problem Solving

1. Becoming aware of a situation or event that is labeled a "problem"
2. Identifying the problem in exact terms
3. Defining all terms
4. Establishing the limits of the problem
5. Conducting a task analysis so that the problem may be subdivided into discrete elements for investigation
6. Collecting data that are relevant to each task
7. Evaluating the data for apparent biases or errors
8. Synthesizing the data for meaningful relationships
9. Making generalizations and suggesting alternatives to rectify the problem
10. Publishing the results of the investigation

If you decide to use a problem-solving experience in your classes, you must realize that it will usually last for days or even weeks. During that time, other learning may be accomplished as well—for example, using reference books, requesting information, interpreting data, presenting progress reports to the class, and taking responsibility for carrying out a task.

Examples of Problem Solving   Let's look at two case histories of real problem solving that took place in elementary schools in Washington, DC, and Massachusetts.

Our first example is taken from one federal education official's personal efforts to help break the poverty cycle and to instill an appreciation for basic school subjects that can ultimately improve students' economic well-being. Recall the national stock market simulation that we discussed briefly in Chapter 8. Robert Radford (1991) of Washington, DC, wanted to help children attending the Amidon Elementary School do the following:

◆ Gain insights into the U.S. economic system.

◆ Understand the concepts of compounding interest, increasing the value of money over time, and capital appreciation.

◆ Practice the concept of delayed gratification (to break the poverty cycle).

In the Amidon project, intermediate-grade students were introduced to economics and business principles in practical ways. To demonstrate understanding, each student had to provide an example of the topics or concepts being discussed. Next, stock market activities were introduced. Students examined *Investor's Daily, Value Line Survey,* and *Barron's Financial Weekly.* The students read and reported on findings and even computed the Dow Jones Industrial Average.

Through hands-on experiences, they studied and discussed business cycles. They tracked selected stocks, graphed fluctuations in prices, and compared industrial stock profiles to that of the market as a whole. These real-life activities made a vivid impression on students of their need to master arithmetic, reading, social studies, and language arts.

Teachers and students decided together to purchase Philadelphia Electric Company common stock (currently called PECO Energy, a subsidiary of the Exelon Corporation). Money to purchase the shares came from gifts from 75 individuals who wanted to help with this project, along with the support of 17 companies and corporations. Each graduating class purchased a number of shares of common stock of PECO Energy, which were then placed into trust accounts for each student.

To take the exercise a step further, several students attended the annual stockholders' meeting. With their peers' proxies in hand, the delegates cast their votes and presented issues to the stockholders at large.

Accompanying the real-life component of this project was a stock market simulation game. Each child received a hypothetical $50,000 portfolio containing 10 different stocks. Students tracked their portfolios each week and thus acquired additional drill and practice in arithmetic and decision making.

Is this an example of real problem solving? John Dewey would applaud it. The project illustrates how students can be exposed to an *experientially* rich curriculum that helps them understand how to better themselves *in their own immediate future*. Having a trust fund will undoubtedly encourage these children to pursue socially valued occupations and professions.

Finally, the Amidon project illustrates how *affective* objectives may be integrated into the curriculum. Every kid feels like a winner, both intellectually and financially. And those feelings have a carryover effect on student behavior, ultimately sparking positive student actions.

In another example, students in a Massachusetts elementary school collected data and presented it to their local school board to show that a major intersection was a grievous safety problem. The students then showed how a pedestrian overpass could be constructed; they even contacted architects to obtain cost estimates. The school board was impressed—and so was the city council, for the walk was constructed later just as the schoolchildren had proposed.

There are many other examples of how teachers and students can use problem solving in the real world. For instance, a class might observe problems in the immediate school environment—parking shortages, long lunch lines, crowded locker rooms, noise—and investigate them with the goal of creating alternative situations. Or you could give students in high school English classes the problem of generating at least three criteria for determining which works of U.S. literature should be added to or retained in the curriculum. Students will learn the difficulties associated with canon building, values, and curricular decision making.

Jennifer Nelson (1998) uses investigative techniques of problem solving by having her students study problems associated with the history of their own school. In a similar vein, Carol E. Murphy (1998) shows how the five themes of geography—location, movement, place, region, and human environment—are used to solve problems associated with the school site. John Harrell, Edwin Christmann, and Jeffrey Lehman (2002) illustrate how the Internet can be incorporated in inquiry lessons. Regardless of whether you undertake an ambitious, large-scope problem-solving project with your

Authentic example: stock market

students or a lesser one, we urge you to initiate problem-solving skills from Day 1. Doing so makes schooling an enjoyable, exciting, and worthwhile experience (see Wakefield 2001).

> **Reflect**
> ◆ What elements of problem solving can be applied to any school-taught topics?
> ◆ Select a problem to be solved. To use problem solving most efficiently, sketch a task analysis chart showing the necessary student skills.
> ◆ Prepare a lesson that incorporates some real problem solving for students.

Discovery Learning

Who really discovered America? Native American people had been here for upwards of 13,000 years, and although Leif Ericson seems to have been the first European to visit our shores, Christopher Columbus got the credit for the discovery simply because he announced it first (Strike 1975). But the territory is named for the mapmaker Amerigo Vespucci because he knew Columbus had landed on a brand-new continent rather than in India. In this vein, Strike's comprehensive analysis of methods associated with **discovery learning**—an inquiry process in which learners pose questions and seek answers—may be of use. Strike (1975) establishes two categories of discovery: absolute discovery and relative discovery. *Absolute discovery* refers to those classic "firsts" in which something is discovered for all humankind—the discovery of the DNA molecule's reproduction mechanism; the discovery of new planets, theories, or synthetic materials. *Relative discovery* means that although a concept or fact is already known by others, an individual has learned it or found it out *for him-* or *herself* for the first time.

Absolute versus relative discovery

Strike (1975) also presents four modes of discovery:

1. Knowing that
2. Knowing how
3. Discovering that
4. Discovering how

Finally, he provides a basic criterion that is essential for any act to be labeled a discovery. The discoverer must communicate both the *what* and the *how* to others. Thus, if you discover the Lost Dutchman Mine in Arizona but do not tell a single individual, you have not made a discovery.

Strike's four modes of discovery are consistent with the 13 major inquiry processes described above. For example, communicating is a major inquiry process and is very much a part of discovery. Also, the model that Strike describes implies that learners must "know" something before they can "discover" something. Content, knowledge, fact, and processes are all very much a part of the discovery strategy.

Although there is much luck involved in discovery, Louis Pasteur's statement that "chance favors the prepared mind" is still valid. The most important discoveries made by scientists—including social and behavioral scientists—are the result of careful observation and systematic research. Discovery makes use of the same processes and skills we describe as being part of inductive inquiry and problem solving. This should come as no surprise because inquiry requires systematic conduct, not haphazard bungling.

Environmental education is a rich arena for discovery learning and problem solving. Students can collect water-quality data using standard, scientifically accepted practices and then analyze and discuss their findings. They *construct* meaning from data (Orlich et al. 1999).

A real-time episode took place when teacher-astronaut Barbara Morgan of Mountain Home, Idaho, went into space in August 2007 aboard the space shuttle *Endeavor*. She answered questions about space asked by students, including 18 children who participated from a NASA *Endeavor* linkup at Boise's Discovery Center (*Idaho Statesman* 2007).

Authentic example: space experiments

Challenge your students to explore selected themes from history (Wilson 2002), genetics (Echevarria 2003), or another area (Kalayci & Cohen 2003). The key point is that critical thought comes before action. Not all discovery learning needs to be as dramatic as NASA experiments. The opportunities for inquiry are limitless. Arthur L. Costa (2008) suggests that teachers integrate the themes of thinking throughout the curriculum. He adds that instruction should be reflective, complex, and relevant. These qualities are all implied in this chapter.

The entire arena of inquiry and thinking, including problem solving and discovery approaches, naturally lends itself to technology applications. See the Video Case on this page for an interesting example.

VIDEO CASE

In the Video Case entitled "Using Technology to Promote Discovery Learning: A High School Geometry Lesson" on the student website, you'll observe how technology can allow students to investigate problems and create their own "conjectures." As you watch the clips and study the artifacts in the case, reflect on the following questions: (1) What techniques does the teacher, Gary, use to encourage his students to discover geometric concepts? (2) How do the students respond?

Reflect

◆ Compare and contrast discovery learning and problem solving.
◆ Prepare a lesson that incorporates discovery learning.

Techniques for Developing Critical Thinking Skills

Implicit in the techniques we present in this section is the assumption that information-processing psychology and schema theory are the most useful explanations of how students learn. **Information-processing psychology** asserts that learning is an interactive process between the learner and the environment, a process to which both contribute; that is, the learner is not just a passive receiver of stimuli (see Snowman, McCown, & Biehler 2009). Schema theory, as we have already seen, asserts that we organize what we learn according to patterns, or *schemas*, that help us make sense of the multiple stimuli we constantly receive. Learning becomes an *individual meaning-building process*, in which the student either relates new data to existing patterns or creates new schemas to understand (see Marzano 1998). These assumptions are also part of the constructivist approach. Starting from this base of instructional assumptions, the teacher behaviors in the Instructional Strategies box below can help students improve their thinking processes. These techniques have proven useful across a broad range of subjects, from primary grades to graduate school.

INSTRUCTIONAL *Strategies*

Ten Teacher Behaviors That Encourage Thinking Skills

1. *Plan for thinking.* Develop units and lessons based on concepts and generalizations.

2. *Teach for meaning.* Connect each lesson to students' experience.

3. *Ask thought-provoking questions:* "How do you know?" "What is the main idea?" "What alternatives can we think of?"

4. *Make students aware of their mental processes.* "From your observations about prices in this chart, what might we infer about supply and demand?"

5. *Explain your thought processes frequently.* "On this tape, I recorded my thoughts as I planned today's lesson. As you listen to it, identify examples of the following thinking skills."

6. *Keep data before students.* Summarize and record student answers on the board or a transparency.

7. *Call on students to explain.* Give students frequent opportunities to explain what they do or don't understand.

8. *Encourage credibility as a criterion.* "Does this make sense?" "Why not?"

9. *Be consistent.* Thinking instruction should be part of each lesson, every day.

10. *Be patient.* Significant change requires at least a semester.

Plan instruction around thinking processes.

The first behavior, which is of primary importance, is to plan your instruction to emphasize thought processes. The resulting plan may bear little relationship to a standard content outline. Most history texts, for instance, organize facts chronologically; however, such a structure does not resemble the way people think critically about history. A more *effective* organizer is to arrange historical facts around selected basic concepts and generalizations, such as elections, economic cycles, events, or technological inventions. Facts must be related to broader concepts or generalizations before they have significance. Thus, effective instructional planning first determines the primary concepts and generalizations relevant to a unit or a course. These become the subjects of discrete lessons, which are planned around the facts needed to understand each concept. If you use the instructional strategies carefully and consistently, with an emphasis on students' understanding rather than on rote memorization, you will develop their thinking skills effectively, and your content coverage will have a meaningful pattern for students.

Strategic Learning Skills   Critical thinking skills are also called **strategic learning**, meaning that students develop a capacity to accelerate their own learning (see Gettinger & Stoiber 1999, p. 952). The box on page 309 lists four major assumptions under which we operate when developing students' strategic learning skills.

> ## Assumptions About Learners and Learning
>
> 1. New skills, knowledge, competencies, and interests are built on previous ones.
> 2. Information is remembered when it is meaningful and gained through active and enjoyable learning.
> 3. Motivation is reinforced when learners feel competent.
> 4. Opportunities must be provided to practice critical thinking and problem solving in various formats.

Following are three specific techniques that you can use to help your students build their critical thinking and strategic learning skills.

1. Integrated Approach Consider a high school unit in U.S. history that focuses on the colonial period. One way to combine content and thinking-skills coverage is to have students prepare a large wall chart listing specific characteristics of several colonies. These might be geographic features, economic characteristics, or social backgrounds and attitudes. From these data, students could infer and hypothesize about colonists' possible attitudes toward future events, such as declaring independence, providing free public education, or abolishing slavery. Similarly, science teachers could help students create a periodic table of the elements through observing, inferring, and generalizing rather than simply by studying a given example.

Note that these activities tend to reinforce many of the thinking skills listed earlier in the chapter. Depending on the instructional emphasis, students could be involved in virtually all thinking processes, from lower-order skills (observing and classifying) to higher-level skills (distinguishing relevant from irrelevant statements). Proponents of this integrated approach assert that such flexibility—the applicability of virtually any subject matter to teach a full range of thought processes—is its primary strength (see Gore 2004; Jones 2003).

2. Think-Aloud Modeling Another method is to use your thought processes as examples. This will help make students aware of their own thought processes (see the fourth and fifth teacher behaviors in the Instructional Strategies box on page 308 and the related discussion of metacognition on page 311). Share with students the thinking steps you follow in planning a lesson, making a conclusion, or performing any relevant activity. Have your students identify the particular skills you use and suggest other strategies you might follow. Such demonstrations can take the forms of printed handouts, audiotapes, or even an unrehearsed problem-solving exploration of a student's question.

Lest you think this idea is simply a theory, we offer Professor Emeritus Glenn Crosby, who taught graduate-level physical chemistry classes by narrating his thought processes as he worked out problems on the chalkboard. You can use this method to interpret writings by O. Henry, Barack Obama, or Langston Hughes, as well as chemistry.

Show students how you think.

Once students understand the think-aloud process, they can pair up and practice it, using selected topics related to classroom issues and the subject matter being studied. A useful exercise is for pairs of students to explain to each other their understanding of an assignment and the steps they will follow in completing it. This exercise uncovers ambiguities in assignments and helps students identify productive thinking and study strategies. Two considerations, though, are paramount in all thinking-aloud exercises: Each student must have as much practice as possible, *and the process of thinking is more important than the product of thinking*—the objective is to identify effective thinking steps, not necessarily to find a particular solution. This technique is ideal for open-ended activities.

3. *Student Summaries* Another technique that has been found generally useful for encouraging thinking behaviors is to have students summarize. Ask students to outline the steps in a math solution, list the causes of a social condition, give reactions to an assembly speaker, and so on. Your imagination is the only limit to the choices. The summary can be made in writing or presented orally.

Considerable evidence (see Wormeli 2004) suggests that the act of writing is itself both an exercise of thinking skills and a generator of those skills. We must think to write—but in addition, when writing, we frequently come up with new statements and ideas we did not think up beforehand. Thus, any writing is probably useful in learning. Writing summaries is particularly effective, however, because it forces the student to develop **criteria**—characteristics used to organize or evaluate ideas or products—for identifying some ideas as more important than others. This activity stimulates and reinforces the highest-level thinking skills (Nickelsen & Glasscock 2004).

Oral summaries are also effective in helping students develop speaking skills that will readily transfer beyond school. Moreover, oral summaries can be part of class discussions that are also essential activities for developing critical reasoning (see Marzano, Pickering & Pollock, 2001; Patrick 2003a). As you incorporate students' oral summaries into your teaching, remember to subtly shift your efforts to an inactive instructional role while the class members assume an active one. Only you will know the difference. When you assign a summarizing activity to a student, observe the four rules listed in the box below.

Summaries challenge students to rate ideas.

Rules for Summarizing

1. To stimulate understanding of the material summarized, insist that students use their own words, not quotations.

2. Limit the length of the summary, whether written or oral, to ensure that students have judged the relative importance of ideas.

3. Have students discuss their summaries, especially the criteria they used for including and excluding information.

4. Have students discuss the summarizing process: What steps did they follow? What dead ends did they come to? What problems developed?

Reflect
◆ How might you organize your classes to use the think-aloud technique?
◆ How could student journals be used to encourage thinking, reflecting, and summarizing?

Metacognitive Skills   Being aware of your thought processes while you are thinking is called **metacognition** (see Leat & Lin 2003 for an extended treatment of this topic). Thinking aloud is one example. Research indicates that effective problem solvers subvocalize; that is, they talk to themselves (see Meijer et al. 2006)—constantly restating the situation, rechecking their progress, and evaluating whether their thinking is moving in an appropriate direction. Undoubtedly you will have students with special and diverse needs in your classes. Harvette M. Robertson, Billie Priest, and Harry L. Fullwood (2001) provide a series of metacognitive techniques to assist these students—and other learners as well.

The following techniques are useful for helping students become accustomed to thinking about and stating their thoughts.

Describing Self-Thought   Perhaps the most effective technique is simply to have students describe what is going on in their minds while they are thinking (Block 2004). Have students practice this technique in pairs for 3 to 5 minutes several times a week to overcome awkwardness with the method (and even to practice cooperative learning). Once they are accustomed to the process, students can recall their thinking processes in larger groups or before the entire class to maintain the skill. You should also model this behavior as often as possible, of course. Connect this technique with the basic questioning model in Chapter 7. Rather than simply stating, "Your response is incorrect," you can ask the student, "How did you arrive at that answer?" That question engages metacognitive action (see King 2002).

Thinking about thinking.

Identifying What Is Known and Not Known   Another approach to metacognitive instruction is to have students identify what is known about a situation or problem, suggest what needs to be learned, and list steps required to obtain the information (Wray 2003). For example, Wray used this type of approach in class to determine whether science is a young person's game; that is, he had his students examine 24 revolutionary scientific figures to determine if young scientists are more likely to make important discoveries than are older ones. Such exercises, done frequently and with attention to identifying relevant processes, will help students use similar steps in their own thinking.

Students identify what is known and what they need to know.

Reciprocal Teaching   One more technique helpful to the metacognition package is **reciprocal teaching,** in which students and teachers switch roles in a lesson. This model was designed by Annmarie Sullivan Palincsar (see Gettinger & Stoiber 1999). Her approach has been used successfully with middle-level students and improves reading comprehension. (Remember the concept of teaching for understanding, discussed in Chapter 3.) Note how this strategy synthesizes several aspects of discussions, inquiry, thinking, and metacognition.

When using reciprocal teaching, the teacher leads the discussion or recitation period on the material the students have read. At that point, the students

VIDEO CASE

For a real-life example, view the Video Case "Metacognition: Helping Students Become Strategic Learners" on the student website. Teacher Julie Craven supports students in reading a difficult newspaper article about China. As you watch the clips and study the artifacts in the case, reflect on the following questions: (1) To what extent are the students aware of what they *don't* know? (2) What prevents them from becoming discouraged?

- - - - - - - - - - - - - - - - - - -

Students get into the mind of a great achiever.

are given four tasks: (1) predict what comes next in the text, (2) generate self-testing questions, (3) summarize the information provided, and (4) clarify any misunderstandings or unclear points. Following these steps, the teacher becomes a class participant and students assume the role of "teacher." This is also a great technique for generating personal interaction (see Puchner 2003; Seymour & Osana 2003).

Analyzing Others' Thinking   You can also encourage metacognition by having students study how others think, particularly persons who are famous for their thinking. Students may be surprised to discover that high I.Q. is not necessarily associated with achievement; the application of intellect is what matters. They could explore and discuss how Curie or Mozart worked, what steps they took, and what things were important to them in achieving. Students can interview accomplished people from their own community, or such individuals can visit the class to discuss what they are thinking while they paint a picture, run a race, or write a newspaper article.

Monitoring Academic Behavior   Teaching metacognition can also include having students monitor their own academic behavior. Do they have test-taking strategies? Are the strategies effective? Might they be improved? What about learning strategies? Do they know whether they learn better from visual, auditory, or kinesthetic stimuli? Do they have strategies to help in each area? All of these questions are relevant to students' school experience. All are areas that you can explore with students as you help them share with one another and provide useful information (see Gallagher 1998; Tanner & Casados 1998). The result will be improved metacognition and application of selected thinking processes.

TECHNOLOGY
Insight

Thinking and Inquiring: Web-Based Resources and Activities

One of the nicest things about being a teacher is the fact that you can be a learner for your entire career, and you can help your students become lifelong learners as well. Using the World Wide Web reinforces this. Because it is impossible to know everything that is available on the Web, one must constantly maintain a learner's point of view. Although we cover many different topics, all under the rubric of inquiry or thinking skills, there are a few Internet sources that provide ideas and resources for inquiry, thinking skills, and metacognition.

Probably the most famous Web-based, inquiry-oriented classroom activities are found on San Diego State University's Web Quest site (http://webquest.sdsu .edu/webquest.html). Bernie Dodge is generally considered the master of the site, which is very popular with teachers and teacher-educators.

Kathleen Cotton of the Northwest Regional Educational Laboratory has developed a series of materials that can help in teaching skills associated with thinking. You can find these at http://www.nwrel.org. Go to the search box on the NWREL home page and type in "thinking" to view several sites on the topic.

Assessing Higher-Level Thinking Activities

We saved the toughest part until last. The challenge of using any higher-level strategy—inquiry, problem solving, critical thinking—is that in most learning episodes there may be no one right answer. Thus, you assess the *processes* involved.

In Chapter 10, we will introduce the technique of using rubrics to evaluate student work. In using rubrics, you establish a set of criteria by which to assess a product, paper, argument, conclusion, or methodology (see Busching 1998; Taggart et al. 1998). The overarching method of inquiry is interaction. Chapter 8 includes two forms (Figures 8.1 and 8.2) that you can adapt to fit higher-level thinking lessons. Perhaps the most critical aspect of assessment is simply to provide feedback to all students so that they will continually improve their use of logic and become more systematic in solving any problem.

In closing this chapter, we want to acknowledge how much time and effort it takes to teach thinking as an integral part of the curriculum, especially with all the conflicting demands of standards-based models. We hope that all educators will begin to integrate the best teaching and thinking strategies into their curricula systematically and diligently. We have confidence that you will address the challenge as one that is intentionally inviting. And, once again, we invite you to visit our website to examine reported effect sizes on several inquiry and thinking techniques. Go to www.cengage.com/education/orlich.

Reflect

A Closing Reflection

◆ How can you integrate the different types of inquiry and the host of skills associated with thinking into your classroom instruction?

◆ In what ways can metacognitive techniques help student thinking?

◆ Review the list of 10 teacher behaviors that encourage thinking skills. How can you incorporate those behaviors into an already crowded curriculum?

◆ If you want to stress the development of thinking skills in your teaching, who else in your school or community must you involve? How can you involve them?

Summary Points

1. The goal of inquiry methods is to encourage students to ask questions, seek information, and become better thinkers.

2. The basic processes of inquiry learning include observing, classifying, inferring, measuring, communicating, predicting, formulating hypotheses, interpreting, and experimenting.

3. Two models for inquiry teaching are guided inductive inquiry and unguided inductive inquiry. Both are based on inductive reasoning, a method of thinking that moves from the specific to the general.

4. Three other methods of inquiry teaching are the problem-solving method, discovery learning, and the use of specific critical thinking

techniques. All these methods may be used to infuse critical thinking skills into the curriculum.

5. Classroom use of any inquiry model or method increases the amount of student-engaged time needed to complete a lesson and adds complexity to unit or lesson planning.

6. Using the integrated approach, think-aloud modeling, and summarizing helps students build their critical thinking and strategic learning skills.

7. Describing self-thought, identifying what is and is not known, reciprocal teaching, analyzing others' thinking, and monitoring academic behavior help students become accustomed to thinking about and stating their thoughts.

Building a Career Portfolio

We want you to have a sound set of ideas and strategies for teaching critical thinking in your classes. Below is a start on which to build that foundation. We offer the following suggestions for inclusion in your career portfolio.

◆ Research and collect reprints of articles in the published literature in your specialty that relate to the concept of "inquiry."

◆ Prepare a list of possible topics that would be appropriate for your students to consider for problem-solving experiences.

◆ What areas in your school would be potential sources for student inquiry? Examples might include the following: (1) Why is the building constructed as it is? (2) What times of day seem to be more chaotic than others? and (3) Has teacher turnover been a problem?

◆ Using the Internet, collect a set of evaluation instruments that would be applicable to inquiry experiences.

Resources

PRINT

This subject is so rich that we found it very difficult to designate only a few references as "must" reading. You may want to review these before you begin using inquiry or thinking strategies.

Campbell, J. R., K. E. Voelkl, & P. L. Donahue. *Report in Brief: NAEP 1996 Trends in Academic Progress* (NCES 98–530). Washington, DC: National Center for Educational Statistics, revised August 1998, 29 pp.
The National Assessment of Educational Progress (NAEP) is the sponsor of a series of tests in English, mathematics, science, art, writing, civics, and history that are administered to samples of fourth-, eighth-, eleventh-, and twelfth-graders and students aged 9, 13, and 17. We consider these tests to be the best indicators of the levels of thinking at which students achieve and teachers teach. Examine the most current reports to understand our plea for higher-level teaching and for ideas on how to reach those levels.

Educational Leadership 65(5): **February 2008.**
The entire issue focuses on the theme "Teaching Students to Think."

Shayer, M., & P. Adey. *Learning Intelligence: Cognitive Acceleration Across the Curriculum from 5 to 15 Years.* Buckingham, England: Open University Press, 2002, 209 pp.
The authors have amassed a long line of developmental research that will inform any teacher who desires to develop age-appropriate cognitive skills.

Starko, A. J. *Creativity in the Classroom: Schools of Curious Delight.* Mahwah, NJ: Erlbaum Associates, 2005, 499 pp.
Creativity is the top of the scale when it comes to thinking. This book provides you with more than enough information on how to encourage that trait in your classes.

Sternberg, R. J., & L. Spear-Swerling. *Teaching for Thinking.* Washington, DC: American Psychological Association, 1996, 163 pp.
This short book is a mind stretcher for the novice, but in it the authors critically examine thinking and creativity.

Wormeli, R. *Summarization in Any Subject: 50 Techniques to Improve Student Learning.* Alexandria, VA: Association for Supervision and Curriculum Development, 2004.
The author, a seasoned teacher, illustrates how you can use one of the more powerful learning techniques in any subject.

INTERNET

Go to the website for this book at www.cengage.com/education/orlich to find live links to resources related to this chapter.

- The Foundation for Critical Thinking has a website that is a "must-read" for developing a wide spectrum of critical thinking methods and implications.
  www.criticalthinking.org

- The School of Chemical Engineering at Washington State University has a website featuring several teacher-designed modules that illustrate inductive, problem-solving, and discovery models for grades 7–12.
  http://www.che.wsu.edu/home/modules/index.html

- Mid-continent Research for Education and Learning (McREL) maintains a site covering topics from constructivist teaching to technology integration. Their index is a useful search tool.
  http://www.mcrel.org/

- The Georgia Department of Education has designed a set of teaching strategies to develop various aspects of critical thinking. Overviews and K–12 lesson plans may be accessed online.
  http://www.glc.k12.ga.us.pandp/critthink/homepg.htm

- The University of Toronto offers a short course related to metacognitive techniques.
  http://snow.utoronto.ca/Learn2/introll.html

- The University of Delaware has an excellent website that provides resources for problem-based learning.
  http://www.udel.edu/pbl/

References

Airasian, P. W., & M. E. Walsh. (1997). "Constructivist Cautions." *Phi Delta Kappan 78*(6): 444–449.

Beatty, A. S., C. M. Reese, H. R. Persky, & P. Carr. (1996). *NAEP 1994 U.S. History Report Card: Findings from the National Assessment of Educational Progress* (NCES 96-085). National Center for Education Statistics. Washington, DC: U.S. Government Printing Office.

Berliner, D. C. (2004). "If the Underlying Premise for No Child Left Behind Is False, How Can That Act Solve Our Problems?" In K. Goodman, Y. Goodman, R. Rapoport, & P. Shannon, Eds., *Saving Our Schools: The Case for Public Education in America*, pp. 167–184. Oakland, CA: RDR Books.

Bigge, M. L., & S. S. Shermis. (2004). *Learning Theories for Teachers* (6th ed.). New York: Longman.

Block, C. C. (2004). *Teaching Comprehension: The Comprehension Process Approach*. Boston: Allyn and Bacon.

Boss, S. (2003). "Course of Discovery: Educators Living Along the Route Traveled by Lewis and Clark Infuse Their Teaching with Modern Tools for Exploration." *Northwest Education 8*(4): 8–13.

Brendzel, S. (2002). "Science on a Roll. Part One: Absorbing Inquiry." *Science Scope 25*(5): 18–20.

Busching, B. (1998). "Grading Inquiry Projects." *New Directions for Teaching and Learning 74*(1): 89–96.

College Board News 2000–2001. (2001, June). "AP Students with a '3 or Higher' Outperform Advanced Math and Physics Students both in U.S. and Abroad." New York City, July 11, 2001. *Full Report:* E. J. Gonzales, K. M. O'Connor, and J. A. Miles. *How Well Do Advanced Placement Students Perform on the TIMSS Advanced Mathematics and Physics Tests?* Boston: The International Study Center, Lynch School of Education, Boston College.

Costa, A. L. (2008). "The Thought-Filled Curriculum." *Educational Leadership 65*(5): 20–25.

Delisle, R. (1997). *How to Use Problem-Based Learning in the Classroom*. Alexandria, VA: Association for Supervision and Curriculum Development.

Dewey, J. (1916). *Democracy and Education*. New York: Macmillan.

Dewey, J. (1938). *Experience and Education*. New York: Macmillan.

Echevarria, M. (2003). "Anomalies as a Catalyst for Middle School Students' Knowledge Construction and Scientific Reasoning During Science Inquiry." *Journal of Educational Psychology 95*(2): 357–374.

Ellis, A. K. (2005). *Research on Educational Innovations* (4th ed.). Larchmont, NY: Eye on Education.

Eylon, B., and M. C. Linn. (1988). "Learning and Instruction: An Examination of Four Research Perspectives in Science Education." *Review of Educational Research 58*: 251–301.

Gallagher, S. A. (1998). "The Road to Critical Thinking: The Perry Scheme and Meaningful Differentiation." *NASSP Bulletin 82*(595): 12–20.

Gettinger, M., & K. C. Stoiber. (1999). "Excellence in Teaching: Review of Instructional and Environmental Variables." In C. R. Reynolds & T. B. Gutkin, Eds., *The Handbook of School Psychology* (3rd ed.), pp. 933–958. New York: Wiley.

Glasgow, J. N. (2001). "Teaching Social Justice Through Young Adult Literature." *English Journal 90*(6): 54–61.

Gordon, P. R., A. M. Rogers, M. Comfort, N. Gavula, & B. P. McGee. (2001). "A Taste of Problem-Based Learning Increases Achievement of Urban Minority Middle-School Students." *Educational Horizons 79*(4): 171–175.

Gore, M. C. (2004). *Successful Inclusion Strategies for Secondary and Middle School Teachers: Keys to Help Struggling Learners Access the Curriculum*. Thousand Oaks, CA: Corwin.

Harrell, J., E. Christmann, & J. Lehman. (2002). "Technology-Based Planetary Exploration." *Science Scope 25*(4): 8–11.

Haury, D. L. (2002). *Fundamental Skills in Science: Observation. ERIC Digest*. Columbus, OH: ERIC Clearinghouse for Science, Mathematics and Environmental Education. ED 478 714.

Hoge, J. D. (2003). *Teaching History for Citizenship in the Elementary School. ERIC Digest*. Bloomington, IN: ERIC Clearinghouse for Social Studies/Social Science Education. ED 479 891.

Holcomb, E. L. (2004). *Getting Excited About Data: How to Combine People, Passion and Proof* (2nd ed.). Thousand Oaks, CA: Corwin.

The Idaho Statesman. (2007, Dec. 31). "Most Committed of 2007: Astronaut Barbara Morgan."

Ishii, D. K. (2003). *Constructivist Views of Learning in Science and Mathematics. ERIC Digest*. Columbus, OH: ERIC Clearinghouse for Science, Mathematics and Environmental Education. ED 482 722.

Jeong, H., N. B. Songer, & S-Y. Lee. (2007). "Evidentiary Competence: Sixth Graders' Understanding for Gathering and Interpreting Evidence in Scientific Investigations." *Research in Science Education 37*(1): 75–97.

Jones, S. J. (2003). *Blueprint for Student Success: A Guide to Research-Based Teaching Practices K-12*. Thousand Oaks, CA: Corwin.

Joyce, B. R., & E. F. Calhoun. (1998). *Learning to Teach Inductively*. Boston: Allyn and Bacon.

Kalayci, N., & M. R. Cohen. (2003). *Integrating Problem Solving with Theme-Based Learning in the "Key Learning Community."* Paper presented at annual meeting of Education of Teachers, St. Louis, January 26 to February 2, 2003. ED 472 968.

King, A. (2002). "Structuring Peer Interaction to Promote High-Level Cognitive Processing." *Theory into Practice 41*(1): 33–39.

Kirk, J. J., & R. L. Orr. (2003). *A Primer on the Effective Use of Threaded Discussion Forums*. EDRS, ED 472 738.

Leat, D., & M. Lin. (2003). "Developing a Pedagogy of Metacognition and Transfer: Some Signposts for the Generation and Use of Knowledge and the Creation of Research Partnerships." *British Educational Research Journal 29*(3): 383–415.

Lyons, N., & V. K. LaBoskey, Eds. (2002). *Narrative Inquiry in Practice: Advancing the Knowledge of Teaching*. New York: Teachers College Press.

MacKnight, C. B. (2000). "Teaching Critical Thinking Through Online Discussions." *Educause Quarterly 23*(4): 38–41.

Martin-Hansen, L. (2002). "Defining Inquiry: Exploring the Many Types of Inquiry in the Science Classroom." *Science Teacher 69*(2): 34–37.

Martinez, M. E. (1998). "What Is Problem Solving?" *Phi Delta Kappan 79*(8): 606–609.

Marzano, R. J. (1998). "What Are the General Skills of Thinking and Reasoning and How Do You Teach Them?" *Clearing House 71*(5): 268–273.

Marzano, R. J., D. J. Pickering, & J. E. Pollock. (2001). *Classroom Instruction That Works: Research-Based Strategies for Increasing Student Achievement*. Alexandria, VA: Association for Supervision and Curriculum Development.

Meijer, J., M.V. J. Veenman, & B. H. A. M. van Hout-Wolters. (2006). "Metacognitive Activities in Text-Studying and Problem-Solving: Development of a Taxonomy." *Educational Research and Evaluation 12*(3): 209–237.

Miri, B., D. Ben-Chaim, & U. Zoller. (2007). "Purposely Teaching for the Promotion of Higher-Order Thinking Skills: A Case of Critical Thinking." *Research in Science Education 37*(4): 353–369.

Mullis, I. V. S., M. O. Martin, E. J. Gonzalez, & A. M. Kennedy. (2003). *PIRLS 2001 International Report: IEA's Study of Reading Literacy Achievement in Primary Schools*. Chestnut Hill, MA: Boston College.

Munson, B. H., R. Huber, R. Axler, G. Host, C. Hagley, C. Moore, & G. Merrick. (2003). "Field Trips Online." *Science Teacher 70*(1): 44–49.

Murphy, C. E. (1998). "Using the Five Themes of Geography to Explore a School Site." *Social Studies Review 37*(2): 49–52.

Nelson, J. (1998). "Get to Know Your School: Involving Students in the Historical Process." *Southern Social Studies Journal 23*(2): 37–42.

Nickelsen, L., & S. Glasscock. (2004). *Main Idea and Summarizing*. New York: Scholastic Teaching Resources.

Noddings, N. (2008). "All Our Students Thinking." *Educational Leadership 65*(5): 8–13.

Nord, G., E. J. Malm, & J. Nord. (2002). "Counting Pizzas: A Discovery Lesson Using Combinatorics." *Mathematics Teacher 95*(1): 8–14.

Orlich, D. C. (1989). "Science Inquiry and the Commonplace." *Science and Children 26:* 22–24.

Orlich, D. C. (2000). "Education Reform and Limits to Student Achievement." *Phi Delta Kappan 81*(6): 468–472.

Orlich, D. C. (2002). "Something Funny Happened on the Way to Reform." *Northwest Professional Educator 1*(1): 1–3.

Orlich, D. C. (2003, June 12). "An Examination of the Longitudinal Effect of the Washington Assessment of Student Learning (WASL) on Student Achievement." *Education Policy Analysis Archives, 11*(18). Retrieved from http://epaa.asu.edu/epaa/v11n18/

Orlich, D. C., J. C. Horne, C. Carpenter, & J. Brantner. (1999, March 27). "Water Plus Science Equals Active Student Learners (W + S = ASL)." Presentation at the National Science Teachers Association National Convention, Boston.

Orlich, D. C., & J. M. Migaki. (1981). "What Is Your IQQ—Individual Questioning Quotient?" *Science and Children 18:* 20–21.

Patrick, J. J. (2003a). *Teaching About the Louisiana Purchase*. ERIC Digest. Bloomington, IN: ERIC Clearinghouse for Social Studies/Social Science Education. ED 479 236.

Patrick, J. J. (2003b). *Teaching the Declaration of Independence*. ERIC Digest. Bloomington, IN: ERIC Clearinghouse for Social Studies/Social Science Education. ED 472 017.

Phillips, K. A., & P. J. Germann. (2002). "The Inquiry 'I': A Tool for Learning Scientific Inquiry." *American Biology Teacher 64*(7): 512–520.

Popper, K. R., Sir. (1975). *The Logic of Scientific Discovery*. London: Hutchinson (8th Impression).

Puchner, L. D. (2003). *Children Teaching for Learning: What Happens When Children Teach Others in the Classroom?* Paper presented at annual meeting of the Educational Research Association, Chicago, April 21–25, 2003. ED 478 759.

Radford, R. (1991, Sept./Oct.). "Young Investors Forum: A Tutorial for Children and Parents." *Washington Parent*, p. 11.

Reading for Change: Performance and Engagement Across Countries. (2002). Programme for International Student Assessment (PISA). Washington, DC: Organization for Economic Cooperation and Development.

Richburg, R. W., & B. J. Nelson. (1991). "Where in Western Europe Would You Like to Live?" *The Social Studies 82*(3): 97–106.

Richardson, V. (2003). "Constructivist Pedagogy." *Teachers College Record 105*(9): 1623–1640.

Robertson, H. M., B. Priest, & H. L. Fullwood. (2001). "20 Ways to Assist Learners Who Are Strategy-Inefficient." *Intervention in School and Clinic 36*(3): 182–184.

Selwyn, D., & J. Maher. (2003). *History in the Present Tense: Engaging Students Through Inquiry and Action*. Portsmouth, NH: Heinemann.

Seymour, J. R., & H. P. Osana. (2003). "Reciprocal Teaching Procedures and Principles: Two Teachers' Developing Understanding." *Teaching and Teacher Education 19*(3): 325–344.

Shayer, M., & P. Adey, Eds. (2002). *Learning Intelligence: Cognitive Acceleration Across the Curriculum from 5 to 15 Years*. Buckingham, England: Open University Press.

Snowman, J., R. McCown, & R. Biehler. (2009). *Psychology Applied to Teaching*. Boston: Houghton Mifflin.

Sternberg, R. J., & L. Spear-Swerling. (1996). *Teaching for Thinking*. Washington, DC: American Psychological Association.

Strike, K. A. (1975). "The Logic of Learning by Discovery." *Review of Educational Research 45*: 461–483.

Taggart, G. L., S. J. Phifer, J. A. Nixon, & M. Woods. (1998). *Rubrics: A Handbook for Construction and Use*. Lancaster, PA: Technomic.

Tamir, P. (1995). "Discovery Learning and Teaching." In L. A. Anderson, Ed., *International Encyclopedia of Teaching and Teacher Education* (2nd ed.), pp. 149–155. Tarrytown, NY: Elsevier Science.

Tanner, M. L., & L. Casados. (1998). "Promoting and Studying Discussions in Math Classes." *Journal of Adolescent and Adult Literacy 41*(5): 342–350.

U.S. Department of Education, National Center for Education Statistics.(2006). *Digest of Education Statistics, 2005*. (NCES 2006–030). Chapter 2.

van Zee, E. H., M. Iwasyk, A. Kurose, D. Simpson, & J. Wild. (2001). "Student and Teacher Questioning during Conversations about Science." *Journal of Research in Science Teaching 38*(2): 159–190.

Verduin, J. R., Jr. (1996). *Helping Students Develop Investigative, Problem Solving and Thinking Skills in a Cooperative Setting*. Springfield, IL: Thomas.

Wakefield, J. F. (1996). *Educational Psychology: Learning to Be a Problem Solver*. Boston: Houghton Mifflin.

Wakefield, A. P. (2001). "Teaching Young Children to Think About Math." *Principal 80*(5): 26–29.

Walberg, H. J. (1999). "Productive Teaching." In H. C. Waxman & H. J. Walberg, Eds., *New Directions for Teaching Practice and Research* (pp.75–104). Berkeley, CA: McCutchan.

Wallace, B., & R. Bentley, Eds. (2002). *Teaching Thinking Skills Across the Middle Years: A Practical Approach for Children Aged 9–14*. London: David Fulton, in association with the National Association for Able Children in Education.

Weinbaum, A., et al. (2004). *Teaching as Inquiry: Asking Hard Questions to Improve Practice and Student Achievement*. New York: Teachers College Press; Oxford, OH: National Staff Development Council.

Williams, R. B. (2007). *Higher Order Thinking Skills: Challenging All Students to Achieve*. Thousand Oaks, CA: Corwin Press.

Wilson, H. C. (2002). "Discovery Education: A Definition." *Horizons 19*: 25–29.

World Economic Forum. (2008). *Global Competitiveness Report 2007–2008*. Geneva, Switzerland.

Wormeli, R. (2004). *Summarization in Any Subject: 50 Techniques to Improve Student Learning*. Alexandria, VA: Association for Supervision and Curriculum Development.

Wray, K. B. (2003). "Is Science Really a Young Man's Game?" *Social Studies of Science 33*(1): 137–149.

Yager, R. E. (2007). "STS Requires Changes in Teaching." *Bulletin of Science, Technology and Society 27*(5): 386–390.

Classroom Assessment

Samantha Alexander, a new teacher at the Salk Middle School, has been reviewing the school board's policy on assessment and testing: "Teachers are expected to provide an objective evaluation of all students enrolled in their classes. Although some testing will be norm referenced and objective in format, we encourage the use of essay and criterion-referenced tests as well. Further, we encourage all teachers to use, as appropriate, portfolios, authentic measures, and performance assessments. This policy does not preclude the use of other indicators in the evaluation process. In addition, teachers are strongly encouraged to use classroom assessment for formative purposes. That is, use classroom assessments to provide students with information they need to learn, self-correct, and meet classroom and district academic standards." Samantha silently muses on how she'll navigate this complex set of assessment options and expectations for use in her social studies and English classes.

You have already had considerable experience with assessment: You were assessed in most classes in elementary and secondary school; you probably took the SAT or other entrance exams before college; and you are likely being assessed in your present classes. But now it's time for you, like Samantha, to start thinking of assessment from the teacher's point of view. This chapter will help you answer these questions.

- How do I coordinate planning, instruction, and assessment in my classes?
- What is the role of formative assessment and what strategies can I employ for it?
- What kinds of assessment tools are available to classroom teachers, and when is it appropriate to use each one?
- How can I construct a variety of classroom assessments?
- What are the principles of grading, and how can I communicate the results of my assessments to students, parents, and appropriate administrators?

SECTION 1   Basic Contexts and Concepts

As a beginning teacher you will be confronted with many challenges in the classroom, including assessment. This section will provide key information to help get you on the right path.

A Continuous Process

Which of the classroom activities listed below do you consider to be assessment issues?

- Observing which students work best together when they sit near each other in the classroom
- Asking students a question to check understanding
- Noticing a student who seems not to hear well
- Giving a quiz on recent instruction
- Noticing that students seem bored and restless during a lesson
- Giving a final test covering a unit
- Assigning grades to students
- Reviewing yesterday's lesson

All of these activities are examples of what teachers do—formally and informally—to monitor and guide student learning. They gather information, interpret it, and then make decisions about whether and how to respond. Thus, assessment is a continuous process whose primary purpose is to improve student learning (Gronlund 2006). This chapter is offered to help you plan, organize, implement, and interpret classroom assessments to become a more effective teacher. The insights provided here will help you think about classroom assessment as a powerful tool to enhance student learning. There are many reasons it is important for you to know about assessment to be an effective teacher. Several of them are noted in the box below.

Main purpose: to enhance student learning

Reasons for Classroom Assessment

1. To provide feedback to students
2. To make informed decisions about students
3. To monitor, make judgments about, and document students' academic performance
4. To aid student motivation by establishing short-term goals and feedback
5. To increase retention and transfer of learning by focusing learning
6. To evaluate instructional effectiveness
7. To establish and maintain a supportive classroom learning atmosphere

Technical and Professional Vocabulary

Before proceeding, let's clarify several terms. It is customary to distinguish among the terms *assessment, test,* and *measurement* in the following ways (Miller, Linn, & Gronlund 2009): **Assessment**, the most general term, includes a broad range of processes by which teachers gather information about student learning. These processes include paper-and-pencil tests, performance and project ratings, and observations. Assessment is in part a qualitative description—making a value judgment in response to the question: How well does the student perform? Assessment can also include testing instruments, such as standardized or large-scale achievement tests.

A **test** is simply a particular type of assessment, usually a set of questions that all students must answer in a fixed period of time and under similar conditions to demonstrate learning. Teachers use tests to determine how well students perform on a specific set of tasks and to obtain comparative measurements of students' performance.

Measurement is a process that assigns numbers to assessment results, such as the number of correct answers or points on a project. It is a quantitative description and makes no statement about the quality of a student's performance. Measurement, as a concept, is typically associated with large-scale achievement tests.

A **norm-referenced standardized test**, such as the SAT or the Iowa Test of Basic Skills, is usually a paper-and-pencil test that has been developed by a major test publisher, standardized for a large population (called a "norming group"), and administered under the same conditions and time limits to all test-takers. The purpose of a standardized test is to rank each individual's

A broad range of processes

score by comparing it with the scores (using measurement) of the entire norming group. Both the norming process and the fact that the same test is given to all takers under identical conditions make the test "standardized."

Two other terms—*validity* and *reliability*—need clarification (see Nitko 2004, pp. 36–76 for a full discussion). These characteristics are of the utmost importance in all assessments, both standardized and classroom assessments. The discussion that follows is focused on standardized, measurement-oriented tests and assessments. In a later section, reliability and validity for classroom assessments are addressed.

Validity refers to the degree to which a test measures what it is intended to measure. A ruler, for instance, is a valid tool to measure the dimensions of a table. The measurements it provides can be trusted in making decisions about where the table will or won't fit, for example. However, a ruler would be useless for measuring the weight of the table; for this task, it is an invalid tool.

Now consider a math test that includes verbal problems. To what extent do the measurements that such problems provide reflect students' reading abilities as well as their math knowledge? To the extent that the test measures more of a student's reading ability, it is less valid as a test purely of math skills. Is there an easy solution to this dilemma? None that we know of—no test is a completely valid measure of achievement constructs or domains. The fundamental question to ask is, "What evidence do I have that the test I'm giving, whether I made it or not, is measuring what I intend it to measure?" Notice also that validity is relative to purpose—a test may be valid for one purpose but not for another. (For an excellent discussion of test validity, see Della-Piana 2008.)

Reliability refers to the consistency of test results. If the same group of students could be retested several times and get about the same scores, then the test can be considered reliable. Obviously, you can't use this method to determine the reliability of a single test because students would learn from each retaking. However, several statistical methods are available for estimating test reliability that test publishers use when documenting the technical (e.g., reliability and validity) characteristics of the tests they produce (see the Print Resources section at the end of this chapter). One general rule for you to remember is that reliability increases with test length. That is, the more questions that are asked on a test, the more information is available on students. As a consequence, uncertainty about student achievement is reduced, which in turn increases consistency or reliability. The box below lists questions you should ask in determining an assessment instrument's validity and reliability.

Does the test measure what it's supposed to?

Are the test's results consistent?

Key Ideas

Validity and Reliability

Validity

◆ Does this test measure what it is intended to measure?

◆ Can I make sound decisions about achievement on the basis of these test scores?

◆ Does this test sample a representative portion of the content being assessed?

Reliability

◆ Does this test give similar results with each use?

◆ Are the results of this test consistent with those of similar measures?

Purposes of Classroom Assessment

As a skilled teacher, you will use classroom assessment in four major ways to accomplish four different, important purposes. These four purposes are discussed below and summarized in the Key Ideas box on page 324.

Placement   Recall Benjamin Bloom's assertion in Chapter 4 that 50 percent of the variability in student achievement results from lack of sufficient knowledge or skill to begin new instruction. Therefore, before beginning instruction, many effective teachers use a **pretest** to assess their students' current knowledge. There are at least three reasons for doing so. First, such a test will identify students who do not have enough prior knowledge to begin the new material; the teacher can then provide these students with prerequisite work. Second, assessing the general level of students' prior knowledge helps determine where to begin instruction and what to present. Finally, scores on a valid and reliable pretest can serve as a baseline from which to measure progress. Depending on the material and the objectives, both multiple-choice and performance measures can be useful as pretests. Placement tests are generally produced by test manufacturers, although they can also be made by teachers.

Pretest is for placement.

Diagnosis   Another purpose of assessment is to determine specific areas of learning difficulty. The tool used, a **diagnostic test**, is most often a commercial product, although teachers may sometimes make it. Its purpose is to identify students' strengths and weaknesses—specifically, what students need to learn in designated subjects. Typically, diagnostic tests are used in conjunction with specialists—teachers of reading or foreign languages, special educators, or counselors and psychologists—to identify problems or to screen for problems.

Formative Assessment   At the heart of your job as a teacher is your students' growing competence and success in learning. Therefore, perhaps the most important kind of classroom assessment you will engage in is that of **formative assessment**—ongoing assessments to monitor your students' progress. The purposes here are twofold: firstly, to verify that learning is occurring and that the curriculum is appropriate, and secondly to provide feedback to students. In the first instance, the primary user of the information is the teacher. Evaluation need not be a formal assessment. Systematic, recorded observations of each student by the teacher (called "anecdotal records" and discussed later in this chapter) can also be used.

Formative assessment is also used to provide feedback to students, to answer their need to know "How am I doing?" and "Am I meeting expectations?" The form of the assessment will be whatever can most reasonably answer this question for the student and provide the quickest possible feedback.

Usually formative assessments consist of daily quizzes, homework, and short tests. Current research shows that timely, relevant feedback is one of the most important factors for improving student achievement (Hattie & Timperley 2007; Marzano, Pickering, & Pollock 2001). Section 2 of this chapter is devoted entirely to formative assessment.

Formative assessment lets students know how they're doing.

Summative Assessment   By contrast with formative assessment, **summative assessment** is an "overview of previous learning" (Black 1998, p. 28). To accomplish this task, the teacher collects information about students over an instructional period or through an end-of-period test or project. A central purpose of summative assessment is to certify completion of projects, classes, and programs. The users of summative evaluation (which often consist of a letter grade) include not only students but also their parents and perhaps future schools and employers. We devote the final section of this chapter to the process of grading because it is perceived by everyone involved to be a major part of schooling. Formative and summative tests are usually made by teachers, although they may be included in the supplementary materials that accompany textbooks or large-scale tests administered by school districts or the state. Summative assessments also have an important instructional dimension that will be discussed in a later section.

Summative assessment includes letter grades.

Key Ideas   Purposes of Classroom Assessment

- ◆ *For placement:* To determine whether the student has prerequisite skills to begin instruction
- ◆ *For diagnosis:* To determine causes (physical, intellectual) of persistent learning problems
- ◆ *For formative assessments:* To monitor learning progress, provide feedback to reinforce learning, and correct learning errors
- ◆ *For summative assessments:* To determine final achievement for assigning grades or certifying mastery

Areas Teachers Assess

Now that you are familiar with a teacher's primary *purposes* for assessment, it will be helpful for you to know about the *kinds* of behaviors, activities, and knowledge you will be evaluating. (As you read this section, you might ask yourself which areas would be most suited to one or more of the purposes of assessment.)

Recall that in Chapter 3 you studied three domains of learning—cognitive, affective, and psychomotor. Effective teachers make assessments in each domain. However, as you probably noticed in reading that chapter, many activities involve more than one domain. Making a wall poster, for instance, is in part a psychomotor activity, but the poster's quality also depends on the students' knowledge of what to include and on their feelings about or motivation for making it. The discussion below, then, uses the term *areas* to identify what you assess, and each area involves one or more of the domains. (These areas are listed again in the box on page 325.) The areas and techniques are

Effective teachers assess in the cognitive, affective, and psychomotor domains.

suggestive but not comprehensive. The techniques mentioned in each category are explained later in the chapter.

Knowledge and Conceptual Understanding   The cognitive area is the one that we usually associate with testing. It is a very broad area, however, and you will use different assessment methods for different types of knowledge. It is particularly important to identify objectives here before considering assessment methods (see Chapter 3). If, for instance, the objective was memory work—learning math facts, perhaps—then you should test students' recall of information, either orally or in writing. However, if the objective was conceptual understanding (of a concept such as photosynthesis, for instance), such understanding is best evaluated by having students explain the concept in their own words, either orally or written; by having them identify examples of the concept; or by having them create new examples of it. Ask yourself, "How can each student demonstrate understanding?"

Thinking   We place this domain in a separate category, although some teachers refer to thinking as a skill. In the sense that one can improve one's performance at it, thinking *is* a skill. However, thinking seems to be much more than just a skill, and assessment can involve multiple-choice tests, problem-solving exercises, and oral or written explanations. Make sure that you have a definition of thinking that works for you. "What indicators will I look for to verify that students are thinking?"

Skills   There are many types of skills—physical, learning, social, thinking, math, problem solving—and a wide variety of tools can be used to assess them. Various kinds of paper-and-pencil tests may be appropriate for math or problem solving, whereas a demonstration is a reasonable way to display physical education skills. Portfolios may well be the assessment tool of choice for art, composition, or drafting classes, whereas performance may be the first choice for a music class. The point is to consider all the areas in your curriculum that involve any kind of skill, and then ask yourself, "What can each student do to indicate progress?"

Attitudes   Especially in relation to building a group spirit and sense of interdependence in a class (see Chapter 8), it is useful to inquire about students' feelings toward one another and about school in general. Attitude inventories, anecdotal records, and checklists can provide considerable data without compromising confidentiality or privacy rights. Ask yourself, "What evidence or student behaviors show positive attitudes in class?"

Areas Teachers Assess

◆ Knowledge and conceptual understanding ("How can students demonstrate understanding?")

◆ Thinking ("What indicators show what and how students are thinking?")

◆ Skills ("What can each student do to indicate progress?")

◆ Attitudes ("What evidence or student behaviors show positive attitude in class?")

Direct Links to Planning and Instruction

Now that you understand several core concepts about classroom assessment and the primary contexts for your decisions about that assessment, we want to take another brief look at planning and how it relates to assessment.

Ideally, assessment planning should be an integral part of your instructional planning, not a process added on at the conclusion of instruction. Done carefully, such "whole-package" planning will ensure that instructional outcomes are clear to you and your students; that instruction is sequenced rationally; that instruction and assessment are congruent; and that your assessment measures all of the intended outcomes. Recall from Chapter 3 that this process is called "curriculum alignment." When all three elements match—that is, when instruction and assessment focus on stated objectives—alignment exists.

Build assessment into instructional planning.

The other point that is critical for you to remember is that all three instructional processes inform one another. That is, your planning decisions will undoubtedly require adjustment once you actually teach from them and reflect on the day's instruction. Likewise, your ongoing observing and monitoring of your students' learning—daily classroom assessment—should directly affect instructional decisions. Have students learned the intended concepts well? If not, where does the problem lie—in the instructional methods, in students' background preparation, or perhaps elsewhere? Which of the methods you have selected seems to generate the most motivation and interest among students? What are an individual student's strengths and weaknesses in a specific area? The answers to all of these questions, gleaned through assessment on a continuous basis, will affect both the next lesson's planning and its instruction.

A few other comments about assessment and the planning process are in order. Some teachers find it useful, once they have written their objectives, to begin their planning with the assessment phase. They specify how students will demonstrate achievement of the objectives and then work back and forth between the instructional plan and the assessment plan to determine what must be included in the teaching (see Wiggins & McTighe 2005).

Sometimes teachers enter the instructional planning cycle at the learning activity phase. Having found an activity that stimulates student interest and enthusiasm, the teacher specifies which objectives the activity will attain and develops assessments to monitor and measure achievement.

Teach what you test, and test what you teach.

Planning the assessment while you are planning a unit's instruction and activities is the best way to be sure that all the parts fit together and support one another. Below are three general pointers about assessment and planning.

Begin with Report Cards   One practical way to plan assessments is to begin with the report cards that you will eventually be expected to prepare. What information is expected there? How often? Are letter grades used? Do you need to prepare comments? Are there check-off items? What sorts of data will you need to prepare report cards? How might you obtain all the required information? Does your school district key its standards to specific lists that form the report card?

These questions may sound simplistic and obvious, but we have seen many instances in which beginning teachers didn't ask about report cards until a few days before they had to prepare them—which is too late! Because you will be expected to document student progress at least four times a year, both practicality and professional responsibility require that you prepare adequately.

Consider the Timing Timing of assessments is a next step in preliminary planning. Four strategies can help ensure that tests are timed to maximize their contribution to learning (Dempster & Perkins 1993). First, newly introduced material should be tested at an early stage. In this way, students are motivated to begin study immediately, and you, as the teacher, have information on student progress. Second, frequent testing encourages continuous study and reduces test anxiety. This strategy helps to maintain student motivation to study and attain the learning expectations (rather than procrastinate and worry about failure). Third, tests should be cumulative, with each test including some material from earlier assignments. Fourth, frequent testing aids retention.

Test often; test new material quickly.

The effective teacher, then, builds a preliminary calendar around required assessments for administrative purposes and necessary assessments for maximum learning gains.

Assessment of Special Needs Students Students with disabilities and students who are English-language learners pose particular challenges to the classroom teacher. Fortunately, most school districts and state departments of education have policies and other resources (including assistive technologies) that can help teachers assess the progress made by these students. This includes accommodations for classroom assessment, large-scale achievement testing, and high-stakes tests.

Peter Airasian and Michael Russell (2008) provide a variety of ideas and strategies for assessment of special needs students. Perhaps the strongest recommendation provided is to incorporate the instruction and assessment of special needs students into the planning process. Students are urged to consult this text for specific suggestions for assessing special needs students.

Challenges to the Proper Role of Classroom Assessment

Brookhart (2004) argues that teachers teach with a core set of operational theories: instruction, assessment, and classroom management. While these theories resonate well with many in the teaching profession, in practice, these theories can conflict with one another. Consider instruction and classroom assessment. Strong evidence shows that, when used appropriately, classroom assessment has a powerful influence on student achievement. Paul Black and Dylan Wiliam (1998), for example, did a review of studies spanning various grade levels, subjects, and countries, and found that effective use of classroom assessment could boost student achievement by as much as 15 percentile points as measured by standardized achievement tests. This is as strong a message about the link between classroom assessment and instruction as can be made.

Common sense, however, dictates that teachers can't teach and students can't learn unless the teacher is able to manage the classroom well. This principle is so important that an entire chapter of this text (Chapter 6) is devoted to this topic. Given the fluid and often unpredictable nature of classroom life, a teacher must make critical, spur-of-the-moment decisions to maintain classroom control. Unfortunately, some teachers have used classroom assessment techniques to maintain this control. This occurs when teachers use assessments for classroom control and student punishment—purposes for which assessments are not designed and should never be used. Examples include "pop" quizzes to punish an unruly class and "settle them down" or taking away credit on a project to punish a student for goofing off. These strategies may well have the near-term effect of gaining classroom control. However, they also have the long-term negative effect of students learning to avoid tests and other assessments because they are never quite sure of their purpose. You as a teacher may want to use them for legitimate instructional purposes, while your students, given their previous experiences, think you may be using assessments for some other reason, such as punishment.

In short, when classroom assessment is not used with student well-being in mind, teachers can damage students' academic well-being and, ultimately, their achievement. Students stop striving for excellence because they are no longer willing to risk trying for a target that could become a weapon, and you lose a potential 15 percentile point gain on standardized tests. In addition, if you use classroom assessments for manipulative reasons, students may begin to lose trust, as well as respect, in you as their teacher. The negative consequences are simply too great to use assessments as tools of punishment.

Punitive testing can damage motivation.

Reflect

The questions below address important issues in classroom assessment. Pool your thoughts with a small group of your classmates and then present your findings to the class.

1. Why is continuous assessment valuable?

2. What facts might make a classroom test or tests either invalid or unreliable?

3. In your experience as a student, what purpose did classroom assessment serve? How does this compare to the purpose it should serve?

4. List the ways that assessment methods might differ in the cognitive, affective, and psychomotor domains.

5. Can you recall a time as a student when a teacher used classroom assessment deliberately to punish you or your classmates? How did this make you feel? How do you think it affected your or your classmates' willingness and ability to learn?

SECTION 2   Formative Classroom Assessment

Classroom assessment can be used productively for far more than the collection of achievement information to assign grades. Of course, assigning grades is an important task teachers must perform. However, when teachers begin to think of assessment *for learning* rather than *of learning*, the power of assessment as an instructional tool is released into the classroom. Paul Black and colleagues (2004) argue that assessment for learning occurs when assessment is used to enhance student achievement.

Assessment not of learning, but for learning

Formative assessment is a type of classroom assessment devoted entirely to the enhancement of student learning and achievement. This chapter offers a variety of assessment strategies that can be used for this purpose. This section (1) provides a definition of feedback and discusses its importance, (2) describes three formative assessment strategies, (3) connects formative assessment to student motivation, and (4) describes the relationship between formative and summative assessment.

Formative Feedback

Much has been written about the connection between assessment and feedback. For students, **feedback**, particularly formative feedback, illustrates the gap between what the student currently knows and understands and what the teacher's expectations are for this knowledge and understanding. Royce Sadler (1998) translates the concept of feedback into simple terms teachers can apply in the classroom. In short, for teachers to assess the quality of student work and provide formative feedback, teachers must (a) have a clear idea of the standard or goal students are expected to achieve, and (b) be able to judge the quality of student work relative to the standard.

To achieve the full benefit of feedback, students must ultimately hold the same understanding of the standard as does the teacher. Students must also be able to assess their individual work and apply a variety of self-monitoring strategies to revise and enhance their work in order to meet the standard.

This is no small task. It requires several years of teaching to fully understand appropriate expectations for students, apply criteria to judge the quality of student work, and model strategies students can use to meet the standard. However, teachers can employ approaches that foster the benefits of formative assessment.

Students and teacher must share the same expectations.

Formative Assessment Strategies

Below is a short list of essential formative assessment strategies you can use in the classroom to enhance student learning (see Black et al. 2004 for more details). The extent to which you will use each technique is a judgment you will need to make based on the class, content of the instructional unit, your teaching style, and your comfort with the procedure.

Questioning. A key aspect of formative feedback is questioning. Questioning is so important that we devote all of Chapter 7 to it. You have learned already that asking thoughtful questions about the learning task and providing sufficient wait time for students to think and generate responses lie at the heart of questioning for formative feedback. This type of questioning can bring all students, not just the high achievers, into the learning process.

Peer Assessment. Ultimately, for students to attain high levels of achievement, they need to be able to self-assess and, when necessary, to employ corrective measures to meet the standard. Self-assessment is typically fostered by feedback to students from the teacher. However, feedback from teachers may not always be received well by students, particularly students who have not achieved well in their schooling. Students can sometimes be more receptive to peers than to teachers, so developing tasks and feedback sessions between and among students can be used productively to enhance student learning. To do this well, teachers need to explain to students how to give useful feedback, perhaps by modeling. For example, suppose a teacher gave a writing assignment to students with a set of criteria for gauging the quality of the writing. Using a student essay from a previous class, the teacher could model the use of the criteria and how to give feedback on performance. With this knowledge and understanding, students could then give one another feedback that illustrates the gap between the current quality of the essay and the expected quality embodied in the criteria.

Feedback through Grading. Grading is clearly a task you must understand and do well. This includes not only the development of semester grades but also the grading of tests, reports, and projects (grading is discussed later in this chapter). The downside of grading is that it can reinforce achievement differences among students. Successful students see grades as connected to effort, while unsuccessful students view grades as evidence that they are losers in the educational system. This is most true when grades are provided without additional feedback.

Studies have shown that written feedback about performance on a task, in addition to a grade, can be a powerful means of enhancing student learning. It can help to encourage students to think about their own performance and achievement, rather than serve as evidence of who wins and who loses. It is not the amount but the type of feedback that has the greatest impact on student learning. Teachers need to have a clear idea of what they want from students, be able to judge students' work objectively against the expectations, and effectively communicate how the student performed (Sadler 1998).

Formative Assessment and Student Motivation

Providing clear feedback to students about their achievement can increase student motivation to succeed. In particular, clarifying the goal or standard and helping students develop a representation of this standard for themselves helps students to take ownership for their success. When students understand what it means to succeed in your classroom, success is no longer a mystery or something held only by the teacher. With shared understanding of success, students are less likely to blame you or something beyond themselves for not meeting the standard. They are more likely to take responsibility when they do not meet a standard on a particular unit and take steps to reach the goal.

Students may be more open to peers' feedback.

Samples of Teacher Feedback

Insufficient feedback (vague; does not help students improve their performance)

◆   "Good effort."

◆   "Nice work."

◆   "Needs revision."

(continued)

> ### Samples of Teacher Feedback—Cont'd
>
> *Useful feedback (gives specific information students can use to improve performance)*
>
> ◆ "When you write your next report, consider using shorter sentences. Your message is lost with such long sentences."
>
> ◆ "When solving these equations, use a different line for each step. Then you'll be able to monitor the process you've used to solve the equation."

These ideas have the greatest potential for low-achieving students. In an environment with little feedback except, for example, grades, low-achieving students see achievement as a futile guessing game and often stop trying. However, when students receive formative feedback they are more likely to try to meet achievement challenges. Thus, the connection between formative assessment and student motivation should be at the forefront of any teacher's thinking and planning of classroom assessment.

Formative assessment helps low achievers grasp the rules of the game.

The Relationship Between Formative and Summative Assessment

As mentioned earlier, summative assessment is a process of "summing up" achievement in some way or conducting a status check on accomplishments at a given point in time. The data obtained from summative assessments are typically used for making judgments about student achievement. Data from formative assessment is more informational in nature. Formative assessment is designed to provide information to students that they can act on to close the gap between where they are and where they need to be relative to the standard. This distinction creates tension for many teachers between judging students through summative assessment on the one hand, and providing feedback to help and support students through formative assessment on the other.

Several years ago Brookhart (2001) found that successful students typically don't make strong distinctions between formative and summative assessments. For them, formative and summative assessment are both part of the school experience and part of the process required to meet their teachers' expectations. In this study, students integrated formative and summative assessment information. They used this information to reflect on how well they were doing at a point and time and what they could gain from this experience for learning in the future. Findings from this study are not trivial. Insights from these students have provided a means to resolve the historical tension between formative and summative assessment. And while this study involved a group of successful high school students in an English class and an anatomy class, Brookhart (2001) argued that the findings likely generalize to other school settings. By implication these findings could also generalize to externally mandated tests.

Combine and synthesize all assessment data.

Biggs (1998) articulated what needs to occur if summative assessments are to have learning benefits for students. First, summative assessments must be aligned with instruction in the same way that formative assessments are aligned. These assessments must incorporate the intended curriculum. Second, the assessments must be criterion-referenced rather than norm-referenced. To be clear, these requirements are for both classroom summative assessments and externally mandated assessments. These requirements provide a means for teachers to construct summative assessments with learning potential. These requirements also provide a means to critique externally mandated large-scale assessments.

Reflect

◆ Think about a teacher you had in high school whom you believe was a good instructor. Did this teacher use assessment to promote student achievement? How was this accomplished?

◆ At what point did you feel as though you understood what "success" meant in this teacher's classroom? Did you then notice a positive difference in your performance?

SECTION 3   Understanding Assessment Tools

Classifying assessment tools is similar to classifying animals or plants—there are many ways to proceed. We saw earlier how assessment can be organized and categorized according to the purposes a classroom teacher needs to consider. Here we lay out a different kind of grouping of assessment tools, organized according to the nature and characteristics of the tools.

Teacher-Made Assessments

As your experience no doubt confirms, most classroom assessments involve teacher-made tests. There are good reasons for this. First, the teacher has monitored the learning experiences in the class and thus has a much better idea than anyone else what needs to be assessed. Second, we assess the learning based on what we taught. If we taught for memory of facts, that's what we assess. If we taught for application, we assess for that. A third reason is that the teacher is familiar with the students as well as the instruction, which may affect the what and how of assessment.

How exactly *do* teachers make assessments? A major section of this chapter (Section 4, "Constructing Classroom Assessments") details that process, but here we offer some overall guidelines to help you produce valid, reliable measures of your students' achievement.

First, as we've mentioned, plan the test as you plan instruction rather than waiting until the instruction is over. Knowing in advance how and what to assess can be an important aid in instruction, especially in keeping it focused and not dwelling too long in some areas and omitting others.

Second, remember that the overall context for classroom assessment involves a variety of methods. You will also be letting students demonstrate their skills and understandings in a variety of valid ways—reports (oral and written), posters, videos, music, plays, stories, models, performances. Sometimes, however, a paper-and-pencil test created by the teacher *is* the most appropriate assessment choice.

Be flexible and creative in deciding on assessment formats.

Third, weave assessment throughout the instruction; don't tack it on at the end. If students are assessed throughout the duration of a unit, you and they will have a much more realistic picture of their understanding than what could be obtained from a single test at the end of the unit.

As mentioned earlier, notions of reliability and validity are important for classroom assessments. Publishers of standardized or large-scale assessments use statistically oriented procedures to quantify reliability and validity. Teachers typically don't have the time and training to perform these statistical procedures. Assessments occur many times throughout the year and are often not standardized, and sometimes, classes have too few students to warrant statistical computation. However, this does not relieve the teacher of the responsibility of ensuring reliability and validity. Richard Stiggins (2008) offers four sets of questions you can ask about your assessments to gauge their quality:

Is the assessment appropriate?

1. What is the purpose of the assessment? Who will use the results? How?
2. What are the learning targets? Are they clear? Appropriate?
3. Assess how? What method? Built of quality or relevant ingredients?
4. Communicate how? Reported to whom? In what form?

In sum, keep in mind that, as a teacher, you are using assessments to communicate to students about their achievement. Asking yourself these questions helps to ensure that you are communicating effectively.

Large-Scale Achievement Tests

Large-scale achievement testing is a big topic, and you'll find many books devoted to it. Excellent coverage of the technical aspects of these tests and interpretation of the several kinds of scores they generate are found in Salvia, Ysseldyke, and Bolt's *Assessment* (2010), cited in the list of Print Resources at the end of the chapter. The following section discusses the strengths of these tests and how you might use their results in your instructional decision making. Next, we treat some of the questions, concerns, and reforms related to standardized tests.

Strengths, Limitations, and Potential Uses Schools use large-scale achievement tests mainly to assess student performance according to districtwide and statewide curricula, monitor student achievement, and assess student aptitudes prior to high school graduation. The primary consideration in using these tests is to be sure that there is congruence between what is taught (the curriculum) and what the test measures. A close study of the test itself and its supplementary manuals will reveal the degree of congruence.

As you teach, always remember that no single test gives (or even claims to give) a complete picture of a student's achievement. Test scores must be supplemented with samples of student work, observation of students, and the quizzes, tests, and assignments that you create for your students. Only then can a professional evaluation of achievement be made.

◀◀ ▶ ▶▶ **VIDEO CASE**

Watch the Video Case entitled "Preparing Students for Standardized Tests: Strategies for Success" on the student website and observe fourth-grade teacher Maria Fenwick as she prepares her class for high-stakes tests. As you watch the clips and study the artifacts in the case, reflect on the following questions: (1) What planning strategy does Maria use? (2) How does Maria mimic high-stakes tests in her classroom?

The following box summarizes the strengths of large-scale achievement tests (Madaus & Kellaghan 1993; Miller, Linn, & Gronlund 2009).

Strengths of Large-Scale Achievement Tests

1. *Technical excellence in questions.* The questions on standardized tests are written by specialists, reviewed by experts on the subject matter being tested, reviewed for bias, and field-tested for flaws.

2. *Extensive technical data.* Standardized tests are accompanied by extensive helpful data on norming, validity, and reliability.

3. *Cost-efficiency.* The development costs of most standardized tests have long since been recovered, which means they can deliver the highest technical proficiency at the least cost per pupil. By contrast, most alternative assessments are not cost-efficient.

4. *Easy-to-use data.* Standardized tests provide separate printouts for class records, individual student reports, reports to parents, and many other uses. They provide a variety of scores—percentiles, grade equivalencies, stanines—for use in comparing each student's score to the norming group's scores. In addition, scores are available to show mastery or non-mastery of specific skills and objectives.

5. *Ease of administration and scoring.* Unlike alternative and most teacher-made tests, standardized tests are extremely easy to administer and score.

6. *Customization.* Standardized tests can be custom-crafted to fit a district's specified objectives.

Questions, Concerns, and Reform   In the 1980s and 1990s, there was a great deal of dissatisfaction with standardized testing. In essence, this dissatisfaction stemmed from the inappropriate use of such testing—using test results to drive the curriculum, using test scores as the *only* indicator for high-stakes decisions, and overemphasizing basic skills in instruction as a result of standardized test results.

Another core problem was that many of the higher-level thinking processes are difficult to assess using a multiple-choice test. For instance, a math test might ask the student to select the correct response from four choices. Does doing so demonstrate the use of the same mental processes as calculating the answer? Many argued that it did not and that the only realistic way to assess such skill is by demonstration. The same arguments were made in

Weaknesses of large-scale tests   many areas, including composition, speaking, foreign language, and music.

As a result of these and related concerns, reformers began demanding increased attention to many issues left out or ignored by the standardized testing movement—instructional emphasis on thinking and problem solving, local determination of learning outcomes, alignment of what is tested with what is taught, and fostering lifelong learning rather than stressing rote memorization of content. The result of teachers' continued dissatisfaction with testing, coupled with school reform efforts of the early 1990s, was a significant change in goals, processes, governance, curriculum, and assessment in the schools (see Linn 1998).

The primary change, in both assessment and curricula (the two cannot logically be separated), was a shift in focus. For many decades, schools had concentrated on classifying and sorting students—ranking them and placing them in various groups. Standardized achievement tests, normed on a national sample, effectively accomplished this. The process was reinforced by a grading system in which the final result was a grade point average and a ranked class standing.

Reform efforts turned away from using numerical scores and averages as indicators of success and toward a focus on each student's competency in the skills that will be most useful in life—being a critical thinker, knowing how to analyze and solve problems, working productively in groups, monitoring one's own learning, and evaluating one's own efforts. In addition, many of today's achievement tests are not norm-referenced but are *standards-referenced*. That is, the tests are built to reflect achievement targets, typically within a state. Scores derive meaning not by comparison with a norm group but by comparison with a fixed standard.

Today, the use of large-scale testing has become more complex and controversial as reform efforts continue into the twenty-first century. Nearly every state mandates statewide assessments with consequences for performance. Known as **high-stakes tests**, these testing policies seek to motivate and challenge students to excel, and hold teachers and administrators accountable for results. The federal government has weighed in with its own set of high-stakes testing requirements (U.S. Department of Education 2002).

The problem with this approach is that the teaching and learning process is often corrupted (see Nichols & Berliner 2005; Popham 2006). Teachers often overfocus on test preparation, skew instruction to the test, and pay particular attention to the form in which tests are constructed by teaching to this form. Because large-scale, standardized tests are predominantly multiple-choice in form, teachers teach to this format. Ironically, much of the impetus for educational reform in the first place is undermined. Teachers don't focus on problem solving and complex thinking. They focus on retention of facts and those achievement targets tested through multiple-choice formats. Keep in mind that it is not the form that is the problem. Multiple-choice formats are quite useful and valid when used appropriately. It is the use of the tests to make high-stakes decisions about students and teachers that is problematic. This testing practice compels teachers to narrow their curriculum and instruction to focus on learning targets that can be tested on current achievement tests, leaving many valuable learning targets out of the curriculum because they are not part of the test.

As a teacher, you will have plenty to keep you busy, necessitating careful choices about outside activities. However, the use of high-stakes tests has direct consequences for you and your students. Thus, working through your local union to understand more about large-scale testing practices and what can be done to improve them will be time well spent (Popham 2006). Ensuring that these tests are aligned with instruction and referenced to a criterion or standard, rather than to a norm group, are critical steps for increasing the instructional relevance of high-stakes tests.

High-stakes tests may have doubtful worth.

Student-Led Conferences

One of the great recent breakthroughs in classroom assessment is recognition of the power that student-led conferences have on student achievement.

Although these conferences can take many forms, they are typically done at midterm as a progress report and include the student, teacher, and parent(s). These assessments are used to discuss a student's performance on various projects, essays, tests, or quizzes. This discussion includes the quality of the student's work, the ways in which the student performed well, and what might be done to enhance his or her future performance.

In a student-led conference, the student takes major responsibility for discussing and evaluating his or her current level of achievement relative to the standard. While this is typically an oral evaluation for the teacher and parents, a student might also convey the assessment in written form.

The benefits of using student-led conferences are, first, that students learn to take ownership for their learning and are held accountable for it. Second, communication among the three stakeholders in student success—student, parents, and teacher—is enhanced. Student-led conferences foster coordination among these individuals, with student academic well-being as the central focus.

Many teachers have known about the power of this technique for some time and have used it successfully for years. On the surface, you might say that student-led conferences could require a lot of work by the teacher. However, there are documented strategies from experienced teachers that can be used to efficiently conduct student-led conferences. Anne Davies, Caren Cameron, Colleen Politano, and Kathleen Gregory (1992) provide an excellent guide to developing student-led conferences. Some of their ideas include ways to get parents involved; strategies to coordinate conference activities in crowded, busy school buildings; and instructional tips to help young children talk about their achievements. These authors have clearly thought through all of the logistical considerations with this tool.

Student-led conferences build accountability.

Voices from the Classroom

Jeffrey J. Sharrock
U.S. History Teacher

Wagoner High School

Wagoner, Oklahoma

Review Game Technique for Increasing Student Interaction and Assessing Student Mastery of Learning Objectives

Regardless of the subject matter, teachers share the common aim of facilitating student knowledge and skill acquisition. While periodic examinations may allow teachers to gauge individual progress, students who perform poorly on these exams usually have not understood course material for days prior, and may have to remediate previous coursework to move forward effectively.

One method I use to assess and improve student understanding on a more frequent basis is through the use of a review game whereby students compete in teams for rewards, such as extra credit or other minor incentives. The rules are simple: Sides or teams are quickly selected and students take turns being the spokesperson in answering questions that I pose. Teams alternate the fielding of a specified number of questions, and the side with the most correct answers at the end of the session wins a reward. To keep the team who is not being asked the next question attentive while their opponents deliberate, I offer the opportunity to "steal" the question if their opponent misses. Because classroom time is precious, question response time is set in advance (usually one minute), but I allow and encourage team members to discuss what their response will be before answering.

(continued)

Voices from the Classroom

Jeffrey J. Sharrock
U.S. History Teacher

Wagoner High School

Wagoner, Oklahoma

Review Game Technique for Increasing Student Interaction and Assessing Student Mastery of Learning Objectives—Cont'd

Interestingly, I have found students who are too self-conscious to participate in standard question-and-answer situations feel freer to speak up when they are able to confer with peers and build consensus first; and for their part, the peers are quick to lend their ideas because the team shares any extra credit if victorious. In addition, when students know the review game will be played at the conclusion of a lecture or other learning opportunity, they display improved attentiveness.

Listening to the student discussion as they reach their conclusions tells me a great deal as to what they understand, and after each question is over I can more effectively reinforce learning objectives by providing a tailored explanation. Finally, repeated use of this, and other oral assessment activities, has raised student scores on my periodic exams, as compared to exams taken after using daily written quizzes to assess progress.

Reflect

◆ While visiting schools, examine a set of various teacher-made assessments. What type of formats are used? Is there a wide variety?

◆ Go to the website of your state's Department of Education and review the various types of high-stakes tests that are administered. Also examine the pass or success rates of various socioeconomic and ethnic groups. What patterns do you observe?

◆ Seek out a school where student-led conferences are being conducted. Ask the principal and teacher if you can sit in and observe one.

SECTION 4 Constructing Classroom Assessments

Having considered why and what to assess, as well as the steps in test planning, we now have a foundation for writing specific test items. Such writing is in part an art, but with some basic techniques, persistence, and practice, the skill develops rapidly. This chapter can include only a small portion of available information. However, supplement your learning with suggestions from the Print Resources section.

We begin with some general guidelines to help you as you map out and structure your test. Then we take a closer look at writing actual test items. We divide item types into the following categories and discuss them in that order:

1. *Short-answer, matching, and true-false items,* for measuring knowledge-level outcomes
2. *Multiple-choice items,* for measuring both knowledge-level and more complex learning outcomes
3. *Interpretive items,* for assessing complex, higher-level objectives
4. *Essay items,* for assessing higher-level outcomes

VIDEO CASE

The Video Case "Assessment in the Middle Grades: Measurement of Student Learning" on the student website shows teacher Martin Somers helping students review for a math test. As you watch the clips and study the artifacts in the case, reflect on the following questions: (1) What techniques does Martin rely on for reviewing the material? (2) What techniques does he use for creating and reflecting on the test?

General Guidelines for Test Construction

Your work in writing a specific test will be greatly facilitated if you follow these six steps:

1. Determine how much importance and instructional time you will give to the major topics to be tested and then create a proportionate number of test items for each topic. For example, if you plan to teach four main ideas and devote equal time to teach, 25 percent of the questions on your test should be related to each topic. However, if time constraints caused you to give two of the topics less attention, decrease their coverage on the test. Yes, you should test on what you taught, even if it differs from what you planned.

2. Decide on the format and item type you will use. Be sure to test the format that you taught. If you teach for concept understanding, don't test for factual recall. Maintaining consistency is more difficult to do than it appears. Fact and recall questions are much easier to write and score than understanding questions—and far more common on tests. Up to 90 percent of secondary school test questions are at the lowest level (knowledge) of Bloom's cognitive taxonomy (Daniel & King 1998).

3. Determine a balance between the available testing time and the number of questions to include. How many questions a student can reasonably answer in a given time is a variable that you will understand with experience. The average high school student can complete two true-false items, one multiple-choice item, or one short-answer item per minute of testing time. Essay items require more time (Miller, Linn, & Gronlund 2009). However, remember that some students work more slowly than others, and time is needed to both begin and end the test. You will get a more valid picture of achievement if you allow plenty of time, even if it means dividing the assessment over several days—another reason for more frequent testing. You must also remember the special needs of your students with disabilities and your non–English-speaking students.

Timing formula for test items

4. Use a matrix, such as the Kaplan's matrix shown in Tables 4.1 and 4.2 (pages 117–118 to help organize your planning. One method is to list main ideas on the left, with headings that indicate the anticipated cognitive level across the top. The Instructional Strategies box on page 339 illustrates the concept with a unit on the U.S. Civil War. The example refers only to objective questions such as multiple-choice or matching. Essay items would be relevant, but we've omitted them for clarity. Notice the strengths of the format in the matrix. Identify main ideas so you can emphasize them in instruction and review them before the test. Note cognitive levels so you don't unintentionally use too many recall items. You can then estimate the time necessary to take the test.

Use matrix to chart content and level.

5. Plan an activity for those students who finish early. Don't wait until test time for this; it always happens.

6. Develop the test items. (We discuss this next.)

INSTRUCTIONAL
Strategies

▷▷▷▷

Objective items have one best answer.

True-false susceptible to guessing

FIGURE 10.1

Sample True-False Format Questions

Example of Planning Matrix

Unit Test, Causes of Civil War

Major Ideas	Number of Knowledge-Level Questions	Number of Understanding-Level Questions	Total Number of Questions
Political factors	3	4	7
Economic factors	2	3	5
Geographic factors	2	3	5
Social factors	3	3	6
Total items	10	13	23

Objective Test Items

Objective items are so called because they have a single best or correct answer. There is no (or very little) dispute about the correct responses to objective items. No professional judgment is required to score them; the real skill involved here is at the other end—in constructing them carefully, fairly, and systematically. Objective items come in two types: the *selection* type, in which a response is chosen from among alternatives given, or the *supply* type, in which the student supplies a brief response. If no clear choice between supply or selection items is specified by the learning outcome, use the selection type. It provides greater control of the response and more objective scoring. But remember to test the format you taught.

True-False Items   True-false, matching, and short-answer items are three types of comparatively simple items useful mostly for measuring knowledge-level achievement. Of the three, the **true-false question**, or *alternate choice question,* is perhaps the least useful. Because these items have only two possible options, students who guess have a 50-percent chance of getting a correct response. The examples in Figure 10.1 illustrate possible formats and uses for these items. Note especially the specificity of the directions.

Directions: Read each statement. If the statement is always true, circle T. If it is always false, sometimes false, or partially false, circle F.

   T   F   **1.** Water always boils at 100 degrees centigrade.
   T   F   **2.** 51% of 40 is more than 20.

Directions: Read each statement. If the statement is a fact, circle F. If the statement is an opinion, circle O.

   F   O   **1.** Other countries should have a Bill of Rights like ours.
   F   O   **2.** A red light requires a motorist to stop.

Directions: Circle the correct choice inside each pair of parentheses.

   1. Give it to (whoever, whomever) you please.
   2. Submit the papers to either the principal or (me, myself).

Matching Exercises   **Matching exercises** are a variation on the true-false format. They, too, assess mostly recall. Their best use is in identifying relationships within homogeneous material. The same cautions and shortcomings apply to matching exercises as to true-false ones. The example in Figure 10.2 illustrates a matching test. Again, note the instructions.

Be careful when writing matching questions. First, use only homogeneous material—don't mingle people, events, book titles, and geographic regions in the same list. This is confusing to the student and tends to provide clues to those who are test-wise. Keep your lists to about eight items and include more options than there are items to be matched. Finally, be sure there is one best option for each item.

Short-Answer and Completion Items   **Short-answer** and **completion items** are supply-type rather than selection-type items. They generally require the student to provide a word, phrase, or symbol. Students are asked not simply to identify a correct choice but to retrieve it from memory—a different, perhaps intellectually more complex, process. Science and math teachers are particularly fond of this format because it seems to directly measure computational and problem-solving skills and can conveniently allow students a place to display their work. Figure 10.3 illustrates various formats.

Completion items can measure comprehension level.

FIGURE 10.2

Sample Matching Questions

Directions: On the line to the left of each name in Column A, write the letter of the statement in Column B that best identifies that person. Statements in Column B may be used once, more than once, or not at all.

Column A	Column B
_____ 1. Cook	**A.** The first European to navigate a southern route around South America.
_____ 2. Columbus	**B.** He made four voyages to the New World.
_____ 3. Da Gama	**C.** The first European to sail the length of Africa's west coast.
_____ 4. Hudson	**D.** His major discoveries were in eastern North America.
_____ 5. Magellan	**E.** He located and conquered the Aztecs.
	F. The first European to locate Australia.
	G. The first European to navigate the Northwest Passage.

FIGURE 10.3

Sample Short-Answer and Completion Questions

Directions:
For each statement, write the correct word or numbers in the blank. If computations are needed, show your work on this paper, numbered appropriately. Spelling will not be counted in your score.

1. A ship is sailing on a compass heading of southwest. If it makes a ninety-degree turn to the left, in what direction will it now be sailing? _____

2. Walnut furniture wood sells for $4.12 per board foot. You need 31 board feet to complete a project. What will the wood cost? _____

3. Write the formula that describes the relationship among current, resistance, and energy in electrical problems. _____

4. What device is used to measure current? _____

5. In the statement $2x + 3 = 6 - 4x$, what number does x represent? _____

Multiple-Choice Items   The **multiple-choice item** is generally considered the most useful objective test item. It can measure both knowledge and higher-level learning outcomes.

Multiple-choice items consist of two parts: a question or problem and a list of possible solutions. The problem, called the **stem**, may be phrased as either an incomplete statement or a question. The possible responses to the stem are called the **alternatives**. The correct alternative is the answer; the remaining ones are called **distractors**. Their function is to distract the unknowing student from the answer while not confusing the knowing student. Creating effective distractors is one of the most difficult parts of writing multiple-choice items.

There are many ways of effectively using multiple-choice questions to assess almost any level of achievement (Bloom et al. 1971). The examples in Figure 10.4 illustrate multiple-choice questions at several cognitive levels. The first question tests factual recall. The second question tests knowledge of a principle. The third question tests application of a principle.

Essay Items

Essays can measure complex outcomes.

The essay item is an excellent way to assess students' higher thinking processes—comprehending and analyzing—as well as skills in organizing and presenting ideas.

Types of Essay Items   In general, there are two types of essay items: restricted response and extended response.

1. *Restricted response.* This is the item of choice when your objective is to assess students' abilities to explain, interpret, and apply information. It focuses on specifics, and the question must be phrased to restrict the response in that way. Note the examples in Figure 10.5. (See Verma & Chhatwal 1997 for an extension of this concept.)

FIGURE 10.4

Sample Multiple-Choice Questions

Directions: Circle the best choice for each question.

1. **Who was the second president of the United States?**
   A. James Buchanan
   B. Thomas Jefferson
   C. James Madison
   D. John Adams

2. **Boyle's Law shows a relationship between**
   A. Density and pressure of gases
   B. Pressure and volume of a gas
   C. Density and molecular weight of a gas
   D. Pressure and temperature of liquids

3. **What should you do if the car you are driving starts to skid on a rain-slicked highway?**
   A. Steer into the direction of the skid
   B. Apply the hand brake to slow down gradually
   C. Turn the wheels in the opposite direction of the skid
   D. Quickly apply the foot brake

FIGURE 10.5

Sample Essay Items

Restricted-Response Essay Questions

1. Explain two reasons leading to the conflict in which Magellan was killed.

2. In one paragraph, explain how sailing vessels proceeded when the wind failed.

3. In no more than one page, explain in detail why Cook and other early explorers had great trouble finding again the islands they had "discovered" in the Pacific Ocean.

Extended-Response Essay Questions

1. A paved, four-lane highway of about thirty miles is to be built across Washington's temperate rain forest. Discuss the possible ecological consequences.

2. Compare England's experience during the American Revolution to the U.S. experience in Iraq. Note specifically the concluding phases of both wars.

---

2. *Extended response.* When you wish to sample your students' abilities to select, organize, and evaluate ideas, this is an appropriate format. As the examples in Figure 10.5 show, the student has great latitude in all of these areas. However, this makes it an inefficient way to measure factual knowledge.

Scoring Responses to Essay Questions   After reading the examples in Figure 10.5 (both the restricted- and the extended-response questions), consider how you would assess them if you were the teacher. Your assessment might well differ from that of your colleagues. Reliability of grading (different graders giving the same grade, or the same grader giving the same grade over several readings) is a major concern with essay items. Extensive experience has shown that consistency of grading (reliability) is not easy to achieve with essay questions, but with careful planning and much experience, a reasonable level of reliability can be attained.

Before writing the questions, decide what learning outcomes are to be assessed (organizing ability, selection of relevant data, comprehension). Then be sure the question is phrased to elicit this objective.

Prepare a sample response, which should include the major points you expect to see, the appropriate format or organization, and the amount of credit to be given for each part or question. Many teachers also extend the sample

Prepare sample responses or a rubric.

into a rubric that shows what superior, adequate, and inadequate responses will contain. (See Table 10.1 on page 348 for an example.)

Use **holistic scoring** for extended-response items. The outcomes being assessed here are global ones, such as organization and selection of relevant material. Since each paper will demonstrate these in different ways, it is necessary to judge each response on its overall quality. Arranging students' papers into perhaps five categories of acceptability for each question provides as much pre-

Holistic scoring assesses work in its entirety.

cision and reliability as you are apt to get. You then total the scores on the separate questions to determine an overall grade. When the categories are carefully defined, and raters understand the categories, considerable reliability is achieved (Stiggins 2008).

Use **analytic scoring** for restricted-response items. Because of the restrictions, you can directly compare responses to the scoring rubric and assign points. As a general rule of grading, it is useful to use quantitative scores (5 points, 4 points) rather than descriptive words (excellent, needs improvement) or symbols (+, smiley face). You will eventually have to combine

Analytic scoring uses a rating system.

your judgments about individual tests and projects into an overall assessment of achievement—a grade. You can do this more fairly, we believe, through a consistent use of numbers.

Develop a coding system that conceals the students' names. This reduces the tendency to evaluate on personal qualities or other work the student has done. Some teachers assign students an arbitrary identification number to use for essay responses. Whatever system you use, you will likely soon recognize particular students' papers. Try not to let that influence your evaluation.

If there is more than one essay question, read all student answers to question 1 before going on to question 2, and so forth. This reduces the **halo effect**— the teacher's tendency to assess a student's performance based on the quality of earlier performance rather than an objective assessment. Also, reading all responses to one question first gives you an overall impression of misconceptions, well-learned areas, and areas needing further instruction.

Reflect

◆ To what extent is matching each assessment item to a specific objective essential?

◆ Obtain a sample un-scored essay response from your school to share with a group of your peers. Evaluate and score the essay without discussing it. Now compare answers. How were your assessments similar? How did they differ?

◆ What techniques can you use to ensure greater fairness in the scoring of essay tests?

◆ To what extent are both objective and essay test questions subjective?

◆ With a few of your peers, list some appropriate objectives for each of the test types discussed in this chapter.

◆ What commonalities did you find among the item types?

Assessing Performance and Products

Many areas of student achievement are more effectively assessed with a performance-based assignment than with a test question. Knowing *how* is often as important as knowing *that*. Language arts teaches speech and listening, both of which are assessed most directly by observing students' performances. The same is true of science lab procedures, social studies community projects, and reports of observations in health or earth science class. Physical education, music, art, home and family living, and the industrial arts are all based on knowing *how*.

Performance-based items do not have a single best response. Instead, students are required to organize and present the material in their own way within the stated bounds of the task. In essence, performance-based assessments ask the student to do whatever will reasonably demonstrate competence. These assessments do, however, require expert judgment from the teacher in what constitutes competence, and they are time-consuming. Performance-based assessment can use the evaluation of either actual student performances (demonstrations) of a task or authentic student products (original creations).

Find out what students can do, not just what they know.

Performances are active demonstrations that assess student learning, such as oral presentations, musical and dramatic performances, and kinesthetic activities. Students can demonstrate mastery of objectives in numerous ways. Oral explanations, for instance, are a key way to improve students' learning and understanding. The more time students spend explaining what they have learned to the teacher or other students, the more effective their learning will be. A mix of formal and informal presentations will provide many opportunities for students. Music, drama, and physical education teachers can give you some excellent suggestions and models.

At all grade levels, students produce **products**—book reviews, term papers, homework assignments, display boards, murals, and posters. The key to assessment is to specifically inform students of what will be assessed—form, content, spelling, design—and then to provide models or rubrics so students will know what an acceptable or superior product looks like.

Several tools are basic to performance and product assessment: rating scales, checklists, anecdotal records, observations, portfolios, and the rubrics that guided the project.

Rating Scales and Checklists   In general, rating scales provide a list of characteristics to be observed and a scale showing the degree to which they are present. To the extent that it is keyed to learning outcomes that can be observed and is used appropriately to evaluate processes or products, a rating scale is a useful assessment tool. See Figure 10.6 for examples.

Checklists and rating scales give students specific feedback.

FIGURE 10.6

Examples of a Rating Scale

Instructions: Rate the presenter on the following characteristics by placing an "X" anywhere on the line under each item. In the comment space, add any thoughts that will clarify your rating.

1. **Presenter spoke loudly and clearly so all could understand.**

1	2	3	4	5
Difficult to understand		Understood most of presentation		Clearly understood entire presentation

Comments:

2. **Presenter maintained eye contact with class.**

1	2	3	4	5
Read notes instead of looking at class		Made eye contact about half the time		Maintained eye contact through most of presentation

Comments:

3. **Presenter made biography interesting.**

1	2	3	4	5
Very few "humanizing" details		Quite a few interesting details		Made subject come to life. We learned what this person was like.

Comments:

Checklists, or "yes-no" rating scales, are useful when a process can be divided into steps and each one checked for its presence. Figure 10.7 gives an example.

Rating scales and checklists have widespread utility in the classroom. They identify specific tasks and portions of tasks and point out strong and weak areas, giving students the information they need to improve their learning. If used carefully, they provide the student with a model or rubric that specifies what an acceptable performance looks like and what its important parts are, as does the checklist in Figure 10.7.

A second value of these performance assessments is their utility in grading. Learning must include the freedom to experiment and make mistakes, but you must grade enough of the students' work to monitor and sustain progress. Also, when it is time to make a summative judgment of a student's achievement, you will use every indicator available so as to make the most accurate assessment possible. Your assessments of achievement can recognize and record that the student did outstanding work on a project, earned acceptable scores on three speeches, is improving in penmanship, contributes readily and usefully to class discussions, functions well as a work-group member, and so on. Like all the other forms of assessment, however, rating scales and checklists have limitations. They can be unreliable—giving varying results when used by different teachers or at different times by the same teacher. A clear statement of the objective to be assessed and the criteria used can alleviate this problem.

Anecdotal Records and Observations   **Anecdotal records** are recorded observations of student behaviors made during routine class sessions and perhaps in the halls or on the playground. What do you observe? Primarily, those behaviors that you can't assess any other way—John seems slow in responding to requests; Cheryl is never asked into groups; Archie doesn't seem well much of the time. A single notice of any of these, and similar behaviors, probably means little, but repeated and recorded over time, these observations can provide insights that will allow you to help students in areas you might otherwise overlook.

Four keys govern the effective use of anecdotal records (summarized in the Instructional Strategies box on page 346). First, don't try to record everything about everybody. Record the unusual, but do it systematically, briefly, and nonjudgmentally: what, where, and when (and your response, if appropriate). Make the note quickly in a couple of minutes during lunch or after school: "4/3/08. Jack hit Sam in the face during recess. This is the 2nd fight between them in 3 days. Each accuses the other of initiating it. I sent both boys to the vice principal, as per school policy for fighting."

FIGURE 10.7

Example of a Checklist

Homework Grading Guide	Yes	No
1. Is the handwriting legible?		
2. Is the response correct?		
3. Are the statements clear?		
4. Were all necessary data included?		

Four Keys to Keeping Effective Anecdotal Records

1. Don't record too much.
2. Be consistent.
3. Record positive as well as negative indicators.
4. Don't draw inferences from a single incident.

Second, be consistent, in both watching and recording. Make a few observations each day, recording them on index cards or notepaper and keeping the notes in your files or some other private place. Although the practice may seem tedious at first, it soon becomes a habit and is quickly done. The first time you alert a parent to a possible medical problem on the basis of anecdotal records, you'll become an enthusiastic recorder.

When you have discipline difficulties with a student—defiance, abusive language, fighting in class—such records can become very important.

Anecdotal records can help you get needed assistance for a student.

Obtaining help for the student (and you) generally depends on following due process for student rights and is greatly facilitated by dated records of all incidents relevant to the problem.

Third, record positive indicators of growth, not just evidence of problems. A surly student's voluntary class contribution, the class bully's politeness to a substitute teacher—these and more can be indicators of growth and should be part of your assessments.

Fourth, don't draw inferences about student behavior from a single incident. The unusual may be simply that—unusual. Patterns, observed over time, are necessary for drawing inferences about health or behavioral problems.

Portfolios   **Portfolios** are collections of student work. The concept of assembling these collections to monitor student progress and to share with parents and administrators is not new. Many elementary school teachers, and some middle school and high school teachers, have done so for years. Although still in their early stages of development, digital portfolios are becoming available. Some educational software companies are developing portfolios that use available technology to provide efficient and comprehensive storage of student work. Until these products are more widely available and properly tested, we recommend a thorough examination of their features and capabilities before purchase.

VIDEO CASE

Teacher Fred Park helps his young students develop new pieces for their writing portfolios in the Video Case "Portfolio Assessment: Elementary Classroom" on the student website. As you watch the clips and study the artifacts in the case, and after you read the interview with Fred, reflect on the following questions: (1) What do students learn in the course of this video? (2) How does it differ from what they would learn from a paper-and-pencil test?

What is new to portfolio usage is the idea that much student achievement can be more effectively demonstrated by a product than by scores on a paper-and-pencil test alone. A collection of these products, if carefully and purposefully assembled, can be a valuable assessment tool.

Focus portfolio on specific learning objectives.

For assessment use, a portfolio cannot be just a collection of student papers. Instead, it must be a demonstration of student effort and progress toward achieving particular learning objectives. (The Instructional Strategies box on page 347 lists the characteristics of a carefully planned portfolio.) Many

Assessment can be individualized.

© Will and Deni McIntyre/Corbis

- - - - - - - - - - - - - - -

Formative assessment is a
positive experience.

- - - - - - - - - - - - - - -

Rubrics: criteria + standards

classes or particular units within a class contain objectives that are readily and effectively assessed with work samples. In social studies and history, maps and charts are basic tools. Students produce these as aids to understanding. Oral presentations are part of most classes, and rating sheets from these can document student improvement. The more you think of objectives, the more ways you will find to use a portfolio to document progress.

To grade a portfolio, assess the student's entries in relation to the objectives specified. Rating scales and checklists are useful here, particularly when the student can use them as guides while constructing the entries.

Portfolios are increasingly used in mathematics classes, partly as a result of the standards adopted by the National Council of Teachers of Mathematics in 1989. Most other content areas have also adopted national standards (see Chapter 3). All the new standards emphasize problem solving and thinking skills, which are more accurately reflected by portfolios than by standardized achievement tests (Far West Laboratory 1992).

Sharing portfolios with parents on special occasions can reinforce a positive link between home and school. Additional perspectives on performance and alternative assessments can be found in the following: Haertel 1999; Herman et al. 1997; Madaus & O'Dwyer 1999; Stiggins 2008.

Rubrics   Especially when students are involved in the construction of the rubrics, this assessment tool can provide readily comprehensible feedback to students. **Rubrics** contain two primary components—*criteria,* which are really categories that describe *what* is being evaluated, and *standards,* which describe the level of achievement and tasks involved in reaching that level.

INSTRUCTIONAL *Strategies*

Designing Student Portfolios

1. Establish how the portfolios will be used.
2. Center the content of portfolios on instructional goals.
3. Translate instructional goals into student performance.
4. Plan the student into the assessment process.
5. Take steps to make review of portfolios more efficient.
6. Use multiple observations to increase generalizability.

Source: Oosterhof 2003, pp. 186–193.

TABLE 10.1	**Rubric for Oral or Written Retelling of a Narrative**	
3	**2**	**1**
Characterization		
Accurately recalls both primary and secondary characters.	Accurately recalls only primary or secondary characters, not both.	Incorrectly identifies the characters.
Uses vivid, appropriate descriptive words when discussing the characters.	Provides limited, correct descriptions of the characters.	Provides no descriptions or inaccurate descriptions.
Setting		
Recalls the setting: both place and time.	Recalls only the time or the place, not both.	Provides minimal information or inaccurately describes the setting.
Plot		
Recalls the action or plot in correct sequence as it happens in the story.	Describes some of the events as they occur in the story sequence.	Inaccurately describes events as they happen in the story sequence or describes events out of sequence.
Conflict/Resolution		
Accurately discusses both the conflict and the resolution.	Discusses only the conflict or the resolution, not both.	Discusses fragmented sections of the story with little mention of a conflict or problem with a resulting resolution.

Name of student: _____

Story: _____

Circle type of response: Written   Oral

Source: Betty D. Roe, Sandy H. Smith, and Paul C. Burns, *Teaching Reading in Today's Elementary Schools,* 10th ed. Copyright © 2009 by Houghton Mifflin Harcourt Publishing Company. Reprinted with permission.

Table 10.1 demonstrates what one kind of rubric might look like (from Roe, Smith, & Burns, 2009). Some guidelines for writing rubrics are listed below.

◆ Base standards on samples of student work that represent each level of proficiency.

◆ Use precise wording that describes observable behaviors in terms that students can understand.

◆ Avoid negative statements such as "cannot make predictions."

◆ Construct rubrics with 3-, 4-, or 5-point scales, with the highest number representing the most desirable level.

◆ Limit criteria to a reasonable number.

SECTION 5   Grading to Improve Student Learning

We end this chapter by considering the summative judgments you make about student achievement (that is, grades) and how you report those judgments to students, parents, administrators, and others.

As an instructional tool, grading and reporting should focus on improving student learning and development by clarifying instructional objectives, indicating students' learning strengths and weaknesses, showing students' personal and social development, and adding to students' motivation (Miller, Linn, & Gronlund 2009). This is certainly more than can be included in the traditional letter grade, but supplementing the nine-week or semester grade with other periodic reports can help achieve these goals. Periodic reports can also establish a positive climate of communication between you and parents, further reinforcing learning and adding to your students' motivation.

We know several teachers, at both the elementary and middle school levels, who send weekly class newsletters to parents. Groups of three or four students prepare them, on a rotating schedule, and the newsletters highlight learning objectives and their accompanying activities. The teachers report that most students enjoy working on the newsletters, and parents appreciate the communication.

Some elementary and secondary schools use checklists containing descriptive statements about students' academic skills, behavior, and attitudes in place of or as a supplement to letter grades, and others use narrative descriptions as a supplement (Oosterhof 2003, p. 219). In addition, some schools hold "portfolio nights" routinely, allowing students to share their efforts with their parents. This adds more reinforcement to students' learning and motivation.

All of the above ideas are attempts to provide more and better information about student achievement than a letter grade communicates. Even so, it seems unlikely that letter grades will be replaced anytime soon. Besides being traditional, they are a convenient administrative tool—for determining honors, promotion, scholarships, and athletic eligibility and for reporting to other schools—which is not readily duplicated by other means.

Principles of Grading

While the issue of grading remains controversial in some quarters and the task of grading complex, there are principles that can be called upon to make the task easier for the teacher and more fair for the students.

No Such Thing as Too Much Data   One of the first principles of grading is that you can't have too much data. No matter how many test scores, homework exercises, and class activities you have assessed, you will likely feel that you need more information to make summative evaluations. By giving your students many opportunities to show achievement, you provide yourself with more data for a fair, professional judgment, and you also provide each student with every possible chance to succeed.

The range of activities you can include in grading is limited only by your imagination. Most teachers include at least the following (not listed in order of importance):

◆ Unit tests

◆ Periodic quizzes

◆ Assigned work done in class

The point of grades is to promote student development and learning

---

Follow the inclusion principle in grading.

◆ Homework

◆ Projects—both group and individual

◆ Papers and reports

The goal is to use a large enough variety that every student finds several areas in which to operate at his or her preferred learning mode and to achieve success.

Some teachers also include conduct and participation in grading. They argue that, especially in elementary and middle school, these are important learning areas—we expect students to learn how to behave and participate in social situations, so we should evaluate students on their progress in these areas. The choice is yours (depending, of course, on your school's policy), but if you intend to include these areas in grading, you should inform all students and keep systematic data on them. This can be done quite easily with checklists, rating scales, and anecdotal records.

Which Assessment Tools?   Having decided on areas and activities on which to base grades, your next step is to determine what instruments—portfolios, objective tests, attitude inventories, checklists—will best provide valid, reliable data. Whatever instruments you choose, use a number system to record data. (Many teachers assign point values to every piece of student work.) This will greatly simplify your efforts to convert all your data to a letter grade.

Keep all your data in numerical form.

Where to record data may puzzle beginning teachers. School districts usually provide a gradebook, but the books don't typically provide enough space to include everything. Many teachers make grade sheets on large sheets of paper, with sections labeled for each type of data, such as Unit Tests, Quizzes, Projects, and Homework. That way, all scores are recorded as you collect them. This, too, is a convenience when you assign term grades. Many teachers also use (and some districts require) a computer grading program, which records whatever you enter, does calculations, and prints out results. With this system, you can tell a student at any time what his or her grade is, or at least that portion represented by numbers. Teachers who use a computer gradebook often keep a backup, either on another disk, on paper, or both.

◄◄ ► ►► VIDEO CASE

View the Video Case entitled "Assessment in the Elementary Grades: Formal and Informal Literacy Assessment" on the student website to see how second-grade teacher Chris Quinn combines formal techniques such as a standardized test with informal ones such as portfolio evaluation. As you watch the clips and study the artifacts in the case, reflect on the following questions: (1) What kinds of information does she get from each approach? (2) Did you observe any novel techniques being used?

Devising a Grading System   Deciding what to record and how to record it are your first steps. Next is adopting a system for assigning grades. Several systems are used, but the *percent* or *absolute* system is common. It works like this: Each graded activity is assigned a total numerical or point value. Student points are recorded for each activity, and at the end of the grading period, the student's grade is based on the percentage of the possible points he or she obtained. A typical example of grades and percentages follows:

Determine grade/point relationship, then weight each activity.

A = 90% or higher
B = 80–89%

C = 70–79%

D = 60–69%

F = below 60%

Having decided what to grade, the next step is to determine the proportion each activity will contribute to the total grade. In other words, do you want homework to count 90 percent or 15 percent or some other portion of the grade? Teachers commonly use approximations of the following weightings:

Tests and quizzes: 50–60%

Classwork: 15–30%

Projects and papers: 10–15%

Homework: 10–15%

If you include participation and conduct, these, too, must be assigned a weight. Conduct in a shop class, for instance, where dangerous machinery is used, would be a reasonably important part of achievement.

Avoiding Grading Errors   You should try to avoid the following errors in testing and grading (Daniel & King 1998):

1. *Using pretest scores in determining grades.* Such scores should indicate only where to begin instruction.
2. *Not adequately informing students of what to expect on a test.* This leaves students trying to decide what's important, which is the teacher's responsibility.
3. *Assigning a zero for missing or incomplete work.* A zero misrepresents achievement and has a profound effect on an average. One alternative is to use the median (middle-ranking) score as an indicator rather than using the average.
4. *Using grades for rewards or punishment.* Achievement of learning objectives should be the only consideration in assigning grades.
5. *Assigning grades contingent on improvement.* A student could improve a good deal but not meet performance expectations. Meeting a specified and well-articulated standard should be the main factor in assigning grades.

You might determine other errors after a few years of teaching

Communicating Your Intentions

Whatever your system, you must explain it clearly—with appropriate handouts and examples—to your students during the first days of class. Students can and should be taught to keep track of their own grades, and a few minutes can be spent one day a week to be sure each student has recorded his or her current scores. At this time, students can discuss questions and difficulties and calculate their grades. Students will know at all times what their progress is, where their achievement is strong, and what areas need attention. There should be no surprises at report card time. Many secondary and middle school teachers distribute a course outline or syllabus that includes a description of the grading system for the class and then have each student and parent or guardian sign it to indicate that they received, read, and understood the contents. This type of communication prevents unnecessary confusion and disagreement and meets our intended goal of making grading more objective in a very subjective business.

With the advent of school reform, report cards have evolved into monumental checklists that parallel various state or local standards. One school district's newly distributed fourth-grade "Student Progress Report" has 11 different categories with a total of 90 items to be evaluated on a five-point scale. A teacher will make a minimum of 450 decisions for each student! Another school district is field-testing an 11-page report card. We leave any reflections on this to you. The sequence of steps outlined in this chapter that we recommend you use as you develop your own classroom assessment approach is outlined in the Instructional Strategies box below. In conclusion, we refer you to the information on effect size on our website, www.cengage.com/education/orlich, where you may be surprised to learn that appropriate uses of assessments as feedback mechanisms have positive effects on learning.

Have parents buy in to grading system.

INSTRUCTIONAL *Strategies*

Guidelines for Selecting and Using Classroom Assessments

1. Be clear about the learning targets you want to assess.

2. Be sure that the assessment techniques you select match each learning target.

3. Be sure that the selected assessment techniques serve the needs of the learners.

4. Whenever possible, be sure to use multiple indicators of performance for each learning target.

5. Be sure that when you interpret the results of the assessments you take their limitations into account.

Source: Nitko 2004, p. 6.

Reflect   A Closing Reflection

◆ Examine a sample of the Iowa Test of Basic Skills or another commonly available norm-referenced standardized achievement test. Copies are often available in the library of your university or your local school district's front office. How do the various questions align with various curricula you have studied for K–12? (Be sure to select the appropriate version of the test.)

◆ Examine the fall issues of *Phi Delta Kappan.* Each fall this journal publishes the annual PDK/Gallup poll about what people think about U.S. schools. What trends do you observe with regard to achievement or assessment?

◆ Select any school district's policy handbook and then examine the section on testing and grading. How do the policies compare with what we have discussed?

◆ Devise a plan for communicating to parents about class efforts and activities. What information will you share? In what way? How often?

Summary Points

1. Assessment is a continuous process whose primary purpose is to improve student learning.
2. Classroom assessments are used for four primary purposes: to determine placement; to diagnose persistent problems; to monitor progress, provide feedback, and correct errors; and to assign grades.
3. Using various methods, you can assess students' behaviors, skills, knowledge, thinking, and attitudes.
4. Teachers have many choices of assessment methods and should select the one that best matches their particular goals of instruction.
5. Formative assessment is devoted entirely to the enhancement of student learning and achievement.
6. Large-scale achievement tests provide a snapshot of student achievement at a particular point in time. They can be more instructionally relevant when aligned to the curriculum and criterion-referenced.
7. Performance assessment tools include rating scales, checklists, observations and anecdotal records, portfolios, and rubrics.
8. Objective test items include true-false, matching, short-answer and completion, and multiple-choice questions.
9. Essay items are an excellent means of assessing students' higher-level thinking processes.
10. The purpose of grading is to improve student learning by clarifying learning objectives, indicating each student's strengths and weaknesses, evaluating the student's personal and social development, and motivating the student.

Building a Career Portfolio

Schools today are eager to hire teachers who can demonstrate understanding and skill with regard to classroom assessment. Although you are just starting your journey as a teacher there are ways to successfully show your assessment competence. For your career portfolio, we suggest that you do the following:

◆ Choose a chapter in this book that you would teach to pre-service student teachers. Develop a formative and summative assessment that you would use as a teacher to assess students. For the formative assessment use one of the strategies discussed in the chapter. Be sure to describe how you would use the assessment to help the student work toward your standard. For the summative assessment you could develop an end-of-chapter test. Be sure to use the principles outlined and discussed in this chapter to develop your test.

◆ After having developed a formative and summative assessment, you can show potential employers that you understand the role of classroom assessment and that you have the skills to develop and employ assessments effectively.

TECHNOLOGY
Insight

Web-based Tools for Creating Quizzes, Tests, and Surveys

A popular method of creating interactive surveys, tests, and quizzes is to distribute them using the Web. One of the powerful features of Web-based surveys, tests, and quizzes is that these tools can be configured to analyze participants' answers and provide immediate feedback. Two of the more popular tools for this purpose are described below:

◆ **Survey Monkey** (http://www.surveymonkey.com/) facilitates the creation and analysis of Web-based surveys. A basic account is free and allows one to create 10-question surveys with up to 100 respondents.

◆ **Hot Potatoes** software from Half-Baked Software, Inc. (http://hotpot .uvic.ca/) helps teachers create interactive multiple-choice, short-answer, jumbled-sentence, crossword, matching/ordering, and fill-in-the-gap exercises delivered on the Web. Hot Potatoes is free of charge for those working for publicly-funded non-profit-making educational institutions who make their pages available on the Web.

Resources

PRINT

The field of student assessment has a plethora of publications to aid the novice in learning more about the process. However, we attempted to identify three that would be of immediate and practical use.

Musial, D., G. Nieminen, J. Thomas, & K. Burke. *Foundations of Meaningful Educational Assessment.* Boston: McGraw-Hill, 2009, 521 pp.
This up-to-date treatment of educational assessment provides beginning teachers with a wealth of knowledge and insights. Connecting assessment methods to achievement targets, e-portfolios, and the assessment of special needs students are a few of the key topics explored in this text.

Salvia, J., J. E. Ysseldyke, & S. Bolt. *Assessment* (11th ed.). Boston: Cengage, 2010, 728 pp.
We suggest using this textbook as a handbook on assessment. The authors wrote the book with novices in mind. Everything you want to know about assessment is here in one source.

Taggart, G. L., S. J. Phifer, J. A. Nixon, & M. Woods. *Rubrics: A Handbook for Construction and Use.* Lancaster, PA: Technomic, 1998, 152 pp.
The authors provide a detailed compilation of rubric examples, models, designs, and scoring techniques.

INTERNET

Go to the website for this book at www.cengage.com/education/orlich to find live links to resources related to this chapter.

◆ Online resources to help you obtain the information you need to evaluate standardized tests can be found in the Buros Institute of Mental Measurements, University of Nebraska.
http://www.unl.edu/buros

◆ Information about standardized tests and other related products developed by the Educational Testing Service may be found at the ETS website.
   http://www.ets.org

◆ A memorandum from the Family Policy Compliance Office of the U.S. Department of Education notes that a parent has the right under the Family Educational Rights and Privacy Act (FERPA) to examine both the test question booklet and the child's test answer sheet for any test, including high-stakes state assessments. You can view the full document at
   http://www.fetaweb.com/04/ferpa.rooker.ltr.protocols.htm

◆ A manual produced by the Kentucky Department of Education provides many helpful suggestions and examples for developing open response and multiple-choice items for the classroom.
   **http://www.kde.state.ky.us/KDE/Instructional+Resources/
   Curriculum+Documents+and+Resources/Teaching+Tools/**

References

Airasian, P. W., & Russell, M. K. (2008). *Classroom Assessment* (6th ed.). Boston: McGraw-Hill.

Biggs, J. (1998). "Assessment and Classroom Learning: A Role for Summative Assessment?" *Assessment in Education, 5*(1): 103–110.

Black, P. (1998). *Testing: Friend or Foe? Theory and Practice of Assessment and Testing.* London: Falmer Press.

Black, P., C. Harrison, C. Lee, B. Marshall, & D. Wiliam. (2004). "Working Inside the Black Box: Assessment for Learning in the Classroom." *Phi Delta Kappan 86*(1): 8.

Black, P., & D. Wiliam. (1998). "Assessment and Classroom Learning" *Assessment in Education: Principles, Policy and Practice 5*(1): 7.

Bloom, B. S., et al., Eds. (1971). *Handbook on Formative and Summative Evaluation of Student Learning.* New York: McGraw-Hill.

Brookhart, S. M. (2001). "Successful Students' Formative and Summative Uses of Assessment Information." *Assessment in Education 8*(2): 153–169.

Brookhart, S. M. (2004). "Classroom Assessment: Tensions and Intersections in Theory and Practice." *Teachers' College Record 106*(3): 429–458.

Della-Piana, G. M. (2008). "Enduring Issues in Educational Assessment." *Phi Delta Kappan 89*(8): 590–592.

Daniel, L. G., & D. A. King. (1998). "Knowledge and Use of Testing and Measurement Literacy of Elementary and Secondary Teachers." *Journal of Educational Research 91*(6): 331.

Davies, A., C. Cameron, C. Politano, & K. Gregory. (1992). *Together Is Better: Collaborative Assessment, Evaluation and Reporting.* Courtney, British Columbia, Canada: Classroom Connections International.

Dempster, F. N., & P. G. Perkins. (1993). "Revitalizing Classroom Assessment: Using Tests to Promote Learning." *Journal of Instructional Psychology 20*(3): 197.

Far West Laboratory. (1992). "Using Portfolios to Assess Student Performance." *Knowledge Brief.* San Francisco: Number Nine.

Gronlund, N. E. (2006). *Assessment of Student Achievement* (8th ed.). Boston: Allyn and Bacon.

Haertel, E. H. (1999). "Performance Assessment and Education Reform." *Phi Delta Kappan 80*(9): 662.

Hattie, J. E., & H. Timperley. (2007). "The Power of Feedback." *Review of Education Research 77*(1): 81–112.

Herman, J. L., et al. (1997). "American Students' Perspectives on Alternative Assessment: Do They Know It's Different?" *Assessment in Education: Principles, Policy and Practice 4*(3): 339.

Linn, R. L. (1998, Nov.). *Assessments and Accountability. CSE Technical Report 490.* University of California, Los Angeles: Center for the Study of Evaluation.

Madaus, G. F., & T. Kellaghan. (1993). "The British Experience with Authentic Testing." *Phi Delta Kappan 74*(6): 458–469.

Madaus, G., & L. M. O'Dwyer. (1999). "A Short History of Performance Assessment." *Phi Delta Kappan 80*(9): 688.

Marzano, R. J., D. J. Pickering, & J. E. Pollock. (2001). *Classroom Instruction That Works: Research-Based Strategies for Increasing Student Achievement.* Alexandria, VA: Association for Supervision and Curriculum Development.

Miller, D. M., R. L. Linn, & N. E. Gronlund. (2009). *Measurement and Assessment in Teaching* (10th ed.). Englewood Cliffs, NJ: Merrill.

Nichols, S., & D. C. Berliner. (2005, March). *The Inevitable Corruption of Indicators and Educators Through High-Stakes Testing*. Tempe: College of Education, Arizona State University, Education Policy Studies Laboratory.

Nitko, A. J. (2004). *Educational Assessment of Students* (4th ed.). Englewood Cliffs, NJ: Merrill.

Oosterhof, A. (2003). *Developing and Using Classroom Assessments* (3rd ed.). Englewood Cliffs, NJ: Prentice Hall.

Popham, W. J. (2006). "Assessment for Learning" An Endangered Species?" *Educational Leadership* 63(5): 82–83.

Roe, B. D., S. H. Smith, & P. C. Burns. (2009). *Teaching Reading in Today's Elementary Schools* (10th ed.). Boston: Houghton Mifflin.

Sadler, D. R. (1998). "Formative Assessment: Revisiting the Territory." *Assessment in Education: Principles, Policy and Practice* 5(1): 77.

Salvia, J., J. E. Ysseldyke, & S. Bolt. (2010). *Assessment* (11th ed.). Boston: Cengage.

Stiggins, R. J. (2008). *An Introduction to Student-Involved Assessment For Learning* (5th ed.). New York: Macmillan.

U.S. Department of Education. (2002). *No Child Left Behind*. Retrieved January 22, 2002, at http://www.ed.gov.

Verma, M., & J. Chhatwal. (1997). "Reliability of Essay Type Questions—Effect of Structuring." *Assessment in Education: Principles, Policy and Practice* 4(2): 265.

Wiggins, G., & J. McTighe. (2005). *Understanding by Design, Expanded* (2nd ed.). Alexandria, VA: Association for Supervision and Curriculum Development.

Glossary

accountability The application of a business model to schooling with emphasis on high-stakes testing.

acculturation The combination of processes that introduce a child to his or her culture, including customs and social patterns.

active learning Any of a wide range of teaching strategies that engage the learner in the instruction taking place, such as working on problems in small groups, as opposed to passive methods such as seat work or listening to a lecture.

advance organizer A frame of reference for a lesson, such as a chart, study guide, list, or graph, that presents the main facts, concepts, or generalizations to be learned.

affective domain The area of learning that encompasses ethical, emotional, attitudinal, and social knowledge.

algorithm A special method of solving a specific problem; for example, a formula.

alternatives The different possible responses to a multiple-choice test question.

analysis The process of discovering relationships, interactions, and causality among ideas, concepts, and situations.

analytic scoring The assessment of student performance by means of a rating system.

anecdotal records Notes written objectively on a periodic basis to track student performance, which may include checklists, student self-reports, and teacher observations.

application The process of employing abstract ideas and concepts in real-world situations, such as hands-on learning and problem solving.

assertive discipline A structured approach designed to assist teachers in running an organized, teacher-in-charge classroom environment, including a discipline plan, classroom rules, positive recognition, and consequences.

assessment The process of evaluating student performance using a variety of measurements, such as tests, observations, ratings, and portfolios.

assistive technology Various items of equipment designed to help students with special needs achieve at a higher level.

asynchronous learning Learning or responses that are usually associated with computer-aided instruction but do not occur within a structured class period.

awareness The ability of a teacher to recognize student needs and demands and adjust the classroom environment to meet them.

behavior modification The process of changing behavior by rewarding desired actions and ignoring or punishing undesired actions.

behavioral perspective An educational approach that stresses changing student actions by rewarding and reinforcing desired actions and outcomes.

bilingual education The teaching of students in both their first and their second language (often Spanish and English) simultaneously.

blog A truncated term for Web log, usually set up by individuals.

Bloom's taxonomy A classification system for cognitive educational objectives.

brainstorming A discussion process in which the leader presents a topic or problem and solicits open-ended ideas about it from all group members.

character development An aspect of schooling that includes discussion of ethical issues and moral dilemmas, with the goal of developing characteristics such as trustworthiness, respect, responsibility, and citizenship.

checklist List-format assessment tools used by a teacher or student to document work completed or skills learned.

classroom clarifier The role the teacher takes during inquiry learning to guide students toward developing logical thinking skills.

classroom management The methods of organization, disciplinary procedures, and routines established by the teacher to ensure positive student behaviors that are conducive to learning and social interaction.

cognitive domain The area of learning encompassing intellectual aspects, such as information processing, memorization, and thinking skills.

cognitive psychology An area of psychology that focuses on inner mental processes rather than behavior.

cohesion The tendency of a group to stick together and support all members.

completion items Test items that contain an incomplete statement and require the student to fill in a missing word, phrase, or symbol.

concept An expression or abstraction based on observations of a group of stimuli, facts, or objects having common characteristics; for example, the concept "animal" encompasses and describes dogs, cats, and elephants.

concept analysis The process of identifying the components of a concept to be taught and deciding whether to teach it inductively (from underlying specific examples to broader generalizations) or deductively (from broader generalizations to underlying specific examples).

concept review questioning technique A teaching strategy that consists of inserting review questions throughout the recitation period.

concrete operational stage A stage of cognitive development (ages 8–11) in which children learn best through visual and hands-on activities.

conditions The specification of what is needed to accomplish an objective.

content The subject matter, substance, or materials of a lesson, consisting of facts, concepts, and generalizations.

content differentiation The process of isolating each fact, concept, or generalization within a hierarchy of knowledge so that it can be learned independently.

content hierarchy A sequence of learning matter that may be closely interrelated and requires a series of definite steps to achieve.

convergent questions Questions that require students to give factual or specific answers.

cooperative learning Learning based on a small-group approach to teaching, in which students are held accountable for both individual and group achievement.

correlation A relationship between two factors, but not necessarily one of cause and effect.

criteria Characteristics used to categorize or rate ideas or products.

criterion measure The third element of a performance objective, which defines the minimum level of acceptable performance.

curriculum alignment The process of making certain that the curriculum is organized and coordinated with what is tested.

curriculum guides Sets of goals and objectives published by a school district to guide teachers in developing instruction by stating what students should learn at each grade level and in each content area.

cyber-bullying The use of information and communication technologies by an individual or group to engage in deliberate, repeated, hostile behavior that is intended to harm others.

declarative knowledge Knowledge of content (*what*), such as facts, definitions, and concepts, as opposed to knowledge of processes (*how*). Also called *content knowledge*.

deductive reasoning The process of discovering specific examples or facts from a generalizing framework; a thinking process that moves from the general to the specific.

definition The presenting of what something means.

democratic discipline A classroom management approach that treats diverse students equally and expects them to take responsibility for their own behavior.

dependent skills Those items of information that are typically taught in a carefully structured or linear manner. For example, one teaches decimals before introducing percents.

desist strategy Discipline technique in which the teacher systematically communicates his or her desire for a student to stop a particular behavior, using either private or public communication.

diagnostic test Assessment tool that pinpoints students' strengths and weaknesses, specifically what students need to learn in designated fields.

differentiated instruction A means of devising or creating multiple paths to achieve learning goals or objectives (*see* **multi-methodology**).

direct instruction Teacher-initiated whole-class learning.

discipline The setting of behavioral parameters for the classroom, both by the teacher alone and in response to teacher-student interactions and situational factors.

discovery learning An inquiry process in which learners pose questions and seek explanations.

discussions Interactive learning processes involving the exchange of information, perceptions, and ideas in a small group.

distractors The incorrect alternative answers on a multiple-choice test.

divergent questions Questions that encourage students to give complex, creative, longer answers.

eclectic Made up of a mix of varied approaches or teaching models.

effect size A statistical notation of comparing independent samples to show evidence of the impact an educational treatment or intervention has on student achievement.

efficacy Effectiveness; the ability to reach a goal or complete a task.

empirical epistemology The process of knowing or learning through observation or experimentation.

enabling skills Facts, concepts, and processes students must be taught before they can learn more complex facts, concepts, and processes.

entry skills The knowledge and perceptions students possess at the beginning of a given lesson.

equity A moral rationale that all children should be given the same opportunities to succeed in school.

evaluation The process of making judgments and supporting one's viewpoints with specific criteria, facts, and values. In education, determining the effectiveness of a lesson or unit in terms of student outcomes.

evaluative criteria Parameters for questioning that ask students to make a choice about where they stand on a given issue or question.

evaluative question Question that asks students to make a personal judgment and then defend their position with criteria that support the position taken.

example A concrete or specific form of a more abstract concept.

exceptionality A condition in which a student qualifies for special services by virtue of his or her physical, cognitive, or emotional characteristics and abilities.

experience The totality of the events and activities in which a student has participated as part of planned learning processes.

extrinsic motivation Desire to perform based on the reward provided for engaging in an activity.

facilitator The supportive role a teacher takes by giving students the skills, materials, and opportunities they need to direct their own learning experiences.

fact The most fundamental piece of information, which is singular in occurrence, occurs or exists in the present time, does not help the learner predict other facts, and is acquired solely through the process of observation.

feedback Information that students can use to improve their performance.

formal operations stage A stage of cognitive development (ages 11–15 and above) in which adolescents develop knowledge through systematic reasoning.

formative assessment A type of classroom assessment devoted entirely to the enhancement of student learning and achievement via specific feedback.

framing The technique of asking a question very precisely, pausing, then calling on a student.

general instructional objectives Statements of what is to be learned that are broad and encompassing.

generalization An inferential statement that expresses relationships between concepts and has predictive value.

goals The broad, general outcomes students should reach as the result of a learning experience, lesson, or unit of study; for example, "Students will learn to appreciate and interpret drama."

graphic organizers Pictures, outlines, sketches, or some pictorial display that help the learner to obtain a quick mental perception or image of the topic.

guided inductive inquiry A learning process in which the teacher provides specific facts or ideas, from which students make their own generalizations.

halo effect The tendency of a teacher to assess a student's later performance based on the quality of earlier performance rather than being totally objective.

hemisphericity The study of where in the brain—in the left hemisphere or the right hemisphere—different types of mental functions occur.

heuristics "Rules of thumb" used to find solutions.

higher-level thinking A multistage construction of meaning that employs analysis and synthesis. Also called *critical thinking*.

high-stakes tests Tests that are administered to students to determine some prescribed level of competence and in which penalties or rewards are provided to students or teachers.

holistic instructional view A model for instructional planning that considers many social and educational factors simultaneously.

holistic scoring The assessment of a student's work in its entirety rather than through judgment of specific parts.

humanistic orientation An outlook that views all students as unique individuals deserving acceptance and respect.

idiosyncrasies Teacher behaviors and habits that interfere with effective classroom interaction.

imposed-discipline systems Approaches to discipline in which the teacher dictates appropriate classroom behaviors and consequences for misbehavior.

inclusion A commitment to provide maximum learning experiences for all students, including those with special cognitive, affective, or psychomotor needs, in regular classrooms. *See also* **mainstreaming**.

inclusive classroom A classroom in which any learner with a disability is educated alongside students without disabilities.

independent skills Learning that can be taught without any prerequisite skills.

independent study Situation in which teachers allow students options of what to study and where the work is done.

individual education plan (IEP) An agreement between a student with special learning needs and his or her classroom teachers, special education staff, and parents that outlines educational goals, procedures, and expected outcomes.

Individuals with Disabilities Education Act (IDEA) Federal act stating that all children with disabilities must have access to a free and appropriate public education.

induction The process of analyzing specific ideas to form more general concepts.

inductive inquiry The process of inferring generalizations from a set of specific ideas or facts.

inductive reasoning The process of studying examples or facts in order to develop generalizations or concepts; a thinking process that moves from the specific to the general.

information processing A means used to learn and remember knowledge.

information-processing psychology A branch of psychology that views learning as an interactive process between learners and their environment.

inquiry discussion group A specific kind of small group in which students develop questioning and problem-solving skills through a process of discovery and analysis.

inquiry process An investigative learning process that includes skills such as classifying, predicting, and experimenting.

inquiry teaching An investigative process of learning in which students are asked to pose questions, analyze data, and develop conclusions or generalizations.

instructional equity The provision of equal learning opportunities to students of both genders and from diverse backgrounds and cultures.

instructional model A detailed organizational scheme of how something is used.

integration The third step in the advance organizer model, in which students see how main concepts and underlying facts are related (vertical integration) or how underlying facts are similar or different (horizontal integration).

interdisciplinary thematic unit A unit of instruction that incorporates various content areas while covering an overall topic or theme, such as "Dinosaurs" or "Seeds."

internalize To make something part of one's unconscious, automatic learning processes.

interpersonal Occurring between people.

interpretation Giving meaning to a new concept by relating it to another, known concept.

interpretive exercise A means of assessment in which students analyze data, charts, maps, or written passages, using higher-level thinking skills.

intrapersonal Occurring within an individual.

intrinsic motivation An incentive, such as pride, self-esteem, and the desire to learn, that comes from within the student.

Kaplan matrix A curriculum planning chart that includes the different levels of thinking in Bloom's taxonomy.

knowledge Recognition and recall of facts and explicitly stated concepts.

learned helplessness A state of being in which students quit trying because they have repeatedly had their efforts neglected.

learning activities Hands-on, interactive classroom experiences.

learning community The concept of a school as a social unit that supports all members—students, teachers, administrators, staff, and parents.

learning deficits Knowledge gaps that students must fill before they begin learning new concepts.

learning modality A way of gaining knowledge or expression through one of the senses—for example, auditory, tactile, visual, or kinesthetic.

learning style The set of cognitive, affective, and physiological traits that a learner exhibits as he or she interacts in the classroom environment and determines how he or she will solve problems. Also called *learning preference*.

least restrictive environment The classroom setting that is as close to the "regular" classroom as possible and still provides the learning opportunities needed to address a student's special needs.

lesson A piece of a unit, in which a given set of objectives or concepts is taught.

lesson plan The specification of what is to be done during class periods.

listserv A term referring to e-mail lists.

mainstreaming Placing and serving children with special cognitive, behavioral, or psychomotor needs in regular classrooms. *See also* **inclusion**.

Maslow's hierarchy of needs A theory that an individual's behavior at any time is determined by his or her needs, ranging from basic physiological needs such as hunger and thirst to the highest needs of self-actualization and transcendence.

master teacher A teacher who possesses much experience and expertise and may serve as a role model or mentor for other teachers.

matching exercises Test items that require students to match words or concepts in one column to statements listed in another column; for example, pairing a word with its definition.

measurement The process of assigning numerical achievement indicators to student performance.

metacognition Conscious awareness of one's own thinking and learning process.

metaphor A figure of speech describing something with implied terms.

mnemonics A strategy for remembering facts by using a device, such as having the first letter of each fact represent a word or sentence.

motivation The desire or incentive to learn something or to behave in a given way.

multiculturalism The practice of including and honoring diverse cultures within school curricula and instruction.

multi-methodology The teaching practice of using a wide variety of techniques during lessons so that every student will benefit from at least one mode of every presentation.

multiple-choice item Test item that contains a question and asks students to choose an answer from a list of provided alternatives.

multiple intelligences The concept that intelligence does not take just one form but exists in eight facets: verbal/linguistic, bodily/kinesthetic, intrapersonal, logical/mathematical, musical/rhythmic, visual/spatial, interpersonal, and naturalistic.

multiple-response questions An instructional technique in which the teacher asks multiple students to respond to a single question, thus encouraging divergent thinking.

negative interdependence A management system that encourages students to work against one another in competition for academic resources and recognition.

norm An unwritten behavioral rule, pattern, or habit accepted by a particular culture or group of people.

norm-referenced standardized test See **standardized test**.

objective items Test items that have a single best or right answer.

objectives The specific steps that must be achieved to realize a broader goal.

online virtual reality Computer-based three-dimensional simulations.

outcome A description of some product or other tangible evidence that learning has occurred.

performance An active demonstration used to assess student learning, such as oral presentations, musical and dramatic performances, and kinesthetic activities.

performance objective A specific, observable outcome students should reach as the result of a learning experience or lesson; for example, "After reading the play, students will write an essay naming and describing five characters." Also called *performance statement*.

physical diversity The variety of individuals' physical traits, such as height, weight, appearance, and physical ability.

planning The process of choosing instructional goals, content, materials, and activities prior to teaching.

pluralism The idea that a society should reflect the diverse mix of racial and other groups of which it is composed.

portfolio A collection of student work that can be used to demonstrate student effort and progress toward particular learning objectives.

positive interdependence A management system that encourages students to work together, with the assumption that the success of each student enhances the quality of learning for all students.

power The influence teachers have over students by virtue of their age, authority, role, or physical strength.

preoperational stage A early stage of cognitive development (ages 2–8) in which children learn through intuition, experience, and concepts.

prerequisite skills The skills or knowledge students must have before they begin a new learning experience.

pretest An assessment given before the start of instruction to determine students' entry skills.

problem A stimulus that requires action to solve.

problem-based learning Technique in which questions are posed for students to solve.

problem solving An inquiry learning process in which students seek answers to a question that is relevant to themselves and their culture.

procedural knowledge Knowledge of processes (*how*), as opposed to knowledge of content (*what*). Also called *process knowledge*.

process objectives Statements that focus on the way students learn (*how*) rather than the specific outcomes of learning (*what*).

products Tangible responses to class assignments, such as book reviews, term papers, or science fair posters.

programmed instruction A teaching method in which skills are presented in small segments, with immediate feedback and continual practice.

progressive differentiation The second step in the advance organizer model, which identifies the basic facts, details, and concepts underlying a main concept or generalization.

psychomotor domain The area of learning encompassing physical movement, including gross and fine motor skills and coordination.

rationale A reason or purpose.

readiness The willingness and ability of a student to begin learning.

reality therapy An approach to discipline in which individuals take responsibility for solving their own problems and begin to reshape their own behaviors to meet selected needs without any threats or implied punishments.

reciprocal teaching A cooperative learning model used to improve reading, in which students play the teacher's role.

recitation A learning technique in which the teacher calls on a different student to answer each factual or knowledge-based question, thus limiting students to one "correct" response.

reflection An active mental process that teachers use consistently as they interact with students and the curriculum, including mental rehearsal prior to teaching, careful consideration of instructional options, anticipation of classroom problems, and quick daily evaluations of which methods worked and did not work.

reflective questions Questions requiring students to develop higher-order thinking skills. A reflective question attempts to elicit motives, inferences, speculations, impact, and contemplation.

regulatory agency An office or board that sets standards, rules, and regulations.

reinforcement A system of rewards that encourages students to repeat positive behaviors.

reinforcer A type of stimulus that has a good chance of increasing a desired behavior.

reliability The degree to which a test consistently measures a given attribute.

response to intervention Known as RTI, this is a three-tiered multilevel approach of helping all children achieve, including those with learning difficulties or in need of special services.

ripple effect The negative effects felt by all class members when a teacher responds negatively to a student.

role An assigned set of responsibilities given to a student as a member of a group; for example, group leader, group recorder, group timekeeper, group evaluator.

role playing A learning process in which students act out or simulate a real-life situation.

routines Daily organizational tasks, such as taking attendance and checking papers, that must be part of a classroom time management plan.

rubrics Examples of different types, models, illustrations, or levels of possible responses that are used as guidelines for assessing student work.

schema A mental scaffold for learning, made up of previously learned concepts to which new concepts are attached.

schema theory An assumption that learners have internal, cognitive frameworks into which they fit new knowledge, concepts, and experiences.

school culture The environment of a school, including its values, management systems, communication styles, and interpersonal relationships.

school ethos The tone of the interactions within a school's environment.

self-discipline A classroom management system that emphasizes student goal setting, individual responsibility, and self-monitoring.

sensorimotor stage A period of cognitive development (ages 0–2) during which children learn through sensations and movement.

sequencing The process of organizing instruction by placing curricula or learning tasks in order.

sex-role stereotyping Making assumptions about students' abilities based on their gender.

short-answer items Test items that pose a question and require students to give a brief, two- to three-sentence response.

simulation An artificial setting or situation that parallels a real-world setting or situation and allows students to practice problem-solving skills.

small group Purposefully constructed set of four to eight students who work together to learn.

small-group discussions Verbal exchanges of ideas and information in groups of four to eight students.

social capital The sum of interpersonal relationships that provide support or encouragement.

standardized test A nationally normed test that compares a student's performance to that of other students across the nation (if norm referenced) or to expected levels of achievement (if criterion referenced).

standards Criteria for what knowledge and learning processes students should be taught in a given subject area, or how teachers should be trained to perform.

stem The part of a multiple-choice test item that poses the question or problem.

strategic learning Student development of critical thinking skills that accelerate learning.

student-initiated learning An instructional technique in which students decide the content, means, and pace of the learning process.

summative assessment A manner of making evaluative judgments and certifying completion of projects, classes, and programs, most often using a letter grade.

synergism The increased energy created when individual elements work together as a whole, smooth-functioning, creative system.

synthesis A process of creatively combining facts, concepts, and learning processes into new knowledge.

task analysis model The process of subdividing the content, concepts, or processes of a lesson into smaller, sequential steps that begin with the least complex and progress to the most complex.

task group A small group of students who work together to complete a particular assignment or job.

taxonomy A set of standards for classifying ideas or objects into hierarchical categories; for example, Bloom's taxonomy of cognitive skills.

test An assessment instrument that requires students to answer questions to demonstrate learning.

thinking A complex act comprising attitudes, knowledge, and skills that allows the individual to shape his or her environment more effectively than by intuition alone.

topics Various subjects used by teachers to help organize their lesson plans.

transfer of learning The application of knowledge or behaviors learned in one setting to a new situation.

translation A thinking skill in which one form of expression is changed into another form.

true-false question A test item that requires students to determine whether a given statement is correct or not.

tutorial discussion group A group of two to four students being taught skills not mastered in large-group class instruction.

unguided inductive inquiry A learning process in which students discover specific facts or ideas by themselves and then make their own generalizations based on what they have learned.

unit A block of lessons grouped together based on related skills, concepts, or themes.

unit plan A detailed plan for providing instruction on a skill, concept, or theme.

universal design The attempt to provide instruction that covers the broadest range of student learning modalities.

validity The degree to which a test measures what it is intended to measure.

virtual reality A computer-generated environment designed to create the illusion of a real setting or situation.

wait time 1 The time between when a teacher poses a question and then calls on a student to answer it.

wait time 2 A silent period that occurs after a student responds to a teacher's question.

Wiki Informational Web page that can be easily modified by users. (*Wiki* comes from the Hawaiian word for "fast.")

zone of proximal development The difference between the intellectual level a child can reach on his or her own and the level that can be reached with expert assistance.

Index